THE
FIVE STAGES
OF CULTURE SHOCK

**Recent Titles in
Contributions in Psychology**

Medieval Psychology
Simon Kemp

Hesitation: Impulsivity and Reflection
Leonard W. Doob

Culture and the Restructuring of Community Mental Health
William A. Vega and John W. Murphy

The Externalization of Consciousness and the Psychopathology of Everyday Life
Stephen T. DeBerry

Self-Representation: Life Narrative Studies in Identity and Ideology
Gary S. Gregg

Hostage: Terror and Triumph
James F. Campbell

From the Other Side of the Couch: Candid Conversations with Psychiatrists and
Psychologists
Chris E. Stout

Counseling in the Asia-Pacific Region
Abdul Halim Othman and Amir Awang, editors

What Wrongdoers Deserve: The Moral Reasoning Behind Responses to Misconduct
R. Murray Thomas and Ann Diver-Stamnes

Using Bibliotherapy in Clinical Practice: A Guide to Self-Help Books
John T. Pardeck

Modern Perspectives on John B. Watson and Classical Behaviorism
James T. Todd and Edward K. Morris, editors

Worlds of Common Sense: Equality, Identity, and Two Modes of Impulse Management
Pauline Nichols Pepinsky

THE FIVE STAGES OF CULTURE SHOCK

Critical Incidents Around the World

Paul Pedersen

Contributions in Psychology, *Number 25*

GREENWOOD PRESS
Westport, Connecticut • London

Library of Congress Cataloging-in-Publication Data

Pedersen, Paul.
    The five stages of culture shock : critical incidents around the
world / Paul Pedersen.
        p. cm.—(Contributions in psychology, ISSN 0736–2714 ; no.
25)
    Includes bibliographical references and index.
    ISBN 0–313–28782–1 (alk. paper)
    1. Culture shock—Case studies.   2. Cross-cultural orientation—
Case studies. I. Title. II. Series.
GN517.P43   1995
306—dc20   93–49711

British Library Cataloguing in Publication Data is available.

Library of Congress Catalog Card Number: 93–49711
ISBN: 0–313–28782–1
ISSN: 0736–2714

First published in 1995

Greenwood Press, 88 Post Road West, Westport, CT 06881
An imprint of Greenwood Publishing Group, Inc.

Printed in the United States of America

The paper used in this book complies with the
Permanent Paper Standard issued by the National
Information Standards Organization (Z39.48–1984).

10 9 8 7 6 5 4 3 2 1

Contents

Preface   vii

1. Experiencing Culture Shock   1
     The Stage Theory of Culture Shock   2
     The Disease Model of Culture Shock   4
     The Growth Model of Culture Shock   7
     Applications of the Culture Shock Metaphor   9
     Conclusion   11

2. Critical Incidents Around the World   14
     The Critical Incident Technique   15
     Applications of Critical Incidents   17
     Critical Incidents of Students Abroad   20
     The Semester at Sea Concept   22
     Critical Incidents Discussion Guide   24

3. The Honeymoon Stage   26
     Introduction   26
     Critical Incidents   27
     Conclusion   77

4. The Disintegration Stage   79
     Introduction   79
     Critical Incidents   80
     Conclusion   132

5. The Reintegration Stage   134
     Introduction   134
     Critical Incidents   135
     Conclusion   199

6. The Autonomy Stage   201
        Introduction   201
        Critical Incidents   202
        Conclusion   243

7. The Interdependence Stage   245
        Introduction   245
        Critical Incidents   250
        Conclusion   263

References   271

Index   277

Preface

Culture shock is a profoundly personal experience. It does not affect all people in the same way or even the same person in the same way when it reoccurs. The critical incidents reported in the following chapters will describe what students on a voyage around the world experienced as they changed in response to the different countries and cultures they encountered. Not all of the students were aware of going through culture shock, but they were very much aware of cultural differences and, in some cases, of cultural similarities as well.

Culture shock happens inside each individual who encounters unfamiliar events and unexpected circumstances. This book will define culture shock as an internalized construct or perspective developed in reaction or response to the new or unfamiliar situation. As the situation changes in unexpected directions, the individual needs to construct new perspectives on self, others, and the environment that "fit" with the new situation. Because culture shock is such a subjective response to unfamiliar situations, it was necessary to provide many different examples for each stage of culture shock across each country setting. The variety of examples demonstrates that culture shock: (1) is a process and not a single event, (2) may take place at many different levels simultaneously as the individual interacts with a complex environment, (3) becomes stronger or weaker as the individual learns to cope or fails to cope, (4) teaches the individual new coping strategies which contribute to future success, and (5) applies to any radical change presenting unfamiliar or unexpected circumstances. Situations of culture shock abroad provide metaphors for better understanding culture shock related to physical health, environmental disaster, economic failure, psychological crises, or any radical change in lifestyle.

The first chapter will introduce the published literature about culture shock indicating what we know and what we do not know about that experience. There is a great deal of disagreement about culture shock and how it presents itself. Some of the publications even discount the construct "culture shock" as a useful concept. The critical incidents were organized according to the stages of culture shock the student author seemed to be experiencing. At the end of each critical incident, the primary "insight" that related that incident to a particular stage of culture shock will be indicated. The reader may well find other insights in each incident that would relate to other stages of culture shock, given the complexity of each cross-cultural encounter.

Critical incidents were chosen for several reasons. First, they provide firsthand accounts of persons going through culture shock while they are in the process of adapting and changing. Second, each incident provides a specific example of a student author's encounter with other cultures. Third, cross-sectional examples demonstrate a change in emphasis distinguishing one stage from another in a growth toward multicultural awareness. Fourth, the critical incidents provide valuable examples for discussion and learning about multicultural awareness by the reader. Fifth, the incidents incorporate the complexity of cross-cultural encounters, through storytelling.

This book is different in several ways from other books about culture shock. First, this book describes a qualitative rather than a quantitative perspective of the experiences of culture shock. Second, the emphasis is on internalized changes in the students as they meet many different cultures and nationalities rather than on matching the student with a single culture over a period of time. Third, the many different examples of culture shock described in each chapter highlight the different ways in which student authors experienced culture shock. Fourth, no attempt is made to provide "right answers" to the dilemma in each critical incident; the emphasis is placed instead on the consequences of alternative decisions.

The critical incidents described in this book were limited to outside-the-classroom experiences. None of the incidents relating to the shipboard teaching were included. It was a decision of the author to focus exclusively on the encounters students had with host country nationals or one another in host country settings because this is one of the more unique opportunities available in the Semester at Sea. The critical incidents described in this book therefore describe only one part of the Semester at Sea experience. At the same time many students were able to relate academic concepts from shipboard classes to the critical incidents ashore as meaningful and practical tools for managing culture shock.

The student authors of the critical incidents were participating in three psychology classes aboard the Semester at Sea *Universe* during the spring semester 1992 voyage around the world conducted by the Institute for Shipboard Education, University of Pittsburgh. The ports visited were Nassau, Bahamas; Caracas, Venezuela; San Salvador, Brazil; Cape Town, South Africa; Mombasa, Kenya; Madras, India; Penang, Malaysia; Hong Kong; Keelung, Taiwan, Republic of China; Kobe, Japan; and, finally, Seattle, Washington, United States of America. Each student in the three psychology classes was required to submit eight critical incidents. Only those incidents by student authors who gave their written permission to let their critical incidents be used in this book were included. The incidents included were selected from 664 incidents. Confidentiality was protected for these critical incidents described in this book by changing personal names into pronouns and omitting other identifying features. The student authors will, however, have no difficulty finding their own critical incidents as they read through this book. The critical incidents selected demonstrated a clear learning insight, presented a unique perspective not duplicated by other incidents, and helped illustrate the dynamics of culture shock.

I want to thank the student authors who agreed to participate in this book project. The following individuals contributed critical incidents. Students in the course "Psychology of Personality" included Prescott Burke, Anouska Cardenas, Camille Collett, Amy Fehsenfeld, Mara Goodman, Ana Gracie, Jason Green, Vincente Grosso, Bonnie Hagan, Alison Haugo, Scott Horowitz, Laurie Hsu, Kiley Johnson, Abigail Leeder, Matthew Mattia, Shanon Melick, Matthew Miller, John Norwood, Kimberly Olszak, Jason Ostrowski, Caroline Pacha, Stephanie Pinola, Jenifer Porter, Sabine Rice, Rachel Rosen, Stacy Sadler, Joshua Seymour, Amy Smith, Kristen Stewart, Susan Wadsworth, Sherwood Wagner, and Annette Zeller.

Students in the course "Small Groups" included Susan Anderson, Cynthia Barsotti, Elizabeth Beattie, Molly Benson, Susan Bratman, Kevin Comiskey, John Dalton, Mollie Eaton, Darcy Feuerzeig, Mara Goodman, Shari Liebermensch, Mark Liff, David Martin, Jessica Martin, Hilary Pfau, April Prohaska, Gregory Queen, Lori Slicker, Tonya Ward, Brett Weiss, Elizabeth Whilden, and Catherine Wilson.

Students in the course "Personality and Social Structure" included Susan Anderson, Erica Bamdas, Barbara Bersche, Kristen Bonesteel, Jerry Coggan, Meghan Dillon, Andrea Drioli, Mollie Eaton, Kori Eldean, Sara Fretzin, Leslie Gill, Ruth Griesen, Michelle Harper, Tia Hoppin, Nicole Jackson, Caroline Jasper, Cathryn Marsico, Karen Michaels, Dona Ring, Jeffrey Rogoff, Jennifer Stack, Megann Vahey, Leander Ward, Jessica Waters, Melinda Watkins, Allison Wells, Laura Yearout, and Marianne Zyla.

I would like to dedicate this book to Mr. Chao-Yung Tung and to his family who have invested in the future by more than twenty years of emotional and financial support to the idea of shipboard university education. Their support has directly benefitted the twenty thousand students who have experienced their Semester at Sea, and indirectly benefitted many times that number of us, for which we are truly grateful.

When I returned from the voyage, some of my colleagues jokingly asked me if I had enjoyed my "vacation" or "the cruise" implying that the Semester at Sea was not a serious venture. I would smile politely and ask them in return to describe to me any one of their undergraduate university courses. Almost none of them were able to identify a single outstanding course in their undergraduate education that was particularly meaningful to them. I then suggested to them that all of the students who had experienced the Semester at

Sea will vividly remember for the rest of their lives the courses they took and the specific insights they gained. If the purpose of education is "remembered learning," then the Semester at Sea provides a very important example of educational development.

THE
FIVE STAGES
OF CULTURE SHOCK

1

Experiencing Culture Shock

Because it is so subjective, the experience of culture shock is hard to convey in rows of numbers or even statistically significant general tendencies of "most" people. This book will focus on the experience of culture shock as described by undergraduate college students visiting different countries around the world. What do people say when they are going through culture shock? What do they feel? What do they think? This book will answer some of those questions in the students' own words as they describe the critical incidents that happened to them in culturally different settings.

Culture shock is the process of initial adjustment to an unfamiliar environment. This psychological construct of culture shock has been used to describe the adjustment process in its emotional, psychological, behavioral, cognitive, and physiological impact on individuals. In a multicultural context, culture shock is a more or less sudden immersion into a nonspecific state of uncertainty where the individuals are not certain what is expected of them or of what they can expect from the persons around them. The term of culture shock was first introduced by Kalvero Oberg (1960) to describe the anxiety resulting from not knowing what to do in a new culture. The familiar cues have been removed or have been given a different meaning, resulting in responses ranging from a vague discomfort to profound disorientation. The recent literature recognizes that culture shock applies to any new situation, job, relationship, or perspective requiring a role adjustment and a new identity. In a broader and more general sense, culture-shock applies to any situation where an individual is forced to adjust to an unfamiliar social system where previous learning no longer applies.

There are at least six indicators that a culture-shock adjustment is taking place. First, familiar cues about how the person is supposed to behave are missing, or the familiar cues now have a different meaning. Second, values the person considered good, desirable, beautiful, and valuable are no longer respected by the hosts. Third, the disorientation of culture shock creates an emotional state of anxiety, depression, or hostility, ranging from a mild uneasiness to the "white furies" of unreasonable and uncontrollable rage attributed to colonials in the last century by indigenous peoples. Fourth, there is a dissatisfaction with the new ways and an idealization of "the way things were." Fifth, recovery skills that used to work before no longer seem to work. Sixth, there is a sense that this culture shock discrepancy is permanent and will never go away.

Experiencing a new culture is a sudden and sometimes unpleasant feeling causing persons to reevaluate both the new host and their own home culture. Until recently, culture shock was assumed to be a consistently negative experience, much like an illness or disease. Oberg (1960) mentioned six negative aspects of culture shock including: (1) strain resulting from the effort of psychological adaptation, (2) a sense of loss or deprivation referring to the removal of former friends, status, role, and/or possessions, (3) rejection by or rejection of the new culture, (4) confusion in the role definition, role expectations, feelings, and self-identity, (5) unexpected anxiety, disgust, orindignation regarding cultural differences between the old and new ways, and (6) feelings of helplessness as a result of not coping well in the new environment.

Others have applied Oberg's framework more broadly to include "culture fatigue" (Guthrie, 1975), "language shock" (Smalley, 1963), "role shock" (Byrnes, 1966), and "pervasive ambiguity" (Ball-Rokeach, 1973). Each of these early definitions has conveyed the meaning of culture shock as a reactive state of specific pathology or deficit which is both the source and result of alienation in a new culture according to the "medical model." More recent explanations of culture shock have emphasized the "educational model," describing the adjustment period as a state of growth and development which-- however painful it might be--may result in positive and even essential insights.

Several different paradigms that are used to describe culture shock are surveyed in this chapter. Later we will describe what was learned from the accounts of students participating in this study which contribute toward a unique and different definition of culture shock.

THE STAGE THEORY OF CULTURE SHOCK

S. Lysgaard (1955) first developed the U-curve hypothesis to describe the adjustment patterns of international students in a host culture. Oberg (1958) described seven stages of adjustment: (1) incubation stage, (2) crises resulting from normal daily activity, (3) understanding the host culture, (4) objective viewing of the host culture, (5) reentry, (6) reverse culture shock, and (7) readjustment to the home country. The initial U-curve adjustment was broadened to a W-curve by J. T. Gullahorn and J. E. Gullahorn (1963) who pointed out how the adjustment process on returning home resembled the original adjustment process abroad. F. Brown (1989) reviews previous stage theories emphasizing the importance of describing adjustment episodes in a context.

Peter Adler (1975) has specified the process and sequence of stages in the culture shock experience based on work by Oberg and others. This approach describes culture shock in more neutral rather than negative terms as a five-stage educational and developmental process with positive as well as negative consequences.

The first stage of initial contact, or the "honeymoon stage," is where the newly arrived individual experiences the curiosity and excitement of a tourist, but where the person's basic identity is rooted in the back-home setting.

The second stage involves disintegration of the old familiar cues, and the individual is overwhelmed by the new culture's requirements. The individual typically experiences self-blame and a sense of personal inadequacy for any difficulties encountered.

The third stage involves a reintegration of new cues and an increased ability to function in the new culture. The emotions associated with this stage are typically anger and resentment toward the new culture as having caused difficulties and being less adequate than the old familiar ways. Because of this outer-directed anger, persons in this stage of culture shock are difficult to help.

The fourth stage continues the process of reintegration toward gradual autonomy and increased ability to see the bad and good elements in both the old and the new cultures. A balanced perspective emerges that helps the person interpret both the previous home and the new host cultures.

The fifth stage is described as reciprocal interdependence, where the person has ideally achieved biculturality, or has become fluently comfortable in both the old and the new cultures. There is some controversy about whether this stage is an unreachable ideal or whether persons actually can achieve this stage of multiculturalism.

There are other stage theories of culture shock as well. S. O. Lesser and H. W. S. Peter (1957) developed a three-stage process of culture shock, including first, a spectator phase on arrival; second, an involvement phase when the person can no longer stand outside the host culture and must become involved; and third, a coming-to-terms phase where the visitor learns how to cope in the host culture. I. Torbiorn (1982) based his four-stage description on (1) the tourist phase, (2) the culture-shock phase, (3) the conformist phase, and (4) the assimilation phase. Although there are differences across the description of stages, the description of culture shock as a stage-based developmental process is shared by most of the persons writing about the culture-shock experience.

This sequence of stages or steps has been referred to as a U-curve, in which the adjustment process moves from a higher and more adequate level through a lower and less adequate level toward a return to the higher and more adequate level of coping in the new culture or cultures. A. T. Church (1982) discusses eleven empirical studies in support of the U-curve hypothesis. These data support the general hypothesis but not full recovery to the original level of positive functioning back home. Five other studies failed to confirm the U-curve hypothesis, indicating that there was no cross-sectional support for the five-stage thesis. In spite of the lack of clear empirical evidence, there is much support for the U-curve as a convenient model for describing culture shock. Because culture shock is subjectively complex, it is difficult to measure accurately.

A. Furnham and S. Bochner (1986) discuss several problems in the U-curve hypothesis about culture shock. First, there are many dependent variables to consider as aspects of adjustment, such as depression, loneliness, homesickness, and other attitudes. Second, the definition of a U-shape is uneven in the research literature that tested this hypothesis because different persons start out at different levels of original adjustment adequacy and then change at different rates. Furnham and Bochner suggest that research should focus on the interpersonal rather than the intrapersonal variables to study the process of culture shock.

The most serious weakness of a U-curve or a W-curve design is the implication of a smooth linear adaptive process, which is quite different from reality. Transformation occurs through a series of degeneration and regeneration events or crises in a nonregular and erratic movement of change. Part of this process is conscious and other parts more unconscious as the visitor seeks greater success in the host environment. As the visitor's internal capacity to cope increases, the individual is able to handle the "stress and adaptation, learning and unlearning, acculturation and deculturation, crisis and resolution" (Kim, 1988, p.57).

There are many examples of U-shaped curves of adjustment in the psychological literature. These include adjustments to retirement, divorce, nursing careers, office jobs, college life, medical school, psychiatric residency, bereavement, economic change, paraplegia, and hemodialysis to name a few (Coffman and Harris, 1984). Some of the parallels between adjustment in these areas and culture shock fit more closely than others, but the typical sequence of events in each case is close enough to be generalizable.

No research to date has attempted to specify the relationships among the various facets of culture-shock in terms of their relative importance, the order in which culture-shock events are likely to occur, and which groups are more vulnerable to one or another type of culture shock (Furnham, 1988). Most of the research has been descriptive with few attempts to explain for whom the shock will be more or less intense or what determines each person's reaction, how long the culture shock is likely to last, and whether culture shock can be prevented.

THE DISEASE MODEL OF CULTURE SHOCK

The earliest descriptions of culture shock compared it to a disease that resulted in temporary or permanent disability but could presumably be cured with the right treatment. Furnham (1988) reviewed the literature about eight deficit explanations of culture shock to demonstrate the weakness of the disease model in each explanation for understanding culture shock.

First, culture shock is described as a grief-like mourning reaction over having lost back-home relationships. However, not all culture shock involves grieving, and culture shock is almost never totally focused on grieving reactions.

Second, culture shock is presumed to be inevitable for all sojourners and cannot be avoided from this fatalistic perspective. However, fatalism does not account for the different rates of culture shock distress experienced by sojourners, and it does not explain how "successful" sojourners somehow escape culture shock.

Third, culture shock is explained as a process of natural selection or "survival of the fittest." However, most research on culture shock is retrospective rather than predictive so this explanation is at best simplistic and not supported by research.

Fourth, culture shock is blamed on unrealistic expectations by sojourners in the new settings. However, there is still no proven relationship between unfulfilled expectations, poor adjustment, and the culture-shock experience.

Fifth, culture shock is blamed on negative life events that interrupt the daily routine in unsettling ways. However, it is difficult to measure life events and impossible to establish causality. Do distressed people cause negative events or vice versa?

Sixth, culture shock is blamed on a clash of values and their consequent misunderstandings and conflicts. However, some values are more adaptive than others, and value conflict itself is not sufficient to explain culture shock.

Seventh, culture shock is blamed on a social skills deficit where inadequate or unskilled individuals have a difficult time adjusting. However, the role of personality and socialization is understated by this explanation, and it implies an ethnocentric bias.

Eighth, culture shock is blamed on a lack of social support, drawing on attachment theory, social network theory, and psychotherapeutic explanations. However, it is difficult to quantify social support and develop a mechanism or process of social support for testing this explanation.

Furnham (1988) went on to acknowledge that even now most people describe culture shock as a stress reaction in which salient rewards are uncertain and difficult to control. A closely related explanation describes culture shock as the lack of reference points, social norms and established rules to guide a sojourner's actions and the actions of others. All explanations highlight the importance of change and adaptation; however, very few writers have emphasized the potentially positive consequences of these changes.

The major assumption in typical explanations of culture shock is that adaptation is guided by uncertainty reduction and the reduction or control of anxiety, again emphasizing the deficit hypothesis in explaining culture shock (Gudykunst and Hammer, 1988). "We may reduce uncertainty without reducing anxiety. We reduce uncertainty by depending on positive stereotypes, favorable contact, shared networks, intergroup attitudes, a secure cultural identity, subsequent cultural similarity, developing a second language competence, and knowing about the host culture. "Reducing uncertainty also is influenced by the appropriate use of uncertainty reduction strategies, the display of nonverbal affiliative expressiveness, attraction, and intimacy. Reducing anxiety, in contrast, is affected by strangers' motivation, strangers' psychological differentiation, host nationals' attitudes toward strangers, and the host cultures' policy toward strangers"(p. 132).

C. W. Stephan and W. G. Stephan (1992) describe how culture shock--or anxiety in intergroup interactions--results from four types of feared negative consequences: first, negative psychological consequences such as frustration or loss of control; second, negative behavioral consequences such as exploitation or verbal derogation; third, negative evaluations by outgroup members such as negative stereotyping or apparent disdain; and fourth, negative evaluations by ingroup members such as disapproval or rejection for having had contact with the outgroup population. The presence or degree of culture shock depends on prior intergroup relationships, cognitions, and situational factors. Positive intergroup contact--indicated by equal status, cooperation, approval by social institutions, and intimacy or important to both groups--are predicted to lower anxiety levels. The more that members of each group know about one another, the less likely they are to depend on stereotypes. The more each situation allows for reciprocal interdependence and the less ambiguity in the situation, the less likely members are to experience anxiety. W. G. Stephan and J. C. Brigham (1985) relate anxiety in intergroup relations to the "contact hypothesis" of intergroup relationships. According to this perspective, four factors emerge as core conditions for reducing anxiety: equal status inside and perhaps outside the contact situation, cooperative interdependence within each group and perhaps across groups as well, support by authority figures, and interacting with other group members as individuals outside their stereotypes.

K. A. Juffer (1987) describes five explanations of culture shock in the literature, four of which depend on the deficit or disease hypothesis. First, culture shock is caused by confronting a new environment or situation. This environmental or situational explanation suggests that all persons will experience some degree of culture shock in a foreign environment.

Second, culture shock is caused by ineffectiveness of intercultural or interpersonal communication. Explaining culture shock as resulting from communication problems causing people to misunderstand one another or predict one another's behavior suggests misperception is the cause of culture shock.

Third, culture shock is caused by a threat to the emotional or intrapsychic well-being of the sojourner. Here the clear emphasis on illness and pathology or disease is apparent in the clinical adjectives used to describe the culture shock experience.

Fourth, culture shock demonstrates the need to modify behavior adequately and to regain positive reinforcement from the new environment. This more behavioral perspective describes culture shock as a reaction to needs and wants, leading to inappropriate behaviors.

Fifth, Juffer (1987) describes culture shock as caused by a "growth experience." This positive explanation of culture shock will be described in the next section where change and transition are seen as potentially positive conditions of growth, development, and learning. The growth explanation of culture shock is described as a normal experience which does not necessarily indicate failure deficit or abnormality.

The current literature on culture shock seems to favor the positive-educational rather than the negative-pathological description of culture shock. While there may be both positive and negative consequences of a culture shock experience it is important to describe the process in a balanced perspective. The importance of a positive perspective of culture shock will be highlighted in the next section.

THE GROWTH MODEL OF CULTURE SHOCK

Although acculturative stress is usually linked to the acculturation process in theories and research about culture shock, the experience of acculturative stress is not necessarily negative. Acculturative stress may be a positive and creative force with an educational impact to stimulate, motivate, and enhance the individual's long-term acculturation. Until recently (D'Ardenne and Mahtani, 1989), there was little or no emphasis on the skills and strengths that people have developed out of their adverse culture-shock experiences. The literature on culture shock was more likely to be problem-bound and problem-oriented than growth-related.

If acculturation is viewed from a unidirectional perspective, it is synonymous with assimilation, directed toward changing cultural patterns to fit those of the host culture. This is the case when attempts to reduce culture shock are focused primarily on acquiring the values of the host culture by members of a minority or immigrant group (Sodowsky and Plake, 1992). E. S. Levine and A. M. Padilla (1980) defined acculturation biculturally in speaking of the Mexican-American's commitment to both the Mexican-American and the Anglo cultures. This biculturality ranged on a continuum from a low to a high commitment toward Mexican-American culture and high toward a low commitment to Anglo cultures. This approach fits with the four acculturation options described by J. W. Berry (1980) of assimilation, integration, rejection, and deculturation. Berry was able to identify the acculturation process being followed by getting positive or negative answers to the following two questions:

(1) "Is my cultural identity of value and to be retained?" and (2) "Are positive relations with the larger (host/dominant) culture to be sought?" The four combinations of response would each indicate one of the four acculturation options.

Acculturation is not necessarily a negative process. The concept is useful primarily to understand the changes that take place when encountering an unfamiliar host culture. Surprisingly little is known about the acculturation process in spite of the extensive anecdotal literature on the subject. D. J. Kealey (1988) found that, in many cases, members of the staff of the Canadian International Development Agency (CIDA) who experienced intense culture shock abroad were ultimately more productive than those who experienced little or no culture shock. This is consistent with Adler's (1975) view of culture shock as a process of intercultural learning, leading to greater self-awareness and personal growth. The educational/developmental approach to culture shock is gradually replacing the perspective of culture shock as a disease. B. D. Ruben and D. J. Kealey (1979) found that the intensity and directionality of culture shock were unrelated to patterns of psychological adjustment. In some instances, the degree of culture shock was, in fact, positively related to ultimate professional effectiveness in the new environment.

J. W. Berry, Y. H. Poortinga, M. H. Segall, and P. J. Dasen (1992) distinguish between the consequences of culture shock. On the one hand, there is the possibility of a relatively conflict-free change in behavior by giving up one role and taking on a different role in a shift of behavior that is smooth and continuous maintaining the quality of life. On the other hand, acculturation can result in psychological conflict and social disintegration that can result in acts of homicide, abuse, general decline in mental health, and deterioration in the quality of life. Berry (Berry et al., 1992) prefers the term "acculturative stress" rather than "culture shock" to emphasize the theoretical links of this process to theories of stress in the health psychology literature.

A. Furnham and S. Bochner (1986) develop the potentially positive consequences of culture shock as part of the culture learning process. Consequently, they advocate a social skills approach to culture shock, where the sojourner learns the skills, rules, and roles that are required in the new setting. Berry et al. (1992) elaborate on appropriate skills for dealing with communication difficulties such as language learning, language dialect learning, turn taking in conversation, exchanging complements, politeness, direct and indirect communication styles, and the appropriate use of nonverbal behaviors. These examples of culture skill learning will increase the sojourner's intercultural competence demonstrated both in the holistic adjustment of the sojourner and learning of appropriate behaviors in more culture-specific terms.

Furnham and Bochner (1986) have identified six classes of predictor variables for determining how and whether the person will be affected by culture shock.

1. The control of conditions for initiating contact with the host culture are important.
2. A range of intrapersonal factors such as age, previous travel, language skills, resourcefulness, independence, fortitude, ambiguity tolerance appearance, and other personal factors will make a difference.
3. Biological factors relating to physical condition and general state of health will determine the outcomes of culture shock.
4. Interpersonal variables, such as having support and a clearly defined role, are important factors.
5. The characteristics of the host culture itself will be an important factor.
6. The geopolitical conditions in the host culture at the time of contact will be an important factor.

Whether culture contact has a positive or a negative effect will depend on these and many other factors. Culture shock may constructively be viewed as a specialized form of learning and educational growth. In this way learning another culture combines the culture-learning model with a social-skills model in emphasizing the potentially positive consequences of culture contact.

APPLICATIONS OF THE CULTURE SHOCK METAPHOR

While we may not be able to explain culture shock adequately, there are generally accepted approaches to dealing with this phenomenon that apply to a wide variety of crises situations, as identified by T. L. Coffman and M. C. Harris (1984).

First, the visitor needs to recognize that any important life transition is likely to result in stress and discomfort as a usual and normal consequence. The pain of culture shock may be seen as less of a deficit or disease by recognizing it as a normal response to change.

Second, the maintenance of personal integrity and self-esteem should become the primary goal of someone experiencing culture shock. Visitors often experience a loss of status in the new culture, where language, customs, and procedures are strange and unfamiliar. These visitors will need reassurance and support to maintain a healthy self-image and to restore their sense of self-efficacy.

Third, time must be allowed for the adjustment to take place without pressure or urgency. Persons adjust at their own rate depending on the situation. Ultimate reconciliation of the new with the old may require a longer period of time than is convenient but which is nonetheless necessary.

Fourth, recognizing the patterns of adjustment will help the visitor develop new skills and insights. By charting the process of changes leading up to culture shock and predicting future stages in a logical sequence, the process may become more concrete and less ambiguous. Depression and a sense of failure should be recognized as one stage in the adjustment process and not as a permanent feature of the person's new identity.

Fifth, labeling the symptoms of culture shock will help the visitor interpret emotional responses to stress in adjustment. Knowing that others have experienced culture shock and have survived or have even grown stronger from the experience can be comforting.

Sixth, being well adjusted at home does not ensure an easy adjustment in the foreign culture. In some cases, visitors may find themselves more homesick if they were much better off back home. It is also possible for people to carry their back-home problems into the new culture, resulting in maladjustment in both the old and the new cultures, while they seek to escape from these problems by going to a new culture.

Seventh, although culture shock cannot be prevented, it is possible to prepare persons for transition to new cultures and thereby ease the adjustment process. Preparation might include language study, learning about the host culture, simulating situations to be encountered, and spending time with nationals from the host culture before travelling there.

In all instances, the development of a support system is essential to help the visitor reconstruct an important identity or role in the new culture. The visitor learns important lessons from culture shock that can perhaps not be learned in any other way. To that extent culture shock actually contributes to the formation of a stronger bicultural or multicultural identity.

The contributing factors of culture shock can be classified into physiological factors, such as fatigue and the body's nonspecific reaction to stress by expending great amounts of energy; psychological factors, such as learning rates, the strength of old habits, and realistic self-expectations; and social factors, such as other people's timetables, the extent of withdrawal, and the availability of support (Coffman and Harris, 1984).

This pattern we have called "culture shock" has metaphorical applications to other crisis situations (Coffman, 1978). Adapting to sharply different life roles, such as divorce, is functionally equivalent to moving into a foreign culture, with many of the culture-shock features. Coffman points out another example in working with elderly mental patients who were moved from one ward to another. Coffman describes how job or career changes, divorce, widowhood, retirement, or disability also share some resemblance to the culture-shock phenomenon.

Discussions of international business describe the adjustment to different environments as a cyclical process (Torbiorn, 1982; Dunbar, 1992). United States managers in Europe were more satisfied than those in South America, a result that was attributed to a greater perceived difference between the United States managers and non-European cultures and has been referred to as the "cultural toughness" of a foreign posting. The greater the perceived differences in the work and social environment, the greater the adjustment, complexity, and culture shock.

Psychological principles, such as the Skaggs-Robinson hypothesis (Triandis, 1971) or the Osgood transfer surface, suggest that any new situation--such as but not limited to an unfamiliar culture--that involves the same stimulus and the same response pattern is least difficult. When both the situation and the required response are different, the learning does not require the "unlearning" of habitual responses. When the same stimulus requires a very different response, the adjustment is most difficult. Therefore, when you are prompted to behave in the new setting by back-home cues, you are most likely to encounter trouble (Brislin and Pedersen, 1976).

The theories of acculturation can be used to conceptualize and study changes of people in a great variety of settings. The culture-shock model offers a promising approach that can be used to understand adjustment difficulties generally and the processes of social change in particular.

CONCLUSION

The current perspective of culture shock makes several generally accepted assumptions. First, culture shock is not a disease but a learning process, however uncomfortable or painful it might be. Culture shock may, however, be connected with disease and pathological states or may result in unhealthy reactions under the right conditions.

Second, by metaphor, culture shock may relate to life crises in a variety of areas other than the experiences of travel to another country. A person experiencing any radical change in his or her life may experience a process of adaptation or accommodation that parallels the conditions described by culture shock.

Third, there is little if any way to measure accurately culture shock because of its complex and multifaceted nature, although the heuristic convenience of the U-curve stage model in describing culture shock is likely to ensure its continuation as a descriptive if not an explanatory model.

Fourth, there are ways to prepare people for experiencing culture shock which will mediate the pain and discomfort resulting from that process. The research in this area includes data both on the intrapersonal and interpersonal levels of analysis. Fifth, culture shock is a frequently experienced phenomenon which, to a greater or lesser extent, is familiar to all persons at one time or another. It is therefore useful and important to gain a better understanding of culture shock to facilitate a better understanding of other cultures and of ourselves in relation to those other cultures.

Most of the research on culture shock has been quantitative in design, gathering objective data from individuals to test one or another theory or explanation of culture shock. The data being reported in this book will emphasize qualitative approaches. The critical incidents that illustrate each of the five stages of culture shock in this book have led to several new insights about culture shock.

First, culture shock does not appear to be a stage-graded progression for the individual students. A student was only slightly more likely to report incidents coded at lower stages early in the voyage and higher stages later in the voyage. Either the U-curve stage-graded hypothesis was not supported by these data or perhaps the complexity of visiting different cultures escaped any obvious measures of continuous stage-graded growth.

Second, culture shock is an intrapersonal phenomenon. The person experiencing culture shock is not merely experiencing an unfamiliar culture but is perhaps more importantly confronting herself or himself. Culture shock is sometimes described as resulting from the encounter between people or a state of mind external from the individual. Most research on culture shock examines the relationship between a particular individual and a single more-or-less homogenous host culture. In this voyage, the individual student encountered a great variety of host cultures and, to the extent that a condition of culture shock existed at all, the adjustment process was internalized and intrapsychic.

Third, culture shock is in response to interpersonal or intrapersonal conflict and examples of dissonance. When culture shock did evidence itself it usually was in response to conflict or dissonance of some sort as a coping strategy for dissonance reduction or conflict management. This sometimes appeared as an internalized "argument" within the person and sometimes as a confrontation with others.

Fourth, culture shock results in learning. It is not always easy to identify or measure the learning resulting from culture shock, but the students on this voyage will have vivid and detailed memories of their culture-shock experiences for a very long time. Students seemed to move from a more externalized locus of control to a more internalized locus of control, venturing out in smaller and smaller groups, requiring less and less reassurance and demonstrating more and more self-esteem and self-efficacy. In some cases, this learning had a positive effect on the student who was free to observe the host culture and participate meaningfully. In other cases, the learning may have had a negative effect where individual students responded to the newly found freedom in less responsible ways. In learning and change the potential for positive and negative results will always present themselves.

Fifth, culture shock is a multidimensional, rather than a simple, process. It should not surprise us that the literature about culture shock is somewhat confusing and even contradictory. The multiplicity of dynamic variables evident in the critical incidents from each of the following chapters will demonstrate elements from all levels of culture shock, even within the same situation. culture shock is not undimensional. In each of the following critical incidents, a particular feature will be identified to illustrate something about one particular stage of culture shock, even though other elements in the same incident could just as easily be associated with other stages. The intention of this book is not to simplify the elegant complexity of culture shock but rather to examine the subjective experiences in their variety of different perspectives. culture shock is a meta reaction both to strangeness and to the awkward feelings provoked by strangeness in an escalation of anxiety. In that way, culture shock resembles any example of rapid social change.

2

Critical Incidents Around the World

When you want to describe an experience as complicated as a voyage around the world the best way to do it is to tell stories. When people ask about the voyage they usually ask to hear one or two stories about extraordinary experiences. These stories are organized to illustrate the profoundly personal process of culture shock experienced during the voyage. While the students who contributed critical incidents in the following chapters were taking one voyage to the many different countries we visited they were taking another voyage within themselves. Because the learning about cultures was so profoundly personal this book will emphasize qualitative data in describing the culture-shock experience through significant stories or "critical incidents."

More than eighty students, who were enrolled in three psychology classes, each contributed eight critical incidents in connection with their coursework. The seventy students who gave us permission to use their critical incidents are mentioned by name in the preface to this book. The critical incidents were classified into categories according to the five stages of culture shock described earlier. One chapter will be devoted to each of these five stages to describe what a sojourner says, feels, does, thinks, and believes while going through that particular stage. The incidents in each stage-category were then analyzed to identify any patterns of response that would help us to understand or explain the phenomenon of culture shock at that stage of the U-curve. Each of the five stages will be covered in a different chapter where the patterns of perception, emotion, behavior, and interpretation will be analyzed.

Because culture shock is such a personalized and complicated phenomenon, a large number of incidents were included to demonstrate ways that different people experience culture shock in very different ways. The resulting assortment of critical incidents provides a wide range of perspectives, organized according to the primary characteristics of the five stages. The objective is to include the reader in the voyage to share vicariously in the many experiences of participating students as they encountered culture shock.

THE CRITICAL INCIDENT TECHNIQUE

The critical incident technique was first described by J. C. Flanagan (1954, J. C. Flanagan & R. K. Burns, 1955) to analyze jobs. The method involves collecting anecdotes describing effective and ineffective behaviors at a particular site or workplace. These anecdotal examples are called "critical incidents." Each incident describes a specific example of success or failure where the observer describes: (1) the events that led up to the incident and their context, (2) what the person did (or did not) do that was effective or ineffective, (3) the apparent consequences of this behavior, and (4) whether any of the consequences were under the person's control to change. When all the incidents are collected, they are content analyzed and sorted by one or more judges into categories or dimensions. These categories or dimensions may be used as tests or become the basis for training programs. Grace Fivars (1980) identified 721 research studies that used the critical incident methodology as of that date, and many more projects have incorporated critical incidents since that time.

The critical incident technique is closely related to the case study method, which evaluates the behavior of a person or persons in a clinical or decision-making setting, examining background, behavior, and changes in behavior over a period of months or years. Case data describe and interpret impressions about the subject from a qualitative/subjective rather than a quantitative/objective viewpoint. Sigmund Freud made the case study method the foundation of his theories while Carl Rogers, Gordon Allport, and other therapists have frequently used the case study method in psychological analysis. Although cases are easier to visualize than numbers, it is difficult to generalize from cases. It is also difficult to separate cause from effect in cases. Finally, the investigator's biases and assumptions will be reflected in the cases reported. Cases are particularly useful when examining an extraordinary situation, when the subject is typical of a defined group, when the case illustrates a special method or experience, and when possibilities are being demonstrated for the future (Burger, 1990). These characteristics made critical incidents useful for conditions to the study of culture shock among students on their voyage around the world.

A major advantage of critical incidents is the focus on observable behaviors. The disadvantages are that it requires considerable time and effort to collect the incidents and to code the incidents in a meaningful way. The incidents also tend to emphasize the extraordinary rather than the average or typical situation, which distorts or exaggerates aspects of the experience. It is sometimes hard to generalize from critical incidents to the real world. It is also difficult to get consensus about the appropriate response in a multicultural critical incident.

Critical incidents are particularly popular in teaching or training about multicultural relationships. In part, this happens because more specific and focused measures are more likely to impose a cultural bias. In part, it is because critical incidents are more open ended and include the complexity of real-life situations where persons from more than one culture come into contact. The critical incident methodology has been used to develop and to measure several multicultural competencies:

1. Information source development: Students develop the ability to use many information sources within a social or cultural environment. In collecting critical incidents, information-gathering skills such as observing, questioning the people one meets, and careful listing skills are developed.
2. Cultural understanding: Awareness and understanding of values, feelings, and attitudes of people in another culture, and the ways in which these values influence behavior, are clarified. Critical incidents help illustrate the ways in which values, expectations, and attitudes undergird behaviors.
3. Interpersonal communication: Listening well, speaking clearly, and paying attention to the expression of nonverbal communication, such as messages delivered through physical movements of eyes and face, are highlighted as important aspects of face-to-face encounters in the incidents.
4. Commitment to persons and relationships: Enhanced ability to become involved with people from other cultures may be developed through the process of collecting critical incidents. This involves giving and inspiring trust and confidence, establishing a basis for mutual liking and respect, caring for culturally different people, and acting in ways that are both truthful and sensitive toward the feelings of others.
5. Decision making: Students develop the ability to come to conclusions based on their own assessment of the information available and their identification of the right action or response. This might also be called problem solving, which includes learning to be explicit about the problem, working out steps to a solution, and generating alternatives. In the multicultural situation, it is important to identify what is at issue, the dimensions of the problem, and the alternatives that are personally and culturally available.

There is no substitute for actual experience. The critical incident technique is an attempt to bring actual experiences or events into the classroom as a resource. The incident is critical--meaning important, essential, or valuable--in the way that a part of a machine might be critical to the smooth operation of the machine. The incident is a short description of an event that took place within a five-or ten-minute period of time. A case study, by contrast, is much more complicated and might take place over weeks, months, or even years.

APPLICATIONS OF CRITICAL INCIDENTS

Critical incidents are based on real-life situations and typically involve a dilemma where there is no easy or obvious solution. The objective of critical incidents is to stimulate thinking about basic and important issues which occur in real-life situations. By analyzing the incident, participants can imagine themselves in the same situation, develop strategies to deal with that situation, and become more realistic in their expectations. Rehearsing what a participant would do in a critical incident provides the relative safety of a training situation, requires limited risk taking, and yet provides much of the complexity of real-life situations.

Critical incidents do not necessarily imply a single solution or a "right way" of resolving the dilemma in a situation, but they explore alternative solutions and their implications or consequences. The critical incident reporting format applied by students in this project was organized into six categories.

1. Identify the event or occurrence with as much specificity as possible, the problem to be solved, the decision to be made, and the issues involved.
2. Describe the relevant details and circumstances surrounding the event so that readers will understand what happened: when, how, why and where.
3. List the people involved describing them and their relationships to the observer and to one another.
4. Describe the observer's own role in the situation in terms of what was done or how that person acted, identifying the particular multicultural skill or skills involved, and the choices made.
5. Write a brief analysis of the incident telling what you learned from the incident, stating estimates of the observer's and actor's levels of multicultural skill
   development.
6. Identify the specific psychological construct or concept that is illustrated in this critical incident.

D. W. Sue and D. Sue (1990) have incorporated critical incidents into their book on counseling culturally different clients. Eighteen critical incidents are used to illustrate concepts of cross-cultural counseling in their book. These incidents share three characteristics: (1) each incident illustrates a conflict of cultures, values, standards, or goals; (2) the solutions are not obvious, and the alternatives are deliberately controversial; and (3) each incident includes a description of the conditions or context in which the incident occurred. There are several reasons why Sue and Sue favor critical incidents as a methodology.

1. Trainees can learn change-agent skills early in training by identifying social, cultural, and political forces operating in each situation.
2. Critical incidents provide a laboratory for examining dangerous

situations, personal biases, value differences, and sensitive issues with safety for the trainee and the client.

3. The readers are encouraged to identify as many cross-cultural issues in each incident as possible so that they can see the same situation from different perspectives.

4. The readers can identify conflicts of values among the different characters within each incident and between each character and social institution.

5. The readers are encouraged to become committed to a course of action by examining their own values and biases, and by projecting their own self-reference criterion into the critical incidents.

Critical incidents have been used to do research on work motivation and satisfaction, as a work performance appraisal and as a behavior-anchored developmental scale (Sauser, 1987). One very popular variation on critical incidents for international/intercultural training is the culture assimilator (Albert, 1983; Fiedler, Mitchell and Triandis, 1971) where the target audience and target culture are specified and where the training is designed to match one specific culture with another specific but contrasting culture. Following each incident, the culture assimilator identifies alternative possible attributions about the behaviors from the host culture point of view with one set of attributions being more accurate than the others.

Fiedler, Mitchell, and Triandis (1971) describe an ideal critical incident for the culture assimilator as being (1) a typical interaction between two cultures, (2) apparently conflictful, puzzling and open to misinterpretation, (3) a situation in which a right decision could be made if all relevant information were available, and (4) a situation that is relevant to a specific task, mission, or training objective. The culture assimilator is adaptable to a wide variety of multicultural settings. If the incidents are gathered by sensitive observers, they can reflect a great deal of cultural complexity and understanding.

The research supporting culture assimilators suggests that the following benefits result from its use (Brislin, Cushner, Cherrie, and Yong, 1986).

1. Greater understanding of hosts, as judged by the hosts themselves.

2. A decrease in the use of negative stereotypes on the part of trainees.

3. The development of complex thinking about the target culture, which replaces the oversimplified, facile thinking to which hosts react negatively.

4. Greater enjoyment among trainees who interact with members of the target culture, a feeling reciprocated by hosts.

5. Better adjustment to the everyday stresses of life in other cultures.

6. Better job performance in cases where performance is influenced by specific cultural practices that can be covered in the training materials.

R. W. Brislin (Brislin et al., 1986) has developed a general culture assimilator not directed toward a specific bicultural relationship but with a more general and unspecified target audience. These materials were developed to help people adjust to any other culture. Brislin and his colleagues identified 100 critical incidents according to nine broad categories:

1. The historical myths people brought with them to another culture.
2. People's attitudes, traits, and skills.
3. Their thought and attribution processes.
4. The groups they join.
5. The range of situations in which they have to interact.
6. Their management of cross-cultural conflict.
7. The tasks they want to accomplish.
8. The organizations of which they are a part and, given an understanding of the above.
9. The process of short- and long-term adjustments.

The emphasis in this culture general assimilator approach is to avoid thinking of a particular target culture but rather focus on the participant's own internal and intrapsychic state. This approach emphasizes commonalities across cultures. The culture-specific and the culture general assimilators supplement one another in training. Although the general culture assimilator cannot be precisely accurate to a particular bicultural relationship, Brislin advocates the general assimilator under five different conditions.

1. When a culture-specific training program is not available, the general assimilator can be useful.
2. The general assimilator provides a basis for covering culture-specific information in newly developed programs by guiding resource persons in their training of sojourners.
3. The general assimilator integrates a great deal of specific information without overwhelming the participant.
4. The general assimilator encourages the development of a multicultural perspective across cultures.
5. The general assimilator provides a way to involve students in courses through specific incidents and examples.

Brislin's general culture assimilator organized the 100 incidents according to eighteen general themes:

1. People's intense feelings of anxiety, disconfirmed expectancies, belonging, ambiguity, and confronting prejudice.
2. Knowledge areas about work, time and space, language, roles, importance of groups, rituals, hierarchies, and values.

3. Bases of cultural differences through categorization, differentiation, ingroup/outgroup distinctions, learning styles, and attribution.

CRITICAL INCIDENTS OF STUDENTS ABROAD

The students participating in this book were enrolled in three psychology courses of the University of Pittsburgh's Semester at Sea project. Each student submitted at least eight critical incidents of about two pages each to illustrate psychological constructs in their contact with host countries around the world. The critical incidents were gathered through (1) personal experiences, (2) observing others, or (3) interviewing others about events in the countries visited by the Semester at Sea *Universe* during the spring semester of 1982.

Critical incidents facilitate learning in a variety of ways. A skilled and knowledgeable leader can help readers of critical incidents to become culturally aware of their own values, expanding their awareness to contrasting worldviews and generating new or alternative counselor intervention strategies. The critical incidents are useful to stimulate small group discussion where different members of the group compare and contrast their different reactions to the same incident. Critical incidents are also useful for individual study and learning on one's own by studying each critical incident from several different contrasting perspectives. Some of the critical incidents lend themselves to role playing where group members take on different roles in the incident and interact with or without a script. The incidents can be used as an orientation or introduction to a topic, such as study abroad. The critical incidents can be used to set up debates on pro and con alternative interpretations of an appropriate response to a situation.

Critical incidents can be used as homework to develop analytical skills, where students are asked to "spot the concept" hidden in the critical incident. Critical incidents can be used as pre and post measures of learning about cross-cultural skills in a particular area. The critical incidents may become the basis of a test to measure the outcomes of training or for selecting candidates to a particular position. The collecting and writing of critical incidents is itself instructive, requiring the participant to observe the situation carefully. The critical incidents in Sue and Sue (1990) are accompanied by a detailed discussion guide about the issues implicit within each critical incident.

The use of videotape enhances critical incidents. P. B. Pedersen (1988) developed a 200-page casebook on mental health problems of unaccompanied refugee/entrant minors together with a one-hour videotape of four incidents in the casebook. In the instructions to users of these critical incidents, several guidelines are provided to potential users of critical incidents.

1. Allow the participants to apply their own expertise to the discussion of each situation. If participants are not allowed to contribute their own

insights, they will become much less motivated. The participants who are attracted to a discussion of critical incidents typically have a great deal of insight to contribute, and this valuable resource should not be overlooked.

2. Focus on the quality of the discussion rather than on getting through all of the critical incidents in a limited period of time. Each group may cover only one or two of the critical incidents that fit their particular interests and needs. The leader should preview the incidents ahead of any discussion so that the group can begin the discussion of the critical incident on the aspects that apply most directly to them.

3. The critical incidents should always be distributed either in written, audio, video, or all three forms if possible. Using an audio and video as well as a written form of the incident allows a more thorough discussion of the issues.

4. Focus on aspects of the critical incident that raise questions in the group discussion giving an analysis of each aspect and how each aspect relates to other aspects. This is especially true when dealing with videotaped critical incidents.

5. A discussion of each critical incident may well begin with a discussion of the stressors implicit within the incident context. Readers or viewers of each incident should be coached on what to look for in the incident. If the reader or viewer is given an agenda or a task, he or she will participate much more actively and may well find additional insights in the process.

6. Identify mental health indicators within each critical incident that demonstrate psychological processes. These indicators might provoke discussion and stimulate thinking about how the characters in each incident are affected.

7. Identify learning outcomes for the participants as a result of using the critical incidents. The barriers, stressors, mental health indicators, and other materials in the incidents will provide source materials for a group to develop its own appropriate learning outcomes.

8. Keep the discussion of each critical incident focused on how participants can realistically accommodate the complex reality of acculturation in a complex multicultural setting. Maintain a practical perspective of the issues involved.

9. Follow a schedule of activities in discussing the critical incidents so that the discussion can proceed in an orderly manner, with stated goals, realistic expectations, focus themes, anticipated outcomes, and practical advantages of studying these critical incidents.

V. F. Calia and R. J. Corsini (1973) coach the reader of their book, *Critical Incidents in School Counseling*, to participate actively rather than passively in the incidents and the accompanying consultant commentaries with the following directions:

1. Ask yourself how you would have handled the situation differently.
2. Tell the characters in the incident how they should have behaved, explaining why your approach is better than the one they used.
3. Read the consultant's commentary on the incident carefully before entering into a debate with what that consultant had to say.
4. Do not hesitate to disagree or argue with the consultants when you believe your view is more appropriate.

The incidents reported in the following chapters are reported in the student's own words, with pronouns substituted for names to protect the student's confidentiality. Consequently, these incidents do not follow the same format as each student tells his or her story in his or her own special way. There will not be a single right answer provided as would be true for a culture assimilator. Each of the incidents contains many elements, but a special insight will be identified for each incident to demonstrate one aspect of that particular stage of culture shock. The reader will no doubt find other insights that might more appropriately be related to other stages of culture shock, given the complexity of each incident.   There are many different interpretations of each critical incident, and it would be very difficult to identify a single "right" interpretation. However, the stories written in the student's own words should help the reader understand the subject experiences of culture shock, stage by stage.

THE SEMESTER AT SEA CONCEPT

This brief historical description of the Semester at Sea concept was abstracted from the book *Discovery* by author and photographer Paul Liebhart in 1985 and is included in this book with his permission and the permission of the Semester at Sea office in Pittsburgh, Pennsylvania.

Since 1877, when James O Woodruff of Indianapolis, Indiana, planned to send a ship-load of students on the steamship *Ontario* from New York City around the world (but never did) the concept of shipboard education has been alive in American higher education literature. By 1926 James Edwin Lough of New York University established himself as "the Father of Shipboard Education" in a seven and a half month voyage of the SS *Ryndam* to thirty-five countries and ninety cities around the world. For the first time an entire college campus had been sent around the world.

Although some students continued to enthusiastically endorse the success of this voyage even fifty years later not everyone was enthusiastic. New York University fired Dean Lough after 27 years of service. Andrews McIntosh, the financial backer had his own idea about how a floating university should be run and took over the operation himself. The McIntosh group sponsored the

"International University Cruise, Inc." (IUC). A modified version of the voyage arranged stays of two to four weeks in selected ports so that students could spend more time among the people there, even though it disrupted the classwork. The original University Travel Association, Inc. (UTA) attempted to set up a competing program but there were only 300 applications and both programs had to be postponed until 1928. Sydney Greenbie succeeded McIntosh in 1928 when both UTA and IUC sent out ships of students from New York around the world and shipboard education was launched as a permanent university alternative.

Shipboard education became a more permanent feature in a charter contract with the Holland America Line to create a university on board the *Seven Seas* in February 1963. The *Seven Seas* was a 12,574 passenger ship converted to an escort aircraft carrier during World War II. The "hanger deck" provided classrooms in the new student ship. Each voyage was to last one semester with plans to sail every semester on a different around-the-world itinerary. The original idea was to make the Seven Seas an independent university with the home campus at Ramona near San Diego offering a regular four year degree program. In 1965 the *Seven Seas* affiliated with Chapman College to secure recognition and accreditation. Chapman College developed the "World Campus Afloat" concept of shipboard education over the next ten years and twenty-one consecutive voyages serving over 9,000 students. By 1966 the Holland American Line also exchanged the old Seven Seas for a new ship called SS *Ryndam*, the same name as the original floating university. Each semester a curriculum of about 100 courses were offered for undergraduate students, emphasizing humanities and the social sciences. Courses were transferable to other universities and faculty came from other universities as well. However, the program continued to lose money and depended on subsidies from the Holland America Line.

Mr. Chao-Yung Tung's career extended from starting as a shipping clerk in Shanghai to becoming one of the world's leading shipowners. He was also an international banker, film maker, computer distributor and patron of the arts. He was a modest man in spite of all these accomplishments whose motto was "the greatest ship is friendship," and a true idealist. He believed in the value of education and supported the concept of an international university. In 1970 Tung met with the World Campus Afloat representatives and began working out the concept of the Seawise Foundation Ltd. to purchase a ship and convert it to a university afloat. The first prospective ship was the RMS *Queen Elizabeth I*, purchased in 1970 by the Seawise Foundation Ltd. After a year of work and six million dollars invested a fire broke out on the ship in Hong Kong harbor and it sank.

Tung had also purchased the liner Atlantic from the American Export Line for Chapman College to use as an interim campus and this ship was named the SS *Universe Campus*. This was the ship that carried thousands of students in the 1970s and 1980s. The SS *Universe* became the ship best known as a university ship.

By the end of the 1975 voyage it appeared that Chapman College was going to terminate its connection with World Campus Afloat. Two WCA administrators, Dr. M. A. Griffiths and Dr. John Tymitz with backing by C. Y. Tung set up the Institute for Shipboard Education as a nonprofit educational corporation and they called the program Semester at Sea. In the spring of 1976 the University of Colorado affiliated with the Institute for Shipboard Education to grant academic credit and issue transcripts for participants in the shipboard program. This affiliation lasted until the fall 1980 voyage.

The University of Pittsburgh was the next academic sponsor through their Center for International Studies in an agreement signed in 1981. Although C. Y. Tung passed away on April 15, 1982, his eldest son Chee Haw Tung reaffirmed the dedication of the Tung family to carry on the shipboard educational effort. The SS *Universe* continues its historical voyage in giving meaning to the lives of its family. Michelle LeBaron, a student on the first Semester at Sea voyage in 1977 describes the meaning of the voyage in her own words:

"For the individuals involved, the voyage has been so much more than the touching of four continents, six seas, and ten countries. It has, like a microscope, brought into sharp focus priorities and ideas, and broadened our awareness. The decks have been a backdrop for a personal voyage of self-discovery. Immediacy and intensity have marked human relationships formed with others as well as encounters we have faced within ourselves. It is in this personal sense that the meaning of the trip is translated into each individual's life. In returning to familiar faces and places, we carry with us new perspectives and resultant energy, injected like a current into our lives. An experience has been ours which cannot be measured in seconds or even light years--it has touched our lives with a mark that is timeless."

Each spring and fall semester the SS *Universe* carries approximately 400 college students around the world for a rare opportunity to learn about their world directly from the world's people.

CRITICAL INCIDENTS DISCUSSION GUIDE

As you read the critical incidents in the following chapters you will have an opportunity to learn both from the student who wrote that critical incident and from others in your discussion of that incident from your various perspectives. The discussion guide below will help facilitate a meaningful exchange with you, the student author, and others in your group about the stages of culture shock.

1. Was the incident authentic?
2. Did the incident illustrate an important issue?
3. How difficult was this incident for the student author?
4. How difficult would the incident be for yourself?
5. How effective do you think the student author was in the incident?
6. How effective would you have been in the same circumstance?
7. Can you generalize from this incident to other learning insights?
8. Was the incident placed in the appropriate "stage" of the culture shock sequences?
9. Have you ever experienced a similar incident?
10. Based on the incident describe your picture of the student author.

3

The Honeymoon Stage

INTRODUCTION

To gain most from experience need to be aware of inner self & culture time

Most if not all descriptions of culture shock indicate a progression of attitudes regarding one's self and others from a lower to a higher level of development. The typical description of progression takes the form of a three-to five-stage U-curve starting at a higher stage of fascination, adventure, optimism, or excitement called the honeymoon stage. This is followed by feelings of inadequacy, disappointment, disillusion, alienation, and self-blame as the direction of progression drops from a high to the lowest point on the U-curve. Finally there is a reorientation or recovery stage where the new situation is viewed in perspective, positive and negative elements are balanced, and the person's morale is restored (Coffman and Harris, 1984). As pointed out earlier, the actual progression of culture shock is seldom as neat and orderly as a U-curve suggests. Only rarely will a person achieve as high a level of functioning in the host culture as in the previous home culture, suggesting a backward J-curve as perhaps more authentic.

If the U-curve hypothesis described culture shock perfectly then one would expect all students to write critical incidents illustrating the honeymoon stage in the first several ports of Nassau, Caracas, or San Salvador, and incidents illustrating bicultural/multicultural perspectives in Hong Kong, Keelung, or Kobe. That did not occur. Although there were slightly more stage-one critical incidents earlier in the voyage and slightly fewer stage-one critical incidents later in the voyage, the individual students seemed to report incidents at each level regarding each port, country, or culture.

There are several possible explanations for this apparent confusion. First, some cultures or countries may seem more familiar than others, resulting in different reactions. Second, culture shock may be multidimensional so that one aspect of the student may be functioning at a higher level than other dimensions. Third, the U-curve may be two-directional, where the student may regress as well as progress on this developmental curve. Fourth, the scoring or measurement of the critical incidents may be faulty or inadequate. Fifth, the sample may be too small, disguising a general trend or tendency which would become more pronounced with a larger number of observations for each student author. Sixth, there may be U-curves within U-curves so that having achieved a level of understanding raises new problems, and the student author starts over again. Seventh, there may be intervening and unaccounted variables in the culture shock experience related to individual differences. Eighth, this apparent confusion of stages may be the result of visiting many ports briefly rather than one culture or country for a longer period of time.

This chapter and the following chapters will organize critical incidents written by student authors on their voyage around the world in five stages to illustrate the different experiences of culture shock. Each of these five stages will provide vivid examples of a type or category in the culture-shock experience. As we understand the experiences of culture shock from the viewpoint of the student authors, we may develop a better understanding of this profoundly personal and subjective phenomenon.

The first stage describes experiences where differences are intriguing and perceptions are positive. The emotions are typically excitement, stimulation, euphoria, playfulness, discovery, and adventuresomeness. The behaviors are typically guided by curiosity, interest, self-assurance, and the collecting of interesting experiences or impressions. The interpretations are those of a tourist, insulated by her or his own culture so that differences as well as similarities are adapted to the person's original status role and identity. There is very little seeming regard for the effect or impact the visiting student author might have on this new environment, and little attention is paid to the consequences of this encounter. The student is usually having a very good time and feels little fear or apprehension about the host culture. The encounter is more likely to be viewed as the end point than the beginning point of a developmental changing process. The student expresses a right to enjoy the host culture with little responsibility for the consequences. The few inconveniences encountered merely add to the adventure and provide something to tell people back home. The novelty of this unusual and exotic setting comes through clearly in the incidents in a sense of freedom, and "unfreezing" of previously constraining rules. The visitor has retained the security and stability of a back-home identity without having to follow all the back-home rules and regulations.

CRITICAL INCIDENTS

Bahamas

Safe and Unsafe. Before boarding this ship about eight friends and I went to the Bahamas early to spend some time there. None of us knew each other, but we all went to the University of Pittsburgh. The first night there we took a taxi to this restaurant in the city of Nassau. We all had a very nice dinner and decided to walk around a bit. My friend and I went into this store to look around. When we left the store, our friends were nowhere to be seen. We went in and out of the neighboring stores. During our search, we got off the main road. We were now walking in a neighborhood that seemed to be unsafe. The two of us were getting scared. All kinds of people were approaching us and yelling at us. All of a sudden this guy approached us and said it was unsafe for two girls to be in the area alone. We told him that we were lost and wanted to catch a taxi. He told us to follow him and we did. As we were walking with him, people were still calling to us and he just told them that we were with him. He got us to the main road and put us in a taxi.

My choices were to trust or not to trust the man in the street. I could have kept walking until I found it myself. Instead I trusted this man. It was hard because I was scared. Women are told not to trust men when they are alone. I learned that you have to trust some people. If I hadn't trusted this man, who knows what would have happened.

INSIGHT:

The two students were so caught up in the "new situation" that they became lost before realizing it. In the excitement of being in a new place it was easy to unintentionally wander into potentially dangerous situations. Although the danger might be exciting to talk about later, at the time it created a lot of anxiety.

Drug Money on the Bus. I was riding on a bus into town in mid-afternoon. The bus system in the Bahamas is very efficient and a meeting place for many people. The bus drivers are very friendly and full of useful advice. Two young men got on the bus and sat down. The bus driver got up from his seat and asked them for their fare. The two men replied that they did not have any change. The bus driver asked them to get off his bus. At this point one of the two guys produced a Bahamian $100 bill from his pocket. "Got change?" the young guy asked while waving the bill in the driver's face. The other guy started to laugh. "Got any change old man?" "Does anyone have any change on this stinking bus?" asked the second guy. The bus driver ordered the two off the bus and apologized to his passengers.

It did not occur to me what was going on until after I heard some older women talking in the back of the bus. The two boys were drug dealers and the bus driver and many of the passengers knew it. Nassau is a very small town and a sudden increase in wealth is noticed by all. The bus driver was showing his disapproval of the boys' new occupation. And he was patted on the back by many of the townspeople as they exited. I only understood the significance of the driver's act after a friend explained to me that the Bahamas was a trafficking spot between Cuba and Miami for drugs.

INSIGHT:

The student observed elements of a local drug culture and the public reaction without getting involved personally. Since the student did not know the rules it was easy to say or do the wrong thing and unintentionally offend host culture persons.

Venezuela

An Ugly American. The critical incident about which I am going to write involves my observance of the behavior of a group of what some would term "ugly Americans": A group of Semester at Sea students acted unpardonably in a foreign country. As a friend and I observed the behavior of these rude people, we made a comment to them about controlling themselves while in another country. The response to our comment was extremely defensive, almost irate.

This incident took place in the terminal outside of the ship in La Guaira, Venezuela. Many students were sitting around the terminal, drinking beer and rum--"having a good time." A few students overdid it in the terminal and began to get out of hand. Two of these students, walking towards the ship (still in the terminal), hopped up on a large conveyor belt and stomped across the length of it, ignoring the reprimands of a Venezuelan store clerk who had seen them. They walked away, laughing, and proceeded to kick over a garbage can, spilling trash on the floor. This, to them, was hilarious--they kept walking towards the ship. One girl out of this group turned the can back up and put a few cans back in it; otherwise, the floor was still a mess. The friend with whom I was walking said to a friend of the guy who knocked over the can, "Don't act obnoxious in a foreign country, it's embarrassing." Very defensively, the guy replied, "What are you, a world traveller? What other countries have you been to besides Venezuela?" She answered, "That's not the point. The point is you're acting obnoxious." "Oh, you're travelled? Where have you been Miss World Traveller?" he asked. She simply ignored his irrelevant question and turned her back. Unfortunately this entire incident was witnessed by three of our new Venezuelan friends from Simon Bolivar University. My friend the "world traveller" turned to them and said apologetically, "Please don't remember that part." It's too bad, but I'm sure that the incident won't be easily forgotten by any of us.

I feel that this event is very critical in terms of the great responsibility each of us has as travellers in every country we visit. We will leave an impression of our own country. Every traveller must realize this responsibility and act accordingly, if we do not, then we are truly "ugly Americans." Through this event, I have learned that even one person's inappropriate behavior in a foreign country (or anywhere for that matter) leaves a lasting impression on others and reflects on the U.S. in a negative light.

INSIGHT:
The group of drunk students seemed to feel no responsibility toward the host culture or toward other students from the ship. These naive students were unaware of the consequences of their unthinking behavior in

Venezuela and sometimes embarrassed fellow country persons by their insensitivity.

American Defenses. I attended a field trip on Monday which took place at Instituto de Estudios Superiores de Administracion Institute (IESA) in Caracas, Venezuela. At this institute they are training MBA's. It is the only institution of its kind in Venezuela. There are 200 students who are enrolled in the two year program which is both stressful and rigorous.

When we arrived at the institute we met the five students whom we would be talking to. Two Semester at Sea students were assigned to one IESA student. I was paired off with a girl from Semester at Sea and our Venezuelan counterpart.

After talking for awhile I finally got up enough guts to ask him the question that I had been dying to ask. "What do you think of Americans?" His response was quite startling to me and came as quite a shock for which I was totally unprepared. He said, "Americans are materialistic, spoiled, stressed and family life doesn't seem important." I didn't really have a response to this, I just sat there. What came next really surprised me, the other SAS student completely agreed with him!

I felt very threatened and upset. I couldn't believe that they were saying this. I'm sure that there are plenty of Venezuelans who think exactly the same way. I learned from this experience that I am proud to be an American. I didn't know enough about his culture to say anything for which I am gravely sorry.

I will not sit somewhere and listen to someone put down my country, the place I live, love and learn. Americans have their faults but so does everyone else. I will not be called spoiled because I can achieve the goals I want. I come from a place where I am given the freedom to speak what I believe, say what I feel and learn what I choose to learn and I will not put this system down. I am very grateful for where I come from.

This Venezuelan student is very proud of his country and its people and did not run them down, he actually loved them. We need more of that in American culture, we need to decide who we are, stand by it and love it for its assets as well as its faults.

INSIGHT:
The student became defensive of American ways before learning why the Venezuelan was being critical. It came as a shock to the students that people in other cultures didn't all have positive opinions about Americans, especially when confronted directly with this bias. It was possible to learn from people who disagreed with the students if they were willing to try and see things from the local viewpoint and to listen.

A Walk on the Beach. While we were in Venezuela, I attended the overnight trip to Angel Falls. There were approximately 35 students total in our group. However, one of the day trips to Angel Falls later got stranded there and ended up spending the night as well. There were also about 35 students in their group. After dinner most of the students went up to the bar and started drinking; I would estimate 55 out of 70. I was one of the 15 or so students not drinking so I was sort of hanging around talking to a couple of other girls who weren't drinking either. A couple of hours went by and most of the students were really pretty drunk. One of our guides (a Venezuelan) came up to the bar and said he had a surprise for us. He and some of the other guys that worked there wanted to take everyone down to the beach to have a bonfire, but we would have to drive there. It was about 11:15 and I wasn't sure if I wanted to go. I talked to the two friends I had been hanging around talking with and they said they were going to go, so I decided I would also. My gut feeling said that it wasn't a good idea as we got on the bus. I felt extremely uneasy, but I didn't want to stay in the camp virtually by myself either. There were only about 15 guy students, and the rest females. There were about 15 Venezuelan men going who were workers from the place we stayed at.

We started down the dirt road which was really dark and bumpy. The further we went, the more uneasy I got, but everyone else seemed to be having a good time, so I didn't do anything. All of a sudden the bus stopped, it was pitch black except for the moon and a light off in the woods. A couple of the Venezuelans jumped down and went off into the trees. At this point I was almost in tears, and I didn't really know why I was so frightened. A girl next to me said under her breath, "Oh my God, they're going to rape us." I could feel the panic come up into my chest and throat and I didn't know what to do. I couldn't walk back in the dark, through the woods to the camp, but I didn't like the situation I was in either. Then there was sort of a commotion to my right and I heard a girl ask if someone would walk a group of girls back to the camp. I immediately jumped down and asked, "Is someone going back to the camp?" One of the two girls I had been talking with earlier was in tears. Four of us were quite relieved when someone offered to walk us back. The rest of the group went on to the beach. The next morning we heard that everything went fine at the beach.

INSIGHT:

The student felt pressured to go along with the group against her better judgment and then was frightened by the possible consequences of her decision. It was easy for the student to get swept away by the group and find herself in an unpleasant or even frightening circumstance. The first mistake of being swept along was compounded by the mistake of overreacting to the potential threat through panic and feelings that she had lost control of the situation.

Should I Run or Should I Stay. I was on my way to the ship because the deadline to re-board the ship was 22:00 and it was 20:00. In Venezuela I was at a friend's house and her father was taking us down to the ship. We decided to leave early just in case there would be traffic or any other problems. The situation is that I was in the car and the traffic was not moving at all. The people from the surrounding cars had their music on and they were dancing. This began to worry me because there was only a few minutes left, and there was still a long drive to go to the ship. We heard that there was a fire and that was what was holding up the traffic. I had to decide either to stay in the car and wait until the cars started moving or take my belongings and start running. I decided to start running with my friend. I was so nervous that I started giggling. After a while I realized that limousine was going through the traffic with six cars in front and another six cars behind it. It was the President. He was trying to get away. He was going toward the airport. As I was running I heard there had been a coup. I realized then that this was the real reason for the traffic jam. I decided to stop for a while and take some pictures of this event although I was dead scared.

Finally the traffic started moving again. I relaxed when I passed two other students who were also heading back to the ship. My friend's father finally caught up to us and we jumped in the car. We had 20 minutes to get to the ship, but by now the traffic was flowing smoothly.

We arrived there just in time. Many people had no idea what had just happened in the city. It was a great experience to share with my friends. Looking back on the incident, I was scared when I heard the traffic jam was due to the coup; however, I thought of it as being present at a historical event. I don't really know what made me stop and take pictures of the traffic jam and the President's limousine, especially knowing how much I had to lose if I was late for the ship.

INSIGHT:

There is a dreamlike quality to some of these students' experiences that sometimes puts them out of touch with reality. As a tourist it was possible to lose perspective and become so detached from the surrounding reality that even a violent revolution became a photo opportunity. There was an "unreal" quality to the initial encounter of other cultures which caused the students to unintentionally put themselves in danger.

Venezuelan Nightclub. When my friends and I were in Venezuela, we went to the restaurant/night club called "Weekends." It was a very big place, with two full bars. After a while, the atmosphere grew loud and jubilant. There was a band playing rock-n-roll American music. Many of us wanted to dance. The place was crowded and there was only a small dance floor in front of the stage. No one was dancing but my friend and I assumed that dancing in this bar was customary.

We got on the dance floor and started dancing around having a good time.

We were getting stared at and knew that people were looking at us strangely, but we ignored it and just continued to have fun. The issue involved was whether or not we should dance in a crowded Venezuelan bar when no locals were dancing.

There is no question we made the wrong decision by (1) choosing to dance and (2) ignoring the strange looks we were getting from the locals. After a few minutes, the manager came over and stopped us, explaining that it wasn't appropriate for us to dance there while people were still eating. He also told us that we could have no more to drink!

Luckily, I speak Spanish which saved us from further embarrassment. We handled the situation as well as could be expected but we nevertheless felt like dumb Americans. If I had it to do over again, as I will have in many future experiences in foreign countries, I would take on a "low profile" in clubs and watch the way the natives act because they know appropriate behavior in their country.

I learned that I should not make assumptions, especially in public places where I risk offending someone or embarrassing myself. I know that my cross-cultural skills are developing rapidly. Having travelled all over Europe, lived in Paris, Germany, and Greece, I know that it takes time to understand the ways of the different people and their mentalities.

INSIGHT:
The two students acted without thinking or paying attention to the patterns of appropriate behavior by local Venezuelans in the club. The students assumed their back-home rules also applied abroad and didn't observe the local customs carefully enough. The tendency to impose their own values was exaggerated by excessive consumption of alcohol and resulted in an embarrassing situation.

Being an Unwelcome Visitor. The critical incident that I will describe occurred in La Guaira, Venezuela. A group of four girls (including myself) decided to venture up into the mountains of La Guaira to see how the Venezuelan people lived. The reactions that we received from people varied a great deal. At the bottom of the mountain people were very friendly, but as we made our way towards the top people became more and more hostile. Because we were foreigners (which was obvious from our backpacks, light skin, etc.) many people stared at us, and sometimes even followed us for awhile. We ran into the scary incident as we reached the top of the mountain. We realized that the poorer people lived at the top. As we walked around the top of the mountain we came upon an area where people were hanging out. As we got closer the atmosphere changed. As a group we immediately felt the tension. Looks of uncertainty and confusion about what to do next were interchanging between the four of us. The next thing we noticed was a woman who was pointing at us, shaking her head and saying something over and over in Spanish. At first I wasn't sure she was directing her comments at us, but as her face grew meaner and her words louder, we knew we should get of there fast. It was mainly through body language and a few spoken words that as a group we knew that we were in a bad situation and should turn around and head back down the mountain.

I glanced around at the other girls in the group to see if they were also feeling uneasy. Through our eye contact and facial expression our group exhibited fear. The only words spoken were, "I think we should go." We all agreed and understood our danger without needing to go into in-depth communication.

INSIGHT:

The group of women students seemed to feel they were travelling in a "capsule" where they could observe locals without getting involved. The students got so caught up in the excitement of an adventure in a foreign culture that they failed to see themselves as the locals might see them. It was important to monitor the verbal and nonverbal cues, especially when the students didn't understand the language, so they could better see themselves as others saw them.

Brazil

Misunderstanding at the Office. This even occurred in Salvador, Brazil. The first day we were in port a group (made up of roughly 12-15 people) went together to change traveller's checks for local currency. Because so many students had the same goal, the bank lines were over two hours. Our group decided to find an alternate plan. After receiving a tip from an IESA faculty member, we went to another building a few blocks away. It was here we were met by security guards and ushered upstairs.

The room where we were taken was relatively small. It had six desks, all with computers, printers, and phones. There were three men working diligently, and one working *very* hard to accommodate us in English.

He explained that he could help us change our money, showed us the rate of exchange on his calculator, and explained (as best he could) that he had sent a runner for money, and the exchanges would take about twenty minutes. We agreed and thanked him in Portuguese.

The critical incident occurred when one of the guys from our group started reeling off a quote from a popular American movie. The quote was humorous, and naturally we all started laughing. Our simultaneous laughter and outburst was offensive to the office workers and the gentleman helping us. They all seemed peeved that we cracked up, and I can imagine how they felt. There was a really awkward moment that followed. The Brazilians must have thought we were making fun of them, and I can understand their resentment, especially after they had gone to such lengths to accommodate us.

The clash of personalities was *so* painfully obvious. Their conservative, business-like atmosphere was shaken by what appeared to be rude tourists.

INSIGHT:
The students did not intend to offend their Brazilian banker hosts, but the group laughter was received as insulting nonetheless. The bankers felt they were going out of their way to accommodate the visiting students, and laughing, casual behavior might well have indicated that the bankers were not being taken seriously.

The Candomble Ceremony. In Brazil, I went to a Candomble Ceremony. The ceremony was held in a small room. There were many people crowded into the small room. There was a long line of people standing and waiting to bow down before the altar. As I walked into the room I found myself to be at the back of the line. I did not realize that the line was for people waiting to bow down before the altar. I thought the line was of people who were waiting to sit down. Before I knew it I was at the front of the line, and a Brazilian woman said, "You must kneel and make a prayer." I said, "Oh, I'm sorry, but I am not a member of this religion." I then went to sit down in the back of the room. The woman looked at me in a strange way.

I went to the Candomble Ceremony to get a glimpse of the Brazilian religion and culture. I am a member of the Catholic religion. I chose not to bow in front of the altar for two reasons. The first reason was because I am a member of a different religion than these people and should not worship in the place of another religion. The second reason was because I did not want to kneel down when I didn't know what "god" I was kneeling down to. The consequence of my decision was that the woman, and possibly some of the other Brazilians present, looked at me oddly. I think that I might have offended her or her religious rituals.

INSIGHT:
By not finding out what was appropriate ahead of time, the student who stood in line to pray at the Candomble Ceremony risked embarrassing herself and her Brazilian hosts. Allowing tourists to attend religious ceremonies puts the dignity of the ceremony at risk when visitors unintentionally disrupt that ceremony.

Surf's Up. We were driving up the coast of Brazil, up the part that stretches some way north of Salvador, in a van that we had rented, complete with driver, for an astronomical amount of money. I had managed to persuade my friends to let me bring my surfboard, which was clogging up the space in the car, and had told them to drop me off wherever there were waves. They were planning on going as far up as a hippie colony which had in the past been frequented by the likes of Janis Joplin and Jimi Hendrix, and where it was not possible to surf. We rolled into this spooky town on the ocean fronted by the ghost of a western hotel that had been abandoned in the middle of its construction, leaving the skeletal remains of a high-rise towerblock. There was a break outside this hotel and we parked right by it.

"Here we are," said the driver, as eight smiling faces turned around to catch a last glimpse of me before I set on my way. "See you later," they said in unison, somewhat ready for me to get out so that they could have a little more room to move, as the surfboard would be leaving with me. But there was something going on in my head that pinned me to my seat. All of a sudden, I grew overwhelmed by an intense feeling of nervousness that crept towards terror.

"My God," I remember thinking to myself, "I'm really doing it. I'm getting out of this van (which had, I suppose, been acting as a sort of shield) leaving this driver, my guide, and leaving my friends, all for the sake of surfing." Where was I going to stay the night? What if something happened to me? I didn't speak Portuguese, how was I going to communicate with these people? These fears, coupled with the eeriness of the town, were then keeping me from leaving the vehicle. I had to get out, therefore, making an important decision. Should I just swallow my pride and tell them I didn't want to go? Tell them that I was insecure about the situation I was getting myself into? No, I couldn't. It seemed that such a decision required more guts than the simple process of getting out of the van and watching them drive away, knowing that they would be back to pick me up tomorrow. But I figured out a way of buying more time to decide.

"You know guys, this hotel doesn't look open," I said, pointing to the deserted ruin, "Could you at least drive me to one that is?" I heard a few huffs and a few puffs from the front of the van. This was an impatient group, but I didn't blame them, as we had been travelling for quite some time. But, after a moment of consideration, they agreed. We spent a while driving about the town, which was one of those towns where chickens roam the streets and the inhabitants just hang out on the side of the road and stare at things. Eventually we found a bamboo shack of a hotel with a thatched roof, exactly the kind of place that this doctor had advised us not to stay at, and I was now faced with a new decision. Did I want to stay there? If I did, I risked getting strange diseases talked about in pre-port tips where weird flies laid eggs in your foot that eventually hatched into maggots that would appear out of nowhere and probably really freak you out. Also, by staying at a place like this, I could risk getting shot by some bandito, as this seemed to be exactly the kind of place where things like that happen. But on the other hand, if I didn't get out of the car and check into that hotel, I risked losing serious face, something I didn't want to do so early on in the trip. Yes, I was being driven to action by my ego.

"OK guys, I'll see you tomorrow," I said, sliding my surfboard out of the back of the van. A moment of silence occurred while I was doing this and I got the feeling that my friends were genuinely surprised I was going through with it. "OK. Have a good surf," someone said. The van rolled off in a cloud of dust. I was left standing there, at which point I felt horribly alone and helpless. Had I made the right call? I gulped a big gulp. Then, to my relief, something happened. All of a sudden I heard the noise of the van rolling backwards and stop right where it had dropped me off. My friend stepped out.

"Wait up, I thought I'd join you. This seems like fun!" he said. I felt relieved and suddenly extremely comfortable with my new surroundings. We had a great time, the two of us, got near perfect surf, met and hung out with some of the locals who spoke pidgin English, and I came to a realization that travelling wasn't so bad really. I was making my situation out to be a lot bigger of a deal than it actually was. I could have easily have done it on my own, but having a companion made things a lot easier, especially in overcoming the initial culture shock that I experienced in the new environment.

INSIGHT:
The student was not ready to leave the safe security of friends in this strange and foreign place. It was difficult for the student to be separated from the group. Travelling with a group of friends was much more secure then going off on his own, at least until he got comfortable with the host culture.

The Market Place. The first day in Brazil, my three friends and I ventured into the city of Salvador. One of the first places we went was the main market place. The market was an enormous building filled with vendors, and a restaurant. The building consisted of two levels, both levels packed with people. In the front of the building there were more vendors selling outside. In the back of the building, outside, there was a large overhang. Under the overhang there were dancing, music, and a few wandering Brazilians selling their products. We went under the overhang to avoid a thundering rain. Everyone else in the near vicinity had the same idea, subsequently the area was packed with people. It became crowded quickly, and from what I could tell we were the only Americans. On one side of this area was a round stage. This is where the Brazilians were playing music, and dance boxing. This interested us, so we started to push our way toward the stage. Before we could get close enough to see, we were interrupted by a wandering vendor. The vendor approached us, and proceeded to pull out a large machete. This startled us, and quickly we said, "Pardon us," and continued toward the stage. As we walked by the vendor, he was visually upset at our quick departure, and mumbled Portuguese words at us, with a sneer on his face. This hurried our efforts to get farther away from him. We finally came in view of the stage. We stood about twelve to fifteen feet from the dance boxers. We proceeded to be tourists, and pulled out our cameras, which of course attracted some unneeded attention. At the same time the dancers stopped dancing and motioned us to come closer to the stage. We walked forward and I could feel a hundred eyes watching the "Americans." We stood right in front of the stage, with everyone's eyes on us. The dancers started up again, and the music rolled its rhythmic beat. Our cameras were now clicking, and we began to feel slightly more comfortable. Then suddenly, the music stopped, and the dancers approached us. All they said was "Money" and held their hands out. In this one moment a thousand thoughts raced through my mind. "I don't want to take my money out in front of a hundred eyes," "Is the guy with the knife behind me," "No one else is giving money," "Should I run." In that moment, my friends and I got in a tight circle, turning our backs to the stage. In a time of about five seconds, we decided to walk away, in one tight unit, and keep our eyes peeled. I could hear the dancers yelling at us in the background, but all I could think about was getting further away. After shoving back through the crowd, we entered the street, with rain falling upon us. Even though I was becoming drenched, I was glad to be in the rain and away from the crowded overhang. Safe from the beckoning of the dancers, and safe from the knife man.

INSIGHT:

The students did not understand the implicit contract they made with the dancers by showing pleasure and taking photographs. The students were also perhaps more of an event to the spectators than the dancing the students came to see. These students took something of value--such as a photograph or an experience--without being aware of the need to give something of value back in exchange.

Trouble with Tokens. During my stay in Brazil I needed to make a local phone call. My parents were arriving in Salvador on this particular night and I wanted to contact them at their hotel. If I tried to call collect the operator would just hang up on me. The only way to call them was by using special tokens. I was travelling with one other person and between us we only had one 50,000 cruzeiro bill and one 50 cruzeiro bill. We were not having any luck in finding anyone who would break the 50,000 cruzeiro bill let alone someone who had a token. Finally we came across a vendor who seemed that he would be able to help us. Although he did not speak a word of English we were able to get across to him that we wanted a token for the phone. We then proceeded to hand him the 50,000 cruzeiro bill and he suddenly had a blank look on his face. Another man that was there immediately started shaking his head saying no, no, no and then mumbled something in Portuguese.

There was also a little boy behind the counter, perhaps the son of the first man. His eyes lit up seeing the bill. The first man then tried to count out the change. A token costs roughly 300 cruzeiros. After the man was finished counting the money, I knew he was trying to shortchange us. I had a choice of trying to get the proper change or the 50,000 bill back or just letting it go seeing that it was only a couple thousand cruzeiros.

As we were doing this, I could tell they thought we must be stupid, rich Americans who didn't need the money anyway. Imagine, trying to get a token worth hardly anything with a 50,000 cruzeiro bill. By the look on the little boy's face, I guessed he had never seen such a high bill. I also noticed the annoyed look his father gave him at the boy's reaction.

After a big hassle the man gave us what he thought to be the proper change. My friend started to walk away, but he and I both realized that we had been short changed. We turned around and recounted the change in front of the vendor. We were three thousand cruzeiros short. The vendor then got annoyed with us and gave us back our 50,000 bill.

Even though I didn't need the money and I'm sure the vendor did, I would have done it again. I felt cheated by the man, It was a matter of principle. I was offended because I thought he insulted my intelligence.

INSIGHT:

The students fed the local stereotype of a "wealthy gringo" by conspicuously displaying the large sum of money without realizing the negative effect this would have. The students were sometimes insensitive to their comparatively great wealth in comparison to locals in the host culture and the ways that wealth might inspire hostility toward the rich students. It was important to avoid any extravagant or conspicuous display of wealth to prevent unnecessary bad feelings.

Crying Man at Dinner Table. One of the nights in Salvador, Brazil, a group of friends and I were eating dinner at a restaurant. A man approached our table and started to speak to us. The man was speaking in Portuguese and we could not understand. However, we understood that he was begging and wanted money. He continued with his plea as we just stared at him wide-eyed. The man then produced a bill and continued explaining in his native tongue why he needed money. For some reason I assumed it was a doctor's bill. All of us were shocked at being approached. The man carried on until he started to cry and sob. At this point someone escorted him away from our table.

We were all speechless and basically did nothing but stare at this man the entire time he was at the table. I think to some extent we felt secure in the environment we were in and were really surprised when this man approached us. We were confused because in the United States there would have been no way this man would have been allowed anywhere near the door of a restaurant to beg from the customers.

When the man approached us we had to decide what to do. Relying on our instincts we did nothing but assume that someone would quickly remove him. The time he was at our table was probably a total of two minutes, but it seemed forever. I felt awkward because I could not understand the man. I wondered if the people around assumed us to be "rich gringos" and in us ignoring the man, thought us to be heartless. We felt secure because dinner in many ways is a familiar experience then this man approached us and we assumed that he would be quickly removed and we would not have to deal with him.

INSIGHT:
The students did not know if they were expected to give money or not and were frozen by indecision. The students often expected to be exploited in a foreign country. They also expected to be insulated from situations where that exploitation might happen. When the students were confronted by situations which might be exploitative they often didn't know how to respond.

The Invitation. While at a bar called Zouk Santana in Salvador one night, I met a Brazilian named Reini and we hit it off. We traded addresses and phone numbers. He asked me to call him the next day. I called him and a friend and I met him for dinner. After dinner we were all planning to go to a party in the streets in Barra, but Reini needed to go home first. Reini gave us a choice-- either we could go with him to his apartment, or we could meet him later.

The big decision was whether to go with him or not. The problem was not one of safety because my friend and I trusted him. The problem was that we were not sure if it was customary for us to go home with him after meeting him the day before. We didn't know if he was offering just to be nice, or if he genuinely wanted us to accompany him. He spoke good English, but it was not good enough to express social correctness or incorrectness. Also, Reini was trying not to force us in either direction and let us decide for ourselves. On the one hand, I really wanted to see his apartment and gain insight on Brazilian lifestyle, yet I didn't want to offend him and make a wrong impression without being aware of it. All of this happened in a span of about one minute.

My friend and I decided to go to his apartment. I think my decision was based on the desire to see a different angle of Brazil and the opportunity which presented itself. Reini did not seem offended and was happy to show us around his apartment and gave us photo albums to look through. He called a friend while we were there and I can only imagine what they talked about.

INSIGHT:
The excitement of an adventure with a mysterious stranger was too tempting for the student to turn down. When the students didn't know the rules in Brazil they were forced to rely almost entirely on intuition or a "best guess" about what to do. If all the risk was eliminated then much of the learning would be sacrificed as well.

The Topic of AIDS. A group of us were in Manaus, Brazil, for a school trip to the Amazon. This was the departure night and we were at a group dinner. The dinner was just about over. I walked down the street to a small bar where several students were standing in front. They were with about ten prostitutes. The prostitutes were in their teens and one spoke English. One of our classes discussed the hatred and fear of AIDS in Brazil, and since I am a health educator in my home institution, I was curious about what these women felt about it.

I questioned the one young woman who spoke English and I gave her my card which has the heading "AIDS RESEARCH LAB." When she saw that she began to cuss and curse at me. This occurred in front of the bar on the sidewalk. Many people walked up to see what was happening. The prostitute shouted to her friends and they all looked at me in disgust. The woman tore up the card and threw it at me. I tried to explain, but to no avail. I quickly left and hopped on the bus.

INSIGHT:
The student was insensitive to the fear and danger of AIDS to these prostitutes and mistakenly assumed they could/would be as objective and detached as he was. The students were sometimes insensitive to the feelings of locals, and treated a topic as "interesting" when from the local perspective it was much more serious. It was important for the students to pay their dues and become accepted before exploring the really serious local problems.

Batman Returns. When my friends and I opened the door to our hut in the Amazon village, a few bats swooped down as if to ward us off. We literally ran screaming from the hut, as if we had seen a huge grizzly bear. When the bats didn't leave, we went to talk to someone at the front desk, telling him that he needed to get the bats out of our room. He kind of laughed at us, but nevertheless went to our hut and "chased" the bats out with a stick. As soon as he left, we agreed to go into the room and put our things away. Of course, the screaming bats were still there. After we yelled and hooted and ran outside again, one of the hotel workers approached us.

"Girls, this is the jungle. The bats won't hurt you. But don't forget where you are," he said with a smile. Needless to say, that was a slap in the face for me. One of my friends continued to carry on and insisted that she wouldn't go in a room with bats in it. From that point on, however, I felt so awake and aware of where I was. We never did get the bats out, but they didn't bother me in the least. I slept, showered, and changed with them hanging right above me. No problem!

One of the things I learned from this experience in the Amazon is that each place has its unique characteristics and they must all be fully appreciated. I loved the hot dense air in the Amazon. I loved the insects and the tarantula and the strange trees and leaves and plants. I loved hiking through the Amazon rain forests--the largest ecosystem in the world and the earth's greatest treasure. My point is that the bats are a symbol of the unfamiliar.

INSIGHT:

The students quickly overcame their fear of bats when reassured by the locals that this was normal and not a dangerous situation. Conditions that locals viewed as minor inconveniences were sometimes treated as devastating by students. Locals judged the students' character by how quickly the students adapted and adjusted to local conditions, differentiating the inconveniences from real dangers.

Swimming with Piranhas. I was on the Amazon trip and we went piranha fishing the second day there. In our motor-powered canoe there were ten of us and we had one driver. Our driver lived in the Amazon and knew an enormous amount of inftion concerning one's survival there. He said that you can swim in the Amazon as long as you are not bleeding. So, after fishing for about two hours it became unbearable outside. The sun was beaming down, and we had nothing to help us cope with the heat, except for a river with piranha fish in it. As a result of this unexplainable heat, people were beginning to contemplate the possibility of swimming in the Amazon River. There were three other people, besides myself, that were thinking of swimming in the Amazon. I didn't know any of these people before today. They all seemed like really cool guys, but whether I could trust them or not was still up in the air. I did however feel secure with the driver and felt that I could trust his opinion. The driver was about 22 years old and has lived in the Amazon all his life; thus knows what it takes to survive there. To no one's surprise, the most outgoing guy on the canoe was the first person to jump into the water. The driver looked at the rest of us and said, "What are you waiting for?"

After hearing what the driver said, I began to really feel secure about swimming in the Amazon. It was the most incredible feeling knowing that I was actually swimming in the Amazon. If there is a next time, I would do things the exact same way as I did the first time.

INSIGHT:

The students who went swimming with piranhas took chances they would never take back home. It was just as easy for the students to overestimate as to underestimate danger in Brazil. Sometimes the same behaviors that would be safe for Brazilians who knew the rules were dangerous for visiting students.

The Importance of Nonverbals. Although my stay in Brazil was very short, I was still able to experience a number of critical incidents. One particular incident occurred which involves the existing cultural differences in body language and gestures.

The incident occurred on my return from the Amazon trip at the airport in Manaus. My friend and I were thirsty for something to drink so we decided to walk down to the food counter at the end of the terminal. Surprisingly, even though it was 1:30 a.m. many people were in the airport walking around and waiting for their respective flights. My friend and I went up to the younger man behind the counter and I attempted to order a large orange juice through broken Spanish mixed with English slang and hand motions. There were two other men behind the counter as well who were trying to help out their coworkers in understanding what exactly it was that I was ordering. Becoming frustrated with the language barrier, I continued to try to visually describe a large drink using my hands and then pointing to the sign to where it said orange juice. My friend meanwhile was trying to explain it to the two other employees using Spanish. The men stared blankly for a few minutes and then suddenly one understood. The climax of the incident occurred when I had to stop him from putting ice in my glass. I shouted, "No, no ice!" The employee looked at me confused. Then I said, "No hielo." In Spanish this means no ice. No luck. Now the employee thought I wanted to cancel my order until I tried to order the drink again. This cycle of utter confusion and miscommunication continued between the five of us for several minutes until I started to try to use my hands to say zero (okay sign) ice with my fingers. Unknowingly, I had just nonverbally told this man to go screw himself. The gesture that is considered an appropriate one in America had a radically different meaning in Brazil. The man's reaction wasn't anger or outrage but just confusion. He realized that we were tourists and were probably unaware that we were unintentionally insulting these hard working men. Finally, everything was figured out and I got my orange juice--with no ice!

INSIGHT:

The waiter probably understood the well-meaning but confusing communication by the student and excused it because of the student's ignorance. It is dangerous to assume that nonverbals have the same meaning in all cultures. While locals often excused students as "not knowing any better" it was a good idea to monitor the use of nonverbals to avoid embarrassment.

Losing Your Appetite. This critical incident took place in Salvador, Brazil. A group of us decided to go out to dinner our last night in port. We just told the taxi driver that we wanted beer and food and let him take us where he desired. We ended up in a very beautiful part of Salvador. Up by the water and the beach. There were quite a few restaurants to choose from, but we chose a pizza place close to a pre-Carnival party. There were tons of people in the streets dancing, loud music, drinking, eating; the environment was very festive. We were all in great moods as we sat down to enjoy our dinner. The waiter brought us our beers and while we waited for our food to arrive we enjoyed ourselves watching the dancing and listening to the music. I couldn't think of a better way to spend our last evening in Salvador. Our pizza came quickly and just as we began eating a very unfortunate thing happened. A young boy who was dressed in rags approached our table and stuck out his hand in request for money. He then pointed down to his foot which was severely cut and very bloody. All of us looked at him and at each other in shock, not used to seeing such a sad and horrifying sight. Before we had the chance to decide what to do in this situation, the boy was being pushed away by what looked like to be the owner/manager of the restaurant. We all sat in silence unable to eat or speak about what had just happened. None of us had had the time to give the young boy any money and at the same time we didn't know if that was the correct thing to do. We all experienced huge mood swings. It took quite awhile before we could once again enjoy ourselves.

Because of our lack of knowledge and understanding about what to do in situations such as poverty, the conversation of what occurred was kept to a minimum. This is not to say that it did not deeply affect us. I believe that each one of us throughout the evening never got the picture of the young boy out of our minds.

INSIGHT:

The partying students were forced to face an ugly and painful reality of local culture in the crippled beggar. When the students didn't know what to do about a problem situation the temptation was to ignore it or pretend it didn't happen. This served to insulate the student from the local culture and prevented learning about serious local problems. The guilt and pain of poverty or injustice were usually so strong that the temptation for students to ignore local problems was very strong.

South Africa

To Ride an Ostrich. I went on a Semester at Sea trip in South Africa. On the second day of our visit we went to an ostrich farm. There were about twenty students on the trip. At one point during our tour of the ostrich farm, we were taken inside a corral of about thirty ostriches. Our tour guide explained to us how dangerous a kick from an ostrich could be--an ostrich kick could even result in death! Our guide then caught an ostrich with a long rope and placed the ostrich in a small holding area so our guide could show us how ostrich feathers are plucked. Now, during the catch and seizure of the ostrich the ostrich seemed very angry and seemed like he could get violent. When our guide was showing us how to pluck the feathers, the ostrich even bit him on the head! I was a little bit nervous about being in the same corral with thirty other ostriches by this time.

Then our guide announced to us that we could ride the ostriches if we so desired, and he gave us a demonstration. Now, during the whole trip I was very excited about actually being able to ride an ostrich. I thought that riding an ostrich would be something that I would be able to do only in South Africa, and I should definitely do it. Besides, it was a great opportunity and I would probably never have another opportunity to ride an ostrich. However, I watched as practically each student rode an ostrich. I saw two students get thrown over the heads of their ostriches, and I was scared. I had the choice to either ride an ostrich, or not ride an ostrich. I chose not to. If I could make this decision again I would chose to ride the ostrich.

INSIGHT:

The short-term risk of riding an ostrich seemed greater than the long-term risk of going without that experience in South Africa. While it was a good thing to be cautious about risk taking in a foreign country, to avoid all risk meant losing out on the unique experiences, insights, and adventures of being abroad in the first place.

Saved by a Taxi. On our third night in Cape Town we ended up at Bertie's Landing Bar. We were just relaxing and having a couple beers before we went back to the ship. There were four of us girls and myself.

Anyhow, we met a few people from South Africa who seemed pretty okay. But then suddenly instead of four girls and three guys, there were about twenty guys all around us. They were so fascinated by the fact that we were Americans; they had never met any before. Well, by this time the bar had closed up. We were left on the outside deck with all these guys from the Transvaal area. We decided that it was time to leave, so we said goodbye and went to the front of the bar to catch a taxi. Little did we know that taxis didn't just show up in that area. We did not have access to a phone because the bar was closed. The guys all came out of the bar and offered to take us home. We knew that we didn't want that, because they were more than a little drunk and there were so many of them. We then had to decide what to do. We needed to get back to the ship, which was about a half mile to a mile away, but we, of course, wanted to get back alive. As we were discussing our options a taxi drives up. We immediately ran over to it to see if he would take us home. Apparently he had been called for another group of people, but when he asked us if they were still inside all four of us replied, "No." This was not in fact true. We all knew very well that there were some people left on the deck, but we had all realized that this was our way out of a bad situation.

We all agreed that we needed a taxi, no matter what we had to do to get it. We did not even need to consult each other on the issue of taking someone else's cab.

INSIGHT:

The students didn't hesitate to take the cab called for someone else even though they recognized this as selfish and impolite. It was unfortunate that they were not able to find a solution that would meet their needs for a safe ride home and still not be impolite to others.

Smile and Say Cheese. My friends and I went on the field trip "Poverty under Apartheid" on the last day we were in Cape Town. Approximately fifty people travelled in two big buses to a small school, a colored township and community center, an Operation Hunger Soup Kitchen and a black residential squatter camp. Each stop was more shocking than the last. For me, the most devastating sight was the squatter camp.

Although we were at the squatter camps for the least amount of time (15 minutes), it left the most dramatic impact on me. Squatter camps exemplify one of the lowest levels of poverty in the world. They are overcrowded acres of land filled with illegal one room shacks made by black families themselves from scrap metal, tin, cardboard and wood. Extended families of six to ten people crowd into these one room shacks with no electricity, no running water and no bathroom facilities. They are not governmentally funded (like the colored townships) until their existence has been noticed by the government as a health problem. Only then will the government provide minimal health aid which usually results in a community toilet to be shared by about 20 other black families. Newspapers cover their walls for insulation.

Our bus stopped alongside the highway at a squatter camp. Our tour guide said, "You can step off the bus to take a quick picture and get back on the bus." My roommate didn't have any more film left in her camera so she stayed seated on the bus. I and several others got off the bus to take a quick picture. To my surprise people actually started to walk towards the shack-like homes of the blacks! I stood behind and watched as the critical incident began when members of our group decided to invade the private lives of the humble residents. My roommate decided to get off the bus because the "invasion" lasted longer than expected. She walked down to where all the commotion was to find a breast feeding mother lying on an old beaten up and torn mattress on the floor inside the rusty tin shack. A very old and sick looking man who was blind in one eye stood in the corner while two babies crawled around on a dirt floor crying.

As if the shack wasn't crowded enough, several people pushed through to get the pathetic sight on videotape. Others had the gall to say, "Smile and say cheese," as they flashed their cameras. My roommate was very upset to witness this incident as an outsider as the rest of us acted like ugly Americans entertained by the "freak show."

Reflecting back on the incident, it really had a powerful impact on my life. It made my biggest problems seem insignificant and it shamed me into realizing all that I have taken for granted. In my analysis of this incident, I feel like I have benefitted immensely by being exposed to a different level of development.

INSIGHT:
Some of the students experienced poverty as a form of entertainment which did not affect them personally. It was easy for tourists to judge a local

situation by the foreign students' back-home standards. A more adequate response, and also perhaps the most uncomfortable, was accepting locals on their own terms and conditions.

He Bit Me. The event occurred in Bertie's Landing, in South Africa. This is a small pub which turned out to be the meeting point for Semester at Sea students, including myself, and a group of ten South Africans who were going to take us sailing on their yacht. We had met them a few days prior and decided to get together and have a few beers before leaving. We went sailing and then returned to Bertie's Landing for dinner. About fifteen minutes after returning, the critical incident happened.

I was standing near a table talking to a guy. There were three people sitting at a table directly behind me. I was talking to the gentleman when all of a sudden I felt someone bite my rear end. I turned around absolutely flustered and asked why had someone done that. The table was filled with laughter, and nobody seemed to want to volunteer an explanation. I then saw myself faced with a very tough situation, and I was unclear as to how exactly I was going to deal with it. I decided to laugh it off and continue with my conversation as if nothing had happened. It was a very difficult situation, for had I been in the United States, I would have smacked the guy. I felt too uncomfortable and confused in general at this point to register any different response than to just ignore the entire situation.

INSIGHT:
The local who bit her took advantage of her being a temporary visitor and disoriented by local customs. The students were sometimes considered "fair game" by the locals who knew the students would be moving on and not likely to make a scene. Making fun of tourists or baiting them was a local sport and a way to prove one's superiority. The very people whose livelihood depended on student visitors might have the most hostility toward these students.

Flying High. Two of us returned to do a freefall jump two days after we were in Cape Town. Two people that we had met picked us up by the ship at noon. The 45 minute drive to the airfield filled me with anxiety about going topless, especially in front of another student from the ship. My friend loved to skydive and she wanted to take another dive after having done it only two days prior.

I wanted to do a freefall to feel how different it was to fall without a parachute for almost one minute. Our two other friends were skydivers from South Africa that we met at the airfield on the first day who we became close with during our stay.

I was more or less the center of attention since I was to go topless. I acted excited about it although I was internally chewing myself out for having accepted the dare. I knew that if I had been in the U.S. I would have never accepted, but the rush of excitement from being in South Africa made me do things that I normally wouldn't.

There I was, 5,000 feet in the air, in a little plane attached to a professional skydiver. I was to take this tandem freefall dive topless. It was cold, -10⁰ F, and by the time we reached 9,500 feet, my shirt was to be off. I had been dared and I don't like to turn down a dare. Would I be so concerned with my naked chest that I would not be able to enjoy the jump? Was it so bad to decline a dare? Would I be disappointed in myself if I didn't fulfill the promise I made?

At 6,000 feet I still had my shirt on. I was strapped to the instructor with my back against his stomach. All of a sudden, his hands began to unfasten my straps--I knew what he was going to do. Should I stop him and back out of the dare or should I let him do it and help facilitate my decision by going along with it all? Well, I let him do it!

At 9,500 feet we jumped out of the plane and the speed of 110 mph did not even make me cold because I was so hot with excitement. It was an amazing feeling to hear the loud whistling of the air and to wonder if the parachute would open successfully and all will be well or death will take over. The landing was perfect and I ran topless in the field for a few minutes after landing and did not even feel shy anymore.

INSIGHT:

Skydiving topless on a dare was exciting and attractive exactly because it was such an outrageous and irrational thing to do. It was easy for the students to leave familiar constraints and inhibitions behind in their home cultures and suspend the rules during their adventure abroad. Collecting outrageous adventures was encouraged by a "can-you-top-this" attitude when comparing experiences with other students. It took students awhile to recognize that host cultures had rules also.

Black and White. During my stay in South Africa I had the opportunity to see many beautiful areas of this country. On my last day there I decided to see the less fortunate areas of South Africa. I hired a driver for the afternoon to take me through the various townships and squatter camps. Before we left, Joe, my driver, warned me that some of the areas could be dangerous so we had to be careful about what parts we entered.

The critical incident I will describe occurred in an area called Crossroads. This is one of the more violent areas. At one point I asked Joe if I could get out of the car to take a picture. He thought I would be safe so he got out of the cab and stood next to me. We were on the sidewalk looking out on hundreds of shacks. Many of the people that lived in the area were standing outside near us. There was one man who was standing near a piece of wood that had sheep heads on it. He was looking at us very strangely. I began to get nervous because he had a very mean look on his face. I asked Joe if I should be afraid and he said we were fine. Suddenly the man began yelling something in his tribal language very loudly and then started walking briskly towards us. I immediately stopped taking pictures and looked to Joe to see what we should do. The look on his face only increased my fear because he too looked afraid. The only words he said to me were, "Get back into the car, roll up the windows and lock the door." He stood next to me the whole time. He first helped me into the car and then once I was safe he got into the driver's side. We drove away safely. When we looked back, the man was standing on the side of the road still yelling at us. Joe and I both gave a sigh of relief. I asked Joe if he knew what the man was saying, but he didn't know their language. He just replied by saying, "I'm not sure what he was saying, but it was very evident that he didn't want us there. To ensure our safety, I thought it was best to leave."

INSIGHT:
The picture-taking student didn't intend to insult the local, but that was exactly what he did by not treating him as more than a photo opportunity. As the students learned about the host culture they became aware of how complicated it was. The ways in which students and locals perceived one another were important for determining how they interacted.

Man on the Sidewalk. Four of us walked down the main street in Cape Town, South Africa, on a hot, humid late afternoon. We had been walking all over Cape Town trying to find some hooks for our hammocks. Several times we had stopped to get drinks and a bite to eat. I wasn't too familiar with the change, so I always used bills. Well, you can imagine, my change pouch was getting rather full. So we bought several newspapers and figured out the coins.

Street after street we saw homeless beggars with multiple problems ranging from no eyes to no legs. We had been told not to give money to beggars, it only makes things worse. As the day went on I thought about the fact that no matter how hard they worked I will always have more than they could imagine. I had all this change in my pouch and had no idea what I was going to use it for so here is the dilemma.

We walked past a man selling newspapers. He was just sitting there, not even begging. He was sitting on the ground leaning against the wall - one leg and one eye. What to do? Within the small amount of time it took to walk past him, both the pro and anti were arguing. I thought--(pro) I have so much more than he will ever have; (anti) they told us it would only hurt them to give them money; (pro) how could it hurt him if he could get a good meal; (anti) they will just beg more often; (pro) they are less fortunate and need a helping hand; (anti) will I have enough money to enjoy the day; (pro) it's not fun having something you can't share with others. After all this debate, which took place in about a minute and a half, I went back to give him whatever change I had at the time.

I think he thought I had given it to him for a paper, but when I didn't pick one up and just said hello--he got a big grin and said--thank you. I feel good about where my money has gone.

INSIGHT:

The student's impulsive decision to give money made the student feel good. Students usually didn't know what was expected of them or what they could expect of other locals. The temptation was to insulate themselves against the local culture even though this resulted in unfeeling and unsympathetic behaviors to make sure no one would be take advantage of them.

Being an Uninvited Guest. After several hours of driving around several South African townships, specifically the Crossroads section, several students and the driver decided to get some food and a drink. Our driver felt this was an ideal place to stop because he felt we could experience Black South Africans safely. We parked the car and entered the mall. Immediately the guard at the door glared at us. I continued in toward the supermarket, which was at the end of a long walkway with shops on either side. As we walked everyone stopped what they were doing and glared at us, some stopped talking only to resume after we had passed. On two occasions I was bumped into intentionally because there was ample room on either side of me. I walked in confident and curious, but when I left I was very uncomfortable, unable to look at anyone in the eye.

I felt very alone and helpless in the mall. All three of us walked closely. In a sense we felt that there was power in numbers. At first I felt immune to the prejudice because I am an "American Citizen." This feeling quickly changed. I never looked anyone in the eye, I kept my head down. I could feel the glares directed towards me the entire time. I was an uninvited guest and I did my business and left.

INSIGHT:

By making themselves conspicuous the students unintentionally became targets for the bad feelings of locals toward whites. It was often difficult for students to accept the fact that they were disliked or hated for what they represented even when they had not done nothing wrong personally. Tourists had become symbols of wrongdoing and therefore visiting students shared in the blame for the people they symbolized.

Kenya

Exchanging Help. When in Mombasa, I wanted to call my parents. My friend and I took a taxi to the Castle Hotel, hoping they would have a phone I could use. They had no phone, but recommended I try the phone across the street.

We crossed the street, and I tried to use the telephone. The operator informed me that I could not use "this type" of pay phone. I got off the phone, and we asked a gentleman waiting to use the phone if he knew where we could find other types of telephones. He replied, telling us to go to the main Post Office about three blocks away. We asked the man if it was safe. He offered to escort us.

We discussed what we should do. Should we trust this man? Is he going to charge us money for escorting us? (An hour before, our friends told us of a man who offered to escort them and then demanded money.) We decided that it was not safe to walk by ourselves (after all it was already dark out), and we would be safer walking with a man, especially a local man. But we did not want to have to pay the man nor did we want to insult him by making an accusatory comment about money. We decided it was best to ask if he expected payment from us.

We said to him, "Sir, we don't mean to insult you, but we had an experience with a man earlier who volunteered to take us somewhere, and then he expected us to pay him. We don't have money to pay you and we want to make sure that is okay." Although we told a little white lie, it made the story seem more legitimate. The man laughed and said he expected no payment. He would simply walk with us, as he had to catch a bus near the Post Office.

The man walked with us to the Post Office, waited for me to try to call, lent me his card, which that type of phone required, walked us back to the Castle Hotel and finally invited us for a drink.

In the end, we sat with the man for over an hour discussing politics, books, prostitution, AIDS and other controversial subjects. We exchanged addresses and thanked him. It was the most positive and informative interaction I have had in any of the countries we visited.

INSIGHT:
It was very frustrating for the students when even the simple task of making a phone call required getting help from locals. Recognizing and accepting the need for help was more likely to get results than a pretense of autonomy and independence, especially when one's helplessness was apparent to the locals.

Deciding Whether to Trust Someone in a Foreign Country. I was roaming near the Mombasa post office, looking for a recycling bin to place two Coke bottles that my friend and I had finished. She and another friend were waiting in line to use the telephone at the post office. I must have looked lost because a Kenyan man about 23 years of age stopped, smiled, and asked me if I needed help. He was about 5 feet 5 inches in height of slim build, and didn't seem threatening or dangerous at all. So I said, "I'm looking for a place to put these bottles." He smiled as he took my arm and said, "There's a place right around the corner." At that moment, I wasn't quite sure whether I should run back to my friends to tell them where I was going or whether I should trust the man and go with him around the corner. It was still daylight with a lot of people on the streets and my friends would be waiting for the phone. He was also young, didn't look dangerous, and smiled a lot, so I thought I could trust him. He must have sensed my hesitancy though because I kept looking back and checking to see if my friends were looking at me. He said, "Don't worry. It's just right there." So I went with him. Another reason why I thought it'd be alright to go was because as I glanced around, no one seemed alarmed that I was following this man. Everyone went about their own business and didn't give a second look to us. Thus I felt that this wasn't an out of the ordinary cultural action. The place turned out to be less than 50 steps away and I sighed silently in relief. In the end, the Kenyan man and I talked briefly, exchanged addresses, and left on a happy note. Although this process lasted only about five minutes, I still ponder whether I should have ran back to tell my friends where I was going.

INSIGHT:

The student had very little data on whether to trust the stranger or not, making it a very difficult decision. It was dangerous to assume that a foreign culture used the same cues for communication as were used back home. Students were sometimes more afraid of being embarrassed than entering into a situation they considered very risky.

Late Night Safari. This is not the usual critical incident, but instead a unique incident that could probably only happen while on a safari in Kenya. The experience was not a human-human confrontation, but instead a human-animal incident.

On the second day of our four-day safari, we stayed at Buffalo Springs Lodge in the Samburu Reserve. The lodge was located in the middle of the "bush." There was no civilization in eye-shot distance. We were definitely in the world of the animals, far out of civilization.

The lodge was set up in a way that it was spread out into a large complex. In the center of the complex was the main lodge, which consisted of a restaurant, bar, gift shop, and information desk. Surrounding the main complex were small bungalows that housed the guests. The farthest bungalows were over a hundred yards from the main complex. There were no lights to lead you from the complex to your room, to "protect" you from any possible wild animals.

Earlier in the evening, myself and a friend had decided to venture from our bungalow to the main complex. The sun had already set, but there was just enough light to make out forms. In between the main complex and our quarters there was a path to follow, but without lights it was difficult. It was pretty empty and almost eerie. As we were approaching the main complex, about forty yards away, we heard a loud crunching sound. We immediately stood still in our tracks, and squinted our eyes to see in the dark. About twelve yards ahead of us a huge form began to take shape. The form was rubbing its huge body against a small tree, and then with its weight, snapped the tree. At this time it was obvious we were looking at a huge elephant itching itself against a tree. It was right there! I could almost reach out and touch the enormous animal. Neither my friend nor I knew how elephants behave, whether they are easily frightened or hot tempered, and I didn't really want to find out at this particular moment. I could already see it, "American Student Trampled by African Elephant." I really didn't have any idea what to do, and at the same time I was fascinated and frightened. Should I slowly turn around, and walk away, or should I just stand still. My friend and I just stood still, I don't think it was a conscious decision, but we were more like in a state of shock, and probably couldn't move if we tried. We just sort of stood there, looking at this huge beast in our path, with our jaws hanging on the ground. The longer we watched, the more comfortable we became. We stayed there for about ten minutes watching the elephant lumber through our complex, until we could no longer see the huge animal.

INSIGHT:

The student confronting an elephant at night had no idea how to cope appropriately but knew that a wrong decision could be lethal. Every so often the students expected something to happen as a vivid reminder that they "were not in Kansas any longer." These memorable incidents usually happened by accident and came as a surprise. It was important to be ready when these accidental surprises occurred to take advantage of each opportunity.

No Picture Taking Accepted Here. After flying to Nairobi, my safari group had a several-hour-long drive to our first lodge. About three hours into our drive, the driver pulled over to a gas station in the middle of a small town. He told the six girls in our van to "stay put" while he went to pump the gas. As soon as he left, about ten people, ranging in ages from 30 to about 12, bombarded our van. We had men and women shoving bananas, bracelets, knives and watches in through the windows. Of course, being the tourists that we were, several girls took pictures.

Over to the left of the gas station was another group of Africans sitting under a tree. They looked considerably older than those who had approached our car. They just sat staring at us. Finally the driver paid the gas station attendant and we pulled away from the station. In doing so, he pulled up right next to the elderly group sitting under the tree. The next thing I know, a tiny old black woman picks up a large rock and hurls it at our car. She begins screaming and yelling at us in Swahili and the driver drives away as fast as he can.

I asked Francis what she had said. He said that she was extremely upset because we had our cameras out and she thought we had taken her picture. The thought that a camera would bother her never crossed our minds. In the U.S. no one cares if you take their picture, so we assumed this to be true in Kenya. In order to have understood why she threw the rock, we should have put ourselves in this culture.

INSIGHT:
The students who disregarded local rules about taking pictures should not be surprised at the local anger. Unintentional insults were no less hurtful than intentional ones. Students needed to be particularly careful and sensitive to the rules of their host culture to avoid unintentionally insulting the hosts.

Bartering with a Masai Woman. This incident occurred when my safari group van stopped at a gas station that also had a crafts store. Outside of the store there were Masai women who had their beaded jewelry displayed. There were approximately ten different Masai women selling their work. A friend and I went to look at their things. After looking at their jewelry I thought that I really didn't need to buy anything. My friend had gone back to our van and another young woman approached me and put a beaded ring on my finger and told me that it was a gift. I told her that I couldn't buy anything from her and tried to give the ring back, but she pushed it back on my finger. She then showed me her bracelets. At this point I felt obligated to buy something from her. I liked two of her bracelets and I had to decide whether or not I was going to buy something from her. I had already bought some beaded Masai jewelry at another village so I didn't think I needed anymore, but I did like her two bracelets. Also, because she gave me the beaded ring as a gift I did feel very obligated to buy something from her.

INSIGHT:
The student felt obligated to buy the jewelry by the gift and the Masai woman's friendly manner without knowing how she was expected to respond. Wherever there are tourists there are likely to be locals who make their living trading with the tourists. Sometimes the local traders take advantage of the tourist's vulnerability and ignorance about local customs.

The Foreign Experience. In Mombasa, Kenya, I met two very hospitable Moslems by the names of Redina and Anwar. I noticed on Redina's hands that she had some sort of tattoo in the shape of the moon on her palm. I thought it was very unusual and very beautiful. I asked her about its significance. She replied, "It is a symbol for a special occasion. Mainly, brides put them up their arms and legs the day of their wedding." She said that she thought my coming to Mombasa was a special occasion and asked if I wanted the dye on my hands. I asked her how long the tatoo would last and she said, "Approximately one month." I decided to go with her because I thought it to be a beautiful sign of art. When I got to Redina's home she began painting an intricate design of flowers on my left ankle and foot. It took her about 45 minutes to finish. Then she reached over to paint the other leg. I said to her, "No thanks, one is fine." She replied, "No, you must do both feet and hands." I was restless by this time. It was my last day in Mombasa and I wanted to be exploring. I figured it would take at least another two hours for her to paint my other leg and arm. Besides, I didn't want tatoos on both legs and hands for a month! Redina seemed very upset at my request for her to stop. I had to decide to tell her to continue or leave and walk around Mombasa. I decided to stay because I felt it was very kind of her to take me to her home and put a piece of her "culture" on me. I decided that a month was not such a long time and I did not want to anger my new Moslem friends. If I had been back in the U.S., I don't think I would have let Redina "paint" me. I don't think I would have stopped to talk to her, let alone go back to her house with her. When I return home, I will make it a point to meet someone like Redina, rather than ignore her because she looks different from me.

INSIGHT:
The student saw tatoos as decoration without awareness of its symbolic significance in the local context. Tourists often found significant local symbols, such as body painting, exotic and "interesting," not for its original intended meaning but as something new and different. While there was usually no harm in collecting local symbols some locals considered this inappropriate and even offensive, showing disregard for local customs.

India

The Shot. Two friends and I travelled to Bombay. We saw many sights and had a great time. We went to many temples and Mosques. All the temples that we went to had signs that read "no photography." The last one we went to was beautiful. It was the biggest we had seen and it had the most people in it. However, there were no signs about photographs. I really wanted to take a picture, but my friends and I were not sure how the people would react.

The temple was open. There were no doors, but there were many walkways one could go through in order to enter the temple. It was about 2:00 p.m. and it was very light inside. People were praying aloud and bowing to the figure I wanted a photograph of. It looked like a coffin covered with a pretty silk blanket with flowers all over. The ceiling was mirrored and the walls were decorated with glass figures. The angle in which I was going to take the shot would have the people praying in the background.

My friends and I were the only Americans in the temple. We are all good friends and have travelled together many times. One friend had his camera but he never really thought about taking a picture. (He told me this later.) When

I took my camera out, he said, "I don't know if it is cool to take a picture here." He sounded worried for me and I got the impression that he meant that I should not take a photograph. The other friend was overwhelmed with what he saw at the temple and didn't pay much attention to either of us. My camera was out and I was ready.

The place was silent and I remember thinking that the only thing these people would hear is my camera. The people praying aloud did so in a quiet voice; sort of like a mumble. I don't know anything about these people or their religion. I was nervous, yet anxious to get it over with. At this point, I felt that I had gone this far and the shot had to be taken. I don't even know if it was the photo that was important or just the fact that I had to take a risk to do it. Boom! I took the picture quickly (I raised the camera to my eye and snapped it). Everyone I saw looked at me with a slightly angered look. Two men approached me and said, "No photos, no photos." One had his hand on my camera. I was nervous because I thought he wanted to keep it. I put it in my pocket. At the same time one lady that was praying on the floor got up and moved to the other side of the temple. The two men looked angered as I walked away. I felt bad because I thought I interrupted the lady who was praying. I felt odd, like a foreigner, and then I walked outside. I did so in order to escape. However, even when I was outside I still had an odd feeling. If I had to do this again, I would not have taken the picture. This is not my country so I should abide by their rules and customs. I felt terrible. I remember feeling like I just committed a crime. Even though nobody punished me, I felt that the way I was feeling was a punishment itself.

INSIGHT:
The student's need to take a picture became more important than the dignity of locals at prayer. Students usually didn't consider photography a form of theft but in some cultures it literally meant taking something away with them that did not belong to them. Because students were detached from the local culture, isolated and somewhat insulated they felt free from local rules and customs, even though they were not.

Gender Roles. While I was in India I took a plane to Trichy. After arriving at the airport, I caught a bus to the center of town. As I boarded the bus, I saw an empty seat on the left-hand side of the bus and decided to hop in it. After driving on the bus for a while I was noticing a lot of stares. At first I thought it was because I was one of the only two white people on the bus and the other person happened to be my friend. When she got on the bus she went to the right. Indian people at first looked at her, but they were still staring at me. I thought that perhaps I was doing something wrong. But I wasn't sure what. I had a skirt on that covered my legs. I didn't have any part of my body exposing any more than any other women on the bus. After a while, a man sat next to me. He asked me where I was from and we spoke for a while. I asked him if I was going crazy or was everyone staring me? He told me that everyone was staring at me. He told me it was customary for women to sit on the right and men to sit on the left. I caused the stares myself. I wasn't fully aware of the Indian culture. I put myself in that situation, by being ignorant to their culture. I should have noticed that there were only men sitting on the left-hand side of the bus. After I was told I didn't get up and move to the right because I didn't want to attract even more attention. From that point on, every time I got on a bus I sat on the right-hand side.

INSIGHT:

The student unintentionally broke a local rule and experienced the rejection by locals as a learning experience. Usually the students learned local rules by violating them and having to recover from the violation. Making mistakes was not so serious as long as the students were able to recover from their mistakes.

Meeting a Stranger on a Train. While in India, I participated in a homestay, which was one of the best experiences of my life. A group of thirty participants rode a first-class express sleeper to the village of Erode. As we were boarding the train, ten of us had to wait for another car because all of the compartments were full. My friend and I were the last to get on the train and consequently we were the last to get a compartment. There was an Indian gentleman already there but we went ahead and put our sleeping bags down and our suitcases on the floor. We assumed it was our compartment because there were no others left. My friend put her stuff across from him, so my bed was the one he was sitting on. Meanwhile, my friend left to speak to someone and so he and I were alone.

I sat down next to him, looked at him and smiled. He looked at me and moved away! I was semi-shocked, but I thought that he would be a wonderful teacher about India and I wanted to speak to him. I asked him where he was going and he said to a business conference. I told him that we were going to stay in Erode with a family and he didn't say anything. I became somewhat frustrated, and continued to ask him questions and didn't get informative answers, just one word responses. I asked him where he lived, he answered Madras. I asked him what he did, he said I'm an engineer. I asked him where he was going, he said a conference. It was so hard for me because I thought that I was trying very hard to learn about the people, or at least one person, from India and I wasn't getting any help. Soon afterwards, I gave up and started playing cards.

INSIGHT:

The student tried too hard to make local friends, breaking the rules and being ignored as a consequence. Roles were often defined in great detail by local cultures, and this was especially true with regard to male-female relationships. When the student behaved differently from her expected and prescribed gender role, local persons were not sure how to interpret that behavior.

A Poor Begging Indian Gives an American Student a Sense of Fortune. The first full day I was in India, I travelled to Mahabalapuram with a friend from the States and two students from Madras, India. While walking through the streets I saw an old man sitting by the side of the road with his hands cupped and reached out toward me. Obviously he was a beggar asking for money. Initially I shook my head and walked past him. But, after taking a few steps I turned and said, "I would love to have the man's picture, I think "I'll give him some money in exchange for his picture." I had assumed that the man would want money in exchange for his photo because that was the way it had been in our previous port of Kenya with the Masai tribes. Although the decision to give the beggar money may not appear to be critical, it was because of what followed that vastly changed my appreciation for the life I have been given. I reached into my pocket and pulled out ten rupees, which is equivalent to about thirty cents, and handed it to the old man. He took a brief moment to look at it and when he saw what it was his sad expression turned into a smile. He held the bill to the sky as if he was thanking the gods; then he proceeded to bow his head several times as if to thank me. As he was doing this I took my camera out of my bag and started to focus the lens in order to take his picture. When he realized what I was doing his body language changed from a clutching, poor, beggar to a proud, upright wise man. I took the picture and pressed my hands together in Indian tradition to thank him. Then I turned around and started to walk again with my friends.

I do not think I will ever forget the look on that man's face as I gave him the bill. That single moment changed my attitude towards my approach to the goals I have for myself. I truly believe that the particular moment was one of the most influential moments in the shaping of my personality. Every time I feel depressed or angry I will think of that dignified man in India and the many others like him who have so much less for which to be thankful.

INSIGHT:

The student who wanted a picture of the beggar without insulting him learned enough local protocol to communicate appropriately. The local beggar had pride, dignity, and respect without having material wealth. Students visiting countries where poverty was more evident sometimes applied an absolute measure of poverty according to their own back-home standards rather than discovering the local measures of pride, dignity, and respect which might not depend on material wealth.

Being Yelled At. My brother and I had to go talk to the manager of the Bagdogia airport in India to see if we could use our VISA traveller's checks.

The room was crowded and an American man was sitting in the first of three chairs against the wall, so we would have had to get by him to sit down. We also didn't want to butt in on any business by pushing our way farther into the small office. I stood back in the doorway as to not get in the way of the "superior" male Indian race. My brother leaned up with his right leg up and sitting on the desk partially with his left foot on the ground which was a typical way for him to sit in America. My brother had been sitting for a few seconds when the manager jumps up out of his chair and yells, "Off, Off! What do you think you're doing? You Americans think you can do anything. Sit, Sit! There is a chair. Now sit, sit!" My brother looked shocked and embarrassed and I was kind of stunned and scared. We needed to get on this flight and these people obviously did not enjoy the company of three Americans. The American man looked up at me (I was still standing in shock) and said, "Why don't you have a seat." So I sat down between my brother and the other American man.

My brother was just a bit too relaxed and did not even think twice and was just kind of taking a load off. The manager took it as a sign of disrespect and kind of blew up. My brother was shocked and embarrassed. I was stunned because a man had yelled at a man. I was scared because I just wanted to make our flight and this man could have pulled some stunt and decided to make life and air travel very difficult for us. There was high anxiety, tension, and cultural differences brewing over a hot fire!

INSIGHT:

The student's casual attitude was unintentionally insulting to the already stressed local manager. Students were much more likely to stay out of trouble if they were more conservative in their relations with locals. A casual and informal way of behavior was likely to be interpreted as showing less respect for local culture than would be appropriate. If locals felt the student was disrespectful toward them they were less likely to go out of their way to accommodate the student.

Deciding Whether to Accept a Dinner Invitation or Not. On a twenty minute long bus ride from Presidency College to a farm in Madras, India, I met an Indian college student who was a part of the homestay that the college was offering. His name was Ramesh and he was about 22 years old, about 5'7" and of a slight build. The bus was full of American students with only a handful of Indian college students. Most of the people were tired and fell asleep on the way to the farm. Ramesh was sitting next to me on the bus and neither one of us was tired, so we started talking. He spoke English very well and was open and honest with his opinions so I found it very easy to talk to him. We discussed neutral topics such as relationships, religion in India, and school and we held many similar views.

After about ten minutes of talking, he asked me, "Would you like to eat dinner at my house and meet my family?" I was surprised at his question because I had hardly even met him and he was inviting me over to his home to meet his parents and two sisters. I wasn't used to such hospitality, friendliness, and willingness to extend one's personal area, so I naturally asked him, "Really?" He must have sensed my hesitation to readily accept an invitation when I hardly even knew him, so he quickly added, "Of course, and your friends are welcome as well." I must have been sending out cues of distrust and caution in my slow response, questions, and uneasy mannerisms. He therefore responded and sent out warm cues that made me trust him. He smiled, looked directly in my eyes, and asked me to bring along a friend, just in case I was afraid something would happen. Because of his warm cues, I was able to trust him and responded, "Yes, I'd love to."

I don't think I would have trusted him as much if we didn't have such a smooth conversation at the beginning and didn't agree on so many views. But the fact that he looked directly in my eyes and asked if any friends wanted to come along, made me decide that I could trust this guy and I'd be a fool not to go. I did go and had a wonderful time.

INSIGHT:
The student was unsure how to interpret verbal and nonverbal cues but didn't want to lose a chance for local contact, creating a dilemma. It was possible for students to form friendships more quickly than they might back home. The urgency of time constraints and the unfreezing of back-home inhibitions provided an openness to new friendships from even brief but meaningful interactions.

What's Normal. While I was in India, I went on the Presidency College homestay. I stayed with one other American student. We stayed with a girl named Regi. She was a twenty-five year old travel agent. We spent most of the day with her prior to going to her house. Most of the day was spent going to a variety of different temples and monuments. We ate dinner together along with other students from the college. Around eight o'clock in the evening my friend and I returned to her house.

When we got there, Regi invited her neighbors to come over and talk to us. We spent the next few hours talking amongst ourselves and frequently having Regi translate things for her friends. The critical incident came after these conversations. We were in the bedroom they provided for us, just hanging out. When Regi walked into the room, turned the volume on the stereo up, shut the door and asked us if we would answer a question for her. She asked whether or not it was true that American women carry condoms in their purses on a regular basis. I was shocked; not so much from the question, but in the insecurity I felt about answering the question. I know that pre-marital sex was not acceptable and I felt strange addressing the issue.

I proceeded to answer the question very honestly, and said that some do and some don't. I know she wanted a more personal answer but I felt the extreme cultural differences between us at that moment. We had just finished talking about her arranged marriage and how love marriages don't seem to work and answering Regi's questions felt very awkward.

INSIGHT:

The student learned that attitudes about sex she considered routine were seen as radical and dangerous in India. American students had a stereotyped reputation abroad probably based on films and media coverage of violence and sexual freedom among American youth. Like all stereotypes the American image abroad mixed fact with fiction.

Malaysia

School Children. As we were going to the lower half of the temple there were vendors at arms' reach on both sides. We were hot and aggravated. Actually, I think I was a bit more peeved than the others but regardless, I was ready to leave this temple. All we could hear were the voices of vendors inviting us to their shop. Then much to my excitement the sounds of children's voices filled my ears. They were chanting a small, short school song. I could see a building through the mesh netting of the vendors' stores. Where was the door? Should I go in? We were all making good time getting out of there. Should I break the continuity and make everyone hold up while I tour the school? Within the phrase time of that question, the children began singing again and I was set on seeing the children.

To this moment, visiting those children in school was the best experience of Malaysia. They were so eager to learn and so fascinated with the fact that I was from America and spoke English which was one of their subjects.

INSIGHT:

The school children provided a familiar point of reference to the student in an otherwise strange environment. No matter how strange and foreign a culture seemed to the students there was always some common ground or point of reference to which the students could relate. In many foreign cultures young children and the elderly provided safe and accepting ways of getting into the local culture.

Their Pride or My Safety. Two men I had just met offered to take me down to a store to buy a phone card. As they offered to help me, I showed acceptance with a big smile and eager eyes. I thought we were going to walk together. When they invited me over to their car, I had to make a quick decision based on the trust we had established in the past few minutes. If I went with them, they would have control to take me anywhere. They could take me out to a deserted area and kill me if they wanted to. On the other hand, if I refused their generosity it could be a big insult. I had to risk either their pride or my safety.

I was standing by a public phone in Malaysia trying to connect with an MCI operator. I'd been trying unsuccessfully for at least an hour. It was already about 3:00 a.m. in California, the place I wanted to call. I had to make that call for my peace of mind and to be honest with the person I was calling. I knew it would be difficult to call the following day since we would be travelling for several hours to get back on the ship for departure. The two men were very friendly from the beginning. They asked me all about Semester at Sea, my experience in Malaysia, who I travelled with, etc. I felt they were sincere in wanting to help me.

When they directed me toward the car, I did not want to show them any hesitation. I needed to make a quick decision to trust or not to trust. If I showed doubt, it might insult their pride. I thought about what I had heard about Malaysians being very generous. I did not have vast resources on that opinion, but I trusted them more than I would Americans. I could have told them I didn't want to get into the car, but would be happy to walk. I also could have said I had to run back to my room (hotel near by) to get my friend first. That would have been the safest option, but I took a risk. My gut instinct, which is often suspicious of strangers, told me it was okay to go with them.

I learned from the incident that there are different expectations for trust in different cultures. They offered kindness with confidence I would accept it. It scares me that I felt so comfortable going with them. In a way, I was blindly attributing sincerity to their generosity *because* of our cultural differences.

INSIGHT:

The student inferred generous and positive motives to the two Malaysians more easily than she would have back home. Students were constantly having to make decisions with incomplete and inadequate information. Decisions were made based on the student's inferences rather than actual facts and subjective feelings rather than more objective reasoning.

You Can't Force It. During my stay in Malaysia I went to the Cameron Highlands. Before I got on the train back I remembered I needed to buy a toothbrush so I went into a store and as I was buying the toothbrush there was a book that caught my eye. It was a bright maroonish colored book entitled "The Greatest Is Love." The word love was written in bold capital letters. The title reminded me so much of my dad that I asked to take a look at it. It turned out to be a Bible and I felt obligated to buy it.

As I was sitting on the train I decided to start reading it. I was travelling with one other person and because there wasn't much room on the train, we didn't sit together. I ended up sitting with this Indian family. There was a mother, a grandmother, an uncle and a little girl. Something was wrong with the little girl, she had these white splotches on her face. I think she was embarrassed by them because every time she looked at me, she put her hands to her face. The train left at 1:00 a.m. so everyone was trying to sleep. As the mother slept she held the child in her arms. The love there was touching. As I sat there reading my Bible and feeling spiritual, I decided to say a prayer for the little girl. Then it occurred to me that I could help them. I could give them money. The whole rest of the trip I sat trying to figure out some way I could give them the money. Maybe slip it in their bag when they were not looking. All sorts of crazy ideas raced through my head. Then I couldn't decide if I should just give it to them. Something was really holding me back. At the same time, I felt like if I didn't give it to them, something terrible would happen to their daughter.

Finally, we got to the last stop. Everyone was getting off. Even though I had strong reservations I told myself I had to do it. I got off the train then waited for the family to get off. When they did, I walked up to them and gave the woman some money. She had a confused look on her face. I told her that the money was for her and her daughter. She refused the money. What else could she do. I felt really stupid and walked away.

I'm not sure but I guess what I learned from this is that you can't force it. You have to follow your heart and let things happen naturally the way they are supposed to.

INSIGHT:
The student's motives to do good were honorable but she lacked the skill to translate these motives into appropriate action. Most students were well intentioned, but they usually learned that good intentions were not enough. Wanting to help was certainly a noble motive, but giving help in a foreign culture was as difficult and easily misinterpreted as accepting help.

How She Got Away. It was 2:30 in the morning in Langkwai Island, Malaysia, about 50 feet from the border of the Beach Resort and three of my friends were at the Riverside Bar. Each headed back to the hotel at a separate time, about five minutes after one another. The first friend walked around the bend in the beach and could see just ahead the lights of the hotel. She could also see the figure of a man sitting down on the beach. She thought nothing of it because there were so many Semester at Sea students around, she was sure in her mind that it was one of them. But as she passed the man he reached out and grabbed her wrist very tightly. She said, "Can you please let go of me." He said, "I just want to kiss you." At this point she was panicking in her mind but remained calm on the outside. She thought, "I can't believe this is happening to me. How stupid I was to decide to walk back to the hotel alone-- and what bad luck!" The man twisted her arm around her back and threw her to the sand face first. He then put one hand over her mouth and the other over her stomach. A million things went through her mind--"There is nothing I can do. I am powerless. I just don't want him to hurt me." But still she remained calm on the outside and never screamed. Again he said, "I just want to kiss you." Thinking rationally and quickly she said, "OK but first I have to throw up," and she began to make exaggerated vomiting noises. At that moment the man loosened his grip in an effort to turn her over. She took this opportunity to run. She ran as fast and as hard as she could to the hotel where luckily friends were waiting.

Afterwards she wondered why she did not scream, why she was so rational, and why she got away.

INSIGHT:
The student had not learned what was safe and unsafe behavior, causing her to wander into danger. Sometimes students took risks that local persons found hard to understand, like a woman being alone on the beach in the middle of the night. Many students had the idea that "it couldn't possibly happen to me."

Spring Break. I considered Malaysia to be my Spring Break, so I decided to find a place to stay by the beach and relax. One evening I found myself at a bar with thirty or so other Semester at Sea students. After many hours of social drinking a lady friend of mine and I decided to go for a walk on the beach. This particular evening was very hot and humid so a swim seemed in order. We decided to get back to nature and go au naturel. It was a wonderful time until we got out of the water and found everything to be missing. Everything!

We had put our clothes in a pile on a thought-to-be-deserted stretch of beach and when we got out everything was gone. It was very late so there were not many people around, but our room was right near the front desk. We were also taking the chance that there might not be anyone in the room to let us in.

When I found our clothes to be missing I became very freaked out, but that quickly turned into laughter. Our only option was to use the cover of night to get us back to our room, and hope no one saw us. I wasn't aware of nudity laws in Malaysia, but I knew they do kill drug traffickers so I figured my apprehension by the authorities would result in decapitation. We really didn't have any other choices, but I think I should have hidden my clothing a little bit better.

INSIGHT:
The spontaneous decision to swim nude was exciting because it was risky and an "adventure" to remember. Students loved to collect adventures while abroad to talk about when they returned home. The quality of the voyage was measured by the number of exotic experiences collected. Sometimes students took unreasonable chances in their search for adventure and sometimes the adventures had a happy ending.

Skinny Dipping. The night after going out to some bars on the beach in Langkawi, some friends and I decided to cleanse ourselves in the ocean. It was a warm night, and being 4:00 a.m., there was no one on the beach. Since we were having such a good time and the opportunity was there, we shed out clothes and jumped in to do a little skinny dipping.

My two other friends and I swam around and enjoyed the warm water and big black sky full of stars for a while and then jumped out, only to be confronted with pure blackness and no clothes in sight. We were laughing hysterically at first but after a few minutes we really didn't see our clothes and got a bit worried.

All of a sudden a flashlight was shining on us for a split second and then whoever was walking towards us turned it off. At first we were going to run up to our hut, but instead we turned to closer sanctuary--the water--and just as we jumped back in, the light went back on and we saw a security guard standing there on the sand.

"Hello! We can't find our clothes," I called out. Luckily the man spoke English and was nice enough to search for our clothes with his flashlight and he found them for us.

It was extremely embarrassing and very funny, but I'm glad we didn't decide to simply run away naked! That could have turned out worse, I'm sure.

After we put on our clothes, the security guard asked, "Are you American students staying here for a long time?" Knowing that other students had caused havoc the night before, we were very apologetic and assured him that we would all be clearing out of the island the next day. Surprisingly, he was disappointed that we would all be leaving so soon. He said, "You Americans are so fun-loving. We really enjoy having you here. Please come back next year." It's amazing how hospitable these people are.

INSIGHT:

The students assumed they were alone and could swim nude in privacy without realizing how rare true privacy was in the local culture. In most if not all tourist areas the locals had many funny stories about tourists that they enjoyed telling to one another. The students were almost never unobserved and not nearly as private as they assumed.

Where's My Case. This critical incident occurred on my last day in Malaysia on an island named Langkwai. The last night on the island three other friends and I decided to sleep on the beach so that we would make the 7:30 a.m. ferry back to the mainland. By the time we left the bars, it was already 3:30 in the morning.

The four of us had left our backpacks in a friend's hotel room. The only thing I had on me was a camera case which contained my passport, sunglasses, some money and obviously my camera. The reason I had my case was because I wanted to take pictures since it was my last night on the island.

Several hours later, at 6:30 a.m., I woke up and woke up my friends. As I looked around I noticed my camera case was missing. I asked my friends if they had taken it as a joke and they said that they had not and had no idea where it was. I knew and everyone else knew that I placed the case right next to me before I fell asleep, so obviously it had been stolen. I was so upset and all of us searched around the beach for it, and it was nowhere to be found. What was I to do? Forget about my camera, money, and my sunglasses--all I cared about was my passport.

I couldn't decide whether to go to the police station in Langkwai or to take the ferry back to Penang, go to the ship and talk to someone who could give me advice on what to do. I decided in a matter of five minutes, and with the help of my friends, to return to the ship for assistance. I was sure someone on the boat had dealt with the issue before.

INSIGHT:

This student was careless with his camera case and valuables making it easy for others to take advantage of him. Students usually counted on having a safety net to protect them if something bad happened. It was almost like they were dreaming and could wake up if something bad happened. This sense of unreality sometimes led to carelessness and unthinking behaviors that were hard to explain later.

Scooter Accident. On the last day in Malaysia, four friends and I rented scooters and explored the island. None of us had ever ridden them and were excited for our adventure. We rode around all day all over Georgetown and up north on the island without a problem. We handled the traffic of Georgetown, and we mastered the winding roads of the coast on the way back. We came back to Georgetown in the middle of the afternoon and pulled over to the side of the road to discuss where we were going next. However, the place we pulled over was a crowded bus stop and there was a bus coming and we needed to move out of the way. All of a sudden one of my friends lost control of her scooter, couldn't stop, and crashed into a group of about ten pedestrians.

I was right behind my friend and watched the entire incident happen. All I saw were my friend's legs and arms flailing, her scooter weaving uncontrolla- bly and scared faces of men, women and children as they watched this American girl come flying towards them completely out of control. The whole accident happened too fast for the people to move out of the way and for my friend to avoid hitting them. The next thing I saw was my friend lying on her stomach on her over turned scooter and two children pinned underneath the scooter. People began to gather and the moms were pulling their children out from under the scooter, my friend struggled to get up without burning herself on the exhaust pipe and my friends and I stared in a state of confusion and shock.

I quickly turned off my scooter and put down the kickstand. At this point, everything seemed to move in slow motion. I turned around and my other friends where still sitting on their scooters and the looks on their faces told me that they did not know what to do next. I ran over to the accident and by this time my friend was standing as were the pedestrians. The thought that ran through my head as the accident happened was that we were on our way to the hospital because there is no way that everyone could come away from this accident uninjured. Phrases that I kept saying were, "Oh my God," and "Is everything OK?" and "What can I do to help?" As it turned out, everyone came away with a few scrapes but no major injuries. My friend burned her arm on the exhaust pipe and one little girl lost her McDonald's hamburger. Our choices of what to do were very limited because these people couldn't speak English. We offered money to buy the girl a new hamburger. No one understood and finally one man told us to just go away. We finally did go away with guilt heavy in our stomachs.

INSIGHT:

The careless driving that led to the accident caused pain and suffering that reinforced a stereotype of the visitor as "uncaring." It was easy for tourists to get so carried away by the unfamiliar and new experiences that they put others at risk without realizing it. When the inevitable accident happened it was very difficult to "make things right" after the fact.

Thailand

Strippers. Here I was in the heart of Bangkok with my six friends. We had decided to leave Taiwan for four days. It was about 11:30 at night and we were at the "nightspot" alley. Women (hookers) and men and transvestites and homosexuals were working it everywhere I look. I was trying to keep an open mind because of the shock I was feeling. The boys headed for a strip bar and we girls had decide to go with them--Hell, you're only in Bangkok once, live it up!--became one of our many mottos. My friend kept warning me, "You aren't going to like this." My response was, "I need to at least see it. I'm only here once!" The boys went on in first while "us girls" stood outside trying to gain courage to walk in. Finally we walked in. By this time the sex show was over and there were no girls dancing on the stage. I sat there for about five minutes and then ran out crying. My friends followed.

What happened was these dancing girls were all 13 and 14 years old. The ones in the show are all older, but these were children. They were expression-less as they danced and let men pick them up. I have a fifteen year old sister who I miss dearly and when I saw how horrible these kids looked I started crying because I could identify with their age.

INSIGHT:

The strange culture plus the strange lifestyle of sex tourism compounded the profound impact of cultural shock on the student. Students sometimes got in over their heads before they realized it. They forgot that they were still the same people even in this foreign culture and that they would not be unaffected by exploitation even in a strange culture.

Hong Kong and China

Buying a Slurpee at 7-11. While in Hong Kong my friends and I were always passing 7-11 stores. One of my favorite things from 7-11's are their slurpees. I decided that I needed to stop and get one while my friend and I were walking down one of the main streets (Nathan Road). There were several people in line. When it was my turn to pay, I told the Asian woman behind the counter that I wanted to buy a small slurpee. She gave me what I thought was a questioning look so I told her, more slowly, because I thought that I might have spoken too fast for her to understand that I wanted a SMALL SLURPEE. She reached under the counter and pulled out a sheet of paper with stickers all over it and put it in front of me. I was thinking to myself, "OK, forget it, this person doesn't understand and I'm not going to die without this slurpee, so I'll just go." The woman could tell I was frustrated and so she said something and pointed down at the stickers.

I looked at her and raised my shoulders to symbolize that I didn't know what she wanted and/or meant. By now there were four people waiting to pay for their various items. The woman was frustrated with me too, and realizing that I hadn't understood what she meant, she peeled off one of the stickers. Under the sticker was the price ($4.50) with a slash through it and a new price of $3.90. The woman behind the counter was trying to save me money. When I realized what it was I laughed and the woman smiled as well. The people behind me didn't think it was funny though, and so I quickly paid for the slurpee and filled it up and left.

INSIGHT:
The slurpee was familiar/friendly while the waitress seemed unfamiliar/unfriendly. Not every local tried to exploit the students. It was important to be patient and approach contacts with locals with a positive attitude. Students who expected to be exploited were much more likely to experience exploitation as a form of self-fulfilling prophecy.

A Stroll through the Park. It was Sunday in Hong Kong. One of the crew had warned me of this day. He said it was the day all the Filipinos come out and relax. It's a big holiday for them. Whole families and friends gathered around Statue Park to forget work. A street is even closed down for them because there are so many. I decided to take a walking tour of the island on this day.

As a Filipino-American I was so excited to see so many of my people concentrated in the park. I felt like I was in the Philippines. I hiked up a small hill to visit the "oldest Anglican church in the Far East." It was a cloudy day, maybe even a bit chilly, but the small hike left me covered with sweat. I walked through the park to return to the ship. I had been wearing a windbreaker over my tank top. One thing I have learned about travelling in all these countries is that walking makes me sweat, so I'd better dress appropriately. When I reached the bottom of the hill, a few blocks from the park, I removed my windbreaker in order to let myself dry out.

As I walked through the park, I noticed many of my countrymen looking at me. As was my custom, I avoided their eyes and kept on walking. Their stares did not seem friendly--there was something curious about it. They looked at me as if I were a spectacle. Then I realized that my face could not have been foreign to them. I was one of them. So, in an attempt to be cordial, I met their stares, smiled, and said hello.

Their expressions did not change. They did not smile back or look away. They just stared hard, like they were trying to tell me something, but they would not speak to me, as if they did not want to be associated with me.

As I rounded a corner, I saw two Filipino women approaching me from the opposite direction. They, too, watched my progress towards them. They looked somewhat incredulous. I smiled, bowed my head, and greeted them. They just looked at me. They seemed to be saying something to each other, but their eyes never left me. They almost looked amused, but indignant at the same time. As I got closer, one of the ladies addressed me in Tagalog.

"Aren't you cold? It's a chilly day," she said giving me a once over look. "It may be, but all this walking is making me sweat," I responded then continued on. I looked down and gave myself a once over as well. I was wearing a pair of jeans, hiking shoes, and a tank top. What was wrong with that? Then I looked at everyone else. People wore long sleeved shirts. Some even had sweaters on. No one else wore just a tank top.

I had forgotten how conservative my native country was. I contemplated putting on my windbreaker, but it was so hot. I battled with myself for a while. I wasn't about to give up my comfort for their petty, little hang up. Let them stare. I'm never going to see them again. Then I became curious. Was that really the reason they were staring?

I put my windbreaker back on to see if there would be a change. There was. People still looked at me, because I looked like a tourist with my camera and my clothes, but they smiled when I greeted them. I decided to keep my windbreaker on since I was getting close to the ferry, and much preferred this type of interaction.

INSIGHT:

The student was insensitive to the cues by locals telling her something was wrong. Locals made judgments about the students with very little information, usually limited to what they saw in a casual glance. They drew conclusions based on this inadequate data and they acted on those conclusions.

An Unexpected Visit. The port of Hong Kong was the first port that I really travelled to on my own. My confidence had been growing this whole trip, but after this port I felt like I could go anywhere and do anything.

It was the third day in Hong Kong and I had decided that I was going to get on a train and head out into the new territory. A friend of mine told me there was a lookout point where you could see the barbed wire of China and everything. However he told me the wrong stop to get off and I ended up getting off at LoWu. The only reason to go there is to go into China. Nobody really spoke English so I just got off the train and followed the flow of people. Pretty soon I realized I was going through immigration. I knew I wasn't where I had thought I was but I figured, what the hell, so I went though. I was for the most part in China. I found out it would only take 20 to 30 minutes for a visa so I went to find out about it. I ended up going into the wrong line--I didn't have a visa. These Chinese communists had an intimidating way about them, the man behind the desk started speaking Chinese to me in a loud voice. I didn't understand him which caused him to get annoyed and he spoke even louder. Then one other person in line shouted that I needed to fill out a piece of paper, so I stepped out of line to complete it. I walked over to the right visa line and the man asked me how long would I be in China. I said I didn't know, maybe a couple hours. He gave me an annoyed look then went to the back of his room. I swear I don't even think these people ever smile. I now realized that what I was doing was a little crazy and dangerous. I decided that I was going to head back into Hong Kong. As I tried to get back a guard stopped me. I told him I wanted to return to Hong Kong. Eventually I realized he wanted me to go back upstairs and tell the officer there to call and give me permission to cross. I did and then was able to cross back into Hong Kong. There was some paper work on the other side but I was back. It was exciting. I had never felt nervousness from people looking at my passport before. I felt like I was in one of those movies where people are trying to get out of Nazi Germany or Communist U.S.S.R.

INSIGHT:

For the student, going to China was an adventure based on motives the local might judge to be frivolous. There was sometimes almost a voyeuristic quality to tourism by the students, a little like window peeking from the viewpoint of the host culture. This was especially true when the students didn't seem to have a good reason for being in a country. In the absence of a clear role or place, locals sometimes assumed the worst about these strangers who "didn't belong."

Taking a Picture. We had arrived that day at Peking University. We toured the campus and took pictures of everything. I wandered off with two other Semester at Sea students. One friend dropped his camera by accident outside the student cafeteria. He took a picture, without looking though the camera to make sure it was still working. Immediately after taking the picture, a man and his son ran over to us and began yelling at him. He had taken a picture of them unintentionally and they were irate.

We did not know what to do. We stood there in amazement not even realizing why they were so angry at us. For what seemed like an hour we all apologized continuously but the man did not speak English and no one was willing to translate. He offered them money and this made them both more angry. Finally my friend opened up the back of his camera and the younger of the two men reached at it and ripped out the film. He then proceeded to stomp on it and yelled something at us before walking away carrying the crushed film.

We all stood there in amazement, the incident had actually happened very fast, faster than I could comprehend what he had done wrong. He could have given up the film right away but he did not think that was what had made them so angry. His offering money angered them more, they took it as an insult, and our continuous apologies meant nothing.

INSIGHT:

The student unintentionally put local students in danger by unthinking behavior with his camera. The visiting student in a closed society like China faced little real risk beyond being expelled, while the locals sometimes faced great danger. The student was likely to be unaware of what was really going on and could easily put locals at great risk unintentionally. Tourists don't have to be malicious to be dangerous.

Republic of China (Taiwan)

Renting a Motorcycle. This critical incident occurred the second day we were in Taiwan. A group of four of us took the train from Taiwan to Toroko Gorge. Upon arriving there at 6:00 p.m., we happened to notice that the main form of transportation there was motorcycle and mopeds. All of us decided that we either wanted to rent motorcycles or a car. A car just seemed so boring to me because when you are on a motorcycle and the wind is just hitting you in the face, it just provides such an adrenalin rush accompanied by a feeling of excitement. I happened to have ridden motorcycles my whole life and I have driven a car since I was 16. So, what should I do? A car provides us with a lot of conveniences because all of us can fit in it and we wouldn't have to worry where everyone is. On the other hand, it would be quite costly and considering that our next port was Japan, we really had to try to save our money. But we all decided that we each had enough money for the rest of the trip and that we could definitely afford to rent a car. We really had to make a decision soon because both the car rental place and the motorcycle/moped rental place were going to close within a half hour and we needed some form of transportation to get to our hotel which was on the top of Toroko Gorge. The whole time we were discussing what we were going to do, I just couldn't help myself from thinking how much fun it would be to rent a motorcycle and carve though the Toroko Gorge on one. But, I kept on reminding myself how dangerous they are and that if I happened to have an accident I would be so upset and it would definitely have a tremendous effect on the rest of my journey. But all of us kept on talking about how much fun the motorcycles would be and how renting a car would be so dull and that it wouldn't add any excitement to our trip through Toroko Gorge. So, we all agreed that we should most definitely rent motorcycles and that we would all drive under control. I guess what helped me and my friends come to a decision was that we decided we were most likely only going to be at Toroko Gorge once in our life and that we should experience it the best way we thought we could and that way was on motorcycles. This journey is a once in a lifetime experience and I don't want to have any regrets.

INSIGHT:

The student knew that renting motorcycles was dangerous and less responsible, which made that decision more attractive to him. A typical student rationalization for risky behavior was that this is "once in a lifetime" and there will never be another chance to repeat the experience. Students sometimes tended to be self-indulgent toward their sometimes crazy behavior.

Running a Red Light. We had been in Taiwan for just under two days now and it was late Thursday night (10 p.m.). We had not eaten in at least ten hours and we were in search of McDonald's. We were about 180 kilometers south of where our ship docked just outside the town of Hualuan. Hualuan looked fairly big on the map so we were hoping we could find something to eat. The Taiwanese do not drive anything like Americans and their streets signs and road maps are only in Chinese. We were driving down a dark street when we came upon an intersection. I, who was driving, did not see that there was a light directing traffic. I was watching the road and looking at the policeman up ahead on the far side of the intersection. I could not figure out why the police were there and thought maybe we could not go straight. I proceeded through the intersection apparently running a red light. The policeman waved me over with a light stick, so I pulled over. I asked the other three girls in the car why they thought he was flashing me over. I was thinking we could not go down the road. They all laughed and said, "No, I think it was the red light you just ran." I replied, "I just ran a red light? Why didn't you tell me there was a red light. I didn't even see it!" I sat there very nervous as the police officer walked up to my window. I didn't know what the penalty for running a red light was.

Was he going to take me to jail? Was he going to make me pay an outrageous fee? What!

I did not know if I should play dumb or try to talk my way out of it. I was wondering if he was even going to speak English. Maybe they search cars in Taiwan. I did not know. Everyone just sat there quietly. I rolled down my window and he looked in the car and smiled. I said, "Hi!" He said, in shaky English, "Do you know you ran a red light?" I said, "I did?" And then just looked at him. He muttered something in Chinese to his partner, laughed and then looked back at me. I chose just to sit there. I did not know what to say. He said, "Lady, you need to drive more careful," and waved me on. He walked back to his car laughing. The four of us also laughed and I drove away.

INSIGHT:

Her unintentional but careless breaking of the law by driving through a red light could have had serious consequences. Locals often forgave students for misbehavior that would never be forgiven for another local. In part this was a way of helping the students have a favorable experience, in part an expectation that students always acted crazy, and in part perhaps the thought that it was just not worth the trouble.

Hiking Down Toroko Gorge. I was involved in a critical incident in Taiwan. I was hiking down Toroko Gorge with two other Semester at Sea students. We had all of our backpacks with us and we had been hiking for about three hours. It was about 5:00 p.m. and we were only about half way down the mountain. It was beginning to get a little dark and we were starting to wonder if we would make it down before dark. At about 5:30 p.m. we all started to get pretty nervous. We knew we had to figure out a way to get down before it got dark. There was not anyone around to ask for help and we were not sure how much longer we had to walk to get to the bottom. Cars kept driving past us on their way down the mountain, but we were not sure if it would be safe to hitchhike. Finally we decided to stop and discuss the situation. One of us said, "We need to figure something out or we are going to be stuck out here all night." I said, "Maybe we should try hitchhiking." Even though I think we had all been thinking about it, I was the first person to suggest it. Another one said, she did not think it was safe, but it was probably safer than walking down in the dark. At this point, we saw a car coming toward us and one of our group members stuck out her hand. The car stopped. We all ran up to the car and looked inside. The driver was a man and he was about 26 years old. He was nicely dressed and the car was extremely clean. I asked him if we could have a ride to the bottom of the Gorge, but he did not understand me because he did not speak English. He smiled at us and opened the passenger side door from the inside. We all got in the car and he drove us to the bottom of the Gorge and dropped us off. Since the man did not speak English, we all sat very quiet and listened to the radio the entire ride.

I think we made the correct decision because otherwise we would probably have been stuck on the mountain in the dark. While we were discussing the problem we kept thinking about all the movies were people try to hitchhike and never return. Although I suggested that we hitchhike, I was very scared in the man's car. I kept wondering if he understood where we wanted to go or if he even cared where we wanted to go. I kept hoping that he would drop us off in the correct place and not some foreign place.

INSIGHT:
The students felt very vulnerable although they were probably safer than they would have been back home. Not knowing the rules about what the students could expect of others and what others were expecting of the students made the students feel very vulnerable. Not knowing the language and the darkness of night escalated that feeling of vulnerability very quickly. Being in a group of friends however reduced the risk considerably.

Peer Pressure in Snake Alley. While in Taipei, Taiwan, I travelled with three of my good friends. I had been friends with them since the beginning of the trip so I knew no problems would arise during our trip. The first night there we wanted to go to Snake Alley. It was quite hard to communicate with the taxi driver but we eventually did. As we walked down the alley I wasn't sure whether or not I wanted to drink the snake's blood which had been my original plan. My friend kept saying, "Don't go back on your word." When I came to the first snake drinking place I was a bit shocked. Here were seven live snakes dangling from a rope. The MC kept one of the snakes in his hand and kept pounding it on the ground. He kept blurting out words but I had no clue what was being said. But after awhile I figured out that he was asking for volunteers to come up and drink the snake's blood. Finally, after watching him bash the snake over the head several times I decided to go for it. As I approached the platform, I was still kind of apprehensive. Right as I walked on stage he slit open the snake's side and filled up a shot glass full of blood. I then was taken over and seated at a table. There were two shot glasses, one with blood and the other with some type of clear liquid fluid with a pill inside. My friend was still pressuring me and saying I was a punk if I backed out. I thought to myself--"What the hell!" I put the shot glass to my mouth and shot the snake's blood. Actually it didn't taste bad at all. What made me do it was the fact of peer pressure and when again am I going to be in Taiwan in Snake Alley.

INSIGHT:
Drinking snake blood helped the student project a macho image and show off his willingness to take risks. The more outrageous and unbelievable the experience, the more some students were attracted to it. In this setting,

group pressure increased the danger by tempting the student to show off in front of friends. It was important for students not to feel forced by peer pressure to act foolishly.

Rabbit Hunting. I was in Fulung Beach in Taiwan staying at a campground. I was playing backgammon with a friend. It was a long day and I was exhausted. The next thing I know there was a man sitting next to us. He could not speak English and was trying very hard to communicate. Finally he picked up a rock and drew a rabbit on the concrete. He said, "Let's go," which is about all he could say. Then the next thing I knew it was midnight and we were in a crazy search to find rabbits. It was very funny. After a while we told him we wanted to go back. We ran into two more of his friends. The next thing I knew we were sitting with three men, a bottle of wine, beer and food. We were communicating on a small computer translator. Then they invited us to their house. Although they were very kind, it was still three men and two women. We asked them how far their house was. They informed us it was only a five minute walk. We asked them why they wanted us to go see their house. They wanted us to watch American movies with them. After tossing the idea back and forth we decided to accept the invitation. They bought more food to us, made us tea, put on a movie and were waiting on us hand and foot. It turned out to be a good idea that we went with them because the interaction between the two cultures was really interesting.

INSIGHT:
The crazy idea of hunting rabbits at midnight with strangers appealed to the student's sense of humor as a story he could tell later. Some students were lucky enough to make local friends and be included by them in the local group. When this happened it usually was wonderfully accidental and spontaneous and couldn't have been planned in advance.

The Stuffed Rabbit. It was about thirty minutes before on-ship time on our last day in Taiwan. I was riding the express bus back from Taipei to Keelung and minutes earlier I had borrowed a pen from the Taiwanese girl sitting next to me by using hand gestures to show what I needed. As soon as I finished writing my postcard I returned the pen. After she put the pen away, she reached into her bag and pulled out two little furry stuffed animals. She held them up for me to look at. I smiled admiringly at them and then she handed one to me. "For you," she said.

I was amazed. First, by the fact that she wanted to give me something for what seemed to be no reason and second by the fact that she knew how to speak a little, and perhaps even a lot of English.

I did not know what to do. I was not sure if I should or should not accept the gift. It seemed to me ridiculous that someone I had done nothing but borrowed a pen from should be offering me a gift. I did not want to seem rude or ungrateful, but I was not sure if I would feel right in accepting something from a total stranger.

I decided that I had to assess my situation a little deeper. "Do you speak English?" I asked.

"A little," she replied.

"Thank you for this gift," I said. "It is very nice of you to give this to me."

From there our conversation continued and a new friendship began. We talked the whole way home, exchanged names and addresses and thoroughly enjoyed each other's company.

I feel that I made the right decision by accepting the gift. I did not offend the giver and by doing so I made a new friend.

INSIGHT:
Giving the student a stuffed rabbit symbolized friendliness for the student in a strange country. Friendliness was especially welcome when it was not expected. Locals often seemed more friendly toward the visiting students than toward their own neighbors.

Japan

Traveling in a Group. This critical incident occurred in Kobe, Japan. I had decided to travel with these two girls and one of their fathers. I had travelled with them for a day or so in another country and had a great time so I figured why not?! Things started out badly from the beginning. These girls had packed like they were leaving for a month. Guess who got the privilege of carrying all their crap up and down every time we came to a flight of stairs. We started our trip out in Tokyo and stayed in a five star hotel, of course, as these girls can best be described as "high maintenance." Our first full day was in Tokyo and, granted it was raining, all these girls wanted to do was shop. I was kind of bugged by this but didn't say anything because it was kind of nasty outside. The girl whose father had met us in Japan was constantly bitching at him. When we were at dinner she'd be telling him, "Don't eat any dessert, you don't need it" or "Don't order me that, I don't even know what it is!" Her father was apparently used to it and catered to her every need. She would also tell him what the plans were and he would just nod his head yes. All this ordering and whining was really getting to me. I didn't say anything, I would just kind of rub my forehead and look down because this really made me feel uncomfortable. At one point I suggested Hiroshima but one of them said it was too far and they didn't want to sit in a bullet train to get there. I made no retort and just kind of walked away with clenched fists. I was not used to hanging out with people like this and was thinking to myself--I wonder what everyone is doing right now. I should have travelled with others. Finally, the second to the last day I told them I needed to save some money and stay on the ship. It was a good way of getting out of a bad situation. I went on by myself and had an incredible time for the remainder of the time in Japan.

INSIGHT:

Conflict between students demonstrates the wide range of backgrounds and habits individual students bring with them when they go abroad. Some students responded to the opportunity of tourism by seeking out learning experiences with other locals while others focused almost exclusively on their own needs. When the student was affluent, the temptation to focus on his or her own needs seemed hard to resist.

Nightmare on Ropponyi Street. This incident occurred on my second night in Japan. I was in Tokyo with three friends. It was a Wednesday night and we were looking for a place to go and dance and hang out. We were in the nightclub district close to our hotel--known as Ropponyi Street. Many foreigners flock to these clubs in this area as we were told by many. It was about midnight so if anything was going to be happening it would be at this time.

We walked up to a club called Buzz. We took the elevator up and got off. The bouncer was standing at the door and we asked him if just one of us could peek our head in to see if it looked like fun. The man was very rude and told us that it was club policy that he couldn't let us look. It was clear to us that the club must have been dead and he wanted us to pay the door charge of about $15 to $20 U.S. dollars just to get in. We started yelling at him and calling him rude names in English that we thought he wouldn't be able to understand. Apparently he understood more than we anticipated because soon we were basically being escorted down the elevator and out of the club by another man. He and the bouncer were both giving us very angry and dirty looks as well as saying rude things in Japanese I am sure. I could only make out the word "Americans" every other sentence or so.

INSIGHT:

Being the victim of racist stereotypes in Japan was an unpleasant but important learning experience for the student. When locals had a bad experience with one group of students they were likely to take it out on the next group. In the same way students who had a bad experience with one group of locals were likely to generalize that experience to all locals.

CONCLUSION

The first of the five stages is called the "honeymoon" or "tourist" stage of culture shock. In this stage, the students were still encapsulated by their back-home identities and the adventure abroad was still something of an unreal experience to them. In the sixty-two incidents reported in this chapter, this detached attitude is illustrated by a variety of repeated themes.

The most popular themes emphasized an unintentional or unthinking attitude toward the host culture. The bad and even the good things that happened frequently happened by accident rather than by intention. The students often did not think through the consequences of their actions and demonstrated a self-centered or self-indulgent attitude which was insensitive to the needs of others.

A second popular theme was being naive, uninvolved, and unknowing about the local culture as well as about themselves. They had a difficult time seeing themselves as the locals saw them. They were encapsulated and insulated by their own back-home identities which they carried with them, so that they ignored problems they encountered.

A third popular theme was experiencing the new cultures as exciting and as an adventure with a dream-like quality full of spontaneous and accidental surprises which led to weird and outrageous consequences. The students experiencing the voyage from this perspective demonstrated a child-like quality which was at the same time a bit voyeuristic, and self-indulgent.

The students experiencing this first stage of culture shock had a hard time maintaining the illusion that they had not really left home as the voyage progressed and they were confronted with very real differences in the host cultures. Some of the students were through this stage even before joining the voyage or passed through this stage very quickly. A few of the students were able to stay in this first stage of culture shock throughout the voyage. Most of the students visited this stage of culture shock fairly frequently during the voyage as some new experience, encounter, or event, for which they were not prepared, forced them to start over in coping with the host culture. For that reason the examples of the first stage of culture shock were found in the last port as well as in the first port of the voyage. Having survived culture shock once does not mean that it cannot reoccur.

4

The Disintegration Stage

INTRODUCTION

After the novelty wears off, the host culture starts to intrude on the visitor's life in unexpected and often uncontrollable ways. It becomes necessary to solve practical problems in the host culture and move beyond the role of a spectator. This stage involves a sense of confusion and disorientation where differences between the home and host cultures become very noticeable causing tension and frustration. The individual often experiences a sense of failure and self blame for real or imagined inadequacies. The individual may experience an acute sense of profound loss and disorientation regarding what can be expected of others and what others expect of the individual. This sense of being different, isolated, and inadequate seems permanent, together with bewilderment, alienation, depression, and withdrawal. In extreme cases this stage can seem to result in the complete disintegration of personality as the former and now inappropriate identity is discarded and the new identity has not yet been formed.

The critical incidents in this chapter will demonstrate aspects of the disintegration stage demonstrating the impact of differences, contrasts between the new cultural reality and previously learned patterns. This disintegrating perception will be evident in emotions of confusion, disorientation, loss, apathy, isolation, loneliness, and a sense of inadequacy. The behaviors appropriate to the second stage are often depression, withdrawal, avoidance of contact with either host or home culture persons, and a self-blaming embarrassment about being so different from the host culture. Persons going through this second stage will typically have a low sense of self-esteem and no support system in the host culture.

Persons going through the second stage experience pain and helplessness. Because they perceive themselves to be at fault for the pain they are feeling, they are unlikely to seek outside help. The process of disintegration is self perpetuating through self-defeating behavior, and failure becomes a self-fulfilling prophecy.

CRITICAL INCIDENTS

Bahamas

What Does It Cost. I had gotten a taxi in Nassau with one other student from our hotel. The driver almost immediately knew that we were from "the ship" and started asking us questions like how long is the trip, how many people are on it, and where are the places that we are going to? He also asked how much money the trip cost. The other student and I had been asked this question many times before and had simply answered that it cost a lot. Most people seemed satisfied with that answer and did not persist any further. However, the taxi driver was not satisfied. He wanted us to give him an exact amount of money. I didn't feel comfortable discussing this topic with close friends let alone a complete stranger. He started throwing out figures and when he said five thousand dollars we agreed that was the cost of the trip just so that he would get off the topic. He seemed to be flabbergasted by the price and we felt really uncomfortable for the rest of the drive.

INSIGHT:
The student was self-conscious about spending so much money for the voyage, and the taxi driver's questioning made the student feel guilty. As the students became more aware of the differences between themselves and the locals, they also became more self conscious and embarrassed or even defensive about having more resources than local people. The differences seemed to violate their sense of "fairness" even though they were not about to give up their advantages.

Venezuela

The Ugly American. I was given the opportunity to spend the night in a native's home. I wasn't comfortable with this idea because of the horrible conditions of the house in which I would be sleeping. The town was San Fernando, Venezuela, which was six hours from La Guaira; therefore, we needed a place to sleep. The house where we were to stay was dirty, bug-infested and smelled very bad. The reason I couldn't just say "no thanks" was because the house belonged to a relative of our friend/tour guide Pablo. Also, the relative was a very nice older women who seemed pretty lonely.

Although I didn't want to spend the night there, I also didn't want to offend the woman or Pablo. The importance I place on cleanliness where I sleep is more important than for most people I have met. I was prepared to stand my ground.

Keeping in mind the "ugly American," I informed Pablo I didn't feel comfortable sleeping in someone else's house whom I didn't know and that I wouldn't change my mind.

INSIGHT:
The female student had to choose between insulting new friends or her own discomfort. Most travellers had heard about the "ugly American" syndrome and were determined not to make a bad impression on the locals. However, when faced with the choice of making a bad impression or giving up an accustomed luxury, students sometimes chose the luxury and then felt bad about themselves afterward.

Encounter with the Police. This critical incident happened in a park in Caracas shortly after dark. We were confronted by three policemen who immediately started shouting at us in Spanish. After spending almost two months in Baja, Mexico, I've learned that many law officers are incredibly crooked. I've watched people get thrown in jail or have their money or jewelry taken for absolutely no reason. Thus, I've learned that sometimes it is better to run. Police often will not bother chasing you and jail is not a place that you want to be in out of the U.S. (or in the U.S. for that matter). The question in my situation was to either run and hope that I didn't become a moving target, or to stay and hope that the men didn't pull a joint out of their pocket, say it was mine, and either request a bribe or take me to jail.

This was a complex question because I was not sure if my companions would follow my lead if I took off. If they didn't, they would surely be in trouble even though I would be free. Because of this, I decided not to run. It turned out to be the right choice because these men were only into harmless harassment and after about ten minutes we were on our way.

INSIGHT:
Since the student had already had a bad experience with local Spanish-speaking authorities it was easy to become suspicious or even paranoid and expect the worst. Expecting the worst increased the likelihood of bad things happening so it was a good idea not to panic when in this stressful situation.

Brazil

Here Kitty Kitty. I was coming back from a wonderful afternoon of sunning, swimming, eating and drinking at Ithaprica Island when I came across this white and orange cat on the docks. At least I think it was white, actually the cat was covered with so much crude oil that it was almost brown. The orange color in the cat was almost like a rust color. I am not sure if you can picture what an orange and white cat looks like at home but this one looked faintly like that.

It was a young cat, it still had this kind of innocent look in its eyes, almost as if it hadn't realized its fate yet. The build of this cat was one that reminded me of the skeleton models you see in most biology labs. It had skin covering these bones but that's all it was, skin. This cat did not have an ounce of fat on its body which made it almost look like it had been dead and buried for a couple of weeks and had just come back to life and was walking around.

When I saw this cat I immediately stopped and turned around. I remembered having some leftover crackers in my backpack, so I got them out, knelt down and began feeding the cat. As I knelt there so many things were racing through my head. Why did this animal have to be like this, didn't anybody care? Should it live and suffer? Should it be killed and put out of its misery? What could I do, I was only a passer-by. I was so confused that I almost started to cry.

I fed the cat the rest of the crackers, got up and walked onto the ship. I realized there are some things that I have no control over and can do nothing about to fix them. I felt so defeated and beaten.

INSIGHT:
The hungry and lonely cat symbolized something important to the student about herself and others. When lonely and alone it was sometimes easier to identify with animals--who also seem helpless and innocent--than with other people. In countries less attracted to pets than the United States, this sympathy for animals as pets was sometimes hard to understand and could be interpreted as putting animals before people.

Steal My Watch. This incident didn't occur to me, but rather to a good friend spending the afternoon in the street festivals in Salvador. The pre-Carnival parties that took place were quite a sight to see. Three friends were on their own for that part of the afternoon. The two are prime targets for any and all harassment. One has long, brown hair and the other has red, curly hair. Both are somewhat fair-skinned. To get to the point, they looked like your average tourist--sneakers with neon, jean shorts, T-shirts, cameras around their necks, bows in their hair, and sunglasses on their faces. And of course one had a watch on, not of much value, but still, she was instructed by SAS not to wear one. They may as well have taped twenty dollar bills to their foreheads.

In the middle of thousands, literally thousands of Brazilians these two girls were very easily spotted. It would be compared to walking down a street in the opposite direction that everyone else is walking. As they pushed their way though the hot crowd, one of the girls noticed a kid tugging on her arm. Her watch was actually tight around her wrist, but this young child managed to twist her arm over her head and tug until the watch came free. All of this occurred in less than 30 seconds. She was so appalled that she really couldn't do anything except scream at the kid running away. Of course, she could have chased after the boy, but the consequences might not be worth it. What if he had a weapon? Was her $10 watch worth the chance? Apparently not, because instead she just let the incident pass.

INSIGHT:

The female student made an easy target for the boy who wanted to steal her watch. As the students became aware of how different and isolated they were, many began to see themselves as potential victims. When they were exploited they were likely to accept whatever happened and resign themselves to being helpless even though that would not be their response back home.

The 4:00 a.m. Jitters. The night was filled with lots of activity. It was Friday night in Salvador and I can remember thinking to myself, "Wow I can't believe I'm here." Partying in the streets of Brazil until 4:00 a.m. was certainly not something I thought I'd be doing a year ago, but there I was and having the time of my life.

When the night began there was a large group of us, seven or eight. We sat at two adjoining tables at an outside cafe and listened and watched the live entertainment of the natives. Students from the ship were numerous and it seemed in a way we were the majority in this particular area, at least for awhile. As the clock ticked away and more beer was consumed the large group I was a part of began to dwindle in numbers. Where it once was comforting to be surrounded by friends, now I was a bit uneasy with only three of us.

My roommate and friend from home was aware of the change of atmosphere and knew by the look of my face I felt the same way. A third friend didn't seem affected by the situation. This both bothered me and helped me feel a little more relaxed. It was now 4:00 a.m. and we were the last students on the streets of this area. The Brazilians were abundant and though not hostile were aware that we were aliens and for the first time this fact really bothered me.

Then, suddenly about fifty yards away a fight broke out between two Brazilians and the aggressor had a gun in hand. The police were nowhere to be found and neither were taxis. We knew what we were going to do, but couldn't leave without the third friend. A decision had to be made and fast. Staying in this place was not smart, but neither was leaving the friend who at this point in time was in the middle of talking to a Brazilian young man at a table just down the way. He wasn't aware of the fight so felt no anxiety, unlike the two of us.

INSIGHT:

The fight emphasized how foreign and alien the students were and how vulnerable they were in an emergency situation. When the full impact of being aliens in a foreign culture and the implications of isolation became clear to the students, it was hard to deal with the situation.

Losing My Watch to a Child. After a day of shopping and sightseeing in the upper city of Salvador, my four friends and I were preparing to descend in the elevator to the lower city and return to the ship for dinner. One of my friends was ahead of me to my right, another friend was right next to me on my right and two other friends were several steps ahead of us preparing to go through the turnstile to enter the elevator. I had a bag of previous purchases in my left hand, and was reaching into my right front pocket for the fifty Cruzeiros bill I had put there several minutes earlier in preparation for the elevator ride.

As I pulled out my bill, I felt a sharp, painful, surprising yank on my left wrist. Although my bag was in my left hand, I realized immediately that someone was trying to steal my watch. Instinctively, I screamed, while at the same time grabbing at the hand of the thief with my right hand. I raked my considerably sharp fingernails up his wrist and arm before realizing that my attacker was a small child. Staring back at me with large, startled eyes, he released his hold on my wrist and ran off. I was too stunned by the entire incident to follow. I realized, however, that my scream had drawn the attention of every individual in the line to the turnstiles. My friends surrounded me as I was overcome by a mixture of rage (at having been victimized), shock (at the suddenness of it all), and even embarrassment (at having screamed in a public place and attracted attention).

INSIGHT:
Being attacked by a small boy resulted in mixed feelings of anger, embarrassment, and perhaps even guilt for the female student. There was a sense of confusion and disorientation, knowing she was different but wanting to be accepted. These mixed feelings were most apparent in the emergency where she acted spontaneously.

Attacked in Salvador. As I approached the gate to enter Salvador, I was bombarded by hundreds of children. They were all grabbing at me, yelling and trying to sell me things. I had not been forewarned of this and panicked.

The children were trying to sell ribbon-like bracelets to me. Time and time again I said no. Then one child said, "OK, here is a present for you--free!" I tied it onto my wrist in a double knot. There he stood trying to charge me two dollars. I was about in tears when finally my cousin came to the rescue. We were all by ourselves travelling into Salvador.

As this boy and several others were yelling at me, their father came up and was screaming strings of Portuguese at me. He was also trying to sell a toy boat. I have no fingernails at all so I couldn't get the ribbon off. My cousin began to untie it when they all started yelling and grabbing me. They were trying to sell us more and more. We kept flapping our hands around us. It looked like we were swatting flies. I kept reaching down and grabbing at my fanny pack to make sure they hadn't stolen anything. Finally, we escaped and practically went running across the street.

The children had all been small and scraggly looking. They were unkept and dirty. I pretty much blanked and stood there.

INSIGHT:

By showing interest, the student started the bargaining process attracting a "swarm" of young boys selling souvenirs who overwhelmed the student. The feeling of alienation became so strong that the locals were described as animals, birds, or insects who were attacking her. It was hard to know or even care about what would be "fair" under those conditions.

Should I Stay or Should I Go. My critical incident happened in Rio. This incident involved my friend and myself. It occurred on a Friday night at about 1:30 a.m. We had a very long day. We went to the beach, had lunch, went sightseeing and went to the shopping mall and then had dinner. We decided to go out to a nightclub at about 1:15 a.m. because it was our last night in Rio and we wanted to make the best of it.

My critical incident happened in the taxi cab on the way to the nightclub. Our taxi driver did not speak one word of English and we had to show him on a piece of paper where we were going. We were on our way to the club and we passed a dead body on the side of the street. He was lying flat on his back with a hefty bag laid on top of him. My heart stopped a few beats and I became nervous. I had never seen a dead body on a street before. The road became very crowded with kids and after a few miles it was quiet. Then all of a sudden we were apparently in the prostitution district. There were prostitutes everywhere. At this moment I felt that this was a critical incident. I did not know if I should go forth or turn back. For one brief minute I questioned the situation. I became scared as I have never felt before. I normally am not nervous in situations like this considering I live in New York City and walk the streets all the time. I decided to go forth and enjoy myself.

INSIGHT:

The female student was probably not used to dealing with violence face to face and had a difficult time when confronted directly and unavoidably with violent behavior resulting in death. Her response seemed to be, "Since I can't do anything about it I might as well ignore it."

Left Alone. Our group had just returned from the four day Amazon Adventure. It was 2:00 p.m. and we had about six hours left in Salvador. I went into the old city with two friends. We spent the day shopping and exploring. We ate at a really tasty restaurant but it was getting late and I had promised my mother that I would call her before I left Salvador. She worries quite a bit! So after dinner, the three of us separated and I went to use a public phone while they shopped around. I talked to my mom for about ten minutes and then, with the help of modern technology, she called my grandma on the three-way calling line. As I was talking, a man came up to me and warned me that I was not safe by myself because the area gets dangerous after dark. So I was a little concerned but I was really enjoying talking on the phone. (I was a tad-bit homesick!)

About five minutes later a man came up very close and was staring at me and making weird expressions. At this point I was truly scared! I told my mom that I was being stared at by this suspicious man. Of course, I was not worried that he would understand me, he just didn't appear to be the bilingual type. He appeared to be very uneducated. I told my mom and grandma that I loved them and I went off to find my wandering friends. I did not have any luck finding them so I sat down in a well-lighted outdoor restaurant hoping that they would appear. After about twenty minutes, they still did not show up. The Portuguese man kept approaching me and talking to me. I would tell you what he said, but since he spoke in Portuguese, I didn't understand one word. So, here I was, in Salvador, Brazil, with no money, because I had spent it all, and I couldn't speak nor understand Portuguese.

I had no money so I couldn't afford to get back to the ship by taxi or by bus. Because I couldn't get back to the ship I would miss dock time and maybe miss the ship altogether. I didn't even have money to get to a nearby hotel and I was alone, so walking was not an option. After scaring myself to death, my friends showed up at the restaurant. I was close to tears and they were pretty worried themselves.

INSIGHT:

The student was a little homesick and feeling very vulnerable in this lonely place at night. Being homesick made her even more vulnerable. It was easy to contrast the dangers of this foreign country with the safety back home. If she had panicked under those conditions it would have been easy to make things worse and to focus on the catastrophies that might occur rather than to plan a way out of the situation.

Losing My Temper with a Young Brazilian Boy. Shortly after our ship arrived in Salvador I departed for a bank by myself. When I got out of the port I was immediately approached by several children who were trying to get me to buy Brazilian "good luck" bracelets. One child of about twelve years kept following me even after I had told him no. He kept repeating the cost of the bracelet--one dollar, one dollar. I politely responded no but he continued to follow me. I tried a new approach which was to ignore him. After a minute or so he started draping the bracelets over my shoulder and saying, "One dollar." Without thinking too much I made what I view as a critical decision and I yelled at him, "No! I don't want your fucking bracelet!"

Immediately the boy stopped and stared at me. I couldn't tell if he wanted to cry or he wanted to hurt me. All I know is that stare seemed to last forever and it made me feel terrible about my lack of patience. Finally the boy turned and left me alone.

Once I saw the look in the boy's eyes I knew I had made a mistake. Instantly I felt like the "ugly American" who had given into culture shock only moments after getting off the ship. I did not know at the time about the thousands of homeless and starving children in Salvador. I only viewed this child as a pesty boy looking to rip off a tourist.

INSIGHT:

The student's spontaneous burst of anger broke the rules of how visitors are supposed to act. The student probably felt like relations with locals were a sort of game, where the student was gradually "worn down" and lost. The need to win once in awhile became so strong that the student broke the rules of the game and attacked the child directly.

The Smiling Clerk. Flying home from Rio, I was sipping my water (no ice) completely unaware that my luggage was not flying with me. Once we had landed and I realized that I did not have my backpack I spent an hour in a small smokey room trying to communicate with the lost baggage clerk. I left the office feeling fairly confident that my luggage would be safely returned to me.

I had been able to communicate fairly well with the clerk though an interpreter. They found my luggage still in Rio. It was to be flown in on the next plane and then driven by a representative from VASP Airlines to the ship. Everything appeared very professional.

I was very concerned about my bag because my credit cards, room key, and money were in it. I was willing to stay at the airport until it arrived but the clerk convinced me to go back to the ship. This was my mistake; I trusted that the clerk was working in my best interest because of her professionalism. I respected her authority and did not want to cause any more conflict, so I went back to the ship.

I left the airport thinking this lady was going to do everything possible to get my luggage for me. The clerk saw my leaving as meaning that she had completed her job because I was no longer a burden to the airline. I know now this is how she felt because I was given a wrong number to call and the address she had for the ship was wrong. I thought we had the same goal in mind, to return my luggage to me. But she merely wanted me and the group I was with out of her office.

INSIGHT:

The student who lost her luggage felt betrayed by the airline clerk who broke her promise to find the luggage. Because students were so transient and troublesome it was easy for locals to not take them seriously. It wasn't as though they would get repeat business from the student or would even meet her again, making one student's luggage a relatively low priority in a busy day.

The Jungle Comes Alive at Night. As I walked back to our hut in the

Amazon in complete darkness my imagination ran wild. The jungle comes alive at night. There are hundreds of different sounds and animal calls, yet one is blind to the rest of the creatures. I was scared to sleep in our hut that night. I think it had to do with the fact that earlier in the afternoon we had bats, a tarantula, and lizards in our hut. This isn't mentioning the huge green spiders on our porch! I have never liked spiders all that much and every time I thought about going to sleep I would think of the twelve inch tarantula in our place during the daytime. I couldn't even understand what was going to be living there at night.

As I approached the hut with two other girls my heart was throbbing. The three of us seriously stood outside the door discussing who would enter first. Finally I entered, however reluctantly. The other two followed very closely and then we realized there was no electricity. So in pitch blackness I was feeling for the candles and matches, hoping that that was all I felt. I finally found some and lit all three immediately. It looked as if I was exorcising the place of evil with the candles. I inspected every inch of the hut, shook my sheets and clothes, and then pushed the three beds together and away from the wall. (A bit ridiculous, but at that time and in my state of mind it was logical.) There was nothing else to inspect so now it was time to jump into bed. My friend and I looked at each other and we were contemplating whether or not to go to sleep or leave the hut and go to the main village. Neither of us had slept for two days and we were exhausted, but I was more frightened to remain at the hut than not to sleep. We were heading to the door and then something stopped me and I thought to myself, I am in the Amazon and if creatures are going to crawl on me then let them because I'll never know if I am sleeping. So I cocooned myself with a sheet so absolutely no part of my body was showing and went to bed. The darkness was still ominous and the sounds overwhelming, but I decided to remain because it wasn't the easy way out.

INSIGHT:
Hiding from real or imaginary danger seemed to work for the student. In this strange and unfamiliar surrounding, her imagination tended to run wild. It was difficult to separate those sounds and creatures that were actually dangerous from those that were merely strange.

Ribbon Bracelets. One day in Salvador, Brazil, just outside the entrance to the Mecades Models a little boy was trying to sell me a ribbon bracelet. These colorful ribbons have the words "Lembanca do Senhor do Bonfim da Bahia" (Souvenir of Our Lord of Good Ending) printed on them. Supposedly if a friend ties these around your wrist with three knots when the ribbon falls off three wishes will come true.

The little boy kept begging for me to buy a set of three for a dollar. I kept saying, "No." Finally he put his arm around my shoulders and was saying, "Friend, friend." At this point I felt uncomfortable with this boy hanging on me. I tried to make him let go of me. My friends started to walk away so he would get the message that we were leaving. I was getting frustrated and scared because he would not let go of me. I started saying, "Let go!" I grabbed one of my friend's hands and they tried to pull me away from him. Then he grabbed my hand and proceeded to tie one of the ribbons around my wrist. I was angry and said, "No." I tried to pull the ribbon off over my wrist. Meanwhile, the boy had started to say, "You owe me a dollar." I persisted in trying to pull the ribbon off. He placed his hand out to be paid. I had no intention of paying for the bracelet he had tied on my wrist over my objections. My friends grabbed me by the hand and we started to leave. I was still trying to pull the bracelet off. The boy followed us and had a hold on the bracelet to tear it from my wrist. My friends wanted him to leave us alone. He persisted to pull on the ribbon. We ducked into the station for the elevator to the upper city, and only once we were through the turnstile, which you had to pay to go through, did we get rid of the boy.

INSIGHT:
This student allowed herself to be manipulated into a situation where she would have to buy the bracelet. The boy who sold the bracelet to her had learned by experience how to manipulate tourists successfully. She was at a disadvantage because she had never experienced the seller's techniques, but the seller had practiced on hundreds of previous tourists.

The Culture Bus. Three of my girlfriends and myself had gone to visit Arembepe, Brazil, for the day. The stop we had gotten off on to go to the town was not on the schedule, but we were dropped off anyhow. The bus was to pick us up again at 5:00. When 5:00 approached, we saw a bus pull up to the town. People were getting on it, so we did too. We thought it must be our bus because no other buses were passing through. As the bus moved along, we stopped at a small local village, other people got on, and the bus kept going. Suddenly we realized that we were not on the correct bus and that we had picked up a local bus. As we got further into the countryside, we got very panicky. We could not get off the bus because we would be in the middle of nowhere. We had no choice but to ride in the "sardine" packed bus until we came to a place of some civilization. We asked if the bus went to Salvador, but people looked at us baffled. I had never felt so car sick in my life and thought we would never see the ship again. I thought that for the rest of my life I would be caught in backward, tiny villages and no one would be able to find me. After two hours on the bus, we were approaching main highways. Suddenly the bus stopped. We were in Salvador--at the correct bus station that we had wanted to go to. We had never been so relieved.

INSIGHT:
The students felt lost and helpless not knowing where their bus was headed

and not knowing how to regain control of the situation. Simple tasks like taking a bus became very difficult in this foreign country, especially when they didn't speak the language. Giving up control was a frightening experience and it was easy to panic.

A Helping Hand. I was eating dinner at a pizza parlor with three other people from the boat, and a little boy about eight years old came up to me and asked me for money. I could not help myself from noticing his bloody right foot that looked as though it was broken, and the fear and pain he had written all over his face. I wanted to give him money, but I knew that once I gave him some money, all the other little kids would be flocking to our table asking for money. But I felt as though this kid was an exception, and that it was my duty to society to give to the poor and needy.

This was going to be our last meal in Salvador, Brazil, because we had to be back on the boat in two hours, since we were leaving for Cape Town, South Africa, later that evening. So the four of us decided to go to this pizza parlor on the ocean where there was live music and dancing going on. There were tons of people dancing, especially little Brazilian boys. Our table was outside, facing in the direction of all the live music and dancing going on. As soon as we sat down, all the kids kept on trying to sell us different kinds of things; such as gum, peanuts, candy, and even toothpicks. Obviously we looked like tourists, considering we each had cameras, and so the kids saw us as fresh bait. We decided not to buy anything from these kids, because as soon as we bought one thing from a kid the rest of them would be hounding us all dinner long to buy something from them.

INSIGHT:
The students were afraid of being flooded by needy people if they helped one of them. Where would they stop? How would they set limits? The student chose to just ignore all of them so that they didn't have to make any decisions.

South Africa

Crossroads. The first day in Cape Town, South Africa, my three friends and I hopped into a taxi. The taxi driver seemed very friendly and introduced himself as Adam. We then proceeded to ask what one should do and see while in Cape Town. He proceeded to run down a list of about ten must things. First off he mentioned the townships. I had heard all about the townships, but was a tad bit scared of going into one. I heard earlier in that day that two white people had been walking through one of the townships and were beaten to death. Adam had told us that he knew many people in the township of Crossroads, so we decided to have him take us there. Even though we were a little apprehensive, we decided to head to the townships. On the drive there we asked Adam many questions about apartheid and why the whites were treating the blacks in the way they did. He told us that the majority of the money in South Africa was held by 10% of the white population. And that they felt that if one's skin color was black that they must be uneducated and worth exactly nothing. As we started to drive there we passed several of the colored people's neighborhoods. Just looking at these made me begin to have second thoughts about entering the townships.

As we approached within one mile, Adam spoke to us about not showing any fear on our faces as we drove through. He then asked us the one question which I was hoping to avoid. He said, "Are you guys sure that you want to drive through Crossroads?" I had kind of assumed a leadership role because I sat in the front seat. For the last two minutes I was having mixed emotions, but without any hesitation in my voice I blurted out, "Let's do it." We entered Crossroads, and I was overcome with a feeling which can't be explained. It wasn't happiness or fear, but rather something like shock. There were rows and rows of shacks all lined up. Outside the houses there were several children and adults. Adam said something to them about us taking their pictures. They must have said something positive, because the next thing we knew they were all smiling and posing for a picture. All the children were so happy. They didn't know how bad they had it. At that point, I can honestly say that I've never witnessed something so sad in my entire life. I felt for each of these black people which we saw and wanted to help every single one of them. As we started leaving the outer limits of Crossroads, Adam asked each of us how we felt. We were basically speechless, unable to express our thoughts. Well, I had just seen something which will forever change my life.

INSIGHT:
When students accustomed to having wealth encountered neighborhoods accustomed to poverty it was overwhelming. They assumed that the residents felt like they would feel if they lived here, rather than seeing the residents on their own terms.

The Tutu Controversy. Five girls, including myself, decided to go to a restaurant called Spurs, in South Africa. We were seated and our waiter came over to take our drink orders. He realized we were Americans and began to ask us about our plans while in South Africa, where we were from, etc. He was very nice, and we asked him about places to see while we were there. Then, after our meal, one of the girls mentioned that Desmond Tutu had been on our ship. The waiter's expression changed dramatically. We could tell his entire opinion of us had changed within one minute because of one sentence. He yelled to his friends, "Hey, guess who was on their ship for nine days, Tutu!" Three other waiters came over and they all began to laugh and ridicule Tutu saying things like, "Yes, the man who lives in the biggest house in Cape Town who helps no one." "He is not a leader of the blacks, he causes more problems than relief for them." We were all shocked and embarrassed. None of us had thought about how Tutu was viewed in South Africa, or that he might be viewed differently by different groups. Our waiter then asked us about what he said to us. I then began to answer his questions vaguely and as uncontroversially as possible, and the other girls quickly caught on. As he saw we were not going to say anything of interest he left, and so did we as soon as we could. I also must add the fact that we received a number of strange glances as we walked out.

INSIGHT:

The students expected all South Africans to share their very positive impression of Bishop Tutu and his work. They were surprised and embarrassed by meeting some who disagreed. They were surprised when issues that seemed clear-cut to them were actually controversial. When confronted by this inevitable controversy, they withdrew to avoid further embarrassment.

Catching a Cab. After a fabulous day sight seeing and a night on the town, I was separated from my friends and had to get a cab home--no big deal, but I was a little worried, seeing it was the first night and I was totally unfamiliar with Cape Town. A cab came after about ten minutes of trying to wave one down, and the driver was obviously drunk. I made the initial choice of getting in without thinking. I knew it was a mistake, but I wanted to get back to the ship. The driver, with the slurred words, asked me if I wanted a lady for the night. "No thanks, I've got to get back. I'm really late" I said. I could see the ship getting closer, and as we approached it I was feeling some relief. "Hey wait, where are you going? That's the ship," I told him as we raced past the stop.

"Come, let me show how lovely these ladies are my friend, only for 100 U.S. dollars." "I really can't. I'd love to, but I can't. I have no money and I'm late." I wasn't sure if this guy was getting angry or not, but I was getting really scared. He took me to this building that was lit up with a sign reading The Cachet Club. "Go in and just look, I will wait here," the driver told me. I wanted no part in the Cachet Club and no part of this driver, so what was I to do. I got out of the car and luckily a taxi was across the street. It was either go for it and risk ditching the original driver or dealing with his drunkenness. I grasped some courage out of nowhere, ran to the new cab, and shouted "The ship, now!"

INSIGHT:

The student went out alone and got into the wrong cab, which predictably resulted in undesirable consequences. Abandoning the cab and escaping in another cab could also have had even more undesirable consequences, escalating the problem.

Which Way Do I Turn. This incident occurred on my first day in South Africa. I was with a friend from Semester at Sea. We had just been dropped off at Green Market Square by a cab driver. We began to walk down the main street towards the shops and restaurants. I guess we looked like tourists. We both had backpacks on, sunglasses, shorts, T-shirts, and tennis shoes, and of course our cameras around our necks. I spotted a telephone booth in the distance, and both of us were anxious to call home to our parents. I allowed my friend to use the phone first while I stood right outside. It was beginning to rain a little, so I moved in closer to the covered area next to the booth. After a couple of minutes three black men approached us. They seemed to be in their early 20's and they knew that we were not native to the land. They began to ask us for change so that they could call their moms. I remember one saying, "Just one rand so that I can call my worried mother." They acted as if we were really naive. They didn't appear homeless or poor in the least. Each was dressed in jeans and a simple T-shirt. My friend was getting very annoyed because he was trying to talk to his mom on the phone and the three guys wouldn't shut up. They knew that we were from the ship, because he asked me when our ship was leaving and where we were going to next. They began to make me feel very uncomfortable.

They asked me how much this semester costs. The question made me uncomfortable so I replied that I didn't know and told them that my parents had paid for it, and I wasn't sure of the exact cost. He then noticed my watch on my hand. It made me a bit nervous because it is quite expensive and he obviously knew this. He asked me how much I paid for it, and I told him that it was a gift. He then asked if I would trade him my watch for his pad of paper that he held in his hand. I told him that I couldn't because it was a gift and I also needed it. This had now been going on for about two minutes or longer and I was becoming angry, scared, and annoyed.

My friend had finally finished his conversation on the phone. He was fully aware of what had been taking place, because he kept rolling his eyes at me and making hand gestures while on the phone. When he hung up he didn't know whether to offer me to use the phone next or if we should go. I knew that in order to use the phone that I would have to deposit coins, and I had already told the men that I didn't have any coins. We were both very annoyed and decided to tell the men goodbye and we began to walk towards the closest store. The entire situation was very uncomfortable for both of us.

INSIGHT:
The students saw themselves as a crop to be harvested by the locals. This can lead both the locals and the students to see one another as enemies rather than friends. This bad experience probably created a perceptual bias by the students that was hard to change.

A Guilty Conscience. In Cape Town, South Africa, I participated in a field trip called "Poverty Under Apartheid." Approximately 45 Semester at Sea students and faculty travelled in two buses to visit several sights where the detrimental effects of apartheid are evident. On our first stop we visited a one-room school house with approximately 15 children ranging roughly in ages from 6-13. All the children greeted us with handshakes and lined up in 2 lines on either side of the entrance way to their school. None of the children spoke English very well, but they had rehearsed several songs in English and sang them with great enthusiasm for our entertainment. The little boys were dressed handsomely in suits while the girls looked pretty in colorful dresses and big bright bows in their hair.

The principal was a black lady who had worked at the school for 15 years. She spoke evangelically of the hope and faith they had about the future and they praised God for the students' enthusiasm to learn. Many of the students have to walk 27 kilometers (15 miles plus) in the hot sun just to get to school and back. One little girl about 6 years old just cries and cries when she finally gets to school after walking several long miles because she is so exhausted.

I could not stop myself from crying. It was heartbreaking to witness that while they are fighting extreme poverty and starvation, they still manage to be optimistic towards the future as well as thankful to God. Their motivation to learn and their determination to make the most of their education was incredible.

Most of the children suffer from malnutrition. Many times the only nutrition they get is one bowl of soup and a piece of bread that the school provides. We were there for their lunch time. The principal called the girls up first to stand in line for soup and bread, the boys were called up later. Each student stood patiently and politely in line for their sole source of nutrition. Our group was told to enter the one-room school house and enjoy a huge buffet of chicken, meatballs, cold cuts, fruits and soda! I cannot even describe in words the overwhelming sense of guilt that seemed to numb us all! I felt sick to my stomach--there was no way I was going to eat the feast in front of us while malnourished children were eating next to nothing! The faculty told us that in order to be polite we should eat what they had worked so hard to prepare for us!

Talking to the other students we decided to fill our plates with food and bring it outside to "share" it with the students as we tried to talk with them and get to know them better. When we offered them our food, each child politely took only one small piece and smiled shyly as we tried to make friends.

The shocking and overwhelming feeling of guilt taught me invaluable lessons that I will remember and live my life by from now on.

INSIGHT:

Encountering the low income neighborhood was like a religious conversion experience in its profound impact. An urgent need to change things that seem wrong and unjust shocked the student into a permanent change of perspective. Being vulnerable to this discrepancy was a painful but powerful way to learn about others.

I Am Unprepared. This critical incident took place at 5:30 p.m. at the railway station in Cape Town, South Africa. Two of us went to the railway station just to see what it looked like. It was very busy and my friend had to go to the bathroom. I was leaning up against a wall, people watching, feeling quite content. I could see people watching me, but I didn't really think about it. I am becoming used to the fact that local people tend to stare when you are a tourist.

At that moment I saw him. It was a little black boy about four years old. He was dressed in dirty jeans with a torn yellow football shirt that said U.S.A. He was pointing at me. He said something to his mother, which I couldn't hear, and she quickly turned him away and began yelling at him, all the while glancing back to stare at me herself. The moment that little boy pointed at me I realized that I, blonde hair and blue eyes, was in a train station filled with black people, in South Africa and that I did not belong there.

I have never felt the feelings I felt at that moment. The fight or flight instinct took over all my thoughts. I thought fight, there are not that many of them. But then reality kicked in and I knew there were just too many. Immediately flight kicked in, I had my escape route all planned. My friend was still in the bathroom and I could not leave him. My options had run out, now what?

I began to quickly assess the situation in my mind. They had to know I was an American, didn't they? Was I just the same as all the other whites to them? What am I going to do if they say something? I can't believe I was naive enough to put myself in this situation. Just then my friend came out of the bathroom. As we quickly left I explained the situation to him and soon his pace quickened.

INSIGHT:
The student was not prepared to deal with exclusion and the anger of local blacks at him as a white. He had a hard time thinking clearly, much like in a bad dream. There was a confusion of motives and internal dialogue voices which were more emotional than rational. The feeling of being unprepared to deal with differences at that magnitude led to his feeling of helplessness.

White South Africa. Unfortunately, I never had the chance to encounter a township or squatter camp. I knew it would be a great experience. I did though get to experience white South Africa.

At home, my family has close friends who used to live in Cape Town. Our friends still have relatives living in Cape Town, and they told me to call them as soon as I arrived.

I called upon my arrival, and they were delighted to accommodate me. They agreed to meet me and my two friends at 10:00 a.m. the next day. We walked off the boat to see a shiny Jaguar waiting for us. I immediately realized I was going to experience the "real" white South Africa.

The host family were incredibly nice people. They wouldn't let us pay for anything all day. They stopped to buy us grapes, fish for lunch, a wine tour, and other exotic snacks. Our conversation was often artificial, and politics was rarely discussed.

The critical incident occurred as we were ending the day. On the way back in to Cape Town, after exploring the whole Cape, we passed a busy bus station. This station was for all the Black South Africans going back to their homes in the townships. Considering it was about 5:00 p.m., the station was busy with people ending their work day. As we drove by an elderly black man was crossing the street with the help of a cane. Our host showed no intention of slowing down, like he never even noticed the man crossing the street. The elderly man realized what was happening and tried to hobble as fast as he could across the street. At this time I was in the front seat, beginning to worry, and hoping we would slow down. No one was talking, and it felt like we were going in slow motion. At the last possible moment, our host slammed on his brakes, and the elderly man sort of hopped and hobbled on to the sidewalk. At this exact moment the car was silent except for our host. Under his breath, he distinctly uttered, "Kafir," in a condescending voice towards the elderly man. Needless to say, the whole incident overwhelmed me and my friends. At the time I just wanted to hide and get away. I could tell that our host's wife was visibly upset with her husband's actions, and embarrassed. For a moment there was an uncomfortable feeling in the air, but our host immediately tried to strike up a conversation like nothing had happened.

INSIGHT:
It was easy to think of racist people as some kind of monsters who were clearly bad and evil. It was a shock to find racism among "nice" people as well. The more prepared the students were ahead of time the less overwhelming their confrontations with racism were.

Poverty under Apartheid. I had been hesitant to go to visit these townships and squatter villages that everyone had been talking about simply because I had heard that it was dangerous for whites to go. I was afraid. I didn't want to cause any more unrest than already existed, and I was hesitant to let the truth be revealed to me face to face about what was commonplace for seventy percent of the black population in this country. Leaving the ship I felt nervous, on edge, and somewhat melancholy. The idea of visiting these people's villages whose homes were made of wood and tin metal strips that were not even fit for animals to live in made me feel corrupt. I was resentful towards myself for being white, for having clean clothes, money, a nice camera and good health when these people were isolated and considered to be less of a people due to their skin color, lack of education and employment.

My mind and heart weighed heavy as we arrived in our first squatter village. Women and children stood in the background washing clothes in buckets and others drifted in the distance. The shacks, if you can call them that, were homes to house a minimum of ten people each. They were without plumbing, electricity, toilet facilities or sanitation. The entire house and its adjoining rooms was no bigger than a ten by ten square foot room. Each was about ninety degrees inside with no ventilation. Children in filthy school uniforms and no socks ran in circles around the eight of us. Most had obvious nose colds and were no older than ten years of age. Their figures were so petite and delicate. They followed each one of us and grabbed hold of our hands. As I towered above them, their dark, thick hair was dense with dust. They would just stand complacently and look up at me with their spirited eyes and smile. I communicated with them by playfully tickling their stomachs, slapping fives, and reading the alphabet aloud with them.

After speaking with a crippled man who was injured by a white policeman in a demonstration this past year, he shook my hand vigorously and said, "Thank you for coming, thank you a thousand times. Please plead for us." I was in shock that he could thank me. For what? I was a white skinned person-- supposedly an enemy that has been suppressing his race for too many years. How could he still have the compassion to thank me, welcome me into his "shack," offer for me to sit on his bed and speak to me about equality. His words are forever ringing in my ears, "I am human too, God created me, God created you. I am as equal as you. God created me too!" As he said these words he raised his voice and vigorously pointed at his chest. Although I didn't know what it was like, to any extreme to be in his shoes, I could feel his pain and I was angry at my race for portraying as "superior" people due to skin color and ancestry.

As fragile black hands grabbed at my body and tugged my shirt, I smiled and slapped fives with them one last time before I got into the van and shut the door. As we drove away about a hundred children ran after the van, dust flying in their smiling faces. Not once was I asked for food, a treat, or money. They knew somehow that I was there because I wanted to see the reality of South Africa and because I cared.

INSIGHT:
When confronted with discrepancies like poverty and injustice it was easy for the student to begin by blaming himself for being who he was. A profound sense of guilt took over. This was a painful but potentially valuable experience as part of this student's education abroad.

Cape Velvet or Cape Fear. This event occurred in Cape Town while riding in a taxi. My friends and I had just gone to a cricket game with our South

African friends from the University of Cape Town. We had been out the night before and were quite tired, so we decided to leave our South African friends and go back to the ship. We were a bit skeptical about getting the wrong kind of taxi, so we went to a hotel so that they would get one for us.

Our taxi arrived and we began to talk to the driver just about what we were doing or had done. We were talking to him about this drink called Cape Velvet that we had had with our friends. All of us loved it and we wanted to buy some. It tasted a lot like a Kahlua and cream milkshake, and it was considered a "ladies" drink in South Africa. We asked the driver if he could take us to a liquor store to buy some, but he said that they all closed at 6:00 p.m. We were a bit disappointed and continued to talk about how much we loved it. Finally the driver said to us that he could try one place that might be open if we wanted, and so we agreed.

The next thing we knew the driver had taken us to Woodstock, and he was driving rather slowly in this residential area. Then he turned the lights off on the car and pulled up slowly in front of this house. He turned off the car and told us that he would be right back. I was so scared that I looked to make sure that the doors were locked, and I could not stop biting my nails. Before the man was able to go too far, my friend jumped out of the car and told him that we had changed our minds and didn't want it.

He returned to the car, and my friend just said to him that we didn't want him to wake anyone up. Then we just asked him to take us back to the port because we had to meet someone there at a particular time. Fortunately everything turned out alright, even though we had had quite a scare. Once we returned to the ship and talked to others about this incident we were able to conclude that the man had taken us to a black market liquor store run out of a person's home.

INSIGHT:
When the taxi driver tried to accommodate the student's wish to buy a bottle of liquor after hours he might well have been puzzled or even insulted when the students changed their minds. The implication was that this taxi driver was not trustworthy and might lead them into danger.

Philip the Gentleman. While I was in South Africa I met about fifteen guys around the age of thirty, and they offered to take me and some friends sailing. A few days later we went, and while I was on the boat I met this guy named Philip. We talked for awhile on the sailboat and then again at the bar we docked at. He and three other guys offered to take us to dinner, and we accepted. So after my friends and I had a few drinks at the bar we headed for the restaurant. My friend and I got into one car, and my two other friends got into another car with the two other men.

The critical incident occurred when after dinner we decided to go to the top of this mountain to look down on the city. The next thing I knew Philip and I were the only two people standing by his car, and my friends had all gotten into the other car and drove away. I felt really uncomfortable at that point, but felt like I really had no options but to get in the car and trust he would take me to the correct place.

About five minutes into the drive he looked at me and said, "American girls are pretty easygoing about going around alone with men they don't know." At that moment I panicked. I wanted to just meet up with my friends. He continued to say, "If you don't mind I want to stop at my house on the way there to pick up a jacket." I got chills down my spine. At this point I felt completely helpless. I didn't want to say no because I didn't want to let him sense my fear, and I didn't want to go with him alone to his apartment. I decided to say I didn't mind, and we stopped by his place. He offered me a drink, which I refused, and we stayed about five minutes while he gathered his things.

Luckily, Philip was a perfect gentleman. I have promised myself since that I would never put myself in such a situation ever again. It was terrifying, and I felt completely helpless and alone. I think he did sense my fear, and he continued to assure me everything was fine. I was only relaxed again when I saw my friends and was back among the large group.

INSIGHT:
The student's new friendship with Philip in South Africa was delightful as a casual relationship but the implications of going with him to his apartment were noteworthy to both Philip and the student. The student put herself in a position where one thing led to another and she didn't feel comfortable going to Philip's apartment, but felt she had no other choice.

Kenya

Am I Living in a Materialistic World. This incident happened at the Nairobi airport. We were waiting for our return flight to Mombasa. The air was humid, but not hot, and the airport was semi-crowded. It was about 7:00 p.m. and it was beginning to get chilly, so I decided to go into the bathroom to change into my jeans.

The bathroom was small, considering this was an international airport. A cheap looking imitation leather chair sat in one corner, and a small wooden table with one of the legs missing was next to the chair. Around the corner were two sinks. They had rust stains from the water, and soap was nowhere to be seen. There were two stalls in this dirty bathroom. I took the one on the right, went in, shut the door and proceeded to change my pants.

When I came out of the stall there were two women standing there and they were holding some metal things that kind of looked like letter openers. They said, "Give me your money." I just stood there looking dumbfounded. The first thing that entered my mind was that they wanted my camcorder. It was very noticeable, I had it slung on my back in the typical camera case. I was not about to give it up. I thought, "Hey, I can fight them, or yell, or scream, or something." I would do whatever I had to do but I was not giving up my camcorder. Then I realized that they probably did not know what it was. They had not asked for it, they just asked for money. I went into my hip pack and pulled out a twenty dollar bill. I then proceeded to go into the back pocket of my hip pack and pulled out sixty dollars more. They were very pleased with the money and left just as quickly as they came.

INSIGHT:

The student valued safety and symbols more than money. She was being changed by exposure to other cultures, and a new set of values and priorities had begun to emerge. The camcorder symbolized all the sacrifices made for the voyage and was important not necessarily for its dollar value but for what it represented.

Physically Held by a Shopowner. On our first day in Mombasa, my friends and I took a cab into town and were dropped off at Moi Avenue. We began to look at the outdoor shops along the road. One man asked me to come look at his shop, so I walked over and began bargaining. After some time I decided that I did not need what he had to sell and I tried to leave, but he grabbed my arm and would not let go. The harder I pulled away, the tighter he gripped my arm.

At this point my friends were scattered among different shops and caught up in their bargaining. I tried to reason with this man and asked him nicely to let go of my arm. This got me nowhere so I tried to yell to one of my friends, but they were too far away and this only made the man grip me tighter. All the while he was still trying to bargain with me.

At this point I began to panic. I wanted to get away from this man and I could not. It was one of my first few hours in Kenya and I was a little overwhelmed as it was. I was definitely not ready to be thrown into a situation where people were so mentally and physically aggressive in their selling techniques.

My friend saw the urgency in my eyes and came to my rescue. She pulled my other arm, so at one point I felt like a rope in the game of tug-o-war. The man realized that he needed to let go and finally did. I felt relief wash over me and decided that I needed a break from these people to gather my thoughts. I found the rest of my friends and we went to get a Coke.

INSIGHT:

The aggressive style of the shopkeepers and the physical contact were very stressful for the female student. When the locals violated her rules about physical contact, negotiation, and aggressiveness it was frightening. The clear notion of being a foreigner was unfamiliar and not a pleasant experience. Although she was not in any actual danger, she might well have thought that she was.

Taking Photos Is Not Allowed. I was in Nairobi, Kenya, and I was with two new friends I had made on safari (they were Semester at Sea students). We had been walking around Nairobi for about an hour and a half and had ended up in the Telex office so one of the girls I was with could make a phone call. I was feeling rather on guard while we were walking around because of warnings of crime in Nairobi and the general sense I was feeling. Inside the Telex office I was feeling fairly safe. I had just changed my roll of film in my camera so I could take a few photos of Nairobi. I thought using the telephone, since we did it in every port, was a Kodak moment. I turned on my camera, popped up the flash, and told the girl waiting with me--while the other girl we were with was on the phone--to smile. I snapped the photo very innocently. The flash went off and I sat back down. I noticed that after I did it everybody started staring at me. I told my friend this and she agreed. This man then came out from behind the counter and started yelling threats of arresting me for taking a photo. I did not know what was going on; I did not understand what he was getting so upset about. My friend and I simply looked at each other and this man in a state of panic. The man then started shouting, "What were you taking a picture of? Who made you take a picture in here? I'm supposed to arrest you for that! Do you want me to arrest you?" And he just kept yelling these same things at me. I tried to say something in between, but he wouldn't let me.

I wanted to explain that I was just taking a picture of my friends and no one made me do it. Finally he let me talk and the only thing I said was, "I don't want you to arrest me. Do you want my film?" I knew it was a brand new roll and so he could have it. He yelled the same questions over again at me and I repeated, "Do you want my film?" Then my friend started to get angry (I was still scared) and said, "She said she'll give you her film." And the man said, "Don't take anymore pictures!" and went back behind the counter continuing to watch us the entire time we were in the office.

INSIGHT:
When the student made the storekeeper angry by taking a photograph she was willing to do whatever was necessary to reduce the conflict, like removing the film from the camera. The photograph was just the trigger that set off lots of angry feelings about tourists, and the film was probably not the real issue.

Being Offered Drugs. We were staying in the Jacaranda Hotel. This was our first day in Nairobi so we decided to go to a shopping area in the town's center. A rattling old Peugeot taxi sputtered up and we got in. The driver was a man in his late twenties with a good understanding of English and a very big smile. During the ride my friend and I talked to ourselves. I saw an anti-drug billboard and asked our driver about it. He said it was no big deal and then offered us some ganja. We both declined saying that we don't do drugs. This is when the trouble began. Our driver became very angry. He said all Americans did because he watched American television. By this time we wanted out of his cab. After telling him this he locked the doors and screeched to a halt smashing up against the curb. When he turned around and thrust a bag of pot in our faces I looked at his eyes and they were very bloodshot and glassy. At that point we realized he was high on something. I pulled out some money, the price we had agreed on for the trip, and demanded to be let out. The driver went crazy, yelling and thrashing about to the point where people on the sidewalk stopped and watched. Because I didn't know if he had a weapon or not I figured my options were either to punch him out or roll the window down quickly and jump out. At that moment he yelled at us to get out. We jumped out and he took off down the street half on and half off the sidewalk into the distance.

INSIGHT:

The driver may have interpreted the student's question about the anti-drug billboard as a request to buy drugs. When the students rejected his offer to sell drugs he became angry at being rejected. It should have been no surprise occasionally to find a local who behaved strangely. The strange behavior may not have had anything to do with cultural differences; the driver may be genuinely strange whatever the culture.

Giving to Charity. A woman merchant was putting a lot of pressure on me to buy something from her stand. I didn't like any of the stuff she was selling so I didn't want to buy anything from her, but she was giving me such a guilt trip I just couldn't walk away.

It had been a long hot morning of trying to fight off all the annoying merchants. I had just bought one of those woven bags and a wooden elephant for my grandfather and we were making our way down the street to the restaurant where we wanted to eat. All of a sudden an older woman grabbed my arm asking me for the "scrunchy" in my hair. I told her I didn't want to trade anything for it because it was hot so I wanted to keep it holding up my hair. She then pulled me to her stand asking me to buy something. She said she needed the money for her little girl. "You're a woman so you should understand," she said. She wanted to take a picture of us--she also took one with my camera. Now I felt as if I owed her something because of the picture! We talked for a few minutes and I gave her a postcard of the ship. I was trying to get out of the uncomfortable position I was in. I didn't like any of the stuff she was selling so I didn't want to buy anything from her. I even tried to walk away but she was too fast, she grabbed my arm and wouldn't let go--I was stuck with no options. She was telling me how poor she was and she needed money for her family. Finally, after being haggled for about ten minutes I bought a small version of the woven bag I had gotten before. I then promised her I would come back later that day (she wanted me to) and practically ran out of there.

I have to say the strongest feeling I felt was that of being trapped. This woman had a firm grip on me, and if I wanted to get away I had no other choice except to be rude. I don't want to go into other countries and experience the same feeling of helplessness, which no tourist wants to feel especially in cultures other than their own. By the last day though I was getting a better feel of how to handle myself in front of the merchants--just put your arms up if they try to touch you and keep walking. The trick is not to stop, because once you do my plan is ineffective.

INSIGHT:
Feeling helpless made the student very vulnerable. She didn't want to be rude. The feeling of helplessness was compounded by feeling guilty, then she became easy prey for the aggressive vendor. As she learned alternatives to being helpless, she became less vulnerable and more able to communicate.

Come into My Shop. I was walking down Moi Avenue in Mombasa Kenya when one of the craft vendors began speaking to me. "Come into my shop, look at what I have." I thought, "Sure, what a friendly person, I'd like to see what she is selling." We talked for awhile about Africa and my experience on the ship while I looked at her crafts. I didn't really want any of them so I tried to leave. "Wait," she stopped me, "you must buy something from me." She looked at me angrily with disappointed eyes. I liked her and wanted to make her happy, but I didn't want anything. "I need to eat," she pleaded, "buy something from me." She was rude to me for taking her time to talk without buying anything. I felt guilty for that and for the wad of money I had while she was hungry. I had to make a quick decision about whether to buy something or ignore her and walk away.

It was my first day in Kenya and my first experience with the sales people there. I did not yet know about their personal pushy approach. I had only a few hours before I would leave on safari which would last until the final day and I had already exchanged extra money for presents. I thought this would be my last chance to buy any presents.

At first I tried to walk away. I knew from my experience shopping that it was normal to look at many things without buying anything. Apparently the shopping culture was different in Mombasa. She expected me to buy something. I found myself thinking, "Okay, what little thing can I buy here? I have to get something so she'll let me leave." I could have just left, but I felt rude so I bought a hand drum. She asked for a ridiculously high price so I got it down to half. I still paid seven times too much for the thing! She was an excellent sales person to make me feel like I had to buy something I did not want for a high price.

INSIGHT:
By entering into a bargaining process and by showing an interest in the merchandise, the student made an implicit promise of an ultimate sale. When she then refused to buy, she broke that implicit promise. Shopping without buying was seen by the vendor as raising false hopes, playing games, or wasting the shopkeeper's time and therefore insulting.

How Two Female Semester at Sea Students Handle Fear, Stress, and Anxiety. My first day in Mombasa my friend and I got a taxi to get back to the ship from town for lunch. We crossed the wide Moi Avenue to get to the taxi stop on the other side of the street. Once we were to the other side a man came up and excitedly directed us to his taxi. The man was very excited and was kind of pushing us into the taxi where his friend was driving. We were trying to set the fare to the port before we got into the taxi, but both men kept saying, "No problem! No problem!" The taxi was old, small, rundown, and had litter all over it. My friend and I were hot and tired and really wanted to get back to the ship. The drivers were smiling and seemed eager to take us for one hundred shillings to the port. My friend and I were a little apprehensive about having *two* males taking us, and the condition of the taxi worried us too.

By the time the price was set and I was trying to explain where we wanted to be taken we were headed towards the port. I had a map of Mombasa with a circle where the ship was and I leaned up to show them where we wanted to go. The man on the passenger side, the navigator, looked at the map and then took it from me to get a better look. Neither of the men spoke very good English and the navigator's response was, "Yes, no problem," but he wouldn't let the driver see the map. The navigator said to the driver, "I know, I know, don't worry, drive!" Well, that little argument was cut short when we were going through an intersection and we had to yield to another car. Our taxi stalled and would not start up again. My friend and I looked at each other with expressions of worry and amusement. We were not feeling very safe in Mombasa and had had a very hectic morning. These feelings of uneasiness multiplied as we kind of coasted across the intersection and both the driver and the navigator kept saying their favorite thing, "No problem!" The driver kept trying to start the car, and when he couldn't the navigator jumped out and went to the back of the car. He tried to push start it, but that didn't work. Then our driver got out, shut his door, leaned in, and told us, "Don't worry, be happy!"

The driver pushed the car from his side while still steering. This was all happening very fast and we remained pretty much silent except for a few stressed and uneasy laughs. It did make us feel better though that our driver seemed really nice. The two men could not push the taxi, and there were some men and little boys sitting on the sidewalk watching these two men pushing two American women in a taxi. The men and some little boys jumped up and helped our drivers push our taxi. I felt uncomfortable not getting out and helping. It was a little like these two white princesses being pushed by their black servants. I did not like the feeling, but we soon came to a gas station. Of course everyone at the gas station, most of whom were men, were staring at our taxi.

By this time, we were laughing about the whole situation and thinking that we'd have to get another taxi, but they pushed the car over to the pumps and we realized we were just out of gas. We had to give the driver some of the fare so he could pay for the gas. The driver and navigator hopped into the car while the attendant was filling up the taxi. The driver asked to see the map and I showed him where we wanted to go. He said, "No problem!" We drove on and the driver, with some input from the navigator, told us that the biggest problem in Kenya is poverty and that this poverty makes people resort to corrupt behavior.

As we thanked both of them and said goodbye the driver told us, "We have shared common problem, we are now friends, good friends!" We smiled, laughed, and told him, "Right, and don't worry, be happy! Thank you! Goodbye!" For being so scared and apprehensive at first it is kind of funny that we ended up being friends with these two men.

INSIGHT:
The good humor of the taxi drivers turned a frustrating series of accidents into a humorous memory. There was no one right way to deal with the fear, stress, and anxiety when things started to go wrong. While a natural tendency might have been to "do something" when the students were caught up in the situation, it was perhaps most appropriate to do nothing and allow the situation to play itself out.

Safari Bargains. While I was on my safari in Kenya we did a lot of driving from place to place. These drives seemed to take forever because we were constantly stopping at the little curio shops along the way. At first these shops were a lot of fun. After a while you get to be an old hand at the game of bartering and it becomes quite boring.

While browsing through one of these shops I saw the neatest bookends. They were carved from olive wood and shaped like gazelles. I made the mistake, which is common for a tourist, of looking just a little too long. They guy knew I was hooked and was not about to let me go until I bought them.

We began at 1,500 shillings. I said to myself, "Nope, too much." I in turn told him that same thought. He began to eye my watch. I thought to myself, okay I paid about 25 dollars for it so I offered the watch and two T-shirts. He said, "No way" and the bartering began.

I do not want to focus on the bartering as much as what was going on inside my head. I did not really know if I wanted to give up my watch. It had no sentimental value but it was still my watch. It was very difficult to try to concentrate on what was going on in my mind with him yammering on and on about making a living. I was feeling guilty. I did not need those bookends. Why did I insist on having them? Should I spend the money or shouldn't I? Were the bookends that important to me? Could I get them somewhere else cheaper?

While all this was going on inside my head the guy is still trying to get me to make a decision. I cannot explain the frustration I felt. I knew that I did not need those bookends, but I wanted them badly. Here we go with the dilemma of wants and needs. I did need my watch, I depend on my watch to get me to places that I need to be. I said to myself, "Hey, you're only going to be in Kenya once in your life. These bookends would be something that you would have all of your life. I could buy another watch just like the one I had when I got home. But once I was home I would never be able to buy the bookends."

After what seemed like a long debate with myself as well as the shopkeeper, I bought the bookends. I got them for my watch, two T-shirts and 150 shillings. I thought about my decision afterwards and began to feel bad. I didn't really need those bookends, but in this instance the want overcame the need.

INSIGHT:
The student felt that no matter what price he ended up paying he was being cheated. The values of personal items like a watch and unfamiliar souvenirs were hard to compare. Even a simple decision to buy or not became complicated by an internal dialogue about whether he was exploiting them or they were exploiting him.

My Confrontation with the Hole. This incident is kind of disgusting, but it was definitely a critical decision. We were in Kenya on our first day of our safari, and we were driving to our lodge. We had been travelling all day, flying and driving, and we were making our last stop before a long and rough drive to the lodge. I couldn't wait to make the stop because I had to go to the bathroom so badly, and our driver informed us that this was our last chance to go. We stopped and I immediately ran to the bathrooms. When we got there, we saw that it was just a hole in the ground, and the stench was almost unbearable. I felt that I had no choice though, because I had to go, and couldn't imagine a long and bumpy ride ahead without having gone to the bathroom. So when my turn came, I held my breath and went in. Just as I was about to relieve myself, this huge bee-type creature came flying straight up out of the hole. I was mortified and stood there for a second wondering what to do. I knew what I had to do--I had to go to the bathroom! But I also knew there was no way I could bring myself to do it, so at that point I decided I would just have to manage in the car ride--I had no idea how, but I was out of that bathroom quickly.

INSIGHT:

The shock of a huge insect in the bathroom became more important than relieving herself in this strange place. While she might be able to accept changes and adjustments regarding everything else, there was a limit. Some rules were just too personal or private to compromise.

India

Walk Away or Make Eye Contact. This critical incident deals with a personal dilemma I faced when a little boy who had elephantiasis of his feet was tapping me on the arm. I had to decide whether I wanted to look down and make contact with him or walk away from him. The reason that this is so critical is because I had already seen the boy before he walked up to me, and I knew that he looked abnormal. I wasn't sure if I was going to be able to handle looking at him or talking to him. This happened at a train station in Agra. I was on my way back to New Delhi. We had gotten off our tour bus and walked right into the train station. We were in culture or reality shock. We had been travelling all day, but this was the first contact we had with such poverty. We had travelled all night and toward the Taj Mahal all day. When the bus dropped us off at this train station it was a completely different scene for us. With regards to this little boy who was tapping my arm--I had seen him earlier and felt my stomach turn. The first impression was that he was kidding --he must be wearing some kind of costume. I walked away when I realized that it wasn't a costume. This initial reaction happened before the actual incident of him coming up and tapping me on the shoulder.

At the moment when the boy tapped me on the shoulder I was forced to make a critical decision. I decided to look straight ahead and not acknowledge him. I was standing with a group of three other students-but he was tapping on my arm. Honestly, I don't think I acted properly. My level of cross-cultural skills wasn't high. I wasn't able to separate my own feelings of how this boy looked to the situation. If I had chosen to look down and smile at the boy I might have made a new friend or found that despite his abnormalities he was still a person. How can I deny another human being who is tapping at my arm? On the other hand, by choosing not to look down at the boy I was avoiding the decision of whether I was going to give this beggar some money or some food. If I gave him some food then he would stay by me and I'm not sure I could have handled that.

INSIGHT:

The student was repulsed by the deformed boy and wanted to get away from this extreme discomfort. Avoidance was a typical response to this potentially overwhelming experience. Establishing contact with this disabled boy was unfortunately seen as embarrassing, painful, and possibly disgusting, so avoiding contact seemed the lesser of two evils.

A Walk through the Slums. Somehow the poorest city in the world is still called "The City of Joy." Going to Calcutta was a very heartrending, sad, mentally tiring and amazing trip. Three of us arrived in the center of the city after a nerve-wracking cab ride from the airport. We got out of the taxi, loaded our backpacks and began to walk with no clue as to our direction or destination.

The city in its entirety is impoverished and destitute. It is a common sight to see the sick and dying lying on the side of streets, in front of hotels, and in the congested downtown area. On one four-hour trek through the streets of Calcutta, we realized we had not seen one foreigner nor had we witnessed a "nice side" of town as opposed to a low-income area. Our walk had ended up in a market place that was both a slum worse than any I had ever seen in the previous foreign countries I visited and in parts of the United States, but also a residential squatter colony. It was almost as if we had looked up and we were in a part of the city where no tourist ever dared to go. All three of us looked at one another and each of us felt somewhat intimidated. None of us spoke a word to each other and walked forward with sweat streaming down our faces both from the heat and nervousness. What would it have looked like to those living in this poverty-stricken slum if we had abruptly stopped and turned around to return where we had originated? It was more than obvious that we were foreigners and that we had no idea as to our whereabouts. I think all of us desperately wanted to turn around and just forget what we had seen and move on, but we could not speak to one another. Our fear was holding us back. As we passed naked, filthy children playing in cow dung and women cleaning clothes in the stagnant, murky water that had collected alongside the side of the dirt road, we were stared at aggressively. No one smiled, no one spoke to us, no one moved. It was as if we were animals in a zoo and they could not take their eyes off of us. I was more threatened by the idea of not knowing where we were and what the people were thinking than anything else.

We had walked too far into the slum to turn around and go back, so we decided to keep pressing forward. We moved slowly so as not to appear anxious and threatened, although our faces most definitely told another story. I had bought about fifty United States dollars in fruit from various people along the way not only to give out to the children and beggars but also to help alleviate some of the resentment and tension in the air. As we walked and I appeared generous by giving fruit to random individuals, more and more people approached me asking for a piece. Within a matter of fifteen minutes, all of the fruit had been given away and the people's outlook towards us began to change. They no longer stared at us coldly as we passed, but we frequently received some shy smiles from a few and even several waves from others. I turned around and looked over my shoulder and we were no longer the sore thumb that had previously stuck out. The people had gone back to their chores, talking amongst themselves, and just relaxing. It appeared to me that we were uninvited guests in their home, however filth-ridden and destitute it might have been. To give money would have emptied our pockets, but in some small way they appreciated our small donation that gave them contentment and nutrition.

My walk through the slums was such an incredible experiential learning that I never would have experienced it if we had turned around and returned to an area where we felt "safe." The gentle, kind faces of the residents of the slum when we offered them our fruit is scarred in my memory.

INSIGHT:
Giving fruit helped the students feel less guilty and mediated between the students and the locals. Perhaps because they felt vulnerable, the students had a very high need to be accepted. Giving away fruit was one way to gain acceptance, and at least it signified a wish to contribute something in exchange for being allowed to visit.

Dealing with Beggars. Looking back on my trip into India it seemed as though I experienced one critical incident after another. As American tourists my friends and I were approached by many beggars. For most of us being faced with this sort of poverty was very hard to deal with. Each time we were approached by a beggar we were faced with the decision of whether or not we should give him/her money. It was hard to justify denying these people a few measly coins, but at the same time once one coin was given out suddenly you were swarmed by other beggars in the area.

There was one incident that had a dramatic impact on me. We were on our way back to Madras after spending a day in Pondicherry. Our car loaded, we decided to stop in a small village for something to drink. Our driver was excited to show us the famous temple that was in the village. We all bought sodas and went over to the temple to check things out. We soon made our way back to the car and were bombarded by beggars. It started with two older men, and then children approached us followed by mothers with their children. We were all suddenly surrounded by these men, women, and children all wanting money from us. It was very scary, overwhelming, and sad at the same time. None of us really knew how to react in this situation. We knew what would happen once a coin was given out. At the same time we didn't know how to escape these people who were grabbing at us, sticking out their hands, saying things to us that we didn't understand, and to add to it all many were deformed, bloody, and very sickly looking.

Our driver advised us to make our way back to the car. We were all in a state of panic because of what was happening. As we moved the people moved with us becoming more desperate to receive money. Their grabbing and vocalizing increased as did our anxiety. Each of us began to feel stress about the situation and started ordering each other to do things with heightened voices. "Don't give them anything!" and "Get back to the car." We frequently yelled. When we finally did make our way into the car, hands were reaching through the windows, and the car was practically surrounded. It was at this point that we felt fairly safe, relieved, and that's when we gave many of the men, women, and children coins, and then made our way to Madras.

INSIGHT:
To these students the problems seemed so overwhelming and impossible that they felt helpless to make any difference. However much they gave to them, it was not enough and only created conflict between those who got something and those who did not.

Giving to Beggars. My last day in Madras (and my first day in Madras) I went on the city orientation. Our guide took us to the Shiva Temple. It was a beautiful structure with many poor people outside of it. Upon leaving the temple a few people came up to me begging for money. I did not want to give them money, but I wanted to give them something.

I asked one of our guides to find out how much the bananas were. He told me, and I bought one dozen bananas. I started to distribute them to people. I gave one to a little boy. I saw more hands. I took another banana and gave it to another child. Within seconds there was a swarm of people around me. All the hands were reaching for me. People were grabbing the bananas and me. I got scared. My heart started beating faster. I could not control the bananas, and I could not get out of the mob of people. I swung around; some of the bananas were still in my hand. I handed one to a man who had no fingers, and then a few bananas that remained were ripped from my hands. When it was apparent to the people that I had nothing more to give (or to be taken) the mob started to disperse. But many hungry people stood around asking for more.

Through the entire scene, I had had a bag on my shoulder, a camera on my neck, and a watch on my arm. Somehow I just knew something would be gone. I examined myself, and much to my surprise, none of my material possessions were stolen from me.

The only thing stolen was the feeling that I had helped. In the end I resented trying to help people who were starving. The only time I felt threatened in India was when I tried to help. I also felt guilty for the mere fact that I regretted trying to help. It seemed like a vicious circle with no way to win.

INSIGHT:
It was not easy for the student to help local people and do it in the right way. The urge to help was not misplaced, but the assumption that it could be done easily was certainly a gross oversimplification.

Blackout at the Train Station. I went on the Taj Mahal trip. After two days of nonstop travelling with no sleep and constant sightseeing we ended up at the train station in Agra waiting to catch a train back to Delhi. It was about 8:00 at night and everyone in the group was exhausted and emotionally drained. We thought that our train would be there in about fifteen minutes, but it ended up being an hour and a half late. This was our first experience with beggars and the complete poverty of India. Children surrounded the group begging for money and food, and no one was quite sure how to handle the situation. A boy wandered through our group with elephantiasis of the legs and feet, and one girl broke out in tears. We were all trying desperately to just keep our peace of mind and wait for the train. Suddenly the lights went out. It was pitch black.

The tension in that train station skyrocketed. Everyone from Semester at Sea grabbed on to the closest friend, and we gathered in small clusters of three and four guarding each other and our back packs. The group was about forty people and we all became very close at that moment, not just physically but mentally as well.

I was in a fluster. My heart was breaking at the sight of the poor children and the deformed boy. It was all I could do to keep my wits about me. I couldn't meet anyone's eyes and needed to sort out my thoughts. At one point me and about four friends concentrated on learning the lyrics from "The Muppet Movie" song, just to get our minds off the situation. When the lights went out it was my first impulse to grab my friends. I called out to my friend and the three of us huddled together. We talked about positioning our backpacks and clung tightly to each other.

INSIGHT:
Poverty, beggars, deformity and illness made the students feel guilty but also feel glad that they don't have to put up with these conditions permanently. A bit of home, like the song, helped keep these intolerable conditions temporary and become a source of self-preservation which further distanced the students from the locals.

How Much to Give. It was the first day we arrived in Madras, India, when this critical incident occurred. I got off the boat with three other buddies and we had no idea what we were going to do, because the boat arrived at night instead of in the morning. We did know one thing, and that was that we needed to get a cab. So, after we got off the boat we began to walk towards where everyone (kids, adults, cab drivers) were, and then the incident occurred. A little boy around the age of eight came up to me, not my friends, and asked me for money. I then looked to my friends for guidance, but they were about fifteen yards in front of me so I couldn't receive any help from them on what to do. If they had been next to me I most definitely would have asked for their input on this situation. At this moment in my life I was extremely confused because my little group couldn't come up with any idea, nor a decision on what to do in India.

I was thinking that maybe the four of us should split up in two groups so a decision could be made, and so that travelling could be made a little more conducive for all of us. I also must admit that at this point in time I had very little patience and just didn't feel like dealing with others, let alone my friends. So when this little boy came up to me and asked me for some money I was quite delirious and confused, to say the least. But when I looked into this eyes I began to feel for him and his people. He looked so helpless, and especially hungry. His clothing was all worn out and he had no shoes on his feet, let alone socks. He looked so dirty and ragged, and I suppose it was due to his environment.

I really had a hard time deciding what to do, whether it was because of my state of mind or just the situation of this poor little boy. I decided to give him a couple of United States dollars and then he walked away. The next thing I know tons of little kids came up to me and start begging me for money. To be honest, it didn't click in my head that this would happen once I gave the kid some money. I could have just walked away from the kid the first time he came up to me and thus I would have avoided all the other little kids begging for money. But I think that I gave into the kid because I was so delirious and confused about what was going on.

INSIGHT:
The student was confused by the beggars and feelings of sympathy toward the small boy without anticipating the consequences. The shock of poverty was overwhelming to the student who felt he had no choice.

Cultural Alarm Clocks. I had the opportunity to do a homestay at a professor's home. I slept on a straw mat next to the main room where the host and his wife slept. The morning involved many decisions about proper behavior under completely unfamiliar conditions. I could not sleep well and I kept thinking that I had to be ready for my ride back to the University at 0600. The professor had told me the night before that his wife would heat bath water for me. At 0500 I woke up and realized that the main light was on but no one came to get me. By 0530 the light had been turned off and I still hadn't been prompted to get up. I didn't know how it was done in India-if a host would wake up his guest or if that would be considered a violation of privacy, especially because we had only just met. By 0600 I was worried about my departure time. I walked quietly into the main room where the professor's wife was asleep but the professor was not there. The morning activities on the street were already alive.

I went back to my room and sat down feeling completely lost. I had to make a decision to relax and wait or to get up and organize myself to go. I went back out and the wife jumped to her feet as if I had caught her snoozing in class. She didn't speak any English, but in a hurry turned on the lights, rolled up the mat, and lead me to the outside latrine at the back of the house. When I came out the professor had returned from the temple. I asked him about my ride and he answered that it would come shortly. He then asked if

I was ready. I said "Yes." In Tamil the wife told him I had not yet bathed. It seemed like I had been disrespectful in not taking the bath prepared for me, even though I had no idea that it was ready. It was obvious that I was much more concerned about my time than my host.

INSIGHT:
Wanting to do the right thing as a guest required that the student know the rules about host/guest relations. It was possible to learn those rules by experience, making mistakes and learning from them, but it was also possible to prepare ahead of time with some homework so that the student could anticipate what was expected of her rather than "assume the obvious."

Being Fed. The main issue involved was the eating habits of the Indian culture. I had attended a welcome reception in India and met several students. A few of the male students and I were talking together. They offered me food-- I refused though they got me a plateful anyway. I did not care to eat the food, but the students kept feeding me with their hands anyway. My main dilemma was how to stop eating without offending the people.

I was standing with two students from India. They both spoke English very fast and I could not communicate well. They were excited to show off their culture and have me try some of the cuisine. They tried some of the food and really seemed to enjoy it. They next offered some to me. I shook my head "no," which really means "yes" in the Indian culture. After that they fed me with their hands. I tried to motion for a drink because the food was so spicy, but they thought I meant I wanted more food and they continued to feed me.

My reaction was to excuse myself for a soda. I had failed to realize that every time I shook my head "no" they thought I was saying "yes." Additionally, I was not ready to mesh with the culture and eat with my hands, let alone anyone else's.

INSIGHT:
The student faced a dilemma. Eating together in India was an important part of being accepted. By indicating a desire to be accepted but refusing to eat mixed messages were being sent that were hard for the local students to interpret. Rejecting their food could easily have been interpreted as rejecting them personally.

Stuck on a Train. I was literally "stuck" on a train, all alone, on my way from Bangalore to Hyderabad--about a seventeen hour train ride. All of a sudden I felt lost. I was in a foreign country where I did not speak the language and looked nothing like the dark hair, eyes, and complexion of all of the bodies that surrounded me and continued to stare at me after four hours of being on the train with them. Feelings of fear, anxiety, complete unawareness of who I was, uncertainty of getting back to the ship, and a desire to return to the ship and see some familiar faces filled me. However, I knew that I was on a train bound for another part of this country called India. How could I get back to Madras in a hurry before I had an anxiety attack?

I boarded a train towards Hyderabad. I went alone into India in hopes that I would be able to submerge myself into the people's culture and benefit from the learning experience. I planned on taking an overnight train and return to Madras by another overnight train the following night. I bought a 5:00 p.m. train ticket. I decided to sit in the caboose which was restricted to only women --I felt it would help avoid any hassles or intimidation. I sat all alone with my backpack on a small wooden bench. There were many Indian women and their babies and children--many of whom were screaming bloody murder.

I sat and smiled at all of the women. Many of them made a generous effort to communicate with me. I enjoyed their company and gave their children some candy that I had brought with me. They stared at me, which I found to be quite amusing-until it continued for many hours.

Travelling alone was my biggest mistake. If I had the chance to do it again, I would definitely go with a friend. Only one Indian lady had the proper English skills to communicate with me. She first addressed me by saying "Hey sister." I looked at her and smiled. She asked where I was from and what I was doing--especially alone. I slowly explained to her that I was on a ship with many university students.

After about four hours on the train, around 9:00 p.m., I felt an urge to get back to my clean room on the ship. I felt that if I could just sleep, waking up in the morning would be fine as we were to arrive at 10:00 a.m. I put my head against the dirty train's window and began to fall asleep until I felt something hot splash on the side of my leg.

I looked down to see that a small, naked child had defecated a sticky excrement on my leg. That's when I went to pieces. I held my composure and calmly wiped the foul-smelling substance from my lower leg and kept cool. At the next stop I found a conductor at the station and explained to him that I had to return to Madras. He told me that it was impossible to get a train in that direction until a station located about four hours away. He told me to board the train again and get off there. I reboarded with slight tears in my eyes. I tried to smile to the women, who had still not taken their eyes off of me, and sat calmly.

The following four hours proved to be some of the hardest and longest of my life. Many thoughts on how to return to Madras entered my mind including calling the ship from the next station phone and have them come get me or even hiring a private plane to fly me to Madras.

I somehow made it to the station and got back to Madras the following day at 3:00 p.m. I learned much about myself. Especially that being surrounded by foreigners with nobody to talk to is very difficult. I think that I have found my greatest fear, it's not death but loneliness.

INSIGHT:
The student felt completely alone and strange among the other Indians on the train by both language and culture. Loneliness was a profound and terrifying experience, especially in a crowd of people. Being isolated by the Indian natives was the worst possible punishment even though the student had willingly put herself in such a vulnerable position.

Tearing the Saree. My roommate and I did a homestay in India through the Rotary Club. The family we stayed with was extremely hospitable and friendly. We stayed with them for two nights and two days. They had two daughters, Prianka and Rasicka, who dressed us up in Indian sarees! I wore bangles on my wrists, a bundy on my forehead, big Indian earrings and a beautiful deep red saree with gold thread stitching. The saree I wore was what an Indian would wear to a wedding or a formal occasion. Even my hair was braided like the Indian women with a black hair braid attachment. My friend was dressed up as well, and together we went out to dinner with their family to a restaurant on the beach. It was a lovely dinner and we enjoyed a variety of Indian cuisines and interesting conversation. At the end of the night they dropped us off at their guest house where we spent the night. As we were getting ready for bed my friend noticed a rather large rip in the saree she was wearing. It was about six inches long and it was similar to a "run" in a stocking.

She was stunned when she discovered the damage that had been done to the saree she had worn that night! It was an awful situation to be in because we had already felt guilty and undeserving of their overwhelming and generous hospitality. How could we ever thank them enough for all that they had done for us? And how could we ever explain to them what had happened to their very expensive and formal Indian dress? The thought literally made my friend sick to her stomach because there was no easy answer. It wasn't like she could go out and buy another one nor could she give her enough rupees to replace it.

The situation was almost unbearable and I tried to think of something to say to make her feel better, but all I could think about was how glad I was that it wasn't me. (That's awful to admit but it's true!) I felt guilty because I couldn't really put myself in her position, so I agreed with everything she said and kept my personal opinions to myself. She began to say things like, "I couldn't have made this rip in my saree because I would have heard it tear. Maybe it was already ripped before I even put it on. I really don't think I did it." And in all my effort to make her feel better, I agreed.

Then she said, "I'm not going to say anything to them about it because I really don't think I ripped the saree." In my heart I felt like she should tell the truth, but if I were in her shoes I would have probably done the same thing. I realized how easy it was for me to say what I think she should do in a difficult situation when I wasn't the one who had to deal with the consequences. So I decided it was her situation and her decision to make about how she was going to deal with it.

She decided not to tell them about the rip she discovered in the saree she wore. So the next morning we folded the Indian sarees and put them in a bag in a way that hid the rip and gave them back without a word of our conspiracy.

INSIGHT:

The students were faced with hard choices in another culture, particularly when they had established good relationships with the local family. While avoiding embarrassment was understandable in the short term, a valuable long-term opportunity to take responsibility and gain self-respect was missed.

Feeding the Fish. While I was in India on an field trip to the temples of Malabalapuram and Kalaparum I was approached by an old Indian woman who wanted me to go down to a large pool where I saw Indians bathing and "cleansing" themselves in "holy" water. I told her I didn't want to go because I didn't have any money. "No money" she said over and over again, but I still didn't want to go down the steep steps that led to the pool. She grabbed my wrist tightly and pulled me towards the steps. Her strength took me by surprise and I almost lost my balance as she forcibly dragged me down the steps. I gave into her persistent demand in order not to fall over and I followed her down the steps to the edge of the pool. There she had me sit down on the last step and gave me handfuls of puffed rice to feed the fish. There were several small fish that swarmed over the rice I had thrown into the dirty water. After the old woman had given me several handfuls of fish food, she put the basket of rice aside and turned to me with her hands out stretched and said to me, "Rupees Madame." I was upset, scared, and shocked because I found myself separated from the group I was with, and she had promised me "no money" before. I honestly didn't have any rupees to give because I hadn't had a chance to exchange my money. I found myself in a bind I didn't know how to handle and I became angry. I said, "I told you I don't have any money. I don't have any rupees to give you!" I searched for something, anything to give to her so that she would leave me alone, but all I had with me was my video camera, and my thoughts were so confused that I considered giving it to her! What would she do with a video camera? She doesn't even have electricity! There was no use in trying to explain to her the random thoughts that flooded my head at that moment. I wanted to give her something, but I had nothing, nothing to give. I found myself in a frazzled state and all I could do was to get up and leave. I felt sympathy and compassion for her, but I was distressed and my actions communicated hostility as I stood up abruptly and walked back up the steps as fast as I could in an attempt to rejoin the group I became separated from.

INSIGHT:

The student was helpless to show her gratitude and frustrated by her helplessness. When locals looked at the clothing, cameras, and toys that the students carried with them it was hard to believe that the students really didn't have any money on them. If the students don't give money then they must be miserly and stingy rather than generous.

The Little Girl. My friend and I were going through Madras in a cab. It was the last day at port, and India had done a number on me. I was tired and emotionally drained. I loved our stay, though disturbing at times. As we were driving we came to a stop, a girl about five years old came to our window. She was filthy and carrying her little sister of about two. She was the most beautiful little girl I had ever seen and was standing in the middle of a very busy street. She begged us for anything. I had remembered being told not to give to these kids and to look the other way, but I just couldn't. The cars started to leave and it became very dangerous on that street for anyone, especially a little girl.

I reached into my pocket and pulled out a coin. I don't recall how much it was but I decided to give it to her. As I reached out the window our cab had to pull away and my outstretched hand was too far for the girl to reach. It was too late. We were gone and that little girl stood there in the middle of busy traffic with her sister. The cars buzzed past her without a care and I watched as we drove out of sight. I couldn't turn away from that little girl, and her face is still in my head. As I got onto the ship hours later my heart felt as though it was in my stomach. India had indeed done a number on me.

INSIGHT:
The students missed an opportunity to help the small girl. It was easier to look back and figure out what the student should have done than it was to think clearly and act promptly on the spot. Because the student missed an opportunity to do the right thing, he will remember it and live with it forever.

How to Give. While in India I was faced with the decision that many other people were faced with. This decision was the decision to give to the beggars. I will recall one incident that had a major impact on me, and how I handled this incident.

The place was outside the Mother Teresa Orphanage in Calcutta. Four of us were visiting. We were waiting outside for them to open the doors, and to give us a tour. While outside, many children approached us asking for money. They would put their hand out for money, and then taking it to their mouth, as if to say "I'm hungry." Decision: Should I give them money or not? Why shouldn't I? I can afford a few rupees, enough to feed them for days. I know I shouldn't. I have been told do not give to the beggars-but these were children, hungry children. Why shouldn't I give to them I kept asking myself. Maybe they will give it to their parents and they will not get any food, or maybe they will buy bad food. I didn't know the reason, but I could not leave them without money or food. I decided to go to a corner store, ten children at my heels, to purchase a couple loaves of bread to hand out to them. I figured, for whatever reason, I should not give them money, but there was no reason not to give them food. I handed out slices of bread to them and they ate it up without hesitation. While eating they still had their hands out for money, but it was time for me to go. From the inside of this orphanage I saw many people gathering outside where I was handing out bread. Mothers with babies, young children all looking in to see when we were to come out. We left and headed straight for the cab, leaving those hungry children behind.

INSIGHT:
It was easy for the student to feel guilty in spite of all the excuses and rationalizations he could come up with when confronted by poverty. Feeling guilty was not a satisfying end goal of that encounter but it opened the opportunity for an internal dialogue and learning about larger problems that also need solutions.

Seeing a Dead Man. While in India several people, including myself, bought tickets for an eleven hour overnight bus ride from Madras to Madauri. We figured that by doing this rather than taking a flight we would not only save money but really see India at a first-hand basis. We had food and water as well as the entire back row of seats. The entire night was spent trying to communicate with the locals on the bus. They were amazed with our presence. We all had a great time communicating through hand signals and pictures. The morning was beautiful. The fiery orange sun rose over the lush green pastures dotted with palm trees. It was a beautiful sight. Several minutes later we pulled into our first town. This was our first glance at an Indian city in the daytime, because we had arrived the evening before.

Driving through we came across a man who had just been run over by a bus. I was sitting right at the window so he was only ten feet away. I was speechless. I wanted to help but we continued on. The man, who looked like he was in his mid sixties, had been run over by some kind of large automobile. He was lying in a fetal position on the side of the road. There was blood running down the gutter and his body was void of any life. I had never seen death that close before and my pulse and breathing quickened. I wanted to get up and try to do something but I was frozen in my chair. What stunned me the most was that everybody in the street and sidewalk continued on their way. They paid no attention to the dead man in the street. As the bus drove by I saw one woman step over the flowing blood and continue on her way.

INSIGHT:
There was an unreal, dreamlike quality to the student's experiences in India. Even death became "interesting" in a detached sort of way. The

experiences were so vivid that the students were immobilized by them.

Malaysia

Cheezy Temple. We were on our second day in Malaysia and we decided to break away from our hotel and go sight-seeing. We were at the Golden Sands Hotel. Three of us rented a cab for the day. I must say it was a hot day. The air conditioning wasn't working very well in this little white scrap metal taxi, so all the windows were lowered. It took us a good thirty minutes to get to our first destination--a temple. I strongly suggested to only look at it from a distance. I was not at all impressed. So with a combination of heat, long drive, and unimpressive temple--I was not in a good mood.

The entire area was a tourist trap--nothing else. I don't even think the place was ever used as a temple, only a tourist attraction. Anyway, as we walked in, bad mood and all, we passed an overweight dark skinned woman sitting on the floor. She was leaning against a large pillar. As I got closer I noticed she was peeling and it was raw pink skin underneath. Apparently she had been severely burned and the peeling is the aftereffect. As we got closer someone in the group said, "Don't even look." We all kept walking as she shook the cup with only a few coins in it. As I past I felt coldhearted and completely rude to not even acknowledge her existence.

We walked around for awhile then back out the same way which would lead us to the lower half of this temple. As we rounded the corner the area was familiar and I remembered this is where "she" was. It's like I hadn't acknowledged her, therefore, giving her no identity which in turn caused me to treat her as an object. This feeling was highly discouraging! Why and how was she burned? Did she do it for the money? Was it an accident? Regardless of her reasoning--what was my problem? Why wasn't I giving her money? As soon as I realized my selfishness I began to reach for my pouchful of change.

INSIGHT:
By depersonalizing the injured woman and ignoring her the student felt badly about herself as she looked back on it. In her role she had set up a protective shell that kept her contacts with locals superficial and pleasant while she ignored or avoided locals who didn't fit that stereotype.

Birthday Confusion. It was the morning of April 1st and I was awakened from my good night's rest at the Golden Sands Hotel in Malaysia by a telephone call. I drowsily picked up the phone, "Hello."

"Hello, this is the front office. May I ask whom I am speaking with," responded a female voice with a thick Malaysian accent.

"This is me."

"Hello, uh, there is someone in your party with a birthday today?" the voice said with a half question-half statement tone.

"No, none of us have a birthday today."

"Uh, yes, It says on your registration card that you have a birthday today."

"Well I am registered and it is not my birthday!" I said, starting to get a little annoyed by being awakened for such nonsense. "My birthday is January 4. Is this some kind of April fool's joke?"

"Excuse me Miss, but it says here on your registration card that your birthday is April 1," she responded. She seemed to be as confused as I was by that point.

But then it clicked "Oh, I get it! I'm sorry. In the United States we write our dates with the month before the day, not with the day before the month. My birthday is 1/4/72, which to you is 4/1/72. So, it's really not my birthday today but thank you anyway."

"Oh, I see. I'm sorry for the trouble."

"Me too. Goodbye."

"Goodbye."

I got off the phone with a huge smile on my face. It was funny to see how different customs can cause so much confusion. It was also interesting to reflect on my initial reaction to the confusion. I was annoyed by the call because I thought the caller was either playing a joke or had made a mistake, but in actuality the caller rang just to be nice.

INSIGHT:
The student was already disoriented by being in an unfamiliar culture. It was easy to put a negative interpretation on any ambiguous communication. The confusion made her feel vulnerable, as though these strangers were likely to take advantage of that vulnerability.

Decision Making. While I was in Malaysia five of us Semester at Sea students rented a car. We drove to a town named Tiping. It was a town where there weren't many tourists. We met this one guy. He was Malaysian, but I can't remember his name. He told us he would drive with us and show us around. We were a little hesitant to allow him but he was persistent, so we agreed. He drove with us most of the day. At every location he wanted someone to take a picture of me and him. At first it was okay but after awhile I became uncomfortable. Whenever we sat down he had people move so he could sit next to me. He was always so close to me that it seemed like he was always invading my space. I didn't want to be rude or misread things, so I didn't say anything. After a whole day of this I was really annoyed and uncomfortable. I didn't know what to do. I wasn't sure if it was culturally correct to tell him to stop. I didn't know enough about the culture to know if it was a male dominant culture. Keeping all this in mind I decided to lie and tell him and the rest of my friends that I felt really sick in the stomach and I needed to get back to the hotel. He seemed to believe this and gave his address to one of my friends to give me, then he went on his way.

INSIGHT:
Situations that would be easy to handle back home were difficult for the student in an unfamiliar culture like Malaysia where back-home strategies might not work or might be misinterpreted. Feeling inadequate to deal with the young man's attention turned even small problems into large ones.

Just One More Spoonful. "Good golly," I thought sarcastically, as I forced a spoonful of gut-churning Chinese concoction into my mouth. The three University of Malaysia students purchased this test of endurance for me so I could try the local cuisine. I was eager to try...a spoonful. What I had before me was comparable to Lake Erie as far as my stomach was concerned. As my new friends looked on eagerly, I forced a smile and said thank you, dreading the next few moments.

Now don't get me wrong, I love trying new foods, but the idea of squishy, runny foods all together does not excite me. Let me go into detail. In one small bowl there were eggshell colored chunks of dense tofu (bean curd) which could have been tolerated except for the ice cubes and watered down maple syrup stuff that gave it a sickening sweet taste. I dislike soy, and as for maple syrup, I eat my pancakes dry.

Now if I had been in a restaurant I would have tried it and pushed it aside. The problem, however, was with my new found friends and their opinion of Americans in general. As I took each gulp by gulp and smiled, muttering "It's good, different but good." Yeah, I lied, but sometimes that is better than telling the truth. And the truth was that there was a war inside my mouth-- between my tongue and the tofu. As the glue tasting particles dispersed in my mouth they then bounced off the roof of my mouth and collided with the melting, cold ice cubes. Finally, getting into a pattern of squashing the mixture to the roof of my mouth and straining it through my teeth it dawned on me that I was culinarily miserable.

My mouth and stomach were telling me to save myself the agony and spit it out; my brain and heart, however, were telling me to grin and bear it. The problems were my feelings on social etiquette and the fact that I've seen ugly Americans.

The deal with social etiquette has to do mainly with table manners. In my nineteen years, I've seen many a person spit out that last bit of masticated taco salad and spit out olive pits to last me a life time. For some of you, I am a Miss Manners with a bad attitude, but offensive table manners are my pet peeve. I also could not have spit it out without having tiny tofu particles, mixed with thick saliva, come oozing down my chin before it hit my small napkin.

In the end I decided to eat the majority quickly as to not afflict myself too badly and not to offend my hosts. Yes, I know this tofu eating incident sounds a bit well, nonsensical but it's not. I realized how seriously I take myself and how I would like others to perceive me. As for my hosts, I greatly appreciated their kind offering and respected the fact that they come from a different culture that values different foods.

INSIGHT:
The student's food tastes were very personal, private, and culture bound. Even when she wanted to like the tastes, that was not always enough to overcome her physical reaction. Sampling different foods was a good way to learn about cultural differences, but it wasn't always easy.

The Restroom in Malaysia. I was at a restaurant and needed to use the restroom. When reaching the bathroom I found a picture of a person in a long skirt on one door and a person with a short skirt on the other door. The problem to be solved was which one meant women.

The figures were stick figures with no other clues to the sex except for skirt length. We were in Lankauai Island in Malaysia. This is a very conservative area. The restaurant was very small with few people who spoke English.

I was basically the only person involved along with whoever could be behind the wrong door. No one noticed my hesitation, although there could have been more involved if I had chosen incorrectly.

I chose the long skirt door, although I was nervous it might be long pants. Knowing a little about the Moslems' belief that women should be completely covered I deduced that the bare legs would not be a female. I would do the same thing again.

INSIGHT:
As the student became aware of the rules in Malaysia, she became more self-conscious even about going to the bathroom correctly. Once she became aware of local customs and was determined to behave appropriately, she still had to read the cues accurately to avoid an embarrassing situation.

Hong Kong and China

The Bracelet. During my stay in Hong Kong I was fortunate enough to take a side trip into China. The highlight of my trip to China was my visit to the Great Wall. Although I had a great time there, an unfortunate incident occurred. I was outside the entrance to the Great Wall shopping at the vendor stands. My friend called out to me from a vendor nearby, "Can you please come over here and help me pick out a bracelet?" I immediately went over to him and started looking at the many bracelets the vendor was displaying. He picked one up and said, "I like this one, but can you even put it on your wrist, it looks small?" I started to pull the bracelet over my wrist and it broke into five pieces. At that moment I did not know what to do. Should I walk away? Should I offer the vendor some money? Should I continue to stand there and help my friend select another bracelet?

I felt awful that I had broken the bracelet. One of my first inclinations was to blame my friend because he is the one who wanted me to help him pick out a bracelet. He also was the one who asked me to try it on. After approximately thirty seconds I realized I was to blame. Next I got mad at the vendor. He started yelling at us to pay ten yuan. I got very defensive and yelled back, "It's a cheap bracelet. You are trying to rip me off." I handed him some money and the vendor continued to demand more money. I felt like I was being cheated, but I could not communicate with the vendor.

INSIGHT:
Even though the student had broken the bracelet it was difficult to take responsibility, especially in an unfamiliar culture where she was less sure about what was fair. It was easier to get angry, both at herself and anyone else involved in the situation. The anger and self-blame escalated a small mistake into a much more serious confrontation.

Stanley Market. I was involved in a critical incident in Hong Kong. I was with three other Semester at Sea students at Stanley Market and we were walking around shopping at all the stores. We all walked into a small China shop and were looking around. I picked up a small China box and as I picked it up I noticed the clasp holding the lid on was broken. As I went to set the box back down the sales lady walked over to me and started looking at me very funny. She then picked up the box and pointed to the clasp. She started telling me that I had to buy the box since I had broken it. At this point I realized I had a very serious decision to make. I could either argue with the woman, walk away from her shop, or buy the box. I told her that I did not break the box, but she started to get very angry and kept telling me that I must buy it. I felt very uncomfortable and people were beginning to stare at us. I asked her how much the box cost and handed her the money. Then we all left the shop very quickly. As I left the other shoppers in the shop were watching me.

INSIGHT:
The student was easily embarrassed when she was already not sure of herself in an unfamiliar culture. It was easy to accept blame for breaking the box even when she was sure she was being falsely accused, just to avoid more embarrassment. Accepting unfair blame also made her feel even worse about herself.

Going to the Bathroom. This critical incident is one that happened to my friend. It took place at the Great Wall in China. She had to go to the bathroom really badly. She finally found the restroom and got in line. It was really crowded and everybody was pushing their way through to the front. She decided to push her way through too. She got in line at the farthest away stall and waited.

After a few minutes a short little Asian bathroom attendant came in and started screaming and yelling at everybody. My friend had no idea what was going on so she just kept smiling and nodding her head.

After the woman finished yelling, women began squatting over a bucket that was less than a foot away from my friend's feet and began going to the bathroom. Obviously the woman had yelled at them to use the bucket since it was so crowded.

My friend was absolutely astounded. She didn't know what to do. The thought crossed her mind to just hold it and go to the bathroom later but she really had to go quite badly. She decided to keep waiting in line and try and ignore the women peeing at her feet as much as possible. She finally got in the stall, did what she had to do and then darted out of the bathroom.

INSIGHT:
Some of the student's habits and customs, like how you go to the bathroom, were unreasonably hard to change and especially likely to embarrass her in another culture. Some culturally learned patterns were just too private to adjust, whatever the local customs might have been.

An Embarrassing Moment in Tiananmen Square. While on my Peking University trip our group saw the sights, many of them unforgettable: the Great Wall, the Forbidden City, the Summer Palace, etc. But one will be especially memorable, our visit to Tiananmen Square.

Four of us ventured out with some free time from our tour. We were all let off at Tiananmen Square and we had a good hour to do what we wanted. So we headed straight for the square. First we tried to get into the Mao mausoleum but the guard would not let us through. As we tried to communicate with him we noticed a group gathering around the square with guards blocking off the perimeter with string.

Curious as to see what was going on we wandered over and joined the crowd. As we looked into the square, the people around us stared at us. One of us caught the attention of an adorable Chinese baby and started to take pictures. After snapping a few shots she handed the baby a basketball card. Everyone around had been watching her, so she handed them out to the people around her.

About five minutes and fifteen cards later, the police came over and slapped the many outstretched hands away. Since we had no clue about what was going on in the square we decided to leave. We had not even gotten fifty feet away and one policeman came running after us. We stopped and he started to speak in Chinese. We told him we did not understand. My friend is the kind of person who wants to meet all and do all. So she figured he might want to trade a pin or something for basketball cards.

This could have been true because he kept muttering, "Card, card." But unless the whole police force were big Larry Bird fans, I could not understand why there were so many police around us. You see, at this time we not only had several policemen around us but several more Chinese people also huddled around to see what the action was. Finally, one police member broke out and said, "You in trouble." Still everyone was basically clueless until I figured out that these policemen were worried that my friend was handing out political propaganda. I stated this to her and she then showed them the basketball card. They looked at us blankly. So she started to pantomime out basketball while saying "Swish, swish." They figured it out, laughed and let us go. We left quickly.

INSIGHT:
In a society where nothing happens by accident or chance and where everything has a meaning, it was easy for the students to have their casual and spontaneous behavior misinterpreted. It was easy enough to get into trouble on purpose, but as travellers it was even easier to get into trouble by accident.

Republic of China (Taiwan)

Get Out of My Seat. I was on a train on my way from Toroko Gorge back to Keelung, Taiwan. The train ride was approximately three hours. I had been asleep in my seat for about one hour when I felt someone nudging my shoulder. I woke up and was startled to find a Chinese man, around the age of twenty five, telling me in Chinese that I was in his seat. I could not understand the Chinese, but I could tell what he was saying by watching his body language and gestures. I immediately showed him my ticket that said "31B" and I exclaimed, "This is my seat." He responded by showing me his train ticket that also said "31B." At this point I was completely confused. I was frustrated because I could not communicate with the man who was kicking me out of my seat. I was also very tired and impatient because I had been travelling all day, and I did not get any sleep the night before. I was now confronted with a decision to make, should I remain in my seat or should I give it up and let the Chinese man occupy it?

The man in front of me spoke English and he explained to me that I bought my ticket later than the man trying to take my seat. "I don't understand!" I exclaimed. The man in front of me explained that it was perfectly alright for the man to get on the train and demand my seat because he bought his ticket before I did.

After the explanation from the man sitting in front of me, I reluctantly gave up my seat to the man who was still hovering over me. I was not familiar with the way the train system works, therefore, I felt like I was at fault.

INSIGHT:
The local rules regarding train tickets were complex but not chaotic. What appeared to be an injustice was in fact based on a rational set of rules. The student was learning the rules by making mistakes. By not knowing the rules ahead of time the student felt at blame.

Pronunciation and Accent. My last day in Taiwan, I was in Taipei in the downtown area with my two friends. I stopped at a street vendor to buy a bag of these fried donut-like things. I asked, "How much?" He said, "Ford-d!" Well, actually it had more of a "Ford-deen!" which I interpreted as "fourteen." So I handed him a NT$ 10 piece and a NT$ 5 piece. He took it and said "No, no! Ford-deen!" I showed him "Ten (and held up the NT$ 10 coin) and five (and held up the NT$ 5 coin) --fifteen!" He kept saying, "Ford-deen! Ford-deen!" His friend walked over and they were talking in Chinese while I was going to my friends "What the hell is he saying? What does he want?" They started to say the price again, "Four-d'n! --Four-d!" Finally my friends and I caught on that they really could count and were telling us "Forty!" With their accent though and Americans always thinking cheap, I thought they were trying to say "Fourteen!" The whole situation was funny and quite entertaining to all the people on the street. Talk about culture clash and a communication gap! I gave him my "Four-T!" and he gave me his little fried goodies, which turned out to be awful and worth around "Four-teen!"

INSIGHT:
When the student didn't understand what was happening, even a simple and straightforward exchange resulted in a misunderstanding. It was hard to see the situation from the other person's point of view and easier to believe the student was being taken advantage of.

Japan

Japanese Mafia. I was involved in a critical incident in Japan. I was walking around Kobe with two other Semester at Sea students and we decided to stop in a small restaurant on the street for a beer and some rice. When we entered the restaurant we noticed that it was very empty and small. The only other people in the restaurant were a group of Japanese sitting on the floor in a corner table. There were four men and they were all wearing slacks and oxford shirts. As we walked in one of the men got up and walked over to the waiter. Since they were speaking Japanese, we could not understand their conversation. At this point, the Japanese man motioned us to his table and I noticed that his pinky finger had been cut off. We all noticed it and were aware of the fact that he was part of the Japanese Mafia, but we did not have time to discuss anything among ourselves. We knew we had to make a quick decision and either leave the restaurant or sit down at the table. We all looked at each other with odd expressions and one of us said, "Well, we had better sit down." Nobody else said anything and we sat on the floor at their table. We sat and ate a meal with them, but since we could not speak their language and they could not speak ours, the communication was very difficult. After the meal the Japanese man who motioned us to the table paid for the bill and all the men left. After they left we all got up and left the restaurant.

While I was sitting at the table there were various things running through my head. At times I thought they were never going to let us go because they kept ordering us more drinks. They also kept staring at us like they were trying to figure us out. However, at other times I felt like they were just being kind and thought it would be interesting to eat with three Americans.

This incident made me realize various cultural differences between us and the Japanese men. First, I noticed that all of the men attempted to pay the bill, and when the one man finally paid it there was no exchange of money between the men. In America we would probably have divided the bill up equally and everyone would have paid their own portion. Also, I noticed that the men poured each other's drinks. In America I don't think men would pour each other's drinks because each man would feel he had to pour his own.

INSIGHT:
The fear and fascination probably enhanced the student's adventure and she never will know what exactly was happening. It may have been spontaneous generosity, entertaining amusement or something else. All she could do was speculate on the other person's motives and/or whether or not the situation was dangerous.

Asking for a Refund. Four of us travelled to Kyoto from Kobe by train and had plans to stay overnight. We had heard it would be hard to get a room so the first thing we did that morning was check into a traditional Japanese hotel. The lady who checked us in couldn't speak any English but managed to convey to us that the rooms wouldn't be ready until later, so we should just leave our bags with her. Later in the day we had run out of things to do in Kyoto and we all agreed we should try to get our money back so we could head for Tokyo. Our critical decision occurred when we decided to confront the lady and try to get our money back. We tried to tell the lady we wanted to leave, but either she couldn't understand or didn't want to give us our money. Then we decided to lie to her and tell her a friend had been hurt and we had to leave. We were drawing pictures of hospitals and dead people while I was making siren noises in the background. We could tell the woman was getting upset, because her words got faster and her voice got louder. Finally, she said, "Two" and handed back the money for two of us. But as she went to shut the reception window my friend stuck his hand in it, stopped it, and yelled, "No, four!" The woman was screaming at this point. Finally, she pulled out the rest of the money and threw it at us. Then she came from behind the desk and started pushing us out the door.

When we had first decided to try to get our money back I thought it would be fun and a challenge, especially since the language barrier was there. As we started trying to convey to the woman what we wanted to do I was enthusiastic and having fun, but my mood changed when I saw her start to anger. I saw our fun was being had at someone else's expense and I started to feel guilty. It only got worse when we started to lie and I had thoughts of backing off and just staying in Kyoto for the night. Then it occurred to me that the Asian culture places more emphasis on honesty and respect and I feared this woman knew we were lying. I then knew that whether or not we got our money back, we couldn't stay, I would have been too ashamed that I had angered this woman. We trusted her with our belongings all day and she saved a room for us that she probably could have filled earlier in the day. When we left I wished we hadn't made the decision we made, but I couldn't change it. I kind of felt helpless.

INSIGHT:
The students felt guilty. The students forgot that this woman made a living serving tourists, and the students thought primarily of their own needs and convenience. When they found locals who trusted them and that trust was not repaid, they made it much more difficult for that local to trust others like themselves.

Assigned Seats. During my stay in Japan a group of five of us decided to take a train to Kyoto to spend a few days. We bought our tickets, which had assigned seats printed on them, and waited out by the tracks when our train pulled up. We got on car "C" and started to look for our seats--mine was C24. We soon realized that not only was my seat taken, but *everyone's* seats were taken. In the United States nobody ever takes your plane seat, at least not on purpose! We were all very confused and assumed that whatever it was, it was our fault.

The four of us walked up to cars "B" and "A" which were also full. I looked at my ticket stub again and it was still C24. I walked back and the same man was there-only now he was asleep. (I think he was faking it.) I found a woman walking around who looked like a "train stewardess" and I showed her my stub. She calmly took the stubs from my four friends, walked over to where our seats were and told the people that we were there. Everyone got up, *smiled* at us and stood in the back near the door.

Apparently there are two types of tickets sold. Some have guaranteed seating and others (which are cheaper) do not. We should have defined reality by *their* ways, not our ways.

INSIGHT:
The students assumed that they already knew the rules for train seating.

While all cultures are equally "fair," the rules they used to define and regulate fairness were different in Japan and the United States. It was important not to jump to negative conclusions.

Getting Lost from My Friends. We had all gone shopping together at the Ginza and I was the only one who wanted to stay and shop. I told everyone I would just meet them back at the hotel. So later I went to the subway station and got on a subway and then realize that I got on the completely wrong line at the second stop. I was completely panic-stricken and got off then and asked about eight different people to help me, and for once no one in Tokyo knew a word of English. Finally this woman asked where I was going and took me to the right subway and rode the entire way to the stop I needed to get off.

This woman did not know who I was or why I was in her country, but she saw how lost and scared I was in that huge city and went completely out of her way. I don't know if anyone in New York City would have ever helped out a lost foreigner like that.

I had this false sense of security because we were in a modern, industrialized port with a relatively easy and efficient transportation system. I never even thought twice that I would get lost, nor did I think to double check how to get back, which would have eliminated this entire incident.

I felt so helpless when I was lost, but I honestly didn't think I'd ever make it back. I was lucky enough to find the wonderful woman to help me, but I realized how awful it would be to be a foreigner who didn't speak the language in the United States. Everything is written in English only, and everyone is only concerned about themselves and barely even notice foreigners, much less that they may be lost or headed in the wrong direction. I hope I will be more aware of that when I return home and pay back some of the favors people have done for me when I visited their countries.

INSIGHT:
By not being prepared, the student ended up feeling helpless. The student was very grateful to the Japanese woman who went out of her way to help. Having experienced that feeling of being lost helped the student establish empathy with others going through the same experience.

Hiroshima. One of my days was spent in Hiroshima. I found the monuments, park, and museum very hard to handle, and my emotions were swimming. Of all the monuments and museums I've seen on our voyage, Hiroshima was by far the most meaningful.

The whole time I was there, a million Japanese school-children were running around. I presume as part of growing up in Japan, all schoolchildren must visit and learn about Hiroshima.

After a couple hours of visiting the area, I was ready to sit down and take it all in. As I was walking out of the museum, with a thousand schoolchildren all around me, I glanced to my right. Standing about fifteen feet to my right was a Japanese student, maybe fifteen years old. As I was looking in his direction, it shocked me to see him give me the finger and run off. It would have been one thing for him to be with a group of friends in any other setting than Hiroshima, and for him to give me the finger to be cool with a group of friends. In this incident he was all alone, and he had a serious, angry look on his face. I was already feeling depressed by seeing and feeling the effects of the bomb, then this had to happen to me. It was a bit too much to handle at the time.

INSIGHT:

The student abroad was not only an individual but also a symbol of all others like herself, when seen by locals. That means taking both credit and blame for what those others like her have done, whether she wanted to or not.

Walking through the Museum and Peace Park at Hiroshima. I visited the Memorial Park at Hiroshima with two friends. I don't think I have ever felt more of a sense of shame and embarrassment in my life. We first toured through the park to look at the A bomb dome and other monuments. We passed hoards of schoolchildren who would all look at us and point and then laugh hysterically. This happened about five times in one minute. We didn't know if they were laughing out of excitement to see foreigners or if it was because they thought we looked or acted funny.

The worst part was when we went through the museum where they showed the videos and the impact the atomic bomb had on the lives of so many. It was an eye-opening experience as it was, but to make matters worse, this older couple spotted us in the crowd and stopped to point and stare at us with obvious vengeance as if they wanted us to feel the pain they went through. I was with two other friends who felt just as uncomfortable as I did. We all just kind of looked away and tried to hurry through the museum. The others involved were the schoolchildren and the older couple who both singled us out as foreigners in the crowd.

I felt the strongest sense of alienation and humiliation for my country ever. I could not get the older people out of my mind for days. I wanted to go up to the woman in particular and say I was sorry for what happened. Instead, I pretended not to notice them and went on my way through the museum.

I felt very threatened and vulnerable to this situation, and I wanted to hide my face and get out of it as soon as possible. I was extremely uncomfortable.

INSIGHT:

The student's feelings of collective guilt for dropping the atomic bomb may not be rational, but it was hard to avoid. The rightness or wrongness of dropping the bomb was less vivid than the pain and suffering it caused.

Drunken Businessmen. The event that occurred was the observance of highly intoxicated businessmen on the streets of Japan. I would be out late at night with a group of friends and see several groups of men in suits who were so drunk they would be unable to walk or stand up. Some were even getting sick on the streets. We found it shocking due to the fact that other Japanese acted as if it was commonplace for this to occur. If we were in the United States people would stare and whisper about them. It looked as if it was considered socially acceptable for these people to be out extremely intoxicated. We stopped and asked an American who was working in a shop the next day about it. He told us that the Japanese considered it acceptable for executives to get extremely drunk after work because they have such stressful positions and work so hard during the day. It was such an odd concept to comprehend since the policy on alcohol is so different in the United States, especially public drunkenness. The one thing that stuck out in my mind was how everyone is always saying how hard the Japanese work, and I was thinking, "Yeah, but look at what they must do to relax after work."

INSIGHT:
It was tempting for the student to judge the behavior of the Japanese businessmen from other countries by the student's back-home standards, but this was likely to result in misinterpreting the Japanese behavior. It was important to learn the local customs so that different behaviors in Japan could be judged on their own merit.

Getting Propositioned. While in Japan one evening several of my friends and I stopped by McDonalds. As we were eating three Japanese businessmen stopped to talk to me while my friends were ordering. I was being friendly and smiling when all of a sudden one of the men waves some yen in my face, winks, and nods his head in one direction. To say the least, I was horrified.

We had been drinking beer and stopped to sit on the sidewalk when we decided to grab something to eat. I decided to wait for them in the corner and finish my beer. I was staring at the ground when I saw three pairs of shoes and heard a hearty, "Hello!" I smiled at the three men and tried to begin a conversation. After a bit I noticed that one of the men was standing a bit closer to me. Soon after he opened his wallet, pulled out some yen and waved it at me. I must have looked confused because then he waved it again, smiled, and nodded his head in a direction. I couldn't believe that this guy was propositioning me! By this time, luckily, my two friends walked up and realized what was going on. My friend put his arms around me and kissed me on the cheek. He told the man that I was his girlfriend, so hands off. After a short discussion the man left angrily. I realized once again that a woman should be careful alone at night no matter where she is.

INSIGHT:

The female American student's behavior communicating friendliness by her casual manner and smiles was interpreted as an invitation for sex by the Japanese businessman. The Japanese and the American were both following the rules as they understood them, but the result was a serious misunderstanding.

Getting Picked Up. I was sitting on a curb on a main thoroughfare in Kobe, Japan, around 9:00 p.m. on a weekday night. I was dressed in ripped jeans, a black silk blouse, and boots. As I was waiting for my friends to come out of a restaurant I was approached by two Japanese men. Both men were wearing business suits and carrying briefcases. They looked at me as they walked by. They walked about five yards and then turned around and again walked towards me. Once they were standing directly in front of me one of them began speaking in a rather soft tone. I tried to explain that I spoke no Japanese, both verbally and using sign language.

Then the men began talking among themselves. About a minute later the first man pulled out his wallet and showed me his cash. He motioned that I go with them and tried to place cash in my hand. At this point I was furious and horribly embarrassed. I immediately stood up and firmly and loudly said, "No!" As I turned to walk away the other man grabbed my arm and began to laugh. I jerked my arm away and ran into the restaurant where my friends were waiting. I could hear both men laughing as I left.

The men must have thought it was appropriate to offer me money in exchange for "company." There were other Asian girls sitting on the same curb, yet none of them were approached.

INSIGHT:

The student could choose to dress and act as she pleased but she then faced the consequences of being propositioned by the Japanese men who interpreted her dress incorrectly. The student's clothing and manner communicated the wrong message to the Japanese men who no doubt felt confused, uncomfortable and perhaps humiliated as well.

CONCLUSION

The second stage of culture shock highlights the disintegration process when persons going through culture shock tend to blame themselves for everything that is going wrong around them. This stage represents the first real encounter and interaction with an unfamiliar culture after emerging from the protecting encapsulation of stage one. As the students felt the impact of being in strange and unfamiliar cultures during the voyage, their first reaction was often to blame themselves for the misunderstanding and confusion they were feeling. The students who were most sensitive and most fearful of becoming "ugly

Americans" were often most likely to accept the blame for any and all misunderstandings in bending over backward to be generous toward the host culture. This is certainly the most painful of all the stages of culture shock for persons experiencing the self-blame. Some students seemed able to avoid this stage while others had a difficult time getting beyond judging themselves to be at fault for the whole voyage. Most of the students experienced brief encounters during the voyage where they rightly or wrongly believed themselves to be at fault for the injustices they experienced or witnessed.

The sixty-nine critical incidents reported in chapter four illustrated several themes, as indicated by the insight statements following each critical incident.

One theme demonstrated a self-conscious feeling of being lonely, isolated, and alone while being vulnerable to their helplessness. They described themselves as foreign and alien in this strange and potentially dangerous place. They expected to be the victims of the host culture, and they were incompetent to defend themselves against exploitation.

A second theme emphasized the discomfort of being homesick, frightened, and afraid. They described feelings of confusion, embarrassment, and disorientation which overwhelmed them. They saw themselves as weak and worn down by their own guilt and by frustration which immobilized their ability to defend themselves.

A third theme led the students to expect the worst in a pessimistic anticipation of each encounter with locals who were sure to reject the students as undesirable and troublesome in their clumsiness in the unfamiliar culture. Some students displayed
self-blame in judging themselves as clumsy and inadequate.

A fourth theme emphasized the students limited ability and inappropriate beliefs, which were biased and racist. They described themselves and their society as members of a materialistic, immoral, and exclusionary dominant culture who were just getting what they deserved.

Finally, there was a fifth theme of those who felt numb, immobilized, and manipulated by conditions over which they had no control.

The students going through the disintegration stage of culture shock were trying as hard as they could to do the right thing, but it just never happened no matter how hard they tried. It is easy to feel sorry for the students going through this painful process. Fortunately, this second stage is so painful that most students were highly motivated to grow beyond self-abuse and see the voyage in a more balanced perspective.

5

The Reintegration Stage

INTRODUCTION

The third stage is both the beginning of recovery--up the far side of the U-curve--and also the most volatile stage in the culture shock process. Persons coming out of the second stage of disintegration toward the third stage sometimes resemble persons emerging from depression. The anger directed inward during the disintegration stage of culture shock is now redirected outward at "others" who are to blame for the situation. As in psychological depression, anger is frequently the fastest way out of the depressive state. Instead of taking responsibility for misunderstandings, pain, and suffering in the new setting, persons in the third stage are more likely to blame others. Frequently they will blame the persons in the host culture for their own problems with less sympathy and more hostility toward that host culture.

It is ironic that persons in the early reintegration stage will display a strong rejection of the host culture. The individual is likely to depend on stereotyped generalizations to evaluate and judge the host culture person's behaviors and attitudes. The individual is likely to disregard both the similarities and differences between the host culture and the individual's own home culture identity. The hostility an individual in this stage experiences is outside that person's reference points of previous experiences. The individual will perceive herself or himself to be vulnerable or under attack and will be likely to defend herself or himself and take a self-protective position toward the host culture. The host culture people are the scapegoats for all real or imagined inadequacies resulting in typically defensive statements and strategies. It is ironic that this stage of outward-directed anger is the beginning of reintegration.

"Yes, things are getting better but they are not getting better fast enough! I am tired of taking all the blame for everything that has ever gone wrong! I'm not to blame! They are to blame! It is their fault!"

At least there is a growing awareness of contact with the host culture and an ability to express feelings about the experience. The rejection of host culture patterns becomes the foundation for a new identity based on cognitive and emotional experiences with the new culture. In response to this external threat and dissonance the individual is likely to either regress to the more superficial tourist phase or move toward a higher level synthesis and balanced resolution of conflict. Whether the individual regresses or progresses will depend on the intensity of emotions, the degree of stress, and the opportunity to change things. Although persons going through the third stage of reintegration are the most difficult to be around they are also probably the most able to benefit from support.

The student authors of the following critical incidents will demonstrate a rejection of the strange ways things are done in the host culture. The host culture is judged less desirable than the more familiar home culture ways. The student authors will express emotions of outer-directed anger, rage, nervousness, anxiety, and frustration toward the host cultures. The behaviors of students will reflect rebellion, suspicion, rejection, hostility, exclusivity, and opinionated attitudes. Students in this stage tend to interpret their experiences in polarized alternatives of good and bad alternatives, with the host culture being consistently bad and the home culture good.

CRITICAL INCIDENTS

Venezuela

Bad Luck or Bad Planning. After we were well on our way to Brazil, people all around me began to speak about their experiences while in port and what they learned in Venezuela. I spoke with a friend of mine from a small town in the Midwest whose trip to Venezuela she would just as soon forget. From the minute she left the ship to orient herself, bad luck was to prevail during her first experience in a foreign country.

It began with her lack of knowledge about the language, the currency and in general, people in a large city. She and a group of friends got in a taxi en route to Caracas. Once they arrived, the taxi driver charged them an astronomical fee in his currency, bolivars, and none of them questioned his amount. After being deposited in the middle of a slum, the small group of girls wandered their way into an outside mall which sold wood carvings, local foods, and crafts. Unknown to my girlfriend, her backpack had been slit at the bottom and all of her belongings had been stolen, including her camera and some money. This incident affected everyone and they fled the city to return to the ship. This time they chose to take the public bus for seventy-five cents each. When they boarded the bus they realized they were the only North Americans on the whole bus. Feeling somewhat uncomfortable, they all travelled in silence. The driver ran one light, then another, and in the middle of the third intersection a construction truck struck them on the rear passenger side. Within minutes the police and observant people crowded the accident scence and they were pulled aside. The officers yelled at the bus passengers loudly in Spanish and looked through their personal belongings. After an hour

of brutal interrogation for just being on the bus, they were finally allowed to
go.

After I heard the entire scenario in depth, I was intrigued by the idea of
their bad fortune. Were they asking for trouble? Did they look so innocent,
naive and so completely oblivious to this foreign culture? I was sad that all of
those incidents had taken place, but I was especially disturbed by the fact that
their opinion of Venezuela and South America as a broader perspective was
ruined. None had any desire to learn any more about the culture, its people,
or its history. The damage was too deep.

INSIGHT:
Were the bad things that happened to the students the result of bad luck or
bad planning? Their attitude toward Venezuela certainly made a difference,
and their increasingly bad attitude probably contributed toward their having
a bad experience.

Stealing My Cap. Sunday, February 3, at about 5:00 p.m. three girlfriends
and I were trying to flag down a bus in La Guaira when a ten year old boy
stole from us. The boy ripped a baseball cap off my friend's head then dashed
across the street and down the alley. It was evident that he had been
anticipating a break in the traffic to act because of his swiftness and the friends
he left behind laughing. The very quick decision that had to be made was how
to react to the theft.

It was late afternoon so the streets were crowded with people leaving the
beach, like we were. The four of us were a bit weary, wearing sandals and
carrying towels. We were standing on the curb while the boy and his two
friends were behind us about five feet leaning against a fence. He must have
waited for a break in the traffic, then jumped the fence, grabbed the hat and
was off, never looking back. We were all in such shock that we simply
watched him go. Not one of us even attempted to act. We could have chased
him, but with sandals and bags it would have been futile. We could have
confronted his friends behind us, but it also was useless, not speaking Spanish.
It was obvious there was not going to be help from others. Since it was such
an insignificant loss, we almost laughed it off. We all felt lucky more wasn't
taken.

INSIGHT:
The group of students returning from the beach were an easy target for the
bored group of boys looking for some excitement. By snatching the cap the
boy raised his status, and the group expressed its resentment against the
apparently wealthy student visitors.

The Gender Gap. I, like most Semester at Sea students in their first port, was still a bit awed with the whole situation. Similar to many students, I decided to get an academic requirement out of the way early, so on the last day in port I embarked on a psychology field trip to IESA, a graduate level business university in Caracas.

Once there we (the Semester at Sea students) paired up and were assigned one IESA student. From that point on the interaction was totally free flowing. I, being a business major, hit it off with our Venezuelan student, Carlos. We talked about the Venezuelan economy, foreign aid, U.S. intervention, and the gambit of business topics. For the entire time that we had been talking about these topics we had been walking three abreast with Carlos in the middle. After about ten minutes it became apparent to me that Carlos was talking solely to me and almost totally ignoring my partner, who happened to be a female. I took interest in this behavior and switched the topic of conversation to his family to see if he started to pay attention to my partner. When he was talking about his family he at least would occasionally glance in her direction, but would never make eye contact with her or talk directly to her. She was obviously getting frustrated, and not being shy, she piped up. She asked Carlos a few questions about his wife and family that definitely had a feminist tint to them. I found it all interesting, so I immediately shut up and let her go to work to see what Carlos would do.

Carlos, being well educated and even having spent time in the United States, realized at this point that he had shut her out. He entertained her questions, but did not go into much depth when answering them. He was clearly more comfortable talking to me, but being there for psychology and not for business, I thought I would get more out of it if I let Carlos squirm. So whenever Carlos would look to me for a question I would simply ask him a yes/no question and give the ball right back to my partner.

He was clearly not at ease. He could tell something was upsetting her, but I did not think that he ever caught on to what it was. He asked if she was hungry, thirsty, or if there was anything he could get her? She politely declined and continued to grill him.

At the end of it all we parted on good terms, but the moment we were safely on the bus my partner exploded. She was livid at Carlos for his failure to treat her as a fellow student on the quest for knowledge. He clearly treated her like she was on a lower level. I tried to explain Latino "machismo" to her, but she was rightfully pissed off anyway. After cooling down she joked, "Well hopefully I can find something to write about in all that." I did!

INSIGHT:

The behaviors that the female student labelled patronizing the Venezuelan male student saw as normal and appropriate. Neither one intended to hurt the other, but each was interpreting the other person's behavior as hurtful, and neither one was willing to bring the problem out into the open.

To Go with a Stranger. The first day that I was in Venezuela, I went to Caracas. I was shopping and looking around the streets when a man approached us trying to persuade us to buy a hammock. Because we spoke no Spanish and he spoke no English, it was difficult to communicate. A man noticed us trying to have a conversation and came over to us. He asked us where we were from. He spoke English very well, although it was clear that he was from Venezuela because of his dark skin and thick accent. At this point, I was extremely hungry. My friend and I had looked at several menus, but could not interpret one word. It was important to me to find a place that offered something other than meat or chicken because I am a vegetarian. At this point, I introduced myself to the Venezuelan man. His name was Paul. I told him that I was having a difficult time ordering a meal and he offered to take us somewhere and order for us. We went with him to a vegetarian restaurant. While we were there I asked him how I should spend my three days in Venezuela in order to see the most and experience the most. He told us that he was a tour guide and offered to take us to San Fernando, a city seven hours from where the ship was docked. He told us that if he took us it would cost us much less than going through the agency he works for. We would stay overnight in San Fernando, possibly at his parent's home. He was thirty-one years old, and within the few hours we spent with him we consumed around eight beers. He told us we needed to rent a car, and *he* would pick *us* up at 5:00 a.m. the following morning. We had also been drinking, although not really as much as Paul. My friend and I were very confused and knew if we went we could suffer some consequences if things didn't work as planned, or could experience the opportunity of a lifetime. What should we do?

Paul was very friendly and seemed very excited about showing us a good time. We tried not to act too trusting. I thought of the opportunity to be able to communicate through this man to the many Venezuelan people whom I could not talk with without him. My choices were to either say, "Yes, we will go" or "No, we will not." There was no medium ground. We couldn't go for one day because the travelling time was too long.

I felt powerless knowing that if something went wrong it would be out of my control. I also know that if I went I could learn about the aspects that make up Venezuelan culture.

INSIGHT:

It was hard for the student to think clearly and make right decisions when he was overwhelmed by the Venezuelan culture. If he made a wrong decision, it would be very difficult for him to recover and turn things around toward a good outcome. Even at the worst, however, he would be able to salvage some learning and memories from the experience.

Pickpocketed. As my friend and I got off the bus from La Guaira we suddenly felt like intruders, as if some stranger were walking through my yard back in Michigan. Our destination was the Hilton about five blocks away and then down under a walkway where taxis were parked. As we were walking by all these locals they all looked at us like we were aliens from Mars, but we had no problems with anyone until this guy came out from behind this sign that was to the left of where I was walking. He put his two hands on my shoulders and his companion gently put his hand over my wallet that was on my right side. For a split second I though he was greeting me, but I was forced to realize in seconds that they were trying to take my wallet, so I put my hand in my front pocket and grabbed my wallet and his hand that was over my wallet. I was lucky to act that fast, grabbing it in time so that he wouldn't take off with it. After I had grabbed my wallet I gave him an elbow in his chest and the two guys acted like they were looking for something on the ground to cover up for their illegal move that failed.

INSIGHT:

The student's bad experience with the thief increased the expectation that future experiences would also be bad. Expecting a friendly greeting and finding out your pocket was being picked was likely to reinforce their negative attitude toward future contacts in Venezuela.

Brazil

Wild Cab Ride in Brazil. One night in Salvador, Brazil, I, and three other Semester at Sea students were on our way to a restaurant in a taxi. We knew the name of the restaurant we wanted to be taken to, knew the address, and knew that it was supposed to be on the water. The cab driver drove along the shore for awhile until he turned off the main road. At this point I noticed that I did not think we were going the correct way, but thought he probably knew a short cut. Finally he made a turn and started down the hillside back towards the shore, and I was relieved. Then suddenly he stopped on the hillside, parked the car, and jumped out. All of us were terrified. The neighborhood we were in did not seem good, and there was a gang of boys close to the car.

Immediately we all started saying, "What are we doing here? Why did he leave us? Are there people waiting to rob us?" We rolled up the windows and locked the passenger door close to the boys. Then the cab driver came back. He tried to tell us that this was where we were supposed to be. The driver spoke in Portuguese and one of the members of our group spoke Spanish. He told us that the driver said we had arrived and we told him to tell the driver that we did not think we were at the right place. The driver then left us again. While he was gone we quickly decided our options. We decided that in case he was going to rob us there, we were going to run as fast as we could. We felt it was more dangerous to run right then, because of the neighborhood and people around. We also came to the conclusion that if he came out and said again that this was the restaurant, we were just going to tell him that we had changed our minds and wanted to go to a different place to eat.

The driver did return. He, again, tried to convince us that this was where we wanted to be. We followed our plan, and after agreeing we would pay twice as much as we were to have paid he started the car again and took us to a safe place.

INSIGHT:
The students in the cab were very vulnerable. They were at the mercy of the cab driver. Whether the cab driver was trying deliberately to extort more money from the students or whether he made an honest error of misunderstanding the student's destination, the students were likely to put a negative interpretation on the experience and feel exploited.

A Picture Is Worth 1,000 Words--or Is It Cruzeiros? This incident occurred outside of the Mercado Modelo in Brazil. The first day in Salvador my friends and I decided to go shopping, so we went to the marketplace. Before entering we saw some Candomble dancing going on and many people were watching. One of my friends took a picture without any of us seeing her do so, and a man came up requesting money. This man was quite persistent and wanted her to give him $10,000 cruzeiros to help those dancing. I did not realize that she had taken a picture, so I told her to just walk with us and ignore the man. She then told me about her picture and that explained why the man would not leave her alone. At this point, many people were watching what was going on, and we were given a lot of attention. She did not want to give him so much money, but we felt inclined to give him some. All she had were large bills, so I pulled out 500 cruzeiros from my pocket, gave it to him, and then we were able to leave.

INSIGHT:
The Candomble dancer would probably describe this incident quite differently from the student. He would probably see himself and his team as hard working, providing pleasure to visitors and expecting to be rewarded by those visitors for watching and especially for picture taking. The student was having a hard time seeing the incident from the dancer's viewpoint.

The Ugly American. In Brazil I travelled with two other girls. The first thing that we did when we got off the ship was to seek out the nicest restaurant and eat the closest thing to American food that we could find. This was because my friend was getting tired of eating the typical food in the typical restaurants of the countries we were visiting. My friend's attitude about crossing cultures proceeded to worsen. Anytime we took a taxi she would constantly complain about the drivers in Brazil. She would say things like, "They can't drive here," and "we're going to crash."

When there were language barriers she would act like the Brazilians were stupid. She honestly felt that the Brazilians should know our language, rather than she should know their language. The particular incident that really upset us occurred one night in a cab. We entered the cab and said, "Porta." The cab driver nodded (indicating he understood) and proceeded to drive. I asked the cab driver, "What is your name?" He responded, "No speak English." The driver was smiling the whole time and appeared to be nice and friendly. Yet, our friend decided to take advantage of the language barrier and say rude things. She said, "Can you drive better than the other stupid cab drivers here?" She also said, "Your country is dirty and smells." As she was saying these things she was laughing. At first our cab driver laughed, but then he was silent and never smiled again for the rest of the drive. I think he realized that he was the object of our friend's rude self-amusement.

INSIGHT:
The critical student was having a hard time expressing her anger and resorted to rude behavior thinking she could get away with it. The result was to make the cab driver feel bad, embarrass the other students, and gain little or no satisfaction by having inappropriately vented her frustration and anger.

The Traffic Jam. On my third day in Brazil a group of us decided to travel with a "tour guide" to the outskirts of Salvador. Our guide ended up taking us (24 Semester at Sea students) about two hours into the country. We were all separated into three Volkswagen buses as we travelled from a fish market to his country house, to a secluded beach, and to a waterfall. The day had been perfect, and we were all enjoying ourselves. One busload of students left around 4:30 in order to make it back to the ship for "Bahia by night." The second bus, which I was on, left around 7:00 for the two hour bus ride home.

We were about a half an hour into the trip travelling on very bumpy dirt roads when we ran into a traffic jam. There were about four lines of cars parked and abandoned, or stopped, all along this small country road. There was a huge, once a year, pre-carnival party being held at the beach right next to the road. Our driver started to swear and announced that we were never going to get through. He stopped the van, took the keys and left. There we were, six girls and one guy, in the middle of Brazil, and none of us could speak the language. No one started to really worry until about twenty minutes later when the driver still hadn't showed up. The line of cars was able to slowly inch forward but we could not because we had no keys and no driver.

It was at this point that everyone started to get upset. How could our guide not have known about the party? He must have known we would get stuck. Everyone had different reactions from anger and frustration to being a little frightened.

Finally about an hour later our driver showed up and announced that he was going to stay and party and that we were welcome to join him because we were all going to have to stay there overnight! At this point everyone started screaming and yelling--basically causing a scene. This went on for about five minutes and then the middle line of cars started to move. Somehow we were able to make it through the jam in about a half an hour and we were on our way home! I think it was a miracle, we were home by midnight.

INSIGHT:

The student's plans didn't work out just exactly the way they planned them, according to schedule, which made it difficult for the more task-oriented students. The driver might have interpreted this "uptight" behavior by the students as giving schedules a higher priority than relationships and being too rigid to accept a spontaneous opportunity rather than "American efficiency at work."

Our Plane Ride from Hell. My first critical incident was unfortunately a frightening one, and it took place on my trip to Angel Falls. There were about twenty-five of us, all from Semester at Sea, and we had to fly in a very small plane. On the way home was when we had had an amazing and beautiful day. The plane was late to leave, because the pilot wanted to rest awhile after having to make an extra trip between the time he had dropped us off and the time we were to fly back. When it was finally time to leave, the pilot and copilot boarded--with the copilot drinking a beer. Then when they tried to start the engines they just wouldn't start. They tried for a while, and then had an idea. They drove a truck up next to the airplane and tied a rope to the truck, and then the other end to the propeller! Finally they got one engine started this way, and after about an hour they had them both started, and we were off and flying. The point of decision making was when they were trying to start the plane with the truck. They told us that if we wanted to we could stay overnight with the other group. Nobody, including myself, decided to however.

When all this began to happen, I basically just couldn't believe it. I was very scared and wasn't sure if I wanted them to be able to start the engine. I was told, however, that this was basically the only plane that would be able to take us back, whether it was right then or the next day. How I decided to handle the situation mentally was to not think about what was actually happening. I knew it would be better if I didn't, and I'd have plenty of time to think about it when it was over. I also did figure that the pilots must have confidence in what they were doing, because they were dealing with their lives too.

INSIGHT:

The students expected the airlines to require high standards for safety under all conditions and makeshift solutions, such as jump-starting the plane with a truck, seemed totally unacceptable. The students wanted all the excitement and adventure of being outside the familiar culture but with all the guarantees and safety from back home.

Should I Stay Or Go. My adventure to the Amazon was shared with twenty others. We were initially told our accommodations were closer to Manas and we would also travel an hour less than the rest of the group. Travelling with a smaller group attracted others to participate that weren't involved in the organizational plan.

The big group endured a nine hour plane ride from 6:00 p.m.--3:00 a.m. on February 12. We stopped at five different cities along our way to Manas and picked up more passengers at each port. After we arrived in Manas, our field trip group separated from the rest of the group and continued our travels on a bus for a thirty minute ride. We arrived at a small dock to board a small ferryboat in the pitch black darkness for an hour. We arrived at an empty marketplace to meet a bus to take us to another dock. That ride was about an hour of bumpy roads covered with potholes and creaky rusty bridges. On to another ferryboat for a three hour trip that turned into a four an a half hour ride!

Finally at 11:00 a.m. on Thursday, February 13, we arrived at our destination--the Amazon Lodge. We were shocked to see three floating huts in the middle of nowhere. It wasn't what we expected, and it was a grand total of sixteen hours of travelling to get there. Several cabins had thatched roofs! The conditions were not only rough, they were unethical. We were told thatched roofs were dangerous because poisonous spiders and beetles would come down on us while we are sleeping and bite us infecting us with an incurable disease. Needless to say there was no electricity and no running water. We had candles and flashlights in our rooms. The bathrooms were three holes in the ground with doors for privacy. We were told that the accommodations would be satisfactory. We were also misinformed about its location and about the length of time it would take to get there. I almost started to cry because we had just spent nine hours in the plane, five hours by boat and two hours on bus. Our leader had a vote to see if we were going to stay or travel God knows how much more to another accommodation more resembling our expectations.

Fortunately, our group decided to stay and to make the best of it. I was so glad the majority decided to stay. It wasn't easy to have a positive attitude. We were thankful we had good weather, a safe trip, and food to eat. We were all starving when we got there. I made a conscious effort to stop complaining and to only emphasize the good points. I focused myself to be a brave, adventurous and strong individual. If I didn't make this conscious effort to be strong I would have instinctively complained, felt sorry for myself, would not fully participate in all activities our tour guide offered. I would have overreacted about the nervousness I felt about the bugs and bats in our cabin. I would have made myself miserable.

INSIGHT:
The student was able to make the best of a bad situation and turn it around. This was especially important when the student's only other choice was to become bitter and complain about conditions that could not be changed.

A Kiss from a Stranger. I was dancing with a man I had recently met. Beginning to feel uncomfortable with his advances, my friend and I decided to leave. As we said goodbye he asked if he could kiss me. I did not know if he meant on the lips or on each cheek as the Brazilian fashion of saying goodbye. I did not want him to kiss my mouth, but did not want to be rude by not accepting a common gesture. I had to answer quickly because he was moving closer towards me as he asked.

We had met about four hours earlier. Because he spoke English, we got into conversation right away. He and his friend showed my friend and me around for awhile, then we had lunch. After lunch the four of us headed for the central area to dance. When I agreed to dance, the man immediately pulled me close to him. Unsure about the local custom, I went along with him for the song. Only part way into the next song my friend and I decided to leave. This was about 2:00 p.m. We were in the middle of a large crowd of partying, dancing and drinking people under the hot sun.

The two Brazilian men were good friends. We knew more about the man who wanted to kiss me because he spoke English. The other one had bought us a beer and smiled a lot.

I answered with a hesitant, "Yes." That way the worst that could happen was he would kiss my lips. If he intended a simple gesture of goodbye and I said, "No" he would have been insulted. Sure enough, he went for my lips. I pulled back enough to indicate the difference of our intentions. He put his finger on my lips then caught my eyes before we left.

INSIGHT:
The student had a hard time distinguishing between the young man's kiss as a friendly or a romantic gesture. She wanted to express friendliness but not a romantic intention. The student's interaction with the young man became a small contest to see who would win and who would lose. She had the insight to see the alternatives and enough skill to shape conditions to fit her own needs.

A Reaction in Rio. When I was in Brazil I went to Rio on the Semester at Sea trip. The first night there I was in a night club called the Hippopotamus. This was supposed to be the best and most reputable of all the clubs in Rio. I was there with my two friends. The three of us were sitting at a table above the dance floor looking around to get an idea of the club's atmosphere. It was a very broad age range. There were people from the age of eighteen to forty-five, so it was not just a young club.

After we had been there for a little while a man about thirty years old approached my friend at our table. He began to speak to her first in Portuguese and then in broken English. He kept asking her to dance. At first she politely refused, but he became more persistent and began to be very touchy and tell her that she was lying and she did want to dance with him. My friend kept looking at my other friend and me, telling us to help her. We had to speak very loudly because of the loud music in the background, so when I was trying to speak to my friend I had to scream over the music and this man that was screaming at her with his face right in her face. When I got her attention the man was not happy he had lost it so he yelled at me to shut up and swung his hand my way. My face dropped, I stopped talking and just stared in absolute horror. I couldn't comprehend how rude this man had just been to me.

I decided it was better not to react so I sat in silence. I felt as if I was being submissive by not reacting. I felt very out of character because I'm not a passive person.

INSIGHT:
The student was adjusting to an unfamiliar culture of Brazil, there was a sense of playing a role, not being who she really was and pretending to be someone else. The new role resulted in her being less active and more passive, less likely to act in a situation than she would back home. The inaction and passivity resulted in getting angry at others and herself for not being able to express that anger appropriately.

Buyer versus Seller. After visiting the Christ statue on Corcovado Mountain in Rio de Janeiro, I wanted to find a gold charm of the statue for my bracelet. When I finally found one after looking at many different stores, a simple purchase became a critical incident. First, my credit card would not go through the machine. I didn't understand what the problem was, but I had the saleswoman hold the charm while I ran back to the hotel and got my traveller's checks. When I returned, the store had started closing thirty minutes early. Because it was my last day in Brazil I asked if I could receive the change in dollars instead of cruzeiros. Both the salesperson and the manager agreed. I clarified it once again and thought it was settled and, therefore, signed the checks and made them out to the store. The charm was in my bag when the saleswoman came out with cruzeiros. I questioned our earlier agreement for dollars and suddenly neither of them spoke English. Now the question was whether or not I should take the change and leave with the charm, or go with my feelings of being a customer who was being taken advantage of and either negotiate or not make the purchase.

As a customer I tried to negotiate by American standards. I expected that once an agreement had been made it would be upheld and that the store was there to serve me.

The manager showed no emotion and the salesperson looked on from across the room. Neither seemed willing to negotiate. I did not leave a good impression but I was very frustrated because I wanted the charm but it meant giving into values I've acquired through American business practices.

INSIGHT:

The student's transaction of buying a charm was actually very complicated, especially in an unfamiliar culture. When the misunderstanding between the student and storekeeper broke down, the problems quickly escalated and got out of control. Pretty soon the original transaction was no longer the issue but face, honor, and principle become foremost, making the conflict difficult to resolve.

A Matter of Self-Control. In Brazil six friends and I were walking at night down a crowded back street. We walked through the middle of a crowd of about six young Brazilian men, all looking our age, who were sitting on both sides of the path we were following. The first man I passed on my left pretended to sneeze, right as I was in front of him, spitting a large amount of fluid in my face and hair. There were two men sitting next to him that were laughing, hissing and carrying on. Then there were another three sitting on a second car to my right. Precisely the same chain of events proceeded to happen with those three. Well, by this time I was aware of what was going on and could see what was coming as the man took a sip out of a glass just as I was approaching. The issue for me was what to do? My immediate reaction was to turn to the man and slap his face from ear to ear. Would this be a justifiable thing for me to do? Would this bring about good or bad results in the long run?

I reacted in the best way I could. I merely looked to the ground, walked a little further and stopped to wipe the spit from my eyes, without any immediate reaction visible to them. I don't think following through with my gut reaction, of slapping him across the face, would have had any benefit in this situation.

In analyzing the incident, I learned that exhibiting self-control is a way of showing dignity and cross-cultural awareness.

INSIGHT:

To avoid further complications, the student did not want to "make a scene" even when she had been insulted or spit at. There was little to be gained by attacking the locals. As an outsider, it might even be dangerous for her to do so. However, being humiliated and not being able to respond is likely to increase the student's anger toward locals.

South Africa

Stress in a Bar. This incident occurred in a bar in South Africa. I arrived with four friends and took seats at the bar next to three South Africans. As we sat down one of them turned to us and told us Americans were obnoxious, loud and intolerable. I was told not to talk about politics or anything related, so I didn't know whether to defend myself or blow it off--I decided to defend myself.

My four friends and I were having a good time when one of the three men next to us leaned over and said, "I hate Americans. They are so obnoxious and loud." I looked at my friends and then turned back to him and said politely, "I'm sorry if we're being loud, but I don't think you can judge all Americans by one group having fun in a bar." As I was speaking his two friends leaned over and began to try to pull his friend away, but before they could he was telling me how America is just as segregated as South Africa, so why did we act so self-righteous. In my mind all I could do was think--what a racist son-of-a-bitch to tell me that when he doesn't know anything about where I'm from or my own personal experiences. His friend leaned over, apologized for his friend, and said, "Well, I love Americans and I hope you won't hold this experience against my friend or my country." By this time I was riled up, and my friends were trying to make peace and settle the situation. In my mind I thought about the fact that even though I hate the policies of South Africa, here I was in a bar having a great time instead of trying to do something about the situation. I learned that I should have avoided the situation. Because my being there with my white friends, one of whom was South African, I was being hypocritical, which did not help my argument one bit. I also learned that the white South Africans are very defensive about the current situation and feel great resentment towards Americans. I feel I made a bad choice by trying to argue about something so touchy and stressful.

INSIGHT:
The American students resented being stereotyped by the South African in the bar. Being blamed for racism in America seemed unfair to the American student who was personally against racism. Arguing back was not helpful, especially since the South African was already drunk. The student felt helpless and angry.

An Angry Waiter. A friend and I went to lunch at a cafe in South Africa. We were in a bit of a hurry because we were scheduled to meet a tour group in about an hour. We sat down and asked if we could order. Our waiter acted a bit burdened, so we explained our dilemma. He launched into an irate tirade, and blatantly told us that he was disgusted with Americans expecting "the world to fall at their feet." Naturally we were horribly embarrassed and began to walk out. The manager rushed over to us and apologized profusely. We still ended up leaving.

Afterwards, my friend and I were discussing how "out of line" we felt the waiter was and how offended we both were. Later, when I thought about the whole situation I began to realize that something (or rather someone) must have driven the waiter to react in the manner he did. It literally dawned on me that he had probably many more bad experiences with Americans than either of us had had with people of his country. I'm not condoning his behavior; it certainly gave me something to think about however.

INSIGHT:

The first reaction of the two students to being scolded for being Americans was to get angry and leave. The delayed reaction was to recognize that this waiter may have been hurt in the past by other Americans and the waiter was generalizing that experience to all Americans. If that delayed reaction had come earlier, it might have been possible to help the waiter avoid stereotyping in a more sympathetic manner and avoid the embarrassment of being scolded.

Race Relations. The problem dealt with a friend of mine who attended a restaurant in South Africa with two friends from Semester at Sea and four residents of Cape Town. As they were waiting for food, one of the men began to poke fun at the black waitress. My friend began to feel uncomfortable and wondered if she should say anything.

There were two Semester at Sea students present. The previous night they had met four people in a local bar in South Africa. They were invited to join them the next night for dinner at a local restaurant in Cape Town. They accepted and went out to eat. My friend was seated across from one of the gentlemen they had met the previous night. There were six people at dinner. The waitress, who was black, came and took their order. It took some time to wait for the food. As they sat there the waitress passed by several times while she was going about her work. The man across from my friend began to make clicking sounds when the waitress passed by, poking fun at their language. The other members of my friend's group didn't seem to notice, however, my friend was quite offended.

INSIGHT:

Relations between blacks and whites in South Africa were difficult for the student to understand as an outsider. As an outsider, the relations seemed very unfair and hurtful. The student knew enough to see the problem but not yet enough to respond in a constructive and appropriate way.

Heated Political Discussion. On the third night in South Africa, two friends and I went to a small, old town called Stellenbosch. We went to a bar which was popular among the students from Stellenbosch University. We began speaking with a young man and got onto the subject of politics and the upcoming referendum. The conversation took on a debate form and the decision I was forced to make was whether or not to continue backing up my opinion, or to stop talking politics and move on to a different subject. This was a crucial decision to make because our discussion was turning into an argument.

The conversation began with my friend and I asking questions about the referendum. A local man began talking about the United States and how we butt into everyone's business. For example, we had no right getting involved with the Gulf War and we are holding back South Africa's progress with sanctions. He went on to refer to blacks as kafirs and told us he was voting yes on the referendum to end apartheid so that other countries would look favorably upon South Africa and allow them to participate in international sports. I was appalled and ready to fight, but couldn't decide if it was worth the argument.

INSIGHT:

The student didn't stand up for what he believed in. He would get angry at himself but when he did stand up for his beliefs he lacked enough knowledge of South Africa to argue constructively and appropriately. When he began to get angry in an argument with locals, there was even less likelihood of being successful or winning, whatever that meant in this context.

Escaping the Riot Police in South Africa. Four of us had gone over to Bertie's Landing to drink a few beers on our last night in Cape Town. The bar wasn't very crowded so we just sat outside and socialized while watching the seals. As the night went on we met a guy from the riot police. We talked with him for a while and then about twenty others who were with him came up and swarmed around us. It was getting pretty late and the bar was closing. At this point I was getting worried that the four of us wouldn't be able to get a taxi back to the ship because it was getting so late. The guy who was talking to me was trying to get me to have all his buddies walk us back. I was already uncomfortable because this guy kept bragging on how South Africa was a racist nation and how he was a member of the conservative party. He made it clear to me that the March 17 referendum would *never* pass. I tried to get over and talk to one of my friends, but he just kept following me. When I looked down at my watch it was almost midnight and the bar was closing. I finally was able to get all of my friends' attention and let them know we needed to find a taxi. The guy to whom I was talking kept telling me that he and all his buddies would walk us back to the ship (and it was a long, dark walk). I told him thanks but we would just take a taxi. He got pretty upset and started to get a little rude. We had started to walk out and there were no taxis and the bar had closed. They had followed us out to see if we were walking or getting a cab.

At that moment a taxi pulled around the corner. (I have never been so happy to see a taxi in my entire life!) We had a ride after all.

INSIGHT:
Being a stranger in the local setting deprived the student of power, and the student felt quite powerless as a foreigner on top of all the other cultural barriers she had to deal with. There was no clear way to get power back, and under those conditions it was easy to get angry at her own helplessness.

Talking to a Racist Man. One of the nights that we were in South Africa I was at a bar called Alligators. My friend was at the bar getting us a drink and I was waiting for her and sitting on a stool. This guy who was a White South African came up to me and started talking to me. He asked me if I was from the United States. I told him that I was and he told me that I was really lucky to live there and that he hated living in South Africa. He then proceeded telling me that the reason that he hated living in South Africa was because of all the black people. He said that he hates all black people and he wished that they were all dead. I could not believe what I was hearing. I defended the black people for a few minutes and then I had to decide whether or not I was going to stay and talk to this guy or I was going to walk away. I knew if I continued talking to this guy that I would get very angry. It was very upsetting to listen to the racist things that this guy was saying. He admitted to being racist and said that if he had the chance he would kill all black people. He also said that he would die before there was a black ruler in South Africa. I told him that I opposed his views and tried to explain to him that everything was not the blacks' fault. I was in awe and could not believe I was actually talking to such a racist person. I was extremely upset and decided that the best thing for me to do would be to walk away. So I told the guy that I had to go and I walked away.

INSIGHT:
Getting into an argument with the South African was likely to uncover basic culturally learned and largely irrational assumptions that separate cultures. Each person saw the other as totally irrational and fundamentally wrong. It is unlikely that such an argument would result in a constructive outcome unless the persons could find common ground assumptions they shared.

Taking Action against Racial Injustice. While visiting South Africa my friend and I travelled to Seapoint. We stopped at a local Italian restaurant on the main street for lunch and noticed that this small city by the ocean was predominantly white. The few blacks we did see were either doing manual work or hanging out on the streets. My friend and I were sitting at an outside cafe table enjoying our first "real meal" in South Africa and discussing how easy it would be to visit this country and never see the racism. The racial problems, we decided, were so well camouflaged that it would be hard to see by someone not looking for them. Then suddenly a yellow police van pulled up across the street and two uniformed white men jumped out and violently grabbed a handicapped, older black man from off the sidewalk. They threw him into the back of the van while they spat words into his face. Because we hadn't even noticed the black man before this, we assumed that he hadn't caused any sort of disturbance worthy of such brutality. My immediate reaction was utter horror and shock. Looking back now I realize that I had several options I could have taken at that time. Even though the incident occurred in probably a two minute period I could have become verbally or even physically involved, but that would have meant risking my own safety. I could have called for help, but being in a predominantly white area in which racism and apartheid were the norm rather than the exception, this probably would have proved to be futile. So instead of taking action against this blatant display of racial violence, I sat still and watched.

INSIGHT:
The student was shocked to see the police demonstrating what appeared to be blatant racism. While the student was offended and angry he didn't know what to do. The student could see what needed to be done, but he had no idea how to do it.

A Man Put His Hand up My Dress. One night in Cape Town, South Africa, two friends and I (all females) went to a night club called the Arena. There was a big dance floor and you had to walk up a couple of steps to get to the tables and then beyond the tables was the bar. I had on a loose, tank top dress that was above my knees in length. I was dancing with my two friends and we walked off the dance floor to go to the bar. The night club was crowded and we were walking through the tables in a single file line with me in the middle. As we walked up the steps and through the tables a man seated at one of the tables I passed reached up and put his hand up my dress. It happened so fast and the man acted like it was no big deal. He just looked up at me and smiled as if putting his hand up my dress would be a perfectly natural thing to do to an American woman. He was probably in his late twenties with dark hair and mustache and a dark complexion. I was so shocked that I just jumped and said, "Excuse you," and kept walking towards a group of Semester at Sea students.

INSIGHT:
The female student was shocked to be violated by this man in the bar. How could she protect herself against being taken advantage of? It was hard enough to fight back when she was made a victim in her own culture but many times more difficult in a strange culture.

A Warning from South African Undercover Police. A friend of mine and I were at a local South African restaurant called the Casa Blanca, which was located in Sea Point. We had been there for a few hours talking to a local colored man about the political situation in South Africa. Midway through our conversation we decided to go to the restroom where we encountered our critical incident. A few seconds after we entered the restroom, two plainly dressed men entered the room and bumped into my friend harder than a casual brush. He, being a fairly short-tempered person, turned around and said, "Why don't you watch where the hell you're going." At that point I saw a gun in a holster underneath the one man's shirt. I pulled my friend back, and quietly informed him of what I had seen. We both tried to ignore the two men as we went about our business. Right before we were ready to leave the restroom the one man turned to us and said, "You had better think about what type of people you talk to around here and how you talk to them." At this point we didn't know who these men were, we only knew they had guns and we had to make a critical decision about what to do and where to go upon leaving the bathroom. We weren't sure if the two men were referring to our political conversation with the colored man, or if they were referring to our arrogant reaction to them bumping into us. We also didn't know if they would follow us if we left the restaurant. Finally we decided we would go back to our table, make an excuse to as to why we had to leave, call a taxi, and return to the ship. The two men watched us from a distance as we returned to our table, but seemed to have little interest in us when we finally left. Later, when we talked to another Semester at Sea student who had been in the restaurant earlier, we were informed that the two men had been policemen, but he was not sure why they were there.

INSIGHT:
To what extent should the student have challenged the locals with guns? Should they have gone out of their way to avoid involvement, or should they have sought out involvement? As the student learns about other cultures, that decision becomes more difficult because they can see how to get meaningfully involved but not know whether they should do it.

We Should Have Gotten out of That Cab. My two friends and I went to see a play in South Africa one night. We took a cab, and when we were dropped off the cab driver offered to come pick us up. He was very nice and polite. He even walked us in to find out when he should pick us up. After the play was over he was already waiting for us outside. When driving us back to the boat, he was driving very fast. All of a sudden we felt something hit the car, and our friend who was in the front screamed. The cab had hit a black man. My other friend and I were sitting in the back seat and we turned around to see what had happened. We saw two black men crossing the street and staring at us. We then heard the cab driver say, "Bastard, he deserved it." I asked him if he had hurt him and he said, "I hope so!" At this point my friends and I were all looking at each other not believing what had just happened. Our cab driver had just purposefully hit a black man. We couldn't do anything but look at each and say, "Oh my God!" We started laughing nervously and holding each other's hands tightly.

INSIGHT:
By not making a decision this student none the less made a decision. The students could not avoid getting involved either by action or inaction when confronted with a hit-and-run cab driver. Whichever way the students decided they would have to live with it in their memory and justify it to themselves in the future.

Another Brainwashed American. It was my first night in Cape Town, South Africa, and my two girlfriends and I had just returned from a welcome reception at the University of Western Cape. We had decided to move on to "The Pumphouse"--a bar where many other Semester at Sea students had gone earlier in the evening. We ended up meeting three South African men who asked us if we would like to go to a more "local" pub with them after the Pumphouse closed. Because we were excited to "experience the culture," we agreed.

The six of us drove about twenty minutes away to the pub. We grabbed an open table, ordered drinks, and started conversation. One of the guys, who was around twenty-eight years old, asked me what we had planned for our stay in Cape Town. I ran through the various activities--shopping, the wine country, Table Mountain and then mentioned that I was going to a township and "hopefully a squatters camp." With this, he laughed and said "Oh, another American student brainwashed by the Bishop." At this point so many thoughts ran through my head and I had to decide how to respond. I was really offended that he laughed at me and said that I had been brainwashed. What I really wanted to do was lash out and accuse him of being a bigot, but of course I didn't. Instead I innocently asked him what he meant. He told me that he had talked to several other students from the ship who had tried to talk politics with him. Basically, he said that "he was sick and tired of talking about it."

He told me that it was extremely rare for any white student (from South Africa) to venture anywhere near a squatters camp. They had all grown up with the system of apartheid and it was normal for them. Instead of contradicting him, I chose to keep my mouth shut and listen. He went on to tell me that the land used for squatters camps was owned by some white man, and that the "blacks had no right to it." His father had owned land outside Cape Town and it had been "overrun and turned into a squatter village."

Instead of going with my gut reaction--which was to attack and become angry--I just let the situation unfold. I did not (or tried not to) jump to any conclusion about him. It was obvious that he had been raised in a family that supported the suppression of Black and colored South Africans. He had been *socialized* to think in such a way. He had never really been taught anything else and it would have been futile for me to argue with him.

INSIGHT:
The student experienced social pressure to polarize whites and blacks as different and potential antagonists. The student was expected to agree with local whites, and disagreement might be interpreted as treachery or betrayal. By listening to the racist remarks but not getting angry, the student had a chance to learn about the problem from another viewpoint.

A Confidence Man. Well, we were walking back from the Seaman's Mission, you know, and this guy started talking to us. He was telling us how he's going to the States for school in a couple of months, so he wanted to know if we would tell him a little bit abound America. Anyway, he stayed with us the whole time we were walking back, asking all these questions about the States and the boat. I'm trying to get rid of him, because he was getting so persistent with his questions. And these guys, he motioned to the others he had spent the day with, just left me with him. They just walked ahead of us, so I was left talking to the guy. Finally, when we got near the ship, right outside the port gates, he turns to me and tells me that he is a freedom fighter. That he is wanted by the government and is trying to get to America, so he needs some money. Would I give him 4,000 shillings.

I told him I didn't have that kind of money, so he gets really mad, okay. He starts yelling at me, calling me a stupid American, and telling me that I'm selfish and unwilling to help such a good cause. So, I got mad, you know, and I told him that he was stupid for calling me a stupid American because he didn't even know me.

INSIGHT:
The local "freedom fighter" recognized the visiting student as vulnerable and easy to manipulate with friendly behavior and if that didn't work by getting angry and intimidating the student. The student was able to avoid being exploited but not without an embarrassing confrontation with the local.

Credit Card Confusion. While my roommate and I were relaxing at the pool of a hotel in Kenya, a black man who worked there greeted us by saying, "Jambo!" He continued to say, "Are you guests at this hotel?" I said, "No. We just had lunch at one of your restaurants and came down here to relax and cool off at the pool." He said, "The pool is private for guests staying at the hotel overnight only. If you would like to stay you must pay 150 shillings or you can go to the beach" (which was right behind us). My friend said, "We didn't know we had to pay to use the pool, we're sorry." He said, "I can't run this hotel for free. We have to charge outsiders who use our pool to pay the bills."

My friend and I understood and apologized once again. We decided to stay and pay the 150 shillings. My friend paid in shillings, and I wanted to pay with a credit card, because I had very few shillings left. The man said, "I don't have a credit card machine in the pool area. You will have to take your credit card up to the credit office."

I walked through the hotel lobby and found the cashier's office. I explained to them the situation and said, "I want to pay with my Visa to use your swimming pool. Please charge me 150 shillings." The cashier ran the credit slip over my Visa card and said, "You can use this slip as a tab and keep an account of your spending by putting under the category of 'description' pool and under the category 'amount' 150 shillings. And if you want to buy drinks or ice cream you can write them down as well. When you leave take the first copy for your own records and give the pool manager the rest of the copies." He gave me back my card and I thanked him.

I took the slip to the pool manager and told him what the cashier had just told me. The pool manager acted as though he had never seen a credit card or a credit card slip before in his life! He looked bewildered and curiously at the written features on the slip. He was amazed when he noticed the identical copies of the carbon slips beneath the first slip of paper. I was so surprised to see a forty year old man working at a five-star hotel who had never seen how a credit card worked before. It was quite funny actually how smart he thought I was for showing him how it worked. When I showed him where to write down how much I owed them he said, "Aw you're a smart one!" with a smile and handed me back the slip.

I ordered two drinks over the course of the afternoon. They were fifty shillings each. Once again, I explained to the waiter how I was paying with a Visa credit card and wrote down how much the drinks were under "amount" and I wrote "drinks" under "description." Similarly the waiter was curious and surprised to see the xerox copies of the carbon paper slips. I had to laugh at their amazement. During the day the manager came up to my friend and me and asked for the Visa card slip. I gave it to him and he tried to show another employee how it worked. He fumbled for a long time turning it over and looking through the slips before pointing to the Visa sign on the top of the first page.

When they left my friend and I said, "You could probably leave without even paying because you hadn't signed your signature on the credit card slip yet, and until you did it wouldn't be a valid transaction." I was tempted, I must admit, to leave the hotel pool without signing my name on the credit slip because it is their job to know how to accept payment for their own services. By the time they would have figured it out, I would be long gone.

INSIGHT:
The students swimming in the hotel pool were willing to pay for that privilege when payment was requested but were astonished by the hotel staff's inexperience in dealing with credit cards. The students were tempted to take advantage of the hotel just as others had taken advantage of them as vulnerable visitors, but they chose not to do so.

Kenya

Life or Death, Rich or Poor. I decided to split from the group and walk around on my own for a few hours. They wanted to go somewhere and I thought it might not be wise to go with them, since I had to be at the ship around 4:00 p.m. for my Safari! Well, I walked to what I later found out was the fruit and vegetable market. It was not very clean and many people were begging for money.

I met a nice guy in front of the post office. He just came up to me and said "Hello!" I said, "Hi, how are you?" He was very interested in me and where I was from, "What state are you from?" I replied, "Pennsylvania." Our conversation went on for some time.

So, we walked around the corner to a small restaurant and I ordered two sodas and an egg sandwich. I was not sure I should order it but it was hot. At the restaurant we talked more about school in the States. We also talked about my Semester at Sea. Then he told me his name. He said he lived in Sudan and studied in Northern Africa. The whole time he drew pictures of Africa, etc. on my pad. After about an hour he started telling me of political problems in Sudan, naming group leaders etc. Soon he told me he had barely escaped his country alive. He said he was on the "black list," and he needed to get out of Kenya! It was at this point that I realized I was being had and he just wanted money. I got the bill and started to leave. On the way out he kept saying, "Well friend, now that you know my problem, can you give me some money for my problem?" Finally in a mean attempt to get rid of this thorn in my side I gave him 20 ksh. "Not even a dollar," he said. I said, "I'm sorry" and walked away.

Not thirty seconds later I encountered a big man! He had a button down shirt on with two of the three buttons open. The following is what happened, with as much accuracy as possible because I was very scared--make that as scared as hell!

"Hey buddy, who were you talking to in that restaurant?"

"Oh, just a guy I met on the street."

"What did he say to you?"

"Oh nothing. I'm a student from the United States and we were talking about school."

"I work for the President and we have men all around, I'm not alone. If you don't cooperate we will take you into jail." I was ready to "shit a brick."

I said, "May I see your I.D. please? He produced an I.D. I'm sure it was fake.

"If you don't tell me what you said we'll have to take you into jail. That man is a terrorist. It's illegal to talk with a terrorist."

Soon they asked how much money I had brought into Kenya with me. I told them $100 that I changed to shillings. "How many shillings? "Oh, about 2,000, I think." They kept cutting me off in mid sentence. Soon they said, "Well, if you give us the money, since you are a student we will let you go." "Boy-oh-Boy." I did not want to give them money, but did I have a choice?

INSIGHT:
The student was an easy mark for exploitation and could be trapped into a difficult situations without ever being aware of the dangers he faced. Intimidation worked very well when the student was already anxious, uncertain, and not wanting to get into trouble.

Village Visit. During our first day stay in Kenya, I went on a safari to Samburu Game Reserve, Aberdaires and Nyeri. Our group had the option of going to a traditional Masai people's village in Samburu and we decided to go, as they have a reputation for being very diverse cultural people.

We were told before we even arrived that it was necessary to pay two hundred shillings in order to enter the village and take photos randomly of the women and children, their huts, and the crafts they make. Once we arrived, we barely stepped off the vans and several men approached our group of twenty-two and demanded the money. After we paid them, I felt uneasy. I'm not sure if it was because I knew I *had* to pay or because the men practically assaulted us in order to make sure they received the money. We began to walk through the thorned weeds, which were used as a protective measure to keep their animals and children within a boundary. The women were all adorned in their traditional congas and beaded jewelry with their children wrapped around them. They began to sing a traditional song as they stood facing us in a perfect U-shaped figure. After a few minutes, the main chief in charge of these people shouted something at them in Swahili, and then the younger women in the group approached us and grabbed our arms. The young girl that approached me could not have been more than seventeen and she had a newborn wrapped in a conga on her back. She spoke some English and explained to me that she wanted me to see what her living conditions were like in her hut. I was both timid and anxious to go with her, but I went as I figured I would never have the opportunity to go again. We entered an adobe (mud-packed) igloo-shaped hut that was about five feet tall at the most. I sat down on the dirt floor and five women followed me into the small adobe. I felt as if I was going to be robbed because they sat down as close as possible to me. They asked me my name and within minutes they asked me to buy some of their jewelry. "Asked" is actually too subtle, it was more like

"forced" to buy something. I was also told I had to give something to the
woman of the house before I could leave. The ladies selling the jewelry
coaxed me into buying something. They priced the pieces totally out of range
of what they were worth, and when I offered a price they would reject it.
They were not willing to bargain whatsoever. I was angry, claustrophobic,
frustrated and I felt ripped off. I made the decision to buy a bracelet of one
of the ladies' choice. I gave all that I had (which was the equivalent of about
ten United States dollars) and left the hut as quickly as possible. The women
ran after me begging me to give them my shoes, a pen, my bandanna, a T-
shirt, anything. I denied all of their requests.

After we left the village, I became really angry. It was like they no longer
dressed in their traditional clothes or lived in their huts because that was their
way of life. They now did it for money.

INSIGHT:
For the village, tour groups had become a business, and the spontaneity of
observing a local culture was almost inevitably lost. The students then
became a crop to be harvested by the locals who seemed to be selling their
culture. Under those conditions the student felt angry about being cheated
and embarrassed for having contributed to the culture-selling by locals.

Being Friendly. We spent the night at the Ark Hotel in Kenya. My friend
and I were sitting in the bar after dinner ordering drinks and talking to the
people who worked at the hotel about their country. We had taught the
bartender and the game leader how to make Kamikaze shots and had been
drinking free since then. When I was getting up to leave, the game leader
came up to me where I was standing alone and asked me if I wanted to go on
a "private" night safari with just him.

This man that I hardly knew had just propositioned me in what I would
consider a sexual way. This man was a native Kenyan, and even though I do
not consider myself a prejudiced person, I could not even believe a black man
had propositioned me. We were out in the middle of a game reserve miles
away from anywhere. There were no locks on the room doors, and it was a
very small building. I politely declined his offer and took off up the stairs for
the night.

I was not expecting this request to come from this person. I still cannot
figure out why he would ask me that question; what did I look like to him?
Afterwards I told my friend what had happened and she told me that the same
thing had happened to her.

INSIGHT:
The student was interested in learning as much as she could in the short
time she had in Kenya. The Kenyan male misinterpreted her interest. She
had enough skill to get into trouble but almost not enough to get out of

trouble. The decision to decline politely and go to her room prevented an even more embarrassing possibility.

Mombasa Madness. This incident occurred my first afternoon in Mombasa. I was with three girls in a cab on the way to town. The girls were Semester at Sea friends. We were on our way to the downtown district to do some shopping. I was very hot in the cab. We lowered the windows to get some air circulating. One of the girls proceeded to stick her head out of the window to cool off. The driver was driving somewhat recklessly, in my terms. He was weaving in and out of traffic. All of a sudden, she let out a loud, short scream. I became very nervous because she had been taking a risk by hanging out the window. The driver put the brakes on immediately and pulled over towards the cars parked on the road. I still didn't know what had occurred. She then informed me that he had hit a bicycle rider. I then turned to look out the back window and saw a man lying on the street next to his bicycle. She said that she had not been hurt and that the bike rider had been hit by the back end of the car and not by her arm that was out the window. The cab driver leaned out the passenger window and started talking with anger in his voice. He was speaking Swahili, but it was easy to tell that by his tone he was blaming the accident on the rider. The man proceeded to pick up his bicycle and come toward the car. I wanted to get out of the car and help the man, but the driver instructed me to stay seated. I didn't know whether or not to listen to him. In our country it is customary to help out. I was angry that the driver wasn't being sympathetic but rather rude to the cycler. The man was obviously very shaken by the incident because sweat was rolling off of his forehead. They continued to argue back and forth and after about one minute the driver proceeded to drive onward. This incident disturbed the four of us, but the driver acted as if this occurred to him on a daily basis.

INSIGHT:
It would have been easy for the student to get involved defending the bicyclist against the cab driver. Guilt and innocence seemed clear, and it may have seemed cowardly not to actively oppose the cab driver for doing wrong. The more angry the student became, however, the less likely a constructive outcome would become.

Taxi Trouble. My roommate and I just returned from our four day safari to Nairobi, Ark and Samburu. We had one day left in Kenya by ourselves so we decided to go to a nice hotel for lunch and to relax by the pool for the day. It was extremely hot and the pool was refreshing. We had a wonderful time, but at 6:00 we regretfully had to leave to be back on the ship at 7:00. I asked the person behind the registration desk to call us a taxi. While he was calling, we saw a boy (I didn't know his name) from Semester at Sea. He was also leaving and was waiting for four of his friends (all of them girls I didn't know). They had a cab waiting and room for two more for another 200 shillings. The boy said, "You are more than welcome to come with us in our taxi for 100 shillings apiece." Right then, the man who called for our taxi motioned to us that it had arrived, so my friend and I went outside to see how much she would charge us to take us to the ship. We told the boy, "It will probably be too crowded for all of us in one taxi so we'll go in this one. Thanks anyway." My friend asked the cab driver, "How much to go back to the ship?" The cab driver looked confused so she restated her question, "How much to go to the port?" "Port?" the cab driver said unknowingly. "We want to go to the ship, port, boat." She said almost screaming this time. Thinking of other synonyms for where we needed to go. I said, "We want to go to the dock!" as clearly and loudly as I could, but she still did not understand. We were at a loss to communicate and she and I were beginning to feel frustrated. All we could do was repeat the words, "Port, ship, dock" in hopes that when she tried to repeat them she would understand where we wanted to go. Then the boy who offered us a ride came over to where we were trying to communicate and tried to help by saying "harbor." Finally she seemed to understand, but our relief didn't last long because the bargaining for the price still hadn't been agreed upon.

She said, "Five hundred shillings to go to the harbor." We said, "two hundred." She said, "No, how about four hundred shillings?" We said, "Two hundred fifty." She said "Okay, three hundred fifty shillings." We said, "Okay" and my friend got in the back seat of the taxi. I was about to join her when the boy offered to share his taxi with us again by saying, "Come with us for two hundred shillings for both of you, we are leaving right now. Here come my friends and the taxi is right here." I said, "Are you sure it won't be too crowded?" He said, "No, come on!" So I followed him and my friend got out of our taxi and we piled into their taxi. It was a big, black, old fashioned car with two sets of seats facing each other like the back of a limo. It was just big enough for all of us. We piled in three in front and three in the back, and the boy sat up front with the driver. I said, "Thank you for sharing a taxi with us," and a girl across from me said, "No problem."

As we drove out of the hotel parking lot, I noticed three black men who worked there chasing after us screaming something and waving their hands. The woman taxi driver we were bargaining with earlier was driving behind us yelling and shaking her fist also. I told the driver what I saw and said, "What's going on?" The driver stopped and talked to the three men who were chasing us down in a language I couldn't understand. I couldn't tell what they were saying, but it seemed obvious that my friend and I should have gone with the lady taxi driver that the hotel registration desk called for us. I didn't realize we had caused such a scene by choosing a taxi who offered us the cheaper price. I didn't realize until then that we were obligated to use the taxi cab the hotel had called for us.

INSIGHT:
The student was eager to get her way for an advantage. By abandoning the cab that had been called and contracted for, the students were breaking a promise or a contract with the first taxi driver from that driver's viewpoint. Since the student had felt taken advantage of, it was easy to justify taking advantage of locals in return.

An Incident with Some Locals. Four of us had walked to Fort Jesus on our first day in Mombasa. On our way back, we passed through many street vendors crowded with locals. One place in particular was like an open cafeteria with benches and tables in front. A thick crowd lounged around and basically socialized while eating. Two of us walked at a quick pace and were deep in conversation, so we did not notice the others fall behind. After walking a few yards beyond this little cafeteria style establishment, one of us (your basic blond-haired, blue-eyed, all-American fellow, and at least the most obvious one in our little group) who was walking with the others, called out and asked us to rejoin them.

"You guys, come back here. I want to share a very upsetting thing that just happened," he announced. I looked beyond him to see if I could deduce the problem from the look of the people we had just passed. With all the stares he had gotten throughout out little trek, I was sure that the day would not pass without a (critical) incident.

"What's wrong," I asked.

"We were walking through that eating place over there, okay, and the passage is narrow, you know." I looked at the people sitting on the benches. While he explained, they stood and joined their friends at the store counter. They kept a watch over us as they spoke to one another.

"I walk through and the shop owner yells out, 'Hey! How are you doing, De Klerk?'"

"Whoa!" I remarked, ". . . who's De Klerk?"

"He's the white president of South Africa," my friend responded absently, still caught up in his story.

"Did he say anything else?" I asked.

"No, but I'm really upset, you know. Why did he single me out, and why De Klerk when he's doing all these reforms for the blacks in South Africa? I want to go back and say something."

"Yeah right! And just what did you plan on saying?"

"I don't know, but I'm really mad. That was an unfair thing that he said, and I don't want to let him get away with it, you know." The locals' vigil was intimidating. I was the only one standing at an angle that allowed me to see how they faced us with a pugnacious countenance.

"Let it pass," I said, "there's no use in getting into a debate with any of those people. You're out of your league."

"But it makes me so mad, you know!"

"I think we should go, you guys. Our presence is making them angry. We don't belong here; we should just go."

Finally, everyone else turned to see what I had been watching during our conversation. We became aware of the enmity coming from their stares, and decided that our indignation was not worth a dangerous confrontation. We grew scared, for not only were we out of our natural environment, we were incredibly outnumbered. We decided to ignore them and continue on home. We turned around with what we hoped was an air of nonchalance and walked away.

INSIGHT:

Since the student was white, locals might well assume that the student would sympathize with local whites on local political issues. Locals and students only knew one another as stereotypes at this point; only if they got to know one another better would they be able to replace that racial stereotype.

Giving Gifts. It was our last day in Kenya, and I had spent an exhausting day at Wasini Island. Our bus returned us to the ship about 6:00 p.m. I walked off the bus with my backpack and a Semester at Sea itinerary shirt draped over my shoulder. As I disembarked I spotted a Kenyan, Sam, who had joined my friends and me for dinner the night before (we had met him on our first day in Mombasa). He was nice enough to take us to places we wanted to see and give us helpful information for individual travel. He was overly and uncomfortably friendly. It was almost as if he wanted something from us. After talking it over we decided to dismiss this feeling, thinking we were being unfair and unnecessarily suspicious.

As I tried to board the ship Sam spotted me and immediately came over.

"How are you?" he greeted.

"Good, thanks. I just got back from Wasini."

"Oh! You had fun then. I just saw your friends on the ship."

I nodded, "They're on board?"

"Yes," he said, "they are coming down."

"Okay, well I've got to get on and hose down," I said in hopes of making an exit. As I turned to leave he lifted the shirt off my shoulder.

"This is nice."

"Thanks. I went swimming in it, so it's all wet."

"But it is almost dry."

"Yes it is," I replied trying to snatch it away from his hands.

"It's very nice," he said, moving it beyond my reach, "A present for me?"

Something about his tone told me he wasn't kidding. I became very indignant.

"No, no," I answered, making a grab for my shirt, "it's the only one I've got."

I turned back to look at Sam. I looked at my shirt and thought of how petty I might have been. After all, it was only a shirt. Then I realized that there was a principle involved. I did not like the way he was so aggressive with me. It seemed as if he decided I was his friend before I could decide I was his friend. I took that as an invasion of my privacy.

INSIGHT:
As the students got more experienced, they became less naive about instant friendships formed with local persons who approached them and were able to distinguish between true friendship and manipulation. It was easy to become cynical toward all host culture persons who professed friendship after being disappointed by one bad experience.

The Samburu Village. It was our second day in Samburu and we were having a great safari. We had seen tons of animals, many of them very close, and we were having a lot of fun. Our trip leaders told us that if we wanted to we had the option of going to the Samburu village and then going on our game drive, or we could just go on the game drive. We would have to pay 200 shillings to even go, and then we weren't sure if we would have to pay extra to take pictures or what. We basically were given no information about it except that we should not go into their huts, because last year some Semester at Sea students had gotten kidnapped there! They wouldn't let them leave until they bought everything they had to sell. This kind of scared me a little, and other kids were saying that these village people weren't very nice either. The decision had to be made whether we each wanted to go or not. Everyone had their own choice; it wasn't a group decision. I thought to myself never again, probably, would I have an opportunity to go see a village like this, and I had already seen an amazing assortment of animals and would still have a chance to see more later that day. My friends all decided that they didn't want to go, but I decided I just couldn't pass up this opportunity, even if I was a little nervous. Others had decided to go, just none of my friends, but I knew it was something I wanted to do, so I did it. I wouldn't be able to forgive myself if I had passed up the opportunity. My friends tried to convince me not to go saying why should I pay these people money if they were going to be mean, why would I want them to hassle me about buying things from them, and why should I go somewhere where people got kidnapped? Like I said, I made my decision to go and I stuck with it, and as it turned out two of my friends decided to go after all!

By deciding to go to the village I knew I would have to tolerate their constant pulling me and asking of money, but I was willing to put up with it so I could see the village. Later on in the safari, I realized that as I was shopping the vendors didn't bother me quite as much. I learned to either bargain with them effectively or to just walk away if I didn't want anything.

INSIGHT:
The student went to the village knowing what to expect and was prepared for the experience. She wanted to get beyond the stereotype of the Kenyan villagers and learn more about their culture in spite of these barriers. The student had learned not to depend on stereotypes but to make decisions based on the actual situations rather than on other people's prejudged expectations.

India

Touring a Temple. It was my second day in Madras. My friend and I decided to do some independent travelling, so we hired a rickshaw and went to the Kapaleeswarrar Temple.

When we arrived a man approached us and proceeded to give us a tour. I looked at my friend.

"Are we paying him?" I asked.

"I think we should," she answered.

"How much?"

"He seems kind of nice. We should at least give a hundred to each tour guide."

We were not familiar with this place at all. Homeless families littered the area, so we decided it would be better if we had a guide who spoke English quite well. We walked down several streets to the temple.

"Do not give money to anyone," our guide warned us. "People will ask you for money. Do not give money unless I say it's okay." This made me suspicious. Just who was it that we should give money to? I did not want to be bothered with it at the moment. "OK," was my reply.

"In the temple," our guide advised us that, "you must make a small donation to the holy man. I will tell you who he is." I looked at my friend and stopped following the guide. He turned around and saw we were hesitant. I didn't want to pay to see a church. I didn't think that was right.

"Donation is only a little," he added. "You give however much you want."

"However much we want?" I asked.

"Yes," he said, shaking his head from side to side. I took his head movements as a sign of assent. In the little time I had spent in Madras it seemed that this was a neutral gesture, something you did when speaking, especially if you are saying yes. I should have gone with the American interpretation. When we arrived at the temple we were asked to remove our shoes. I did not want to, and did so unwillingly. I started to put them in my backpack, but our guide stopped me.

"Oh no! He," he said, as he pointed to a man standing by the door, "He will watch your shoes for you."

"That's alright," I insisted. "I can carry them in with me. I would prefer to." He gave me a come-on-leave-your-shoes look and said, "Please. You can trust me. Your shoes will be here when we come back."

I looked at my friend and saw that she had removed her shoes. She was watching me, along with some students and temple dwellers, waiting to see if I would resist further. Feeling pressured, I dropped them next to my friend's.

Our guide took us to a small altar of Vishnu's wife. Another man walked up behind us holding a basket filled with a coconut, two bananas, some red powder, and a match. He motioned for me to place my hand on the coconut.

"Wish for something," our guide instructed, "A good life, money, happiness, anything."

"Okay," I closed my eyes and did so. After I did he dotted my forehead with some of the powder. He turned to my friend and made her do the same thing. After we had both made a wish the other man broke the coconut, placed it in front of the alter, and lit a piece of paper. He peeled the bananas and gave one to each of us.

I thanked him for the wishing ceremony and moved on. My friend followed. Our guide and his friend followed a few paces behind us. They spoke low and in Hindi. The former called out to us.

"A little donation for the ceremony," he said. This made me uneasy. I didn't like the fact that he wasn't telling us what things would cost before we did them.

"Is this for the temple donation?" I asked.

"Oh no!," he retorted with a don't-be-cheap look, "This is for the offering to Vishnu." I didn't want to argue the point, so I reached into my pocket. I gave my friend a look of frustration. Both of us had very limited funds and we needed to save some of it to get back to the ship.

"Five rupees okay?"

"No, one hundred rupees each."

"Yeah right! You should have told us beforehand," I said. "I don't have 100 rupees to throw away. Here's ten. That's all I'm giving." My friend handed them fifty.

"Next time," I turned to our guide after the other man left, "you have to tell us if we have to pay to do certain things. I don't like surprises."

"It was only a small donation. That is nothing to you."

"I'm sorry," I said doing a 180 degree turn, "but we're not rich Americans. We're only poor students, okay. Let's get this straight, because if this keeps up we will leave now." I looked at my friend to see if she had anything to add.

"Yeah," she shrugged, "we don't have a lot of money with us. We haven't had much opportunity to convert our money into rupees."

"Dollar bills, then," he said with a come-on-get-real frown. "We didn't bring those with us," I answered. "I talked to a tour guide on our ship and he said it wouldn't cost us much to visit this temple and the cathedral. If there is a problem with that we'll leave."

"No, no. It's okay. I tell you next time." We walked around for a while and soon ran into the holy man.

"This is the holy man," he said, "I told you earlier about giving him a donation."

"Yes," I said, "however much we decide."

"At least 250 rupees each."

"No."

"Why not?"

"I don't even have 250 rupees on me!" My friend was shaking her head and rolling her eyes, "We're getting taken, big time."

"I know," I agreed, "There is no way we are giving him 500 rupees." At this point, I was both agitated and nervous. There were only my friend and I with all these locals in an enclosed temple with only one exit. "We will only give 100 rupees and that's it!"

"One hundred each," our guide insisted.

"No! One hundred and that's all. If that's not good enough we will leave right now."

"Fine, 100," he said looking exasperated with us. He tried to resume the tour, but I was not up to it anymore, "I just want to leave. I just want to go!" I said.

"I know, so do I." my friend said. After some time we finally saw the rest of the temple and returned to the gate. I quickly put my shoes back on, as did my friend. We got up to leave and the guide put his hand up.

"Some rupees for him, for watching your shoes."

"You know," I said motioning with my hand, "I told you I wanted to carry my shoes. He didn't need to watch them. You should have told us."

"Five rupees only." I didn't want to argue anymore. Five rupees was no big deal. What upset me was that they kept trying to bleed us. When they saw us all they saw were dollar signs. My friend and I were willing to give the guy about 250 rupees for his help; he seemed so nice. But when he kept asking for money, I was too indignant give it to him.

"Fine!" I reached into my pocket and retrieved exactly five rupees. I handed it to the guy who watched our shoes and walked out. I didn't even bother to see if my friend was behind me. I was so frustrated. I just wanted to get into a rickshaw and get out of there.

INSIGHT:

The Indian guide probably saw the students as trying to cheat him and the locals out of their fair share. The students saw the guide as trying to cheat them by charging them for every small service. Neither the guide nor the students felt they were treated fairly, and a potentially valuable encounter with Indian culture turned into a negative experience in which everyone felt exploited.

On a Beach in India. One night my roommate and I took a taxi to the beach in Madras, India. While we got out to walk on the beach, the cab driver waited by the taxi for us to return. My friend and I walked to the water. There was practically no one else on the beach. As we started to walk back to our taxi six Indian men approached us and proceeded to ask us many questions. They asked us, "Where are you from? What do you study? How old are you?" I responded by saying, "I am a nineteen year old American who studies Liberal Arts." They asked, "Would you like some food?" (They had a box of food with them.) We politely declined and continued walking back to our taxi. These men kept grabbing our hands and seemed very interested in talking to us. When we got back to the taxi the men asked, "Can we come with you? Would you like to come with us?" We politely said that we were leaving, and then left.

INSIGHT:
The two women walking together on the beach at night in Madras were probably putting themselves in harm's way, and it was not surprising that they attracted a lot of attention from the Indian men on the beach. The women were able to avoid an embarrassing situation for themselves and the Indians by their skill and keeping their cool.

The Head bob. What did the man want? We had, I thought, agreed on a price, and now that our improvised tour, complete with tour guide was over, payment was in order. The only problem was that every time I asked, for fear of insulting him, if the amount was not enough the Indian man would nod his head from left to right several times; a gesture I took to mean he was not satisfied.

I was starting to get frustrated. What did he want? He would not say a price, so it was up to me. Every number I threw out I got what I dubbed "the Indian head bob." What made me really angry is that he did it while all the while smiling in a most friendly fashion. After a couple of minutes I realized a real lack of communication was going on here. I thought the number I suggested was fair, yet still the head bob. What did he want? Finally I just gave him some money, more than I originally had planned, and walked away.

Later while relating the story to some friends, they laughed and said that the head bob meant yes. It was not until that particular moment that I realized how ignorant I had been in dealing with the man. What I had assumed was a refusal had all along been an acceptance.

INSIGHT:
The nonverbal head nod showing agreement by the Indian guide to the price offered by the American student was an attempt by the Indian to accommodate the visiting American. The American student's lack of understanding turned this friendly exchange into an embarrassing conflict to the puzzlement of both the Indian and the American.

My First Night in India. After having gone to the welcome reception in India, my friend and I ran into some other friends who were on their way to a bar. Two of the people we were with said that there was a bar just across the street and we could walk there. The minute we stepped outside the gate of the port people were all over us. We were a group of three men and three women. As we started to head out to the street, kids of all ages were starting to grab us and ask us for rupees. As we walked down the street not only were the kids still following us, but the drivers of those three-wheeled taxis asked us to get in--they wold drive us to the bar. My friend's attitude, and mine also, was to just ignore all these people. After walking a little bit I felt that something had slapped my behind. I was surrounded by so many people it was likely that someone had just bumped me. Then I felt a hand touch my front. At this point I was a little confused and started to wonder if those touches had been accidental.

Right then I felt someone stick his hand between my buttocks. I immediately turned around and grabbed the hand of the kid who did it. He was no older than thirteen or fourteen. I was so mad I stabbed his arm with my nails. He and his friends just laughed at me. Right then I felt really trapped. I started walking with one hand behind me and one across my chest. I could still hear all those kids laughing around us. I immediately caught up with one of our male friends and asked him to walk behind me so no one else would touch me. Right after that we found the bar we were looking for, but it was closed. We were still surrounded by all the people and the taxis that had followed us all the way up the street. Right then some cops showed up and started beating up some of the kids that were around us. I felt so disgusted! I thought to myself, "I'm going to hate India." After the cops threatened to beat more people all the kids started heading down the street. We then asked the taxi drivers to take us to a bar. We had to take two taxis. After we got to the bar we had to wait for the other cab to show up with the rest of our friends. Once we had paid them and were inside the bar, our friends who were in the other taxi told us how on their way there this cop had *thrown* this kid in front of their car! The cab driver had to turn in order to avoid running him over. We were all so upset! I myself felt that I would never be safe in the streets of India.

Even though my female friends and I were all ridiculed by the kids on the streets, we were still disgusted with the fact that they had cops who beat them up all the time and even tried to *kill* them! I felt really sorry for them then, even though I had been so angry at what they were doing to us. I felt sorry that it seemed like society was against them and they would never have a chance to better themselves. Even though they had made me feel trapped as I was walking down the street, that was only temporary. I felt like they are permanently trapped.

INSIGHT:

The student's anger at the local youth for exploiting her quickly changed to anger against the system in which the local youth were trapped. The student's feeling of anger was clear, but it was hard to know where to direct that anger appropriately and who was really to blame.

Physical Contact. We had some serious trouble changing money in India. The few of us who needed to cash travellers checks hopped in a cab and came back to the Semester at Sea ship, "The Universe" to use the onboard bank. My two other friends stayed behind at the travel agency to wait for our driver and car, which would take us all over during the next five days.

Three of us changed our money on the ship and then walked through the port of Madras to get to the street entrance of the port where there were seemingly hundreds of screaming Indian cab drivers, rickshaw drivers, and beggars. By this time we were sure that our friends would be waiting for us. Unfortunately, they weren't. It was *hell* out there.

We three girls were a prime target for this horde of screaming people who immediately mobbed us. They were grabbing at my hair, my body, tugging on my clothes, and pulling me every which way. We got split up because we were each targeted and dragged in different directions. Filthy little children were tugging at my shirt and one literally grabbed onto my leg and refused to let go of it. My compassion for these poor people went down the drain, even though I tried not to get angry and violent! I was completely mobbed--so much so that I couldn't move! Luckily, I am tall and could look over the crowd. I was screaming to my friends, "Where are you? Where the hell are the others?" I had to make a decision to either continue to be attacked and wait for the guys to come, or get out of there fast!

Needless to say, I tore my way away from the people as much as was possible, ran out into the street, literally bumped into a cab that I jumped in, and luckily my two friends spotted me and did the same. Sweating, teary-eyed, dresses torn, and scared, the three of us drove away with people pounding on our windows and running beside the cab--maybe in hopes of milking some money out of us??! What a nightmare.

That was the only negative experience I had in India.

INSIGHT:
From the student's viewpoint, the locals seemed to gang up in a "feeding frenzy" and she began to panic. The panic seemed to encourage the crowd to act more aggressively, and the feelings of panic escalated in a spiral of still more aggressive behavior. Once begun, the chain reaction between the student's panic and the local beggars' aggression was difficult to stop.

Disrespect by Two Indian Men. I was standing in line to get two tickets for my brother and me. I was in the Calcutta airport at the Indian Airlines ticket counter. There were not a lot of people in the airport, but quite a few milling around the front of the ticket counter. It was around noon and our flight left at 1:20 p.m. A woman was behind the desk helping customers and I was the only woman in line. There were two men in front of me. As I neared the counter with the last man in front of me finishing his business, two men (one on each side) just cut in front of me and proceeded to buy their tickets. The whole incident was nonverbal. I knew what men thought of women in India and I did not want to cause trouble, so I did not say anything. The men acted as if it was no big deal and so did the woman behind the counter. I motioned for my brother to come over, and when he walked up in line the two men stepped aside in order for him to get his business done. I guess this was just another day of business as usual in India. I was just kind of stunned and just thought to myself how much I hated India.

I am pretty sure that the two men thought nothing of it, but just that a woman, no matter where she is from, is inferior to them. I, just like an Indian woman, needed to rely on her "man" to get things done.

INSIGHT:

The rules that apply to women and men in India are different from those in the United States. The student judged locals according to the more familiar back-home rules as measures of fairness. Although the student was able to find ways to accommodate the local rules and still achieve a measure of fairness, she resented having to accommodate the local rules.

Gender Roles. The problem I faced was how to deal with what I would call sexual harassment. Women in India are not as visible as they are in the United States. The treatment of women is entirely different. Additionally, women are usually not out at night and certainly not alone. My friend and I were shocked at the treatment we received when we tried to get a taxi late at night.

My friend and I were meeting several friends at a hotel bar. They had all gone ahead of us. We proceeded outside the terminal gate in Madras where we had hoped to grab a taxi. Immediately we were surrounded by men trying to offer us a ride and arguing about a price with us. In this already stressful situation, one of the drivers kept trying to place his hands on me.

My own reaction was bad. I screamed when this guy touched me. In my hometown if a woman was screaming all the people around her would jump in and help. So I screamed to call attention to my friend's and my situation. However, no one seemed to care. If I had to do it again, I would have brought a man with us. In later days I received less harassment when I was with a guy. Additionally, I would have slapped the guy who was trying to touch me.

INSIGHT:

The student was shocked at being touched and resented being stereotyped so easily. She was even more shocked that her screams drew no attention or support from others. She felt helpless and angry at the cab driver and all Indians for being so insensitive.

Offensive Gestures. My entire experience in India can be characterized as being one huge, continuous critical incident. However, a few moments stand out in my mind that I feel illustrate the extreme cultural differences that exist between the East and the West. The incident occurred on the third day of our visit in one of the many historic temples, which was located just outside Kachapuram. I had been travelling with four other Semester at Sea students-- two girls, two guys. The temple itself was known for its majestic beauty and its daily visits from two eagles who were fed by the priests. We all had to climb five hundred stairs in unbearable heat in order to reach the top. Once there, we were ushered in by a frantic man waving his hands and mumbling something. We weren't able to understand him at all because he didn't have a tongue. We followed him to a nearby window that was situated so that gusts of air would flow freely through it. We figured out that he just wanted us to cool off. He then showed us around a few of the prayer rooms and led us to one particular room where he motioned for us to stay. He disappeared and moments later two other men entered the room.

The room itself was made of marble with a large "God" statue in the center with flowers strewn all around it. One of the two men proceeded to tell us the history of the temple and the statue's significance to their religion. Meanwhile, the other man lit a few candles and threw some flowers around the statue. He then picked up a tray and placed some ash and petals onto it.

Personally, I was very intrigued with the ceremony at this point and was quite interested for them to continue. Then the other man who had spoken to us about the history told us each to draw a line of ash across our forehead, so we all obeyed his command. After doing this both men in unison asked, actually more like demanded, a donation. The five of us looked at each other somewhat shocked and disappointed that this whole ceremony that appeared to be so genuine and spiritual might have been a hoax or a play for money.

Frustrated, we looked at each other and asked who had change or some small bills to give them. One of the girls said she had ten rupees, so she pulled it out and motioned to put it on the tray they held out. They shook their heads in absolute horror! They nodded their heads up and down, which we later learned meant no, and said repeatedly, "No!" She looked at them with a confused expression and asked what it was she was doing incorrectly. Unfortunately, their attempt to explain her error in English was a complete failure. So she again motioned to place the bill on the tray, and again they shook their heads frantically. It was only then that they pointed to her hand and said, "No!, No!"

Finally, we understood what she had done. She was putting the money in the tray with her left hand, which in their culture was a huge insult. My friend quickly apologized for her mistake and switched the money to her right hand, and placed the bill on the tray. They both smiled and looked very happy with us and our very generous donation. We smiled back at them, thanked them, and headed straight for the exit, so as to avoid any other ploys for money.

INSIGHT:

It took courage for the student to seek out new experiences in India and be forced to learn the rules along the way. By being open and patient, she was able to interpret the meaning of local Indians and find meaning in her experiences of India.

Is Giving Money to Beggars Right? On the third day in Madras, India, I stepped off the ship's gangway and started walking towards the harbor gate. It was fairly early in the day, so I was not afraid to walk alone. In the distance I could see a group of four Indian kids barely clothed. From experiences of the previous days I knew instantly that they would come up to me and ask me for money. My dilemma was whether to stop and give them some money/food or to just ignore them and walk on by.

As I walked nearer I saw them look towards me and whisper to each other. They walked towards me with their palms face up and each said boisterously, "Madam, moni madam." I guess I knew from the previous days that if I gave anything to one person I would have the rest of the people ask persistently until I gave them all something. I decided that I would not give anyone anything and walked straight on without turning my head or slowing my pace. My face was expressionless and my eyes were fixed straight ahead on the harbor gate. They persisted a little longer but soon realized that I would not change my mind and turned to approach the next Semester at Sea student.

An alternative choice would have been to stop and look through my purse to give them each some change or candy. But I didn't because I knew that there were other "beggars" in the vicinity, and if they saw me passing out candy I would be swamped by people. Perhaps if the children were not all together and noisy, I would have given a little something. But they talked loudly and aggressively, so it didn't seem like they were in need of items as much as others did. By looking at me and whispering to one another they sent cues that they were going to approach me. And from past experiences I knew that they would ask for more if I gave out anything. I sent cues that I wasn't going to give them anything by not making eye contact, not responding verbally or through my actions, and by not slowing my pace down.

INSIGHT:

The student was not willing to be exploited even by deserving poor who would want her to help them. The student quickly learned by previous experience the cues for accurately communicating her intention to locals. This did not necessarily help the student make a "right" decision, but it did help the student communicate in a less ambiguous manner.

Being Offered Drugs. An auto-rickshaw driver in Madras, India, offered me something I could not understand, and I had to choose between being impolite and refusing, or risk buying what might be drugs.

I had returned from my very brief trip from the Taj Mahal to Madras only to find most of my friends from the ship gone. A casual acquaintance and I decided to spend the day shopping and sightseeing. We caught an auto-rickshaw just outside the port gates and told the driver the name of a downtown bank at which we wanted to stop before shopping. He agreed, and we started driving down the street.

Suddenly the driver turned to us and began gesturing and speaking to us in broken English. I caught phrases like, "Do you want. . ." and "You like. . ." I was very uncertain--for all I knew he could have been offering to take us on a sightseeing tour of Madras. My friend was shaking her head and whispering, "No!" to me. I didn't understand why she was being rude to the driver and not making an effort to understand what he was saying. I gave her a quizzical look, but she didn't explain.

"Just say no" she insisted. The driver was by now ignoring her, since she had refused his attempts at communication and was now looking at me expectantly. Finally I decided that perhaps she knew something I didn't, so I shrugged at the driver and said, "No!" The driver turned around in obvious annoyance and continued driving. My friend turned to me and whispered, "Drugs." I was very glad I had told the driver no.

INSIGHT:

In an attempt to adjust and adapt to the local culture, it was possible for the student to create problems unintentionally. Being too accommodating could have been as big a problem for the student as not being accommodating enough.

A Gender Issue. While in India I encountered many new and different cultural traditions and practices. However, I think the most difficult adjustment for me throughout our travel to each of these countries has been accepting people's treatment of women. Because I was well aware of the fact that women are considered to be the inferior sex in India, I was somewhat prepared for the chauvinistic attitude that I inevitably encountered. One particular incident occurred when I was visiting a historic temple in Kachapurary with four other Semester at Sea students; two girls and two boys. We had been having a difficult time finding the temple because we were carrying a map, and we had decided to walk from our hotel in an effort to better see the people and their culture. We were fortunate enough to accidently run into a young man who worked at our hotel and he graciously "offered" to lead us personally to our desired destination. We accepted his offer knowing that he would expect money in return, because we were unsure if we would be able to reach the temple on our own.

Minutes later we arrived at the entrance. We were commanded to remove our shoes by several Indian men standing there. As we did, a man approached us and told us that he would be our guide and tour us around the temple. He asked that we all pay a small fee for carrying our cameras inside with us. We agreed, not really having too many other alternatives at that point, since we did want to see the inside of the temple. One of the two guys I was travelling with introduced himself to our guide and shook his hand. I remember thinking that it wasn't really customary for Indian men to shake hands, but the guide did not hesitate at all to shake it. Because the other guy and girl that we were travelling with were lagging behind at the shoe shelves, it was only my girl friend, one guy friend and myself standing around him.

After he shook the male student's hand, my girlfriend and I both simultaneously put our own hands out to shake his hand. He then looked at our hands, looked at our guy friend and turned his back on all of us. He had blatantly ignored our handshake almost as if he had no need to even explain his actions. His body language and expression clearly illustrated that he felt absolutely no remorse for what we considered to be his impoliteness. Throughout the tour it became more and more apparent that he believed women were inferior to men. For he directed all his attention to our male friends and neglected to make any eye contact or conversations with my girlfriends and me.

This incident clearly addresses the issues of equality between men and women, resulting in anger, frustration, hostility, and ignorance. I have learned through this incident, and others like it, that by accepting another culture's practices I am not necessarily agreeing with it but respecting their right to believe in it.

INSIGHT:

Not shaking hands with the female students might have been a way the guides showed respect for "another man's woman" and not an example of chauvinism. Treating the women and men alike might have been considered very impolite by the guide. It was important to try and judge behaviors from the other person's viewpoint and give them the benefit of the doubt.

Malaysia

A Friendly Ride. After the incredible amount of stress involved in dealing with all the rip-off artists in India, upon my arrival in Malaysia I was very defensive and bitter. When I stepped out of the terminal in Penang I wanted to find a taxi with three other girls to take us to a hotel. When we exited the terminal we immediately were approached by about ten different drivers. We had asked beforehand approximately how much it should cost us, so we knew that every person who asked us was attempting to take advantage of us. Finally, after wandering around the area for a while a gentleman approached us and told us he would drive us for the quote we offered him.

This was the critical incident. The guy was not a taxi driver, but he just rented out his car. After all the social warnings all of the Semester at Sea students had been given we didn't know if we should. We decided to go ahead and take the risk, which was the definitely the right decision to make.

The driver, whose name was Goh, picked up on our sense of feeling uncomfortable because he made light conversation, and at the same time was extremely informative. He ended up showing us around Penang for a few days, and was, in fact, the best tour guide I've had thus far on the voyage. A bonus to that was that he never asked us for any money and let us decide how much it was worth. He was very generous. It restored some hope in me that I don't feel like every country is after our money, and, in fact, some do want us to experience their culture.

INSIGHT:

Something as simple as a cab fare became symbolic of trust for the students in Malaysia. Therefore a very small amount of money could have resulted in heated bargaining to avoid being ripped off. The cheaper fare would not always be a good indicator of trust, respect, and fair treatment by the locals, however, nor indicate that the student was not being exploited.

Going Out to Dinner and Not Having Fun. One night while we were in Malaysia, my friends and I met up with two Malaysian men. We talked for a couple of hours and all of us were having a great time. These men, we thought at the time, were nice. When we decided to leave, the men asked if we would join them for dinner the following night. We agreed and picked a spot to meet at.

Well, in the beginning the dinner was going okay. We met at a Japanese steak house. My friends and I ordered cokes and the guys ordered six rounds of sake. When it came we tasted it just to be nice and then left it there. As the dinner progressed the two men got so drunk it was embarrassing. They finished all of theirs, ours, and proceeded to order more sake. It was awful. We tried to tell them to slow down, but they persisted, saying that they were alright. Everyone in the restaurant was looking at our table. They were so loud and so drunk. All I wanted to do was get out of there. The ceiling really hit the roof when one of the men started to harass the waitress. That did it for me, I wanted to leave. But how could the four of us get up, get this drunk man away from the waitress and pay for our half of the bill? I was scared because I thought that maybe they would come after us if we tried to leave, and we didn't want the restaurant to deal with these drunken fools.

My friend and I excused ourselves from the table to go to the bathroom and decide what we were going to do. The plan was we would play sick and a few minutes later we would hand one of the men our half of the bill. If he didn't accept, we wanted give it to the waitress directly.

Well, we went with our plan. Two of my friends played sick and my other friend and I told the two men that we couldn't leave them. We gave them all the money we had, thanked them, (I wanted to punch them) and took off. I apologized to people as we were leaving and again apologized to the waitress.

INSIGHT:

The four female students were unable to avoid an embarrassing situation at the restaurant with the two Malaysians but were able to leave the scene gracefully. The embarrassment and subsequent anger would have been difficult to avoid, given the overconsumption of alcohol by the men, but the students did a good job of damage control.

The Restaurant. My friends, a group of around ten, went out to dinner at a restaurant in Malaysia. We went for an early meal, because we were supposed to meet more friends at a local club later. Our meal was delightful and service was very pleasant.

The next day a girlfriend of mine wanted to try the restaurant for lunch, as she had been unable to join us the prior evening.

As we walked in we were met by a hostess who told us to wait while she got the manager. Once the manager arrived he explained to us that we were not welcome to dine at the restaurant. I asked him why he had a problem with our business. He proceeded to explain to me that a group of American students had "stormed" the restaurant the night before. He said, "They were obviously intoxicated and were being loud and belligerent." I tried to apologize and remind him that our group had been respectable. He would not, under any circumstances, allow American students back. He let me know that, though it was not we personally who had acted poorly, he was still deeply offended. We were escorted out.

INSIGHT:

The group of Semester at Sea students who had behaved badly the previous evening were an embarrassment to all the Semester at Sea students. All the students were being blamed for the bad impression that one small group had created, and it led to the exclusion of all the students from the restaurant. While it may not seem fair for the manager to exclude all students, it was not difficult to understand.

Who Do We Choose. We arrived in Penang ready for a relaxing, peaceful, fun time. Six of us left the ship as soon as customs cleared us and anxiously walked through the port immigration building in order to catch a mini-bus to take us to Kuala Perlis. As soon as we walked through the security area onto the street we were mobbed by taxi drivers asking us where we wanted to go and telling us how much they charged. It was evident that our transportation situation to Langkawi Island was not going to be as smooth as we had all hoped.

The greedy drivers not only invaded our personal space, but tried to get us into their cabs by pulling our bags, offering to carry them, grabbing our clothing, and not letting go of our hands after trying to make acquaintance with us. I was frustrated before we even left the dock area. I was perspiring heavily, my body was being touched and grabbed from head to toe, and I could not move away from the congested area. I became not only claustrophobic, but seriously annoyed.

After about forty-five minutes of being pestered and shoved around, I was past the stage of being annoyed and was now angry. My friends were just as annoyed as I was by this point of being pestered by men saying, "Taxi here, where you go? Langkawi? I know the way, good price, you come with me." No matter where we turned to get away from this chaos the situation was never ending and lacked improvement.

Finally, when I was about to perspire to death and scream at somebody to vent my frustrations, I pushed my way out of the congested cesspool of cab drivers and walked across the street to gather my peace of mind. After a few minutes, I was approached by a man named Ezy. I was hesitant to look at him, talk to him, or even be near him after my previous experience, but somehow he caught my eye. He just smiled and looked away. As I approached him he was casually leaning up against a mini-bus drinking a coke. I asked, "Will you take eight of us to Langkawi Island?" He said, "I can take you two and a half hours to Kuala Perlis were you catch a ferry to Langkawi, I charge you $25 Malaysian each."

By that point I was ecstatic to meet a friendly, rational driver who appeared to be sane and who did not pester me to hire him. This cab ride was the best time and added to our excellent experience in Malaysia. Ezy ended up picking us up at the ship the morning the ship was to sail. I guess my patience paid off.

INSIGHT:
When the student had been aggressively approached by several cab drivers, it was easy to react angrily toward all locals. Fortunately the student found a local cab driver who was less aggressive and could communicate to the student in a way she found more acceptable.

Thailand

Getting a Cab. During my trip to Bangkok we stayed in a hotel downtown. One evening my friends and I had dinner reservations and were planning on meeting friends around 9:00 p.m.

As we entered the lobby, I asked the lady behind the counter if she "could have a cab sent over." She nodded eagerly and smiled. My friends and I sat in the lobby and waited for our taxi. After around twenty minutes I walked up to the desk and asked if "there was any kind of a problem with the cabby." The lady behind the desk smiled sweetly and motioned for me to have a seat with her hand, and nodded the whole time. After another ten minutes I again approached her, as we were worried about being *really* late at this point. I asked again if "there was anything I could do to facilitate getting a taxi." About that time another hotel employee walked from behind the office area. She rushed over and explained that the woman I had been speaking with did not understand a single word of English. She apologized for the obvious misunderstanding and was extremely efficient about summoning a cab.

When we finally arrived at the restaurant my friend, who is originally from Canada and is working temporarily in Bangkok, explained that Thai, *especially* women would much rather completely and totally avoid a situation that appears confrontational than explain they don't know or understand.

Well, naturally we felt so badly for putting her on the spot, not just once but over and over. We could have apologized, yet we were told that would be to acknowledge the problem, and if we were truly concerned we would smile and nod and pretend it never happened.

INSIGHT:

The students calling a cab caused an embarrassing situation without ever intending to do so. The non-English-speaking staff member did everything she could to diminish the embarrassment for both the students and the staff, however frustrating her nonresponse must have been for the students.

Sex Show in Bangkok. During my trip to Bangkok I had the rare opportunity to see a "sex-show." When my friends first proposed this idea I was disgusted, but I understood it was part of what goes on there, so I decided to go.

Sex-shows in Bangkok are sad because the girls are very young and are usually sold to the establishments because their families believe girls are worthless. After I realized the sadness of the shows I decided to go. We went to the most popular bar called "Supergirls." The guys were joking and laughing as the first act came on, but all I was thinking was that I felt so sorry for this girl who could be no more than fifteen years old. I thought of myself at fifteen and how embarrassed I was to even go to the store and buy my own feminine hygiene products let alone have sex on stage. Just when I thought it couldn't get any worse, I looked over and saw one of the "performers" holding a baby in the corner. I felt so horrible for letting my friends laugh and giggle at the girls on stage, because even though culturally the girl and I were a world apart, as a female I could relate to her position. I'm glad I went to the show because it taught me a lot about how lucky I am to be able to go to college and become whatever I want and that I won't be sold to a strip-joint because I'm worthless. This incident, to say the least, was intense.

INSIGHT:

The American female student was able to identify with the Bangkok bar girls and feel empathy for the pain these girls must have felt as victims. Lacking that empathy, the other bar patrons had less of a problem participating in the exploitation of the girls for their own amusement.

Hong Kong and China

Hong Kong Shop Owner. After getting back from Beijing, my friend and I decided to do some shopping on our last day in Hong Kong. We weren't looking for anything in particular, but instead we were sort of browsing to see if anything caught our eye.

We passed one shop that had a bunch of Walkmans in the window. We peered in to see what sort of technology they had, and I noticed a Walkman identical to my own. I was interested to see if I had paid more in the U.S. for my Walkman. We walked in and I asked the shop owner, "Could I please see the Sports Walkman with the clock and alarm?" The shop owner looked at me and loudly responded, "No, I don't have that." I thought he must have forgotten or didn't realize he had this type of Walkman. So I repeated myself and pointed to the Walkman in the window. This time the shop owner became angry with me and retorted, "I have no Walkman with clock. Leave. You no buy!" With this outburst everyone in the store was looking at me. I became embarrassed and angry. I wanted to yell at the guy and tell him he was wrong. I realized that if I retorted it would just cause more problems. He obviously didn't want me in the store, and I definitely didn't want to hang around.

INSIGHT:
Because the local shopkeeper's livelihood depended on serious shoppers it was easy for them to become impatient with window-shoppers who did a lot of comparison shopping before actually buying a product. The student suffered from a local stereotype in Hong Kong as someone who looks but never buys.

Camera Shopping. My parents met me in Hong Kong. I had their camera, and as they were continuing on to China they needed to get another one. We went camera shopping, and we had a very unpleasant encounter with a local salesman.

We explained to the man, "We need a second camera and we want it to be similar to this one (mine)." The man started showing us cameras of lower quality and higher prices. "What do you have of lower price?" we asked.

"This one is $60.00," the man said.

"What does it do? How does it work?"

"Put film here, winds automatically," the man replied sharply.

"Does it flash automatically or do you have to turn it on?" The man first said that the camera flash was automatic, but a few minutes later he said it wasn't automatic. "You need to push this button and then it will flash." My father and I were getting very angry. My mother was too, but she held it much better. She continued to ask the man questions, trying to be diplomatic and pleasant. "Why should I buy the more expensive one? Tell me the difference between the two?"

"No!" the man replied.

"Will my pictures look different?" my mother asked the man.

"He obviously doesn't know. He has no clue," I snapped.

"I know! I'm just not going to tell you," the man replied.

"Why do you have to be so rude?" my dad asked.

It was the first thing he had really said, and I was surprised it took him so long to blow.

"I'm not rude," the man replied, in a hostile way.

"Yes you are," my dad returned. "Your job is to help us and answer questions, not to be rude and insult us. I wouldn't buy a camera from you if you paid me," my dad said calmly but sternly. Then we walked out. We left very frustrated and aggravated. We also left without a camera.

INSIGHT:

The Americans were used to treating Hong Kong as a place to buy bargains. When this proved false, the student and her family became angry. The increased economic affluence of Hong Kong and the relatively lower value of the dollar have changed things. Americans now may have a reputation of being difficult customers who spend relatively small amounts of money.

The Snotty T-Shirt. I was walking with my friends through the streets of Hong Kong. It was a gray and rainy afternoon and we had taken the bus to the outskirts of the city to explore and shop away from the rest of the numerous tourists. My goal for the day was to find and purchase a plain white, extra large, one hundred percent cotton T-shirt. Now this was not as simple a task as it first seemed to be. I looked in dozens of shops and stalls--but to no avail. Finally I found what seemed to be the closest thing that I would find to my goal--a large, white, one hundred percent cotton shirt. I decided that despite the fact that it was the wrong size, for U.S. $1.00 it was still a deal.

I took the shirt off the rack and brought it up to the woman to pay. Her back was towards me, and as she turned around I was horrified to see that she had her finger up her nose! Before I could stop her she had taken her hand down from her face and grabbed the shirt I was holding with the very same finger that seconds before was lodged in her nose. I was appalled! This incident was completely out of my frame of reference. Before I even realized what I was doing I screamed: "Forget it! I don't want it anymore" and stormed out of the shop.

INSIGHT:

The student's culturally learned habits of personal hygiene were so ingrained that it was offensive to violate them even when the student knew that the locals had different culturally learned habits. The student's sudden anger was probably hard for the shopkeeper to understand.

Cause a Scene in an Asian Country. When the ship was in Hong Kong I flew to Bangkok, and on my way back in the Hong Kong airport I was waiting in line for customs when these two people who were in the line next to me picked up all their stuff and moved over to my line right in front of me. I guess they thought my line was moving faster, but it never occurred to them to go to the end of the line. The decision I had to make was whether to say anything or just keep quiet.

If I said something I might start a scene, and I knew that was the worst thing to do. I was very angry though, and I had been travelling for a long time. I was tired and irritated, so I thought this was extremely rude of them since I had been waiting there for at least a half an hour already and my patience was running very low.

I ended up deciding that the last thing I wanted to deal with was a scene, so I didn't say anything. But I also wanted to let them know what they did was rude. So I did the only other thing I knew how, which was to use nonverbal communication. When the wife turned around and looked at me I glared at her. Her facial expression indicated innocence and that she had no idea what she had done wrong. This irritated me even though I knew it was cultural difference.

INSIGHT:
The student's indirect criticism of line-jumping locals was ambiguous and hard for the locals to interpret accurately. The student could have found better ways to reduce ambiguity in communicating with locals. A less ambiguous way of communicating might be understood as intended and would not require making a scene.

What the Hell. This critical incident still perplexes me! It occurred on the last day of our six-day visit in Hong Kong. I was walking alone from the outlying district ferry terminal in Central to the main ferry terminal to catch a boat back to the ship. I had just spent an hour getting back from Cheng Cheu and was a little dazed as I walked back--mainly from physical exhaustion from all the travelling and touring around I had done in the last couple of days. I was walking along a quaint path next to the harbor among many other Chinese people when suddenly this man walked from the side toward me and kicked me hard in the foot.

Fortunately, even though I was wearing sandals, the kick did very little physical damage (maybe a bruise is my guess). He kept walking and sort of smirked. I was completely stunned that this man, who actually looked like a normal Chinese, between the age of 25-30, wearing casual clean clothes, kicked me on purpose. I know it was done on purpose, because I remember hearing him breathe really hard as he did it, as though he was using all his effort. Because I was so stunned and taken aback I continued walking toward the ferry. A few seconds later when I realized what had just occurred I stopped and turned around and yelled to the man, who was at a stoplight across the street by this time, "What the hell, you ass!" Even though I yelled it loudly no one else around me gave me even a second glance. Maybe it was my imagination, but I could have sworn that the man laughed and smirked to himself and crossed the street once the light turned green. I was so angry and confused about the entire incident that I simply continued walking toward my destination.

Thinking back on the entire situation all I can do is laugh. Here I am walking along in Hong Kong minding my own business and some mystery man comes out of nowhere and kicks me--crazy! Although I was a bit dazed after that ferry ride, I know I didn't cut him off in his walking path or do anything else (break some social rule or custom, etc.) to deserve that.

INSIGHT:
It was difficult for the student immediately to make the right response at the time she was kicked. By the time the student had rehearsed the right response, the opportunity to respond had passed. Under those conditions doing nothing was a better choice than doing something without thinking through the consequences first.

Drunken Problems. It was our last night in Hong Kong and I was out with two friends. We were out drinking heavily into the morning. We left the bar and one of us had stolen about nine glasses, which she could barely carry. We went to McDonalds where she proceeded to pass out! Humiliating! After we had finally woken her up, I asked my friend to get the cups so she wouldn't break them. She yelled and yelled, "Don't break them!" They had only been outside two minutes when a small shot glass (which we hadn't known was in a larger cup) broke. She absolutely freaked! She was yelling, "Dammit, I can't trust you at all! I am going to have to do it all by myself!"

This entire time she was being belligerent. I went to speak with her and she went on and on about friends and how "we were terrible..." I calmly said, "We are your friends, and when a friend passes out in the middle of McDonalds that's when the others take over!" She yelled something, so I started to walk away. We kept a close enough distance so I knew she'd be all right. Once back at the ship I went to check on her and she told me "how her friends had embarrassed her tonight!" I left and let her sleep it off!

INSIGHT:
The student's overconsumption of alcohol was almost certain to result in

problems in a foreign culture. The already vulnerable students became much more vulnerable and much more likely to create unnecessary problems with locals by being drunk.

Coke, the Universal Word. It was late in the afternoon and we were hungry, so we decided to eat. At any other time or in any other place that would have been one very simple task. But today we were in China and neither the waitress, the busboy, or the hostess could speak English. The icing on the cake was that the menu was in Chinese and there were no pictures at all on the menu!

I had been doing so much travelling and was so tired that hunger had taken over. Along with hunger and tiredness comes the "crabbies." The crabbies have no tolerance, and a person with the crabbies becomes very frustrated when they do not get what they want.

I think the waitress was kind of afraid to come over to the table because she hesitated for a very long time. We both must have looked very crabby. She came over and said something in Chinese, which I assume was, "Can I take your order?" I was with my friend and we just looked at each other and then looked back at her. I think that we all most have sat there and just stared at each other for what seemed like forever.

I could feel my frustration level rising and nothing had even been ordered yet. I then attempted communication. I said, in my nicest and slowest voice possible, "Do you have an English menu?" She gave me the nicest smile she could give and nodded her head up and down. I breathed a sigh of relief. But then she just stood there. I just kept looking at her, I didn't know what to do. I hadn't run into someone on this whole trip who didn't understand a word of English. I was backed into a corner which is exactly how I felt. I was getting more frustrated, not at the waitress but just because of the simple fact that I had backed myself into this corner and I could not see a way out.

What to do? What to do? Try again? Speak slower this time, I told myself. While I was speaking slower I also raised my voice level. I guess I thought maybe she couldn't hear me. I don't know why I thought speaking slower or talking louder would help. I could not face the fact that she just could not speak English.

I was running circles in my mind. Speak slower, talk louder, speak slower, talk louder, those were the only solutions that I had. My mind had frozen and I could not think. Just as I was going to begin to try to use a primitive form of sign/body language, I looked on the wall and saw a Coke sign. I thought if they advertise it they must know what it is or means. All I had to say was, "Coke." She knew exactly what I meant. She went to the back, brought out two Cokes and a manager who could speak broken English.

INSIGHT:
The student's inability to communicate resulted in frustration for the

student, which built up to an intolerable level. It was easy to get unreasonably angry when the frustration level got too high and display what locals call the "white furies." Finding something familiar, like a bottle of Coke, did wonders to relieve that frustration.

A Visit to Tiananmen Square. I was on the Semester at Sea trip to Peking University. Our tour bus stopped at Tiananmen Square where we were given an hour to walk around. There were many Semester at Sea students and many more tourists walking around the square and taking pictures. I, and the two girls I was with noticed that a lot of tourists were crowded around a building, so we decided to go toward the building to see what was happening. As we pushed our way to the front of the crowd we noticed that there were several policemen standing there and that the policemen weren't letting the crowd advance any further. We then noticed that police cars were driving through the area. As we were standing in the front of the crowd the policemen began yelling at us in Chinese, therefore we could not understand them, and shoving us away from that side of the square. Eventually the entire crowd of tourists was herded entirely out of the square and across the street. As we stood on the other side of the street we noticed that cannons, along with more cars and more policemen, had been brought into Tiananmen Square. There were also policemen standing directly in front of the new crowd that had formed across the street from were we were standing. We eventually found out that this incident was because a prince from Indonesia was going to deliver a speech at Tiananmen Square later that day.

The Chinese tourists could probably have communicated with the policemen verbally, but it appeared as if there was no communication between the Chinese tourists and the policemen other than the yelling and shoving on the part of the policemen. The Chinese tourists behaved exactly as the Semester at Sea tourists and moved away from the crowd. This surprised me. I felt that I would have communicated with the policemen if I could have.

INSIGHT:
The students visiting Tiananmen Square and the Chinese people with them were all intimidated by the police. While the non-Chinese speaking students could not communicate with the police, it was hard for them to accept how accepting the Chinese people were toward police intimidation. An open expression of anger or resentment toward authority could have had serious consequences.

Waiting in Line. In China I attended an acrobat show with my tour group. During the intermission I had to use the restroom and so did my friend. We went down to the bathroom and found a line of people; so we got in line. As soon as my friend was first in line two older Chinese women walked into the bathroom, walked right in front of my friend and me and began checking all the stalls only to find them all occupied.

At this point I figured they would know why we were all in line and proceed to get in line with the rest of us; I was wrong. These women stood directly in front of the stalls waiting for them to open, and as soon as one did they went in. Needless to say, we were shocked. We did not know what to do. More women came in and walked past the line waiting for a stall to open.

At this point my friend walked up to them and was ready to do the same thing, and she did. As soon as a stall opened she had to shove a Chinese woman out of her way to get in. I was now first in line observing this and I began to laugh. I could not believe what was happening. We had to shove older women who had cut in front of us to go to the bathroom. Well, I realized I would not get anywhere standing in line, so I walked up to the stalls and raced a Chinese woman to the first stall to open.

I could not believe what was happening; it was ridiculous, even chaotic. When I left the bathroom the same thing was still going on. There was a line and then there was a group of women standing around the stall doors ready to race or shove anyone who wanted the same stall.

INSIGHT:
The student knew that the local rules were different, but it was still hard to ignore the rules of polite behavior. There was no easy solution. If the student had stayed in line, her needs would probably have been continued to be ignored.

A University Visit. During my short visit to Beijing, China, I had the opportunity to meet with students from UIBE--the University of International Business and Economics. On my first night in Beijing I attended a "dance party" set up through Semester at Sea and UIBE to allow for interaction between Chinese and American students. At the gathering I met two very interesting (and interested) Chinese freshmen, a girl and a guy. The girl's "English name" was Lisa and the guy's was Roger. I spoke amiably with the two students for about thirty minutes. During this short time we covered a variety of subjects, but only when we came to the subject of schooling and education in America did I feel things become tense among the three of us.

Roger asked me where I attended school, and I told him De Paul University in Chicago. He asked me if it was difficult and whether or not I enjoyed it. I replied that some of my classes were difficult and that overall I did enjoy it. He asked, "What kind of punishment does your school use?" At this I was very confused. I asked him what he meant and he answered, "If you don't go to class or if you are acting out what do your teachers do?" I told him, "At American universities there are few punishments in terms of acting 'out' or for not going to class. If you don't want to attend a class then you don't have to, and most students who go to college do so because they want to, so there isn't much of a disciplinary problem."

He seemed baffled at the notion of that much lenience in the schools. He asked, "So if you don't want to go to class you don't have to, and you don't get punished for not being there?" "Exactly," I replied. He kind of chuckled as if to express his disapproval of our system, and I asked what he was laughing at. He replied that, "Well, in China we are punished and criticized by our teachers if we do not go to class." I do understand that this is an inherent part of the Chinese educational system, especially since a very small percent of Chinese are able to attend college. But, by his demeanor I was picking up the feeling that he felt superior to me just because I went to school in such a liberal environment.

He chuckled and said, "Your education system is not very good then if your teachers cannot punish you." Obviously this offended me and I defended our system by merely stating that, "The United States and China are different in many respects and that neither is better or worse, just different." I felt as if I had to defend my country to this student who was taking such a superior stance in viewing the United States.

INSIGHT:

The student was insulted by the Chinese student's criticism of American education. The student was unable to interpret American education in such a way that the Chinese student could understand the student's culture.

Using a Credit Card. While I was in Beijing, China, with the Peking University trip three of us went in a gift shop at the Forbidden City. None of us had appropriate Chinese money to buy anything with cash, so when we went into a gift shop we asked them right away if they accepted Visa credit cards. Finally we went into a store with clerks who nodded their heads yes when we showed them our credit cards and asked them if we could use them to pay for the merchandise we wanted to buy.

We were so excited because we all wanted to buy T-shirts and postcards, and other paraphernalia of the Forbidden City. We had to hurry because we didn't have much time before we had to meet back on the bus. So we kept the salespeople busy picking out the right size T-shirts with the right design, taking out this and that from their packages and taking things off the shelves. I picked out some M & M's and started to eat them as the lady behind the counter added up our purchases.

I gave her my credit card when she showed me the total, but she just stared at me blankly pointing at the total. I pointed to my credit card and it was obvious that they didn't accept credit cards in their store. I had no other choice but to leave the store with my credit card and without the merchandise I had picked out to buy because I had no Chinese cash whatsoever. The salespeople were enraged that we weren't going to buy everything we had set aside to buy. I was in a bind because I had eaten a small bag of peanut M & M's and didn't have the money to pay for them. Luckily one of us had some small Chinese currency on her and she paid for the M & M's I had eaten and we left the store.

As we were leaving the Chinese salesperson even went so far as to throw the T-shirts we were planning to buy against the wall at the other end of the store! It was a miscommunication that resulted in hostile feelings towards one another on both sides.

INSIGHT:

The miscommunication between the students and shopkeepers resulted from the assumption that a message had been communicated when in fact the message was not understood as intended. The student's wrong assumption led to an embarrassing confrontation that left everyone angry.

View on Hussein. At my Beijing University visit I met a girl named Wong who was very curious about international affairs. We talked extensively about the crumbling of the Soviet Union, and she was always asking me what America's position was on Gorbachev, Yeltsin and the new Commonwealth, and so on.

After walking around her university (a highly security-oriented place) and speaking with her for over three hours, I invited her into my dorm room for a cup of tea. We sat and visited, and the subject turned to the Gulf War. In answering her questions I explained that the American people for the most part supported Bush in his efforts. We are a country extremely concerned and involved with international affairs. America has been criticized for not "finishing the job" because although we got Hussein out of Kuwait he still apparently wields some political power. I shook my head in disgust when speaking of Hussein, and this prompted some wonder in her eyes. I asked her what she thought of Hussein. "Oh! What a honorable man--Hussein," she said, pleased, "I admire him very, very much--the first man to ever stand up to America. A very strong and brave man."

Needless to say, my mouth dropped to the floor. I could hardly believe it. I had a choice: inform her a bit on Hussein in a way she would never hear through the authority-filtered news she explained to me earlier, or I could simply leave her with the mistaken opinion of him.

I couldn't help but tell her that what we learned of Hussein was far from anything honorable. I said, "Do you know anything about the burning oil wells?"

"No, what is this?" she looked concerned. I went on to explain (in the basic terms of my understanding of what led to the war) his stranglehold on America through oil and his desired monopoly on the world's oil. I asked her if she was at all aware of the environmental effects these burning wells were causing. She was very surprised. I went on to talk about the burning down of homes, the unlawful killing of innocent people, and the atrocities this man spearheaded. I told her, emphasizing this is my personal opinion, that I thought the man was crazy.

INSIGHT:

The student's view of world affairs was likely to be different from the local views of Chinese students. It was easy for the student to become a missionary for the back-home view and attempt to teach that back-home view without first learning the local contrasting viewpoint. If the student had been well informed on world events ahead of time, she could have been more articulate in explaining her viewpoint.

Republic of China (Taiwan)

Not to Take Candy from Strangers. My friend and I were on a local bus going to Taipei, Taiwan, from Keelung, Taiwan. I was sitting with a middle-aged Chinese woman. My friend was right across the aisle from me. I was very excited about life and smiling about everything, so I'm sure I looked like a very friendly person. I said, "Hello!" to the small Chinese woman and smiled at her. She smiled back and nodded at me. She took out a little container of hand cream and offered me some. I took the cream and said, "Thank you." She said, "Yes, yes," while nodding her head. We were friends. Later on in the trip she took out a bag of dried fruit candy of some sort from her purse and offered it to me. I was very open and took the bag and offered it to my friend like my little Chinese friend was motioning.

My friend declined, but I took a piece of the candy and my new little lady friend joined me. The candy was like some kind of dried fruit covered with what looked powdered sugar. The candy tasted good at first, but then I started to pucker and tear. It was very sour and salty. I did not want to be rude so I turned to the woman and smiled and nodded. She seemed to be liking her piece. I turned to my friend with this panicked, helpless look of despair over what I was going to do with this piece of candy from hell. My friend was laughing and I was trying not to. My friend said, "Swallow it! Swallow it!" I could not swallow it because I had determined that it was most likely a dried out prune and had a pit inside. I tried to ask my Chinese friend if I should swallow it, but of course she did not understand. It was a pit so I decided that I had to spit it out. I took out a piece of paper and put the pit in it. The Chinese woman then took out a Kleenex and put her pit into it. She looked at me and smiled. I took out some Wrigley's Doublemint gum and offered a piece to her, she accepted, and I hurriedly shoved a piece in my mouth to get rid of the awful taste.

INSIGHT:

The polite student paid a price for that polite behavior. However inconvenient that polite attitude might have been in the short term, the long-term benefits of being polite were probably worth it.

Beyond Frustration. I'm glad I can laugh at the situation now, but at the time I was very embarrassed and frustrated that I could even react like this.

We were in Taiwan at the National Palace Museum at the restaurant. No one there could speak English at all, but the menu was in English. There was a huge communication barrier between us and the waiter, and I think I was frustrated about other things before I came to the restaurant. Anyway, I got frustrated and threw the menu at the waiter. He walked away and we decided it was best to leave and go somewhere else.

I acted completely irrationally, and I took my frustration out on this guy I didn't even know for absolutely no reason.

I think stress was involved, also frustration and anger. I think I reached one of the stages in culture shock that describes feeling anxiety and frustration. I think I was really just taking my anger out on him for other things that were going on, and this incident just triggered it. I'm not saying that's right, but it is some sort of explanation.

INSIGHT:

As the student's frustration built up to intolerable levels, it was possible to become unreasonably angry without even knowing why. A small event became the final straw, and the unfortunate local became a target for every real or imagined offense previously experienced by the student.

Rented Scooters. A critical incident happened to my roommates. This critical incident happened in Taiwan, at the Toroko Gorge (Hualuan).

Basically, the five girls had rented motor scooters to go up the gorge and come down the following day. The girls went to return the scooters the following day and the rental workers had noticed some scratches on the two bikes. The rental worker had wanted eight hundred dollars in Taiwan money, which is forty American dollars.

The critical incident that took place happened with my friend who had given the rental worker her passport as a deposit. She did not have forty U.S. dollars to give the worker, and she could not leave without her passport. Plus, there was the language barrier that had caused even more problems. We gave him eight hundred dollars Taiwan money to pay for her scooter, because she needed her passport.

The critical incident that took place with my other friend was whether she should also pay for the moped or not. She claimed that she did not damage the moped, when in reality she had unknowingly scratched it. After deciding to pay for the moped, she grabbed both passports and all the girls ran towards the train station across a huge intersection. The rental worker grabbed her arm and we helped her get out of her reach. The girls continued to run to the train station with a man chasing them as well until the girls got on the train safely. The reason the woman had grabbed her arm was because she only paid for one scooter and not the other one as well.

INSIGHT:
When the student's miscommunication resulted in breaking the law in Taiwan, the situation became very serious. Running away was an extremely risky and generally unacceptable response for dealing with legal problems.

Pot Stickers. Taiwan was the place I decided that I was going to spread my wings of independence. Yes, I was forgetting about organized tours and was heading out as "the Anthropologist." I tended to all the preparations--I read up on the culture (so not to offend), plotted my course on maps of Taipei and of course, wore comfortable tennis shoes. I walked off the Semester at Sea *Universe* with a "That Girl" kind of attitude. Freedom, intelligence and compassion were all in my grasp. I just had to find them successfully.

So I took the express bus to Taipei and got there about lunch time. Since I had missed breakfast, my stomach was speaking the international language of hunger. And quite frankly, it was embarrassing. Seeing a department store, I decided to go to the basement and observe Taiwanese people at lunch and check out my chopstick abilities.

The basement was filled with everything from apple pancakes to yellow tail sushi. I decided to go with something more regional (when in Taipei). So after fifteen minutes of charades and a lot of pointing I was able to sit down with my potstickers for lunch. Delicious! Many times have I eaten those delectable little pork filled noodle packages in the States. . . but with a fork. It took me such a long time signing out chopsticks and since the ship was leaving the next day, I decided a fork was out of the question.

Using chopsticks was part of getting into the "living like a native" so I'd be acting like a native while observing the natives. Perfect! But I was soon to find out that I would be observed by the natives while looking like a tourist wanna-be fool. You see, those potstickers were slippery little suckers. And the time that they remained in my chopsticks was less than the time that it took from my plate to my mouth. After biting half, the other half would slide out of my mouth, and after skidding across the table, it would hit the floor.

Each time my eyes would slowly roll up to see who was watching. For the first three, I was lucky. No one watched as I sat in silent hungry humiliation. But by this time the basement was filling up with what looked like high school students; they were obviously not much younger than my nineteen year old self.

I decided to try to eat quickly since it was getting late and I was not getting very much accomplished. As I worked on picking up my fourth potsticker, a group of boys set their books down on the table catty-corner from mine. They walked towards me and I tried to blend in with all of the other lunch-time eaters. Unfortunately, I tried stuffing the whole thing in my mouth. The ritual began again. It gingerly bounced off of my lower lip, propelling droplets of soy onto my white shirt, before ricocheting off my arm and onto the floor. Afraid to look up, I kept my head low and rolled my eyes up. They met with the eyes of one boy, the rest had turned away. I couldn't help but blush and laugh. He smiled broadly and walked off.

"Whew," I thought to myself, "they're gone. Now I'll just eat my last few quickly with my fingers and be out of here before they come back." I was content that whole ordeal was over. Or so I thought. A few moments later a styrofoam Chinese soup spoon came over my shoulder and was placed on my tray. I looked up and it was the boy!

I didn't know what to say! I was totally confused. First, I thought, "How nice. He's just helping me out." And then I thought, "Jerk, I'm trying my best to assimilate to their culture and by doing this he's saying, 'Yeah, I don't think so tourist.'" Then I tried to figure out what I'd do if someone was having trouble eating. I thought if it was me I would probably let it go, and not embarrass the poor tourist.

INSIGHT:

The student wanted to fit into Chinese culture and not be obvious, but her skill with chopsticks made this difficult. The boy offering a spoon may have been trying to help, but his offer was received as embarrassing.

Japan

Train Tickets. Two of my friends and I bought bullet train tickets in a travel agent's office in Kobe on the 21st of April. We thought we were purchasing three round trip tickets; Kobe to Tokyo and Tokyo to Kobe with no set date. It took a while to purchase our tickets due to the clerk's broken English. After a while we found out the total cost would be $206.00 per person. We laid down our credit cards and signed away. Little did we know we had to buy a reserved seat for $40.00 before we got on our return train to confirm our tickets. We arrived in Tokyo with ease but our return ride was hell.

We had to take several trains from my friend's apartment in Tokyo in order to catch the bullet train in the Tokyo station. We finally arrived at Tokyo station around 12:50 p.m.--just in time to catch the 1:07 p.m. bullet train. We found a Japanese man who spoke English and he directed us to the correct express bullet train headed for Kobe. We were relieved to find this man because if we did not make the 1:07 p.m. train then we would miss the Semester at Sea ship departure. We were already late. We got on the train with a sigh of relief--"We've made it."

Halfway through the voyage the attendant came around to check our tickets. There was a problem. We did not buy our reserve return seats to complete the purchase of our ticket. We honestly had no idea that this was necessary. The authorities called the police to get on the train at the next stop. They thought that we were trying to pull a complete scam. The police instructed us to go to the ticket office in Kobe and purchase the rest of our tickets. We had no problem with paying the difference we owed but we did not have the time to go to the office. We needed to pay now because it was already 4:15 and we were still on the bullet train. We had to get to the boat as soon as possible because it could set sail at anytime. We could very well miss the boat. When we got off the train, thinking of the time only, we tried to make a run for it. The authorities caught us and brought us to a nearby office where we could pay what we owed. When we arrived at the ship our bags were packed, the telephone lines were disconnected, and the captain was ready to sail. If we had been ten minutes later we would have missed the boat.

INSIGHT:

The students assumed they had followed the rules in buying their return tickets to Kobe. They also assumed they could wait until the last minute and still make the ship before departure. When caught by the police they assumed they could talk their way out or run away, tempting fate with each false assumption.

The Japan Railway Pass from Hell. The first night in Japan I lost my purse and my camera. I was bummed! In my purse I had four rolls of used film, $300.00, my identification, and my Japan Railway Pass. Now the rail passes are not, by any means, cheap. For some odd reason before I went out that night I took my passport out of my purse and in my passport was my rail pass receipt. I figured that since I had my receipt that would prove that I had once had a rail pass and I could, therefore, get a new one. How wrong I was!

We left for the rail station at 9:30 on the last day. Our train was scheduled to leave at 10:20. I went to an information desk and told the guy how my purse was stolen and that my rail pass was gone.

"Sir, how can I get a new rail pass, here is my receipt and my passport. Is it possible?"

He looked at me with a look of confusion and doubt. "Ah, you must go to ticket desk--that way," he stuttered. His English was not very clear.

He was kind enough to take me to the place where I needed to go. The man at the ticket counter was so rude, and he refused to give me a new pass. By this time, I was hysterical. I didn't think that I was going to make it back to the boat.

"I'm sorry Miss, but you have already used the pass. You must buy a new one."

"But I have already paid $300.00 for the one I had," I screamed.

"I am sorry. I can't help you."

I'm sure I used some vulgar language at this point, because I was so delirious from lack of sleep.

INSIGHT:

The student who lost her Japan Railway Pass was unable to see her situation from the viewpoint of the ticket seller who had to follow the rules, and consequently she made an already bad situation worse for herself and the others around her.

Going to a Sushi Bar. I was tired and thirsty, not to mention a little bit sick of being ripped off in Japanese restaurants. I had two hours to kill before my friends arrived and I felt like spending it in a small sushi bar. (I had heard these were inexpensive.)

As I entered, after going down a flight of stairs, I was much relieved to find a full, but quiet atmosphere. I seated myself, as seemed to be the custom, and immediately the waiter approached. I smiled, he did not. Oh boy, here we go again. He told me, in so many words, that I had to leave. "Why?" I asked. That did not sit well with me. I got mad and pointed to one or two empty tables. He still said I had to leave. Fine, I left and went to the next, which was virtually empty. "You have to leave, we are full," said the manager. Now I got angry. What was with these people? What is their problem? And then I knew. I am an American and they do not want me in their restaurants because of it. I could not believe it. I had heard of this, but never thought it would happen to me--a well off white male. I felt anger and indignity being asked to leave. I also had some startling realizations about racism and what it must be like on a much broader scale, especially in my own country.

INSIGHT:
Being blatantly discriminated against was apparently a new experience for the well-off white male student. The Japanese bar managers did not need to explain why they excluded him nor did they defend their decision against his arguments. This no doubt increased the student's frustration.

Americans Find Bank Hours Ridiculous. After the scene in the travel agency, we hurried over to the bank before it closed at 3:00 p.m. It was about ten of three and the teller was nice enough to let my roommate and me exchange our traveller's checks for yen. After giving our passport and checks to her, we sat down and waited for it to be processed. We were the last people she was going to help before closing. At about 2:55, five Semester at Sea students came running into the office making a huge ruckus. The lady nicely told them that they were closing and that she could not help them. The students became loud and obnoxious saying, "I can't believe you close at 3:00! In the United States the banks close at 5:00." My roommate and I could not believe it. I just sat there thinking, "These people represent college students in the United States? I sure hope the Japanese don't think we all act like this." I just wanted to get up and shake them, "This is Japan you idiots--not the United States!!!" The teller was so overwhelmed that in the end she agreed to help them, probably just to get them out of her hair!

INSIGHT:
The frustrated students became very intolerant of local banking rules which seemed inconvenient. It was not difficult to understand why the locals might stereotype all Americans as difficult to deal with after a few bad experiences with these students.

Succeeding in the Japan Rail Office. After arriving in Kobe, most of the students who had purchased a Japan Rail Pass headed over to the Sannomiya Station to turn in their vouchers. My friends and I arrived at the travel office and beat the rush of Semester at Sea students. We took a number, stood back, and waited our turn. It was an easy system and simple to follow. After about five minutes of waiting a herd of students came crashing through the door loudly asking what they needed to do. I told many of them, "You just take a number and wait your turn." In the period of about three minutes the travel office was packed with other Semester at Sea students who were impatient and unwilling to follow the system of taking a number. At this point I was extremely embarrassed by the behavior of my fellow students. How hard could it be to just take a number and wait your turn? Well, it must have been pretty difficult because the Japanese travel agents turned off the number counter and made all of the Semester at Sea students get in a line. I'm so glad our number was one of the last ones called! All the bitching and moaning of other Semester at Sea students was absolutely ridiculous because the system, in my opinion, was very efficient and simple to follow.

I was shocked at the behavior of my fellow Semester at Sea students! It opened my eyes and made me understand why foreign countries view "the Ugly American tourist" the way they do.

INSIGHT:
It was easy for the frustrated students to become so self-centered that the local rules were disregarded. While some misunderstandings in a foreign culture are unavoidable, other behaviors were so obviously inappropriate that they could and should be avoided.

Bombarding the Tourist. It had been a very long morning. We got an early start and took the train to Kyoto to do some heavy duty sightseeing. We had already been to various tourist spots, and the Nijo Castle was going to be our last stop of the morning. Of course there were tons of uniformed schoolchildren, as there were every other place we had been. The Nijo Castle had some really beautiful gardens, and since it was cherry blossom season they were even prettier. Therefore, we spent a lot of time walking through the gardens taking pictures and even posing for an occasional picture with some of the children. Well, around 1:00 our stomachs started growling and our feet were aching, so we decided it was time to go. We got about half way out when a group of about ten schoolchildren came up to us and asked in their broken

English if we would pose for a picture with them. "Sure thing, no problem," we said, we even took a few also. The next thing we know about fifty more students and a few of their teachers were gathering around us to take pictures and have us fill out their questionnaires. We were not too thrilled about this, after all we were really very tired--among other things. We were nice and smiled big for the pictures, promising each other if more come over we will just kindly walk away or not make any more eye contact with them. Anyway, about every other one was holding a questionnaire, so we grabbed one, filled it out, smiled, and walked away.

I feel that it did teach me something (whether true or false) about the Japanese people though. Just from watching these schoolchildren, by the way they acted towards us made me believe that they are selfish. I know that's harsh and probably inaccurate, but regardless that's the impression I was given. To be more specific, my friends and I wanted to ask a group of children if they could take a picture of us, and when I tried to get their attention they ignored me. Yes, I realize they probably are shy. Well, two seconds later one of the girls whose attention I was trying to get came over because she wanted to take a picture with us.

I feel like I'm stereotyping Japanese people, and I don't like that. I can't put into words what's in my head about describing these people except for the term "selfish," which I use very lightly because it's not done in spite. They just seem to be very closed off people unless they want something.

INSIGHT:

The student was accustomed to looking at the local people, but now the students themselves had become the objects of local curiosity. That role reversal can became uncomfortable for the students. When the situation became uncomfortable, it was easy for the student to view the Japanese as "selfish," which may or may not be true.

Club Afrika. During my five days in Japan, we two female students encountered something that made us very uncomfortable and almost angry. A friend and I were walking down a downtown street in Kyoto. It was about 10:00 p.m. and we were looking for a club called Afrika. We were having difficulty finding someone who spoke English who could point us in the right direction. Finally after about a half hour of roaming we stumbled upon two Japanese girls of about twenty-one. We saw them and asked them if they spoke English. They replied that they did. We asked them if they could tell us where the club was, and they pointed down the street and were trying to explain in "bits and pieces" in English where to turn to find the right street. When they saw that we did not understand their directions they started to walk in the direction of the club and motioned for us to follow.

We thanked them for showing us the way and introduced ourselves. They told us their names, Fumi and Ikomi, and expressed to us that it was no problem and could they join us when we got to the club. I was very happy that they'd invited themselves to join us, as I was eager to interact with Japanese youths. However, once the girls got into the club with us my attitude changed.

Fumi and Ikomi sat with us at a small table in the crowded club. There were many people dancing and talking, a majority were Japanese. The two girls engaged us in conversation and finally asked if we wanted a drink. We said yes and each ordered a beer. When the waiter came up with the bill for four beers (one for each of us) the girls, instead of offering us money for their portion of the bill, pointed the waiter in our direction and said in Japanese, "They will pay for it." We were offended that not only did they assume that we were paying for their drinks, but that they rudely spoke their assumption in Japanese to the waiter. Grudgingly, we paid for the four drinks and went on talking to the girls who were otherwise very nice.

When the time came for the next round Fumi asked me, "Do you want to buy us another beer now?" I was very surprised at her audacity and asked, "Buy you another beer? We paid for the last round." She and Ikomi giggled and nudged one another. This action angered me and I asked what was so funny. The girls continued to laugh and nudge each other. Finally, we told them, "It was nice talking to you but we really should be getting back." Ikomi said, as we got up to leave, "We show you the way here, you pay for us." I was shocked to hear this, I thought that they were simply nice girls who were eager to help foreigners. Obviously what I thought and what really was the case were two entirely different things. We didn't want to stir things up at the club, especially since it seemed that they knew quite a few people there. I said, "Yes, you showed us the way here and we bought you a drink. Now we're leaving." She and I left the club.

As we walked back to our ryokan we talked about the night's incident and came to the conclusion that perhaps it was customary for people to do something for someone in return for a favor. I was personally angered however, whether or not this is the custom. The girls seemed to find it quite funny that we paid their bar bill without question and seemed to be testing us to see if we'd "fall for it" a second time.

INSIGHT:
Requesting a favor from the two Japanese women resulted in unexpected obligations to exchange favors. Accepting something of value from the Japanese women required giving something of value in return. This expectation by the Japanese women need not necessarily indicate that they were exploiting the traveller.

No Americans Allowed. "Well," she began by giving me a shut-your-face look, "The three of us were going into this one restaurant for dinner and they wouldn't let us in."

She paused, and I was about to ask her what happened when I saw her expression change. She was both hurt and angered by the experience, so I decided not to push for the rest of the story.

"One of us went in first," she continued, "and this guy inside, the one who welcomes people, grabbed him by the shoulders and threw him out. The rest of us didn't even go in."

"How come he wouldn't let you guys go in?" my friend asked.

"Because we were Americans." I was incredulous. The Japanese, so far as I'd seen, were the most polite and accommodating individuals. There was no way that they were kicked out of a restaurant for their race.

"There must have been some other reason," I quipped.

"Yeah," one of us said, "It must have been your long hair or something."

"But we were all kicked out."

"How were you guys dressed?" I asked. I just refused to believe her story was true. Her reasoning was correct. The Japanese could not have committed such an atrocity.

"Like normal," she admitted, "in jeans, T-shirt, tennis shoes--like what I'm wearing now."

"So y'all were shabbily dressed," I concluded.

"That must be it too," one of us added. "You must not have been presentable enough. They didn't deny you entrance because you were Americans."

"What do you mean we were 'shabbily dressed?' We were not!"

"Have you seen the people in this place? They are always dressed immaculately. What we consider well dressed in the States is still slovenly here."

"No, that wasn't it," she insisted. "He said 'No Americans!'"

"He said that?"

"Yes, he did." I still couldn't believe it. Bigotry was not an uncommon thing for me. I encountered it often living in California. It just seemed so uncharacteristic of the people and an antithesis to what I'd seen.

"Did you say anything to him?"

"No. What could we say? We just left." I later learned that anti-American sentiments were being promoted in the restaurant. They were showing videos of Americans smashing Japanese cars on the television monitors. It was an economic war indeed.

There was nothing they could have said. The problem was between the governments and not the individual people. The waiter's problem was not with them in particular, rather what they represented--the enemy.

INSIGHT:

Not all local persons liked and welcomed Americans. It was both embarrassing and frustrating for the students to encounter rejection for being

American. Just as the students stereotyped locals, the locals were likely to stereotype the students also.

Being Unable to Get a Cab Home. After being in Tokyo one night my friends and I decided to get a cab back to our hotel. We went to the taxi station nearby and showed the piece of paper with the name of our hotel written in Japanese to the cab driver. He shook his head, "No" and kept saying, "Gaijin" and then pulled forward. The same exact thing happened as we tried to hail two more cabs. Within one minute we had been turned down three times, and the subways were no longer running, or there was some big complications. This businessman who spoke English told us that "gaijin" means foreigner and that a lot of Japanese feel hostility towards foreigners. He offered to hail us a cab and was successful on the second try.

My two friends were absolutely livid at the fact that we couldn't even get a cab to our hotel. One of them was quite drunk and was so mad she started yelling profanities at the third driver, and saying how much the Japanese owed to Americans.

I was fully embarrassed by her outburst in the middle of Tokyo, and all the Japanese who were watching. I felt so stupid and self conscious that we were having all these problems. I felt so discriminated against and believed that the Japanese really hated us. I felt as close to being a black in Alabama during the 1960s as I will ever feel. I kept my frustrations under control and was the only one who would talk to the businessman. I really learned what it felt like to be on the other side of discrimination for once and did not like it.

I felt very threatened by this discrimination--even more so because I couldn't understand a word that anyone said, and I felt like they were all talking about us.

INSIGHT:
The taxi driver who had encountered embarrassing situations with other foreigners was likely to avoid future embarrassment by not providing services to foreigners. By becoming angry at this rejection, the students only reinforced the rejecting behavior by the cab drivers and demonstrated why foreigners should be avoided.

Sushi Bars. I found Japan to be a great experience. I met many friendly, helpful people. As in any country there are also those people who aren't so friendly.

A friend and I were walking the streets of Kobe the first night. It was around 9:00 p.m., and there were a lot of people wandering around. We decided that we wanted to sample traditional Japanese food. We noticed a lot of small restaurants were people sat on stools in bar style. The cook never had to walk out of the kitchen, because it was in the middle of the bar. It looked like one of these bars would be a good choice for typical Japanese food, so we decided to venture into one.

I stuck my head through the door, saw two empty seats, and walked in. As soon as I walked through the door a man, presumably the manager, quickly walked towards me. He was excitedly talking in Japanese, of course I couldn't comprehend a word he was saying. I thought he was excited to see a foreigner and got up to welcome us in his restaurant. So I put my hand out to shake his--basically trying to be friendly. He came right up to me, and to my surprise, pushed my hand away. He then physically began to push me out the door while yelling at me in Japanese. The only words of English that I could make out were, "Only Japanese."

Everything happened so quickly, before I knew it I was back in the street. The manager was still standing at the door yelling at us in Japanese. I was truly befuddled by the whole incident. I couldn't understand why he didn't want us in his restaurant. I was dressed nicely, I wasn't rude, and I was ready to spend money in his place. I later found out that the same incident happened to many other students. When I asked a Japanese friend why I wasn't allowed in, he said it was most likely racism. It surprised me that in such a modern society there was such blatant racism. Then again, I think about home and there are definitely places I wouldn't try entering. Racism is prevalent in every society, it's sad, but reality. Sometimes you don't realize where it exists, even after it hits you in the face.

INSIGHT:

It was embarrassing for the student to be refused service and discriminated against. However discrimination is a fact of life in many cultures, and it was important for students to learn how to deal with it.

CONCLUSION

The third stage of culture shock deals with the beginning of reintegration. The students were able to move beyond self-blame toward a more balanced perspective. The students were no longer accepting all the blame and fault for misunderstanding but rather were putting the blame and fault on the locals. In both stage two and stage three there is a polarized good/bad, right/wrong way of thinking about the problems they encounter.

As indicated in the review of research literature on the U-curve hypothesis, some research suggests that persons seldom get beyond this third stage in their accommodation of an unfamiliar culture, suggesting that a backward J-curve would more appropriately describe the typical adjustment process. Some of the students were indeed stuck in this third stage of hostility toward unfamiliar cultures as being consistently inferior to the more familiar back-home cultures. Other students seemed able to move beyond fault finding and fixing blame for misunderstandings either on themselves or on the hosts. Most, if not all, students displayed some brief examples of exaggerated hostility toward the host culture in the seventy-nine critical incidents describing this third stage.

The first theme of critical incidents applies many of the self-derogatory labels from the second stage to the host culture. The host culture was described as "vulnerable, frustrated, rigid, complaining, backward, unsuccessful, irrational, dumb, naive, inefficient, insensitive, ambiguous, unclear, and generally inadequate."

A second theme described the host cultures in a more malicious way as being deliberately hurtful. In this theme the students described the host culture as "patronizing, hurtful, extorting, unsafe, unfriendly, pretending, dangerous, racist, unsympathetic, destructive, inappropriate, unjust, authoritarian, manipulative, intimidating, opportunistic, judgmental, disrespectful, unfair, untruthful, aggressive, impatient, cynical, sarcastic, impolite, intolerable, insulting, offensive, hostile, tricky, prejudiced, and exclusionary."

A third theme described how the students in stage three saw themselves. In this theme, the students described themselves as "unlucky, resentful, exploited, angry, dissatisfied, bitter, misunderstood, insulted, humiliated, stereotyped, a harvested crop, disappointed, trapped, ripped off, and having to defend themselves for their own protection."

Students going through the third stage of culture shock were hard to be around and would tend to "flare" into anger with little provocation. The students were beginning to reintegrate their identity to incorporate aspects of their back-home and the new host cultures, but it was a painful process. In the short term of this voyage, there was not always enough time for students to grow out of this third-stage resentment. As the voyage moved from one country to another, the students were often kept off balance by having to apply what they learned from one culture to an entirely different, new culture. Some, if not all, of the students were able to move toward a more balanced perspective where both their own culture and the host culture were assigned some responsibility for the good or bad things that happened. The critical incidents describing this more balanced perspective are covered in the next two chapters.

6

The Autonomy Stage

INTRODUCTION

The persons who emerge from the detachment of stage one, the self-blame of stage two, and the hostility of stage three are in a position to build a new perspective between their former identity and the new host culture. The person begins to establish an objective, balanced, and impartial view of the whole situation. It is now possible to experience both the positive and the negative aspects of the host culture situation. As in previous stages, it is likely that the individual will regress to earlier stages from time to time but will gradually evolve toward a synthesis.

There is a new sensitivity resulting in new skills and understandings about the host culture and the person's own identity. The need for defensiveness is diminished as the host culture is perceived as less deliberately--or malevolently --hostile. The person is now able to move into new situations with greater awareness of self and others. The person demonstrates an increased competence, and an ability to relax and enjoy the host culture, and is able to articulate this new understanding to others. Sometimes the person overestimates the degree of his or her own adjustment and considers himself or herself an "expert" on the host culture. The individual may overestimate the degree of his or her own understanding in this newly discovered autonomy. However, the individual is now a more fully functioning person and is less dependent on others. The person can see himself or herself as both an insider in some areas and still an outsider in other areas. It is easier to cope effectively even though imperfectly in the host culture. Although the person now has the insight to understand the host culture, he or she may not yet have the ability to act in the most appropriate ways.

The person going through stage four will accurately perceive differences and similarities between the old and new ways as legitimate. The emotions of this stage tend toward self-assurance, a more relaxed attitude, increased warmth in one's relationships to others, and an ability for empathic caring. The behaviors that go along with this stage are typically independent decision making, a sense of being in control, a self-image as an "old hand" in the host culture, a sense of credibility and increased self-confidence in making the right decisions. The person interprets himself or herself as able to negotiate most new and different situations in the host culture with these new-found skills and expects to survive new experiences with greater self-assurance.

Student authors who describe incidents classified as examples of the autonomy stage will be aware of what needs to be done but perhaps not yet be able to act on that awareness. They will typically travel in smaller groups in the host culture and be more tolerant of themselves as well as of host culture people. They have become both the teacher and the student in their interpretations and analysis of the new situation.

CRITICAL INCIDENTS

Venezuela

Trying to Go to Dinner in Venezuela. A group of three of us, all Semester at Sea students, decided to go to dinner in La Guaira. More people were to meet us later in town after they had finished with the student reception. All of us were girls and were concerned about safety. I was the only one of the group who spoke Spanish. We were under the impression that La Guaira was only a twenty minute walk, but decided that it was best to get a taxi because it was dark.

We walked out the entrance of the port building and could not get a taxi. We decided that the best thing to do would be to walk further down the road that led to the main road into La Guaira. One of the girls was particularly cautious and frightened. She wanted to turn back because the people and area scared her.

There was what appeared to be a tour bus close by with a lady who was in charge of the group. The scared girl said, "Ask her if she can speak English. Ask her if she speaks English!" I asked, and the woman looked at me and replied in Spanish. I then proceeded to ask her where we could get a taxi. She answered, and then I translated for the other two. Then, again in Spanish, I asked her if we needed to be careful. Then to double check I rephrased and asked if it was dangerous. Both times the woman replied that it was safe and that a taxi would be along soon if we walked to the end of the entrance road.

I trusted this woman because I assumed she was from the area and knew what she was talking about. The girl persisted that she was scared. She wanted us to give up our plans of going to dinner and return to the ship and eat. I kept reassuring her that we were safe and not to worry. The strange surroundings and the "foreign" language made her very frightened. Finally she agreed to continue with our plans, after I reassured her over and over that the woman said it was fine for us to be in the area.

INSIGHT:

The "strange surroundings and language" made the short trip from the port to the village very frightening for the student who did not speak Spanish. Reassurance by the Spanish-speaking student and other locals did little to reduce the student's fear and anxiety. The Spanish-speaking student experienced the same situation with little fear or anxiety.

Returning the Enthusiastic Greeting. This critical incident took place at the welcome reception in Venezuela. The bus ride took about an hour and all of the students from Semester at Sea were waiting in nervous anticipation for our first experience with students from another country and culture. I don't really know what I was expecting when we arrived but I was in for a delightful surprise. When the buses pulled up to the university, all of the Venezuelan students had formed two lines that stretched up to the entrance of the reception. They were clapping and calling out greetings as I passed through their "receiving" line. From the first moment that I stepped from the bus, with the help of a Venezuelan student, until I reached the reception I had said hello and shaken hands with several friendly and eager students. As you walked through them they would reach out their hands to shake and offer you a smile. They were all so excited to meet and talk with students from the United States. After all of the students from Semester at Sea were seated inside, the Venezuelan students hurried in to find seats at the tables where we were spread out. This all took place within the period of about ten minutes. If you put a number on it there were about seventy-five to one hundred Venezuelan students and about one hundred to one hundred twenty-five students from Semester at Sea. I was surprised at how excited the Venezuelan students were and walked through them in a real sort of daze. I, of course, returned the introduction and greeting, but it took me a couple of minutes to take it all in. The major cross-cultural skill involved here was greeting one another. Greetings ranged from a simple smile, a handshake, to a verbal hello. This was a great learning experience that was valuable to attain in the beginning of the voyage. The biggest lesson that I learned from just the first forty-five minutes of the reception was that you cannot underestimate the willingness of another culture. The Venezuelan students were so willing to share themselves and their lives with us even for such a brief period of time.

INSIGHT:

Because the student had not done anything to earn gratitude from Venezuelan students it was overwhelming to experience the Venezuelans' spontaneous generosity. The student may never repay or return the hosts' enthusiastic gesture but may pass that generosity on to other locals elsewhere when the American students become hosts.

A Dance with Reynaldo. This critical incident took place on the first night that I spent in Venezuela. I was at the welcome reception at Simon Bolivar University, and unfortunately I was placed at a dinner table with all Semester at Sea students. This was a little disappointing because I had gone to the reception with hopes of meeting and interacting with many Venezuelan students. After the dinner the band began to play and one male Venezuelan student approached me and asked me to dance. I was quite unsure of whether or not to accept the offer. I knew no traditional Venezuelan dances, and I was not accustomed to dancing with strangers. Furthermore, the Venezuelan student had not introduced himself to me before extending the offer and, therefore, the situation was even more foreign to me.

I did choose to accept the invitation, and after a few fun dances I learned that my partner's name was Reynaldo. Reynaldo and I spent the rest of the evening chatting about our lives, and at the end of the night we exchanged addresses and promised to keep in touch.

INSIGHT:
By travelling in a group, the American students had a safe context for them to meet local students with a minimum of awkwardness and embarrassment. New friendships were possible that would be much more difficult if travelling alone.

A New Friend. I attended the university welcome reception in La Guaira, Venezuela, and met two young men from Simon Bolivar University. My friend and I ate dinner with them and danced with them some. We decided to leave on the early bus back to the ship because we were tired. As we were boarding the bus, one of the young men, Vitor, asked if he could show us around Caracas the next day. We agreed to meet him at 1:00 p.m. in the Plaza Bolivar. Then we returned to the ship.

The next day we met Vitor, and the three of us had a very dull afternoon. My friend and I were tired and didn't feel like talking much. Vitor took us by metro, bus, and foot to a very modern shopping center--a far cry from the markets we had hoped to visit. Our boredom was compounded by the fact that most of the stores were closed because it was a Sunday.

After several hours of small talk, my friend and I decided to leave for the ship. As we got ready to board a bus back to La Guaira, my critical incident occurred: Vitor told my friend and me that he would miss us. Then he told me that he wanted to give me something, and that I had to accept it. I agreed, thinking he would give me a small figurine like the one I had given a friend of mine the moment before. But instead, he removed a crucifix from around his neck and put it around mine. Then he told me I couldn't give it back, handed me a note (which I later read), and left me standing by the bus to La Guaira with his crucifix around my neck. The crucifix was obviously intended to be very meaningful in a romantic sense. I felt it was inappropriate for me to accept it, but I did so anyway. It was a decision that I made within a matter of three or four seconds, but I still feel that it was the only thing I could have done.

INSIGHT:

The Venezuelan was spontaneously trying to express how meaningful his contact with the American student had been. The American student was unfamiliar with the Venezuelan rules of giftgiving so it was hard for her to know what was appropriate.

Canamia, Venezuela. The circumstances appeared perfectly normal. A group of fifteen young people were sitting at a bar being loud, drinking beer, and playing games. But the beer wasn't Coors, the bartender didn't speak English, and everyone reeked of mosquito repellant. Our tour guide, George, informed us that he was up to something. Ten minutes later George and seven other Venezuelans pulled up behind the bar in a zebra striped passenger trolley, which was pulled by an old green tractor. It was about this time that it occurred to me that I was in the middle of the rain forest with fourteen people who I had just met that day, and I was about to go for a joy ride with them and eight very excited Venezuelans. George, I trusted, he had safely led us from La Guaira to Canamia in a very professional manner. but it was 11:30 at night and we had been very generous in buying George cocktails.

If I would have had more time to think about the situation I would have graciously refused, but I am glad I went along. We travelled along a dusty road for fifteen minutes then hiked through the jungle to one of the most beautiful beaches I've ever seen. We built a huge bonfire, and the Venezuelans proceeded to teach us traditional folk songs until the sun rose. When I think about the experience I would have missed if I had stayed at the camp, I worry about what other cultural experiences are ruined by uncertainty.

When we left Canamia I had learned four Venezuelan folk songs, but more importantly I realized the incredible amount of pride that the Venezuelans have for their country. They take pride in their traditions and history. Another aspect of their ethnographic culture was portrayed as we were asked to remain silent on the way home because we had to pass a church. The Venezuelans love to have a good time and were very eager to make us happy, but everything was done in moderation and they made it very clear to us what was to be respected.

INSIGHT:

Many of the best experiences the students had happened by accident. It was important to be open to spontaneous opportunities that were not planned or rehearsed. The excitement of genuine sharing in an otherwise private celebration with a group of Venezuelans created a very special and memorable experience with the local culture.

The Rules of Etiquette. Throughout my stay in Venezuela I encountered many new sights, sounds, and experiences. Because I had made an effort to study the Venezuelan culture before entering the country, I was in many ways prepared for the existing cultural differences I inevitably experienced. However, one particular incident that occurred the first day of our visit made me question the Venezuelan rules of etiquette and gift giving.

The incident occurred when I was travelling through Caracas with my two fellow Semester at Sea girlfriends. We had been touring around seeing the sights and had decided to sit down to take a short breather. One of my two friends decided she wanted a picture and politely asked a young man sitting alone beside us to take one if he could. He spoke and understood English surprisingly well and afterwards initiated conversation with us. Though there was an obvious language barrier, we were able to successfully address a broad range of topics. The young man was a university student as well and seemed genuinely interested in the American culture and way of life.

We spoke for about one hour when my friends and I decided it was time for us to leave and meet our other friends at the hotel across the street. As we discussed our plans, our newfound Venezuelan friend pulled out from his pocket three coins, which he individually placed in each of our hands. He told us that the government had decided to stop making that particular sized coin because it was simply too small. So the ones already distributed within the public were the last ones left. I was incredibly touched by his generosity and thanked him profusely.

We all got up to leave and then realized we still had our return tickets for the Metro subway that we would not be able to use, so we handed them to Simon and told him that we wanted him to have them since they would be of no use to us now. He looked at us with a puzzled and somewhat insulted expression. We continued to try to explain ourselves, but the expression remained fixed upon his face. Unfortunately, we then left each other at the corner with a sort of abrupt and uncomfortable goodbye.

INSIGHT:
The gifts of caring were symbolic of special positive feelings toward the students. Accepting the special coins from the young Venezuelan implied an obligation and required an appropriate response in return from the students. By giving left-over tokens the students probably insulted the young man. It was important for the student to think through the implications of giving an appropriate gift from the Venezuelan's viewpoint before giving it.

Making Friends. Three of my girlfriends and myself decided to make a day trip into the city of Caracas, Venezuela. As none of us had previously visited the city while we were in port, everything about our visit was to be foreign to us.

Once we arrived safely in the city after a treacherous cab ride, we began to walk. We realized we were in a large South American city not knowing where in the city we were, where we were going or what we wanted to do. With those things in mind, all of our preconceived ideas about how dangerous the city is, that it is not a place for women, the theft, the poverty, the language barrier, and all the other trivial nuances about a foreign country weighed heavily on all of our minds.

As four blond-haired, California girls made our way through the busy streets of Central Caracas, we were terrified to look at anyone the "wrong" way, talk to anybody or be friendly for that matter. As we walked, I quickly looked around the area to see at least the neighborhood we were in. I'm sure we appeared to be four "gringas" who didn't know anything concerning being in a large, foreign city, especially one in South America. Suddenly I felt a hand on my shoulder and I jerked powerfully around, and to my surprise I saw two astonished and surprised men. They were university students as well, or at least appeared to be, and they just smiled at us. Both of them spoke fairly good broken English so we were able to communicate. They introduced themselves as Andre and Isaac and offered to show us around as we appeared lost. However naive we might have been, we accepted their offer and went with them.

We walked a long way through the city, as both pointed out particular points of interest, but we kept walking until we were out of the center of Caracas. Andre and Isaac were about to orient us with the Caracas that tourists don't care to see--they took us to their homes. Their neighborhood was full of small, dirty children and teenagers who were intrigued by the blonde, well-dressed, clean, American tourists in their "barrio." Both of them lived in "ranchitos," as the Venezuelans call them, which were government houses for the lower-income families of Venezuela. Andre invited us into his home, introduced us to his mother and six younger siblings who all graciously accepted us into his domicile. The two-room home was poorly lit, but furnished with three queen size mattresses on the floor, and a table, and nine book crates scattered the main room. I later learned they used them as chairs. It was the most incredible experience to have had complete strangers invite us into their home, that not many would be proud to call it theirs, and communicate openly. They were so interested in learning about the political and economic situation in the United States, the family structure, our morals and our religion.

I find it very interesting to realize now that I felt closer to Andre and Isaac in the four hours we were together than I do towards friends of two years.

INSIGHT:

It took courage for the students to get lost deliberately in Caracas. The many real and imagined dangers were outweighed by the opportunity to meet Venezuelans on their own turf, outside the tourist areas. Being invited into a Venezuelan home was a good sign of having survived a crucial test in the eyes of the Venezuelans and having received a passing grade.

Are You American? While in Venezuela, I went to a bar called Weekends and met two Venezuelan guys: Boris and Jon. As I started to talk to them I had the feeling that they did not like Americans too much. The first question they asked was, "Are you American?" When I told them I was they had a negative facial expression, looked at each other, and then giggled. About to leave the scene, I decided to stick around, ask what they thought about "us," and was ready to change their minds.

It was about 9:00 p.m. and it seemed as though Jon and Boris had a couple of drinks. They weren't drunk, but they seemed to be really relaxed--then again, so was I. (That's probably why I didn't leave.) I was trying to speak Spanish to them, but they didn't want to converse in their language, rather we spoke English. I asked what they thought of Americans, and Boris replied with a hand gesture meaning "so-so." They both had the same vision of Americans because they spoke fluently. They told me that Americans are narrow-minded because everywhere that an American goes they expect everybody to speak English. Well, when I thought about it I couldn't disagree more with them. However, I replied by saying I tried to speak Spanish. I can speak Spanish well, not fluently, but well, but they wouldn't let me. They told me I was different, and suddenly I got the feeling that they started to enjoy our debate, and me. Then they said that Americans go places and always stick together. They pointed to about fifteen students on Semester at Sea that were all in a corner by themselves. Again, they told me that I was different. I agreed with Boris and Jon in the fact that Americans as a whole are uncultured. I told them that I want to live in a Spanish speaking country so I could learn the language fluently. They thought that was great, and the conversation had a totally positive tone to it at this point. Now, for the third time, they told me I was different than most Americans.

INSIGHT:
It was easy for the student to spend time with persons who agreed with them and shared the American student's perspective. It was more difficult but educationally more valuable to learn from Venezuelans whose perspective was different and who did not necessarily agree with the student.

Brazil

Psychology of Small Groups. In Salvador, I met a very nice young man named Sam. Sam was very friendly with my friends and me, and we decided to go out one day. We weren't exactly sure where we wanted to go, but we got on a bus that headed to the main bus station. When we got to the station we looked around and decided that because of the Carnival preparations and the start of summer that we would find somewhere not crowded to go to. However, it was almost noon and we were all very hungry, so Sam suggested that we go to the mall to get a bite to eat. We agreed.

When we got to the food court place in the mall, Sam asked us what type of food we wanted to eat. We said Bahian (local food of course), so he brought us to a Bahian restaurant with a buffet counter. Everyone turned to me, giving me the we-can't-eat-this-because-we'll-get-sick-and-you-explain-it-to-him look.

At this point I had to decide if I was going to say anything. The food looked hot (there was steam), and I certainly didn't want to offend Sam by saying we didn't want to eat in the place he chose. However, I did say that I didn't think it would be a good idea to eat there and tried to explain why. He did not understand, and I think he was somewhat offended, but we eventually ate somewhere else.

INSIGHT:
It was difficult for the student to know how much risk to take when eating local food. Avoiding all local food costs the opportunity of potential friendships with Brazilians and eating everything indiscriminately could result in temporary illness. Food was very important in Brazilian culture and rejecting their food was a symbolic way of rejecting their culture and them personally.

Communicating with a Foreigner. This event occurred on an airplane on the way from Salvador, Brazil, to Manaus. About one hundred Semester at Sea students were on board en route to the Amazon. It was going to be a nine-hour flight. Only about three hours had gone by when a man, about age thirty-five, boarded the plane at one of the five stopovers and sat next to me. He smiled and I smiled back. He was dark haired with a beard and a little rotund with a jocular air about him. He seemed to be a native Brazilian taking a short flight from one city to another. I wasn't sure if he spoke English so I didn't say anything. There weren't any Semester at Sea students sitting in the near vicinity so I kept quiet and started writing a letter. A few minutes later he looked toward me and said in a Portuguese accent, "You Japanese?" I said, "Yes, my mother is Japanese and my father is Chinese, but I was born in the United States." He seemed to understand and nodded his head in affirmation. It turns out he didn't speak English, but through hand gestures, picture drawing, and a lot of repeating, we engaged in a kind of conversation. We started off with where we were going and where we came from. Through key, one-word concepts such as "Amazon" and "Salvador" we got where we were from and where we were going communicated to one another. We also had the use of a world map, which made it easier to "show" him where I originally came from (Los Angeles) and where I've been in the world.

I think both of us were interested in what the other had to say, so despite the language barrier we were able to communicate with one another. There were so many frustrating times when we couldn't get our points across, but we stuck to it using the same hand gestures and words repeatedly until somehow we got our ideas across. I would draw pictures of a calendar when he didn't understand when I said "month" and in that way we learned about each other's families, travel experiences, plans for the future, work and school, and some basic interests.

I think that for both of us this was the first encounter with a "Brazilian" and an "American," and we were both excited to get to know one another and our cultures. I found myself being a lot more patient and selective of the words I used, trying to pick the ones that were most basic. I was more open and receptive and appreciated any trivial point we got across to each other. (I was overjoyed when I discovered, after five minutes of hand gestures, that he had two brothers!) Because of the language barrier we were able to transgress all notions of formal talk and go straight to what we could communicate. Overall, I think both of us were a lot more patient with each other (an important cross-cultural skill) and were more intent on every word we said and heard, and more aware of any clues we could use around us. My other choice could have been to give up trying to talk to him and simply not have cared, but I was glad I got a chance to "communicate" with him and share information. I think this event gave me encouragement to keep trying to communicate with and understand the foreigners I will meet in the various countries. Just the fact that there was someone out there who was willing to struggle with me gives me a lot of incentive to try again next time.

INSIGHT:
Being able to communicate with the Brazilian without sharing the same language required extreme patience for the student but helped to emphasize the importance of nonverbal communication skills. The willingness of both persons to invest effort into communicating became a valuable training experience for the future.

Rio de Janeiro. On our trip to Rio de Janeiro a couple of friends of mine and I decided to go hang gliding. The day before I had talked to two guys who had done hang gliding the previous day. They both said that it was the ultimate feeling and that there was no danger involved. Before I had talked to them I wasn't really sure that I wanted to go, but they reassured me that everything would be fine. For some reason a little part of me was still worried. I decided that I would just wait until tomorrow to make a decision on whether to jump or not to jump.

The next day we were picked up at 10:00 and took about a half hour journey. When we got to the hang gliding site the first guy we spoke to was one of the instructors. He spoke fluent English and said there hadn't been any problems in over ten years. He also said that if you didn't like it then you wouldn't have to pay. But no one had ever not enjoyed it. Now I had no worries and was psyched to hang glide. Next I met my instructor whose name was Paslo. He spoke very little English, but what he could say made me feel very safe. We drove to the top of the cliff and prepared to jump. I felt good but still a little uneasy. Within ten seconds I would be flying. I thought about chickening out, but there was no way I could do that in front of these girls. He asked me if I was ready and I said let's go for it. The next thing I knew is that I was flying over Rio and had never felt higher.

INSIGHT:
The student took chances abroad like hang gliding which he probably would not have taken back home. When the hang gliding adventure abroad had a positive outcome, the student gained self-esteem and confidence for other adventures. Each success increased the potential for future growth experiences in foreign cultures.

Clashes in Courtship. Coming from the United States I am accustomed to dating standards in America. It is easy to recognize what people want or trust when familiar advances or lines are used. In other cultures norms for dating are different. Additionally, there is an added awkwardness in the language barrier.

In Brazil I attended an outdoor bar with several other Semester at Sea students. While on the street we ran into some Brazilian students who knew English and began to have a conversation about the country and customs. I was particularly interested in finding out about one of the student's jobs. He was working in the tourism industry and he spoke English very well. I felt safe enough to be separated from my friends and sit down alone and talk to this gentleman.

The main problem in the situation was that I became too relaxed with Carlos. He had different expectations than I had. I felt I was having a casual conversation with a student who was happy to talk about his country. However, the conversation took a turn in a direction I did not want to discuss. It was clear Carlos would rather be alone than discuss the Brazilian tourism industry. My main fear was that I would be separated from my friends. I became unsure of whether or not Carlos could be trusted and I felt unsafe. I attempted to ask a lot of questions to keep things on a more formal note, but Carlos kept touching me. I was unsure what he intended. Additionally, I did not want to offend him outright by telling him I didn't want to be touched on the shoulder. It all could have been just a friendly gesture. My choices were unclear about what I should personally do, so I tried a safer route. I told Carlos I had a friend I wanted him to meet because I thought they had a lot in common. I then motioned to a male Semester at Sea student who was nearby who then came over and joined us. I introduced him as a boyfriend and within two minutes Carlos asked me if I had any single female friends I could introduce him to.

INSIGHT:
In Brazil the rules for communicating romantic intentions were particularly ambiguous for the American student. The Brazilian who misunderstood was vulnerable to being embarrassed unless the student who was misunderstood could find a way to communicate her intentions accurately before it was too late.

How Important Is Sleep. It was February 1992, the first day we were in Brazil. The bus that took us to the welcome reception did not leave until 9:00 p.m.

The reception was uneventful, but the students were great. At 10:45 two of the male students wanted to take us to Barrah (the place for night life). I was tired and knew I had to get up early, so I gathered a group of five women and said they all could go. No one wanted to go if I did not go. I had to decide within a matter of a minute whether or not to go. My fun side was saying go, but my rational side knew I needed to go back to the ship.

I was the only one talking to the Brazilian students, therefore, I was the only one who felt comfortable with them. I got the group together to go to Barrah, but I thought I was going to go back to the ship. My Semester at Sea friends did not know if it was safe to go with these Brazilians, and the Brazilians had just been introduced to my friends. I had a lot of peer pressure from both the Brazilian students as well as my Semester at Sea friends to go to Barrah. They promised they would have me home (back to the ship) early. I had a hard time saying no. Actually, I could not say no, and so I decided to go to Barrah.

INSIGHT:
It was tempting for the student to fill every available minute with new adventures and opportunities while in Brazil. Each event seemed like the chance of a lifetime and not to be missed. It was important to be selective and recognize the student's physical limits of endurance while in Brazil.

South Africa

Operation Hunger. On my last day in South Africa I went on a field trip into the townships. This one was sponsored by a group called "Operation Hunger." This was an organization that was set up to feed many of the black South Africans who weren't getting enough to eat. For many of them the one meal that they eat a day was the bowl of soup that was given to them by this organization.

The first stop on our trip, and the most meaningful to me at least, was to a school. The teacher had obviously been preparing her young students a while just for this meeting. They had songs that they sang and little dances that went with them. These kids had it pretty hard. One of them had marks on her face that were starting to go away from malnutrition. Many of these kids had to walk over twenty miles every day just to get to school. The most amazing thing about it was that most of the food had been donated to them. They had all this nice food prepared really well for us while they just ate a bowl of soup. None of us wanted to eat it. At the same time we didn't want to refuse it, which I think would be considered rude. What many of us did was to take the food outside and share it among the kids.

I was very touched by these kids and the hospitality of the whole situation. I liked the kids. They were a little shy and very well mannered. It was kind of hard to talk to them. I tried talking to one little boy for awhile and then I took off the hat and put it on his head. I wanted to give him something, so I gave him my hat I had been wearing almost every day on this trip. I felt like that was giving something that was kind of important to me. He took it off his head immediately. He put it back on, or maybe someone else told him to so they could take a picture of the two of us. I kind of felt a little weird about it, like it was for a picture and that I gave him something that he really didn't want. After all, what good really is a hat to him? It isn't going to fill his stomach. But later as I got back onto the bus I looked up the hill at the school and I saw a group of the students walking down with some Semester at Sea students, and I saw the little boy wearing the hat I had given him. He was grinning from ear to ear, and I got this sudden rush of happiness.

INSIGHT:

The poverty of the crossroads township did not always extinguish their hospitality nor even generosity. Students from affluent backgrounds were accustomed to associating hospitality and generosity with material affluence. When the South Africans chose to give the students something of their food and themselves in spite of their limited resources, the gift took on a very special meaning.

A Squatter Camp. Our field trip was titled "The Religious Roots of Anti-Apartheid." Because of the leader's interaction with the people as the priest in Honk Bay, he took our group of ten students and faculty into a squatter camp. As soon as our van came to a stop in the middle of the camp two women approached us. At first five of us were trying to communicate with them. It was not easy to bridge the language gap, and eventually I was the only one standing with them. My hair was down past my shoulders. It came as a surprise to me when both women started combining their fingers through my hair. They stroked it, felt the texture, and pulled it gently. All of this was done with a great deal of affection. I wasn't uncomfortable with the situation, but I didn't know how to react. Never before had a stranger approached me in such a way. But then again, I had never been in contact with two black women from a squatter camp with very different cultural behaviors. My only reaction was to smile at them.

One woman was named Silvia. She was taller than me and built heavily. She had her hands wrapped in the top of her skirt and appeared to be wringing them over and over again. The other woman was much smaller with a young face and big, pretty eyes. Her name was Persila. Both had very short, kinky hair and told me that they were twenty-one years old. Neither of them had children. After exchanging about three sentences, as we tried to talk in English, Persila said, "I like you." I answered that I liked them too and wished we could talk more easily. Then Silvia said, "You're pretty." I said, "Thank you." I looked over in the direction of my group, and almost as if they couldn't fight the urge any longer, they both simultaneously reached for my hair.

My reaction was just to keep smiling. Thoughts rushed through my mind of what I should do. Should I feel their hair? What did it mean? Was it an invasion of privacy? How would they react if I reached for their hair? Did I want to? I know that it was harmless. Then I had a realization. This cross-cultural encounter enabled the three of us to explore what was different. I came to their home to interact and see how they lived. At the same time they were interested in me, and my physical appearance was the most obvious to them. The likelihood that Silvia and Persila came into contact with a white, American woman who was their same age and didn't mind their curiosity or affection was probably very low. My presence in a squatter camp was also highly unlikely to happen commonly. If I had the chance again I would return the gesture and feel their hair. To initiate contact may have shown that I did care, and that I was interested in them as human beings not just something to stare at.

INSIGHT:

The students encountered local South Africans who were more private than themselves and others who were less private in their communications with the students. It was important to interpret accurately the expectations of locals even though their behaviors seemed to violate the students' rules of privacy. It was important to focus on the positive expectations for friendship.

Leah Saves the Day. As we walked down to Pursar's Square on the ship we saw the sign, "Field trip to townships cancelled!" My heart jumped and sank. We stood around wondering what we should do from here. I couldn't bear the thought of leaving South Africa without seeing the one thing I was so interested in. Everyone else just walked away disappointed, but I was close to tears. At this moment my friend walked up and asked if we'd been planning to go on that trip. I replied, "Yes!" We said, "I am going into a township regardless if it's on a field trip or in a taxi." So we formulated a plan. We hired a taxi driver and he took us to the black political party headquarters! It was a rundown, shabby looking building. Everyone in there was very suspicious! We wanted a guide who was comfortable going in. They told us to go home. They would have a meeting and call us in the morning. Back at the ship we were visiting in Pursar's Square and Archbishop Desmond Tutu's wife Leah Tutu came in to chat. We spoke with her a few minutes and told her, "We are just going to rent a car and drive in by ourselves." Well, Leah looked at me and said, "Nonsense, your parents would be mad if I let you go by yourself! Come to tea at Bishops Court and then I will drive you in myself!" We could hardly believe it! We ran, changed, and before you know it we were on the official tour of their house and gardens and having tea with Desmond Tutu! Then Leah drove us into the townships. It was the best day during my entire voyage!

INSIGHT:

The students were truly determined to visit the townships in Cape Town and that persistence eventually paid off, although in an unexpected way. It was important that the students were able to find new ways of accomplishing the visit to the townships in South Africa when the scheduled tour was canceled.

Kenya

Lunch. This incident occurred the last day we were in Kenya (March 11, 1992). We were at the Border Controls between Tanzania and Kenya. We had just gone through Immigration and Customs (showing our passports and filling out a form so we could get back into Kenya). It was lunch time and each van (of eight people) had their own box lunch. We had to wait to cross the border, so we were all sitting in our vans eating lunch. The box lunch (although it was not bad looking) did not really seem appetizing to any of us (mainly because we had eaten a huge breakfast). The lunch consisted of one piece of chicken, one banana, one orange, a half of a cheese sandwich and one piece of pound cake. Each lunch box was relatively uneaten and my friend and I offered to throw them out for everyone.

As we walked into one of the border offices (there was a bathroom and a little cafe in there) I noticed all the children outside along with some women. I thought to myself, either throw out eight boxes full of food or offer it to this woman who was inside with her two daughters. I did not know if I would be offending them by offering them the food. I asked if there was a garbage can around but then I decided to go over to this woman and give her the lunch boxes. I figured that I would feel better about myself knowing that I had at least offered them this food instead of throwing it all out and wasting it.

The woman did not really speak English so I pointed to the lunch boxes and then kind of explained verbally and nonverbally that she could have them. I opened one up and picked up a banana to show her little girl. No one took the food in front of me, but my friend and I thought that once we left they would eat it.

I do not know for a fact if the food was eaten but I assume it was. Although there was no actual communication between the woman and me (it was more like I said, "Here are the lunch boxes. Would you like them or else I will throw them away." The woman kind of motioned for me to put the boxes down and I assumed she would take care of them). Her little girls said something to me and I motioned to them to eat the food in the lunch boxes. I walked out of the office feeling like I had made the right decision leaving the boxes with her.

INSIGHT:

After viewing poverty, the students from a relatively affluent background became acutely aware of how wasteful their own affluent society was. It was not easy to change wasteful habits but finding alternatives to throwing away food was certainly a good start. By observing less wasteful cultures, the students learned a great deal.

Simon Says. This incident was between a man that I met and myself. Simon approached me and wanted to speak with an American. We went and sat at a restaurant. The man started to talk quickly and explain his situation to me. The incident became critical because of the story he was telling me about his situation. I had to decide if I believed him and wanted to help him. Basically the man was explaining to me that he had been a university student in Sudan. At his university he was one of the leaders leading a demonstration that was protesting the government killing of twenty-one Christian children. He was blacklisted from the country and forced into exile.

The sad part of the story was he also had been awarded a full scholarship to Cal Tech in California. He told me that the United Nations was paying for his flight to Los Angeles but he needed to get to Tanzania. He needed to keep a low profile in Kenya because if he was caught he would be deported back to Sudan. He explained that he had walked over 800 km from Sudan to Nairobi. Once in Nairobi they had gone to the university and managed to get enough money for the train ride from Nairobi to Mombasa. Now he was trying to get money to get to Tanzania so he could get to the United States.

This is where the incident became critical! I had to decide if I believed him and wanted to give him some money. If I gave him money I would be helping him out. I might also be a victim of a scam of a man trying to get my money. If I didn't help him I would think about Simon and wonder if he got out or was not deported. I decided to give Simon five dollars. When I got the money out of my wallet Simon motioned that I crumble the money up into a ball and hand it to him discretely.

I think I was interested because his story reminded me of my father. In 1948 my dad got on a night train from Prague, Czechoslovakia. He was leaving the country because of the communist invasion. He managed to get to Argentina through the help and money of others. So when Simon told me his story I was imaging my dad being forced to do the same thing, asking for money. At the moment I had to decide if I was going to give Simon money I actually thought about my dad. Somebody had helped my dad--I should give something to Simon.

INSIGHT:

The student was approached by a young Kenyan in need who may have been genuine. It was not easy for the student to tell the difference. Whether it was a scam or not the young man was probably in need of help. There were no easy guidelines for the student on how to deal with persons in need.

A Village Family. On our third day during our safari the drivers for our group offered to take students to a Samburu Village for a small fee. We had already been on several game drives, so many of us decided not to go. On our way there our group leaders warned us not to go into anyone's home/hut. Last semester several girls had been held in a cabin until they bought jewelry made by the Samburu women. While no one was hurt it was a frightening experience.

When our group arrived at the village we were immediately bombarded with people trying to sell us their jewelry. One woman marched right up to me and asked me my name. She had nothing to sell that I could see, and I was a little taken aback. I told her my name and then asked hers. She said that her name was Grace and that she had three babies. "How old are you?" she asked. I told her that I was twenty, "And how many babies?" "No babies," I said. "Husband?" she asked. "No" and she laughed shaking her head. "You come with me to *my* house," she said. I had to decide whether or not to go with her. The other Semester at Sea students had moved off to another area so no one could come with me. Grace seemed harmless enough, so I decided to go.

Grace showed me the inside of her round hut and it was really interesting. She showed me where they slept, where they ate, and where she kept her things, then I left. Nothing happened and she didn't ask me to buy anything. I am really glad that I trusted my own judgment and decided to go. Just because there was one bad incident didn't mean that the whole village was out to rob us. I think I got the most out of that visit to the Samburu Village. I was not hassled and I think I made a friend. I definitely learned a lot.

INSIGHT:

The student was as much of a curiosity to the Kenyan woman as the Kenyan woman was to the student. When the student was lucky enough to find an openly curious local Kenyan woman, there was an opportunity for a useful exchange of ideas and viewpoints from which both persons benefitted.

On Safari. The first day we arrived in Kenya, a group of about fifteen of us headed to the game reserves of Savo and Ambosgeli for a safari. On the way there I became acquainted with two new people. We each started talking to each other about how excited we were to see all the animals. About an hour into our drive we pulled over at some shops on the side of the road to have lunch. We decided to go into the store and try to become friendly with the people who worked there. We started talking to this woman. She had no idea about what the United States was. One of us said, "We're from North America!" The woman had a pretty confused look on her face when she heard this. So for about the next half hour we all sat around and tried to explain to her what the fifty states was all about.

I said to her, "The states are just like separate countries. The same as Kenya is to South Africa." She still didn't understand what we were trying to say. But I felt that as each minute passed she was beginning to understand us more and more. I think by this time she had gained a little bit of trust in us. She then spoke in her broken English and asked us, "Would you like to try one of the foods we eat?" We all looked at each other and decided why not. She motioned for us to follow her outside to some little shack where a man was cooking something.

As we were walking there I was wondering to myself whether or not this was such a smart move. I mean here we were somewhere in the middle of Kenya about to eat something which we had no clue about. I could tell that my friend was a little skeptical about the situation because he kind of walked at a much slower pace than both of us. As we got to the hut we politely asked what we were about to try. The man replied, "Kenyan sausage." One of us turned to the other and said, "I'll eat it if you eat it." We all decided to give it a try. It had been cooking for some time so we figured that all the germs or bacteria had been destroyed, so it would be safe to eat. The man handed us each a piece of sausage. I still didn't think each of us were quite sure this was such a smart idea, but since we didn't want to offend them we each decided to take a bite of the Kenyan sausage.

As we started biting the sausage and chewing it, I could tell by the look in my friend's faces that, they thought it was as bad as I did. We all started laughing as we chewed. I wanted so badly to spit this sausage out, but I couldn't, just because they would have been extremely offended. We finally finished and politely said, "Thank you." I turned to my friend and said, "Never before have I tasted shit, but that definitely came the closest." It was the worst thing that we've ever eaten. I asked, "What was it?" He told us, "Goat intestines." We all were in shock, we had just eaten goat intestines.

INSIGHT:

No matter how well prepared the students were to deal with different customs and foods in Kenya, there were always those situations that arose for which nobody could be prepared. These unique surprises became stories and legends to help other students prepare for their own surprises.

Talking about Kenyan Politics. In Kenya I went on a safari to Tsavo for a four-day trip with several of my friends. By the second day we had all developed a pretty good rapport with our driver whose name was Salim. On our way to one of the parks another Semester at Sea student and I began to talk to Salim about the history of the political parties in Kenya. He was open to the conversation and willing to give us information about the subject. Soon after we finished the conversation we pulled up to the gate of the park where several guards were standing. As we were stopped my friend and I were talking about several of the things Salim had just told us. I guess we were loud enough that the guards could have heard us because Salim turned around, put a finger to his mouth, and uttered, "Shhh!" Only then did I realize that my friend and I had made a critical mistake when we openly talked about Kenyan politics in front of government guards.

INSIGHT:

The student needed to be sensitive to the unintentional consequences of what was said and done in public in Kenya. This was particularly true when discussing controversial topics like politics. The students who had the opportunity to discuss controversial subjects with locals needed also to learn about circumstances where that discussion was inappropriate.

Face to Face with an Elephant. We were at the Samburu Serena Lodge for our last night in Kenya. We were all hanging out at the bar, but it was getting late and we had to be up at 5:45 the next morning, so I decided to go back to my cabin and go to bed. I was walking back by myself and was a little nervous because of all the talk of violence lately, and, of course, my cabin was the farthest away. All of a sudden I heard this man's voice saying, "Wait! Come back here! Wait!" I was so scared, I couldn't decide if I should run ahead or stop and see what he wanted. All these horrible things ran through my mind, like he was going to rob me, or rape me, or kill me. For some reason though I decided to stop and see what he wanted. There was basically no thought process or reasoning behind my decision; it was just a spontaneous decision because I really didn't have time to think about it.

As it turns out, I definitely made the right decision. The man worked there and proceeded to tell me that there was an elephant right around the corner! If he hadn't stopped me I would have walked right into the biggest elephant I'd ever seen! The guard proceeded to throw rocks in the direction of the elephant, so after some time he finally scared him away and walked me safely the rest of the way to my cabin.

INSIGHT:

The female student's first reaction was a tendency to evaluate the shouts by the Kenyan male in negative terms. It was important to avoid premature evaluations of this situation until sufficient data were available. Assuming the worst about Kenyans was as likely to get the student into difficulty as being too naive.

India

Offering a Silver Dollar. When I was in India I spent most of my time with two friends I had met at the welcome reception. Their names were Narendren and Radah. They took the time to show us throughout the country. When it finally came time to leave I decided I wanted to give them each a United States silver dollar, which I had brought for such occasions. In doing so I made a critical error by just handing them the coins and saying, "Here, I want you to have this." They understood my offer in a different manner in thinking that I was just trying to give them money. Radah responded by saying, "No, no we are fine, we have enough money." My heart fell to my stomach because I realized that I probably insulted them. I quickly explained to them that it was somewhat of a rare coin in the United States and that I wasn't giving it to them for monetary purposes, rather I was giving it to them to keep as a remembrance of our friendship.

Being from the United States my two friends probably viewed me as being very wealthy. I had seen the apartment in which they lived and it was very modest, so I doubt they were from well-to-do families. Thus, we each had these unspoken perceptions of one another. When I offered them the coins it didn't even cross my mind that it would be viewed as a cash offering. I had brought the coins with me for the sole purpose of gift giving, a symbol of the United States. After I handed them the coins, with little explanation, and saw their reaction I understood that they didn't realize the meaning of the coins. They perceived my offering as charity.

It's ironic that I wanted to give them a symbol of our friendship and I almost ended up insulting them.

INSIGHT:

The student learned that many local Indians put a negative connotation on money and people who have money. As a gift to a friend it implied the purchase of friendship and could easily be given a negative interpretation. Without explanation, the giving of money could easily have been taken as a demeaning insult.

Show Us Calcutta. In India a group of us from Semester at Sea were travelling from Madras to Calcutta, and from Calcutta to Darjeeling. On the way back from Darjeeling we stopped over in Calcutta for the night. Our flight left at 11:00 in the morning the next day so four of us from the group decided to wake up early and see as much of Calcutta as possible. We woke up at 5:30, hired a taxi driver and told him to show us Calcutta. We saw quite a bit in that short time, including a one-minute incident that I will remember forever.

We met this man who said that he knew where Mother Teresa lived. We all agreed that we would like to see where she lived, so he took us there. We came up to this door and on the mailbox it said "Mother Teresa in." We knocked and a woman let us in. I thought that we were just going to see where she lived, I never expected to go inside of Mother Teresa's home.

While sitting there watching the daily activities of the fellow sisters, a woman at another door motioned for us to come in. One by one we filed up to the door and entered. A woman was shaking hands with my friends as they walked by. When it came my turn to shake this woman's hand I felt this unbelievable energy rush through my body. This woman who was shaking my hand was Mother Teresa! I didn't realize it until that moment. Once we were inside she asked us where we were from and if we were students. We replied, "Yes, we are students, and we are from the U.S.A." At that moment she blessed us and said, "Thank you for coming," and disappeared into another room. It happened so quickly and it was such an incredible feeling that it left us speechless. On the way to the taxi my friend asked us if we realized what just happened. We all said, "Give us a minute to think about it." I am still thinking about that incident today.

INSIGHT:
Every student had one or two incidents, usually unplanned and spontaneous, that will live forever in that person's memory. The opportunity to visit Mother Teresa as a person of great spiritual power was an example of one such profoundly important experience for these students.

Love. During my stay in India I flew with a group of people up north to the Himalayas. Due to flight schedules we had to cut short our stay there and spend a night in Calcutta. I was a little bummed about this at first, but then I thought it would be interesting to spend some time in Calcutta, a place I knew nothing about.

We woke up at five o'clock in the morning to catch a 10:45 flight. None of us really knew what we wanted to do. One of the people in our four-person group suggested we visit the orphanage that Mother Teresa started. I knew nothing about it, but it sounded like a good idea.

Our cab driver didn't know where it was so he picked up this man who had lived there all his life. He was a Christian and his name was Mark. When we got to the orphanage it hadn't opened yet. Mark then told us he would show us Mother Teresa's home. As we drove there one of the people in our group talked about how great it would be to meet Mother Teresa, especially since he was a Catholic. "That's like meeting the Pope," he said. He had a camera in his hand, "First Tutu, now Mother Teresa."

We got there and one of the sisters opened the door. Mark said something to her and she let us in. As we sat waiting we saw a group of Chinese tourists all with their cameras out. One of the members of our group said, "I want to meet her so bad, yet I don't feel right about it." I knew what he was saying, but it hadn't really dawned on me what we were doing. Mark then asked us to stand up and pointed us in the direction of a room. I was the last to walk through the entrance. As I did I was greeted by a little old woman. I didn't expect her to be right there, and at first I didn't realize who she was, yet I received this sense of goodness and love from her. It was amazing the feeling that she sent out just by reaching out and holding my hands. She asked us about our voyage and we exchanged a few words. I think we were all just really stunned. It couldn't have lasted more then thirty seconds and then she was off.

INSIGHT:
For this student the trip to visit Mother Teresa was a little like a pilgrimage, a search for new experiences and values. When the student was fortunate enough to find Mother Teresa, who symbolized those values, the pilgrimage was a success.

A Drink of Water. A critical incident happened to me outside the dock in Madras, India. My friend and I had walked through the dock area, through the gate, and into the street, looking for the international phone that was supposed to be right there. While we were walking along the street looking for the phone, a horde of begging children clustered around us asking for money. I was carrying my water bottle in my hand and one of the boys grabbed it. He was about to drink out if it, and I reached to him to grab it but then I saw the look on his face. He looked offended because I had given him a look of disgust when I saw that he was going to drink from it. I did not know what to do; whether I should let him drink from it knowing I could probably never use it again or whether I should take it away from him. I decided in a split second to let him drink, and I showed him how to use it.

I think I did the right thing by letting the boy drink from my water bottle, although I am ashamed that I gave him a critical look of disgust. I also knew I did the right thing because I have never seen a face light up as much as his did when he drank from the bottle. I only wished I had given it to him. I took it back after he had drank enough.

INSIGHT:

As the student became more experienced, she also became more aware of the feelings local Indians displayed toward the students. The increased awareness opened new opportunities for learning about India and also about herself.

Should I Drink or Not. I was in Pondicherry, a town in the south of Madras. We decided to visit these houses which were by the beach. The idea was to take some pictures and leave, but this boy invited us to go and see their houses and meet his family. We went in and they put a carpet on the floor so that we could sit down. There were many Indian boys and girls around us. They invited us to have a coconut. The father climbed a tree and got it for us. Then he came down and opened it. They took the coconut water and put it into these metal cups, which were wet. At first we just looked at each other not knowing exactly what to do. We could either say no or just take the risk, even though we would get sick. It would not be nice of us to just leave it there, but then we could also get very ill. There were five of us, and the guys were drinking straight from the coconut, and as a courtesy they put it in glasses for the girls. We decided to drink it no matter what would happen because it was very nice of them to offer this to us. Actually I was surprised because these people were really poor and yet they offered everything they had.

INSIGHT:

Being invited into a local Indian home was always a very special privilege not to be taken lightly. In attempting to be good hosts and be generous, the Indians may have unintentionally said or done something, such as serve fresh coconut water in wet cups, which forced the student to make a decision between being polite and being safe.

The Persistent Friend. When we visited India I attended the welcome reception. After being there for awhile my friends and I were talking to this one group of students in particular. We then sat with them to watch the performance. There was a guy sitting in front of me who was by himself and wasn't talking to anyone. He was also an Indian student, but he seemed very quiet and serious. He turned around and started talking to me. He wanted to know what I was going to be doing in India during my visit. I told him I was going to go to Pondicherry the next day and that I wouldn't be back until the last day in port. He said he was from Pondicherry and that if I was going to go there he would go there also and show me around. I told him I was on an arranged trip and that I probably wouldn't be able to get away. He told me to call him the next morning before I left if I could arrange to see him in Pondicherry. I never got a chance to call him.

On the last day that we had in Madras I was woken up by a public announcement asking me to go to the duty desk for a message. This was through the loudspeaker. I got there and there was a message from this student that said he would be waiting for me outside the gate between 8:00 a.m. and 8:30 a.m. It was 8:45 a.m. when I got the message, so I went back to bed. A few minutes later someone knocked on the door and handed me a note that this guy had given him the day before. I went back to sleep. Then someone else knocked on the door and gave me another note. I started getting dressed so I could go outside and meet him. While I was dressing my name was called through the loudspeaker again to say I had a visitor.

I finally got out there and he said he'd been waiting for me for two and a half hours and that he wanted to show me around. I had already made plans to meet some Indian girls I met on my trip at 12:30 to go shopping. I told him this and he said I could go with him for awhile and then I could go back and meet my friends. After he took me shopping to a couple of places I came back and met my friends. He asked if I minded if he stayed with me. I did mind, but I told him I didn't. Other girls from the ship joined us and then we were a big group. We all did things together for a while, but it was very hard to get anything done with such a large group.

My friend kept suggesting that we go off on our own so we could see more. After a while I agreed to this. I ended up having one of the best days I've had on this trip. He took me where I wanted to shop, and to the jewelry store to get my nose pierced. He took me to lunch, then to his friends' homes, and a temple by the beach. We had such a great time. We talked a lot and I ended up becoming really good friends with him.

We promised each other that we would write at least once a year, and that when he got married I would come back to India and come to his wedding. It was one of the best days ever. I was so happy.

One thing I know now is that it is so important to give people a chance.

INSIGHT:
It was hard for the student to know whether or not the young man was her friend if she didn't give him a fair chance. The Indian who was more persistent was judged negatively by back-home standards in spite of many other positive features which were overlooked. The student eventually gave the local Indian a chance to become a friend and gained from it.

Ganges-Bound or Not. I went to Calcutta with two friends during our short stay in India. On our second full day we ventured to see a sacrifice at the Kalighat Temple and also to visit the first mission that Mother Theresa established for the destitute and dying. Calcutta is home to more than ten million people and is the most poverty-stricken slum city in the world. I say this because it is difficult for me to try and categorize one part of the city from another--as on the whole it was a destitute, depressing city.

We were walking towards the Mother Teresa Mission, which was situated behind the Kalighat Temple, and children of all ages swarmed around us.

They followed us for more than ten minutes pursuing us for money and materialistic items. A few boys caught my eye who just smiled at us and said, "Hello" and waived their hands at the other children to stop pestering us. The two boys spoke very good English. They would grab our arms and aggressively pull us forward behind them. One of the boys, Jamul, continued to ask us, "You like come to river?" We were in the middle of a busy fruit and vegetable market with bustling people everywhere, these children pestering us for spare rupees, it was ninety-five degrees and I saw no water in sight.

Our cab driver who we had rented for the day spoke some English, most of which was broken. He overheard the young boys tying to convince us to follow them to the river and immediately said, "No, bad, dirty, you no go." He tried to get us to turn around and go back to the cab, but things were happening too rapidly. I wondered why he did not want us to go down to the tributary of the Ganges. Was it because it was not safe for a girl to go? Was it just not safe and we had to walk through a residential slum? Was it because he was earnestly trying to protect us from these impoverished children who might try to take our personal belongings or money? We were all clueless, but I was determined to find out what was so exciting about the river and why it was so important for these three boys to take us there.

We followed the boys through many narrow, dark, poor alley openings that were full of sleeping lepers, mothers and crying babies and children running around naked. The further we walked the closer the three of us moved towards one another. The smell of sweat, urine and charcoal smoke permented the confined area. The boys began to run and we followed.

At a distance I saw light even though it was no later than two in the afternoon. The destitute had built canopies over the path not only to keep things cooler but also to support their shacks. As we reached the opening, which felt like we were exiting a long, dark tunnel of filth and depression, we encountered a shrine dedicated to Shiva, their protector. Flowers adorned the white statue and candles were lit at the foot of it. Holy men sat in prayer and young children splashed in the disease-ridden, stagnant water. The Indians just stared at us in amazement. I wondered what they thought of us. Somehow in this quiet, secluded, non-populated area by the bank of the river I felt a sense of peace and solitude.

INSIGHT:

For the student, trust implied risk. Being too trusting was just as dangerous as not being trusting enough. There were no easy rules or guidelines for deciding whom to trust in India. The students developed confidence in assessing each situation on its own merits and made the decision whether or not to trust in a cultural context.

Siesta in India. In India I went on the Rotary Club homestay for two nights. There were three of us staying at the home of an Indian family.

When we first got to Dinesh's home he quickly ushered us to a room which he told us was "ours." It had a TV, which he was very proud of; a big bed, a great view, our own bathroom, and an air conditioner. He asked us when we wanted tea. We all shrugged and so he suggested four o'clock. We all said fine and then he said, "Okay, four o'clock," and closed the door on us. We were very confused because it was only 1:30 and we wanted to go out and see India. We sat in the room for about a half an hour discussing our options. We didn't want to offend Dinesh, but yet we didn't want to just sit in this room for hours when there was so much of India to be seen and only a short time to see it.

I believe we discussed what to do for about fifteen minutes before we came to the conclusion that we would open the door and ask what they were expecting us to do all afternoon. We then opened the door and he looked so surprised. We politely asked what was the schedule for the day and he looked at us in a strange manner and said that it was time for "rest" and that we would "take tea" at four, *then* we could go shopping. We said okay and retreated to our room for our "rest."

We then realized that Dinesh was offering us a cool place to stay during the hottest part of the day. We could go shopping when the heart of the day had subsided. We obviously made a wrong decision by going out and asking him what was up, but to us we were much happier after we at least knew what was expected of us.

INSIGHT:
Being guests in a local home was a special privilege for the students but it also meant following fairly specific rules and routines which were unfamiliar to the students. The students needed to do some homework before visiting a local Indian home about what was expected of them and what they could expect of the hosts.

How Late Should I Stay. This critical incident took place in India while I was on a homestay. I had gone to the home of a professor from the University of Anamali. I had already eaten dinner and we were sitting around talking. There was a ton of people there and they were all very curious and eager to hear what I had to say. Towards the end of the evening the upstairs neighbor wanted me to come up and look at his apartment. I went upstairs and talked with his wife and mother, and his children played some musical instruments for me and danced. After his children were done entertaining me he started asking me questions about my lifestyle--like when I went to sleep and when I got up. I told him that my sleeping habits varied a lot but that I usually was in bed by midnight. He thought that was very late. I then noticed that it was about a quarter past ten. I asked him what time they usually went to bed and he said 9:30 or 10:00. I didn't know if he was hinting for me to leave or not. I also didn't know if it would be rude for me to excuse myself. So finally after sitting there in awkward silence for awhile I finally excused myself and he seemed relieved. I guess that I should have done that about a half an hour earlier, but I didn't know if he would walk me back downstairs or if I would be rude by leaving.

INSIGHT:
The student had trouble reading the cues accurately in the Indian home. Both the Indian host and the student guest were trying to accommodate the other, resulting in an awkwardness or inconvenience to both.

Getting Stuck in India. Two girl friends and I travelled along the southeast coast of India, eventually ending up in Madurai. In Madurai we rented a taxi for a full day. The taxi driver was also our tour guide for the day, and an excellent guide to say the least. We went to temples, shops, a castle, and even his home. It was an excellent chance to see the Indian lifestyle.

One of the shops we stopped at was a fabric store. They had everything from silk to cotton. The shop owner invited us in to his shop. He had beautiful silks for low prices that particularly interested us. He told us to pick the fabrics we liked and he would make anything from pants, shirts, dresses, to even boxers. Consequently, we bought quite a few items. The two girls I was with really enjoyed themselves, buying all different sorts of outfits. The shop owner asked us when we were planning to leave Madurai, and we told him our train left that night at 7:30 p.m. He told us to come back around 6:30 p.m. and he would have our clothes ready. It was now about 1:00 p.m., so we continued on with our tour and planned to come back later that evening. We paid for half of our purchase at that time, and we were told to pay the second half when we picked our clothes up. It all sounded good to me, so onward we went through Madurai.

We had an incredible day, and around 6:15 we headed to the fabric shop to pick up our clothes. When I walked in I noticed the shop owner busy at work. He was stitching our clothes together, which meant he wasn't finished. He saw the concern in my face and he said, "No problem, go to train, and I deliver clothes, no problem." This worried us, how did we know if he would deliver? He could have easily pocketed half of the money we already gave him and never show up at the station. We really didn't have a choice, he obviously wasn't finished with the clothes. Above all, our trusted taxi driver said it was no problem, and was pushing us to go. The three of us had a quick conference and we decided to trust the shop owner and head off. It was really the only thing we could have done.

Our taxi driver showed us to our train cabin and got us settled in. He then told me to collect all the money we owed to the shop owner. After I collected the money he said, "You come with me and you two (the two girls) stay on the train." It was now 7:15 p.m. and the train pulled out in twenty minutes. To say the least I was a bit worried, not so much about getting the clothes but missing the train. It was an eleven-hour train ride back to Madras, and the boat left the next day. I couldn't afford to miss the train.

We walked to the front of the train station and patiently waited for some sign of the shop owner. My watch kept ticking. At about 7:30, with five minutes to spare, I was ready to call it quits. As I turned around to go back to the train, and feeling pretty pissed off, I heard some yelling. I turned back around and saw a man with two bags hop off a moped. He came running up to me with a big smile. I handed him the money, and he tossed me two large bags of clothes. We exchanged thank yous, and I ran for my train. It was now almost 7:35, and I was running through the Madurai train station with two large bags of clothes under my arms; it was like an O. J. Simpson commercial. As I turned the corner I saw my train start moving. I threw the bags on the train and grabbed a railing, swinging myself on the train. If I had missed that train I might have missed the boat.

INSIGHT:

Indian and United States cultures have different concepts of time. The student learned to accommodate and compensate for a more leisurely perspective toward time limits in India. If the student did not compensate and accommodate, then the Indian hosts might draw the wrong conclusions about this student's dependability and trustworthiness.

A Walk through the Slums. On our last day in India I was on the field trip that went on a "walk through the slums." Let me just say this was probably one of my fondest memories of the entire trip. The people were absolutely inspirational. I have never fallen in love with a group of people so quickly! The one incident where I had to make a critical decision was in the middle of this little village. By this time it was done everyone in the village knew we were there. There was one old, old woman who confronted me alone. I was straggling behind the rest of the students. She had a basket of berries, or seeds, or something I had never seen before. She offered them to me. One little kid, who had been by my side since I stepped off the bus, showed me by example they were edible. Well after all the warning about eating in India let's just say I was a little hesitant. My decision was whether or not I'd rather risk the chance of having a little diarrhea or risk deeply insulting this community by not trying what I was being offered. Of course I gobbled one down, even though it may have been one of the most hideous tasting things I've ever put in my mouth, for the reaction I got I'd have eaten the whole basket full.

This was a little community that the government made provisions for and compared to the other slum areas we saw they were pretty well off. They had either little huts or a room in massive concrete structures. There was a school and community center. There were perhaps about twenty Semester at Sea students and one tour guide. The people really spoke very little if any English. At the time of this offering the people were all speaking Tamil to me and gathering around to see my reaction. The one little boy beside me said, "good, good," that was about it. Everybody just giggled and watched. Once I did eat this thing they were so delighted they clapped, and laughed, and continued to talk to me in Tamil. The people were so numerous I couldn't even tell you how many there were. The one little boy whose name I never understood never left my side and would pass friends of his and show them how he could shake my hand, and then they would both giggle and we'd walk on.

INSIGHT:
Acceptance by the local Indians was demonstrated through many smaller and seemingly insignificant behaviors such as eating the berries that were offered to the student. By the student's putting acceptance and friendship in a context, these otherwise abstract terms took on specific meaning and importance for the Indian locals and the students as well.

Eating Etiquette in India. Before reaching India the idea had been repeated many times that the risk of diarrhea was almost one-hundred percent. I decided to bring a supply of granola bars that would last for the duration of my stay in Southern India. The first day was fine, and I had no problem ordering meals at the restaurants we went to. On the second day, however, our group visited Annamalai University who would host us for the next two days. Our arrival was an hour late and lunch had been prepared and saved for us. I sat down at the table next to Sumongoli who was the fifteen year old granddaughter of our guide, Sunithi. Sumongoli was supposed to give me tips on eating off the banana leaf with only my right hand and using my left hand only to drink the water. I saw red flags coming from the medical section of pre-port tips. I thought I'd be able to pass up the food with the excuse of motion sickness from the long bus ride. After three different things were put on my leaf, the host who served it stood in front of me and stared at me. Sumongoli tapped my arm and said that he was waiting for my approval, and that I should start eating. I didn't know what to do. Either I risked becoming sick or acting disrespectful to our Indian host. I looked down at the wet leaf and then around to see what everyone else was eating. Sunithi said, from across the room, "Don't be shy, your hands work better than forks and knives." Of course I couldn't explain it wasn't the method of eating but rather what the food could do to me. I decided to eat the food. I ate a little bit of everything and a lot of the safer, hotter, less-dairy looking food. I didn't drink the water even though a Professor had said my water bottle was rude. I had it next to my chair and waited until after the meal to drink it.

Either I was lucky or the food was prepared safely, because I did not get sick in India, and I enjoyed the food as well as the corresponding experiences.

INSIGHT:
The student had to make a decision about whether the risk of getting sick

was more important than offending the local Indian hosts. For the student, offending a generous and gracious Indian host would have been more painful than the possibility of getting sick later.

Malaysia

To Travel on My Own. On the last day in Penang, Malaysia, I was to go on a Faculty Directed Practicum in the morning but my clock was slow so I missed it. All of my other friends had already left on independent travel plans, so there was no one I knew who I could hang out with for the day. I don't normally go out by myself because I feel that it is dangerous, so I sat in my room for an hour deciding what I should do. I could spend the day doing homework on the ship because I did have a lot of catching up to do, or I could exercise on the bike for a while. I really wouldn't have minded staying on the ship. Besides, I wasn't sure how safe it would be if I travelled alone. I had no idea where I could go and how I would get there--staying on the ship was looking better and better to me. But I also didn't want to spend the last day in port on the ship. I thought to myself, "When will I ever get the chance to come back to Malaysia? And I will have the next five days on board the ship."

After I said that my room looked smaller and less appealing to stay in. In a way I was excited to go off on my own and experience Malaysia my own way. Without other Semester at Sea students I could blend in with the other Chinese natives around me. Vendors and natives wouldn't hold any preconceptions of me as being a foreigner, so I could see Malaysia more as it exists to the Malaysians. All I needed was a little incentive to get off my bed and walk out the door. So I told myself that I would regret staying on the ship and I could have a safe and fun time on my own, and off I went. And I'm glad I went because I had a wonderful, relaxing time walking around Penang at my leisurely pace.

I think my decision was important because it showed that I had the courage to travel independently. I got to observe the Malaysian culture quietly without being looked at (because I did fit in quite well) and feel that I submerged myself in the culture more than if I were with other Semester at Sea students. I found myself pretending that I could understand Malay when people spoke to me and picked up on some habits by observing other people. On the bus to Kek Lok Si Temple, I learned that if I handed a lady sixty sen she would give me a ticket back. So after a few bus rides I felt like an expert at public transportation. Even though I did not do much I felt that just being in a group of Malays helped me experience ordinary Malaysian life. I observed lots of people and their actions. I walked around rural streets and through little specialty shops. I developed my ability to observe and experience cultures without imposing mine on them as well. This way I was able to see how ordinary people live. If I stayed on the ship I definitely would not have left Malaysia feeling as though I actually submerged myself into the culture. I am glad that I got the opportunity to travel by myself, and I think that if I ever get the chance again I would not hesitate to go.

INSIGHT:

As the students became more experienced, going out on their own in a foreign country became less scary and more natural. Travelling by themselves resulted in a very different and often more authentic experience than travelling in a group of other students. Local people became less reluctant to approach them, and students often found the need to approach locals for assistance.

Thailand

Dancing. When we went to Bangkok from Taiwan, we met up with our friend, got to our hotel and decided to go out. We went bar hopping and ended up at a small dance place. I love to dance, so when I saw this group of guys who were also good dancers I was forced to make the decision of whether or not I should ask them to dance.

I was there with eight friends, but I was the one really dancing, so when I looked over and saw this fun looking group of guys, I decided to ask one of them to dance. As I decided to approach them, I stopped and thought--I'm not home, so I don't know if this is the brightest move, and then it also occurred to me that all the guys were black and I didn't know the friends I was with well enough to know how they felt towards blacks. I decided that if my friends had a problem with it that was too bad and I went ahead and approached the group. After I introduced myself and told them where I was from, they told me they were from Nairobi and were on vacation. I was excited to tell them I had just been to Kenya on my voyage, and they were impressed. We had the best conversation and I was very happy that I had talked to them. After a while I introduced them to my friends, and everyone had a great time talking and dancing. It felt really good to know that I had allowed so many people to make new friends, because I wasn't scared and I did what I wanted to do.

INSIGHT:

It took some courage for the American female student to approach a group of males who were strangers in a foreign country and ask for a dance. By risking some embarrassment by being so forward, she ended up making new friends in a meaningful encounter. She was able to find common ground between the strangers from Nairobi and her visit to Kenya which helped to establish a relationship in Thailand.

Hong Kong and China

Directions. As I was walking from my hotel back to the ship in Hong Kong, I asked a young man for directions to a local drugstore. I had the name and address written down and was trying to at least get "pointed in the right direction." We were waiting on a street corner for a light to change and I politely tapped his shoulder and pointed towards my paper. He read the writing (in Chinese characters) and waved me down the street. I thanked him and walked in the direction he motioned. About two minutes later, maybe less, he grabbed my shoulder and tried to explain that evidently I was going the wrong way. When I conveyed to him that I didn't understand what he was trying to say he became frustrated. He kept trying to explain in Chinese (I assume) where the address was located. I finally realized that because I had presented an address in characters that he must have thought I understood what he was saying. I tried to thank him and he seemed as though he really wanted to help, but we were completely *worthless* to each other. We both walked away smiling, and I can only hope he thought it was as humorous as I found it-- language barriers--ugh!!

INSIGHT:
Not knowing the local language is always frustrating, but the student was able to accept the frustration without getting angry and without making the Chinese young man angry. Neither the Chinese man nor the student was effective in communicating a message, but they were able to share some humor about their own helplessness.

Modesty in China. I met a Chinese man one day at a market and began to have a conversation with him. We discussed many topics like football, China, and schooling. We had been talking for about fifteen minutes and I was thoroughly enjoying myself. I then made the mistake of complimenting this man's English and ability to speak clearly. All at once he became flustered, shook his hands frantically at me, would not look me in the eyes, and began to walk away.

I was confused and unsure of what had just happened. I went after the man and asked him if I said something wrong. He hesitantly told me that he was embarrassed by flattery and was a very modest man. Slowly, we resumed our conversation and it took time for this Chinese man to feel fully comfortable around me as he had before I had bestowed the unwanted compliment.

INSIGHT:
The student came from a more individualistic culture where being assertive and aggressive paid off. In a more collectivist culture like China there was more emphasis on individual modesty and fitting into the group with a minimum of disturbance or attention. Students with an individualistic

background often misunderstood locals in a collectivist culture.

Republic of China (Taiwan)

Padu Train. Here we are in a busy city we know very little about; can't read the signs; can't speak the language. Regardless, we wanted to travel to Toroko Gorge. We set out with minimal Chinese written instructions and maximum hope of communication skills.

Four of us set out at 5:45 a.m. for the train station. We already had reservations for the first port. The problem was when and where to change trains. We were all sitting along the window with blank and lost looks on our faces. The others seemed to be doing the majority of the working--figuring out where to go and all. So I simply observed and tried to figure stuff out quietly. Eventually we were all discussing the situation of where to get off and how to get to the next train.

Then we noticed several students who seemed to be paying attention or trying to understand what we were saying. Should we see if they know any English? Well, we can and then find out where and what to do. Otherwise it will take quite a while to get anything right, so we asked. First I said, "Hey guys, don't you think we should just ask?" "Well," they replied, "I'm pretty sure we are right." I had gotten real sick of our stupidity so the deciding factor was when we stopped at some station we did not at all recognize! One of the students was more than just helpful. The verbal exchange was little to none. The only things he could say was "twain (train)" and "yes and no." It was like playing charades. He got off the train with us even though he was on his way to school. He waited at the stop with us, put us on the train going to the proper location and then went to school. It was amazing yet wonderful to find someone so willing to go out of their way to help us.

INSIGHT:
Almost every student on the voyage had stories where locals had dropped their own important tasks to escort the student to her or his destination at a considerable personal inconvenience. The more experienced students did not hesitate to ask for help in the foreign cultures, especially when the surrounding locals could see that the traveller was already lost.

A Kiss from a Stranger. I was at Lionshead Mountain with four friends. After four hours of riding buses and not knowing where we were, we finally had found ourselves at our desired destination. It was about 3:00 p.m. and we were wondering whether we really had time to hike around the mountain before having to go through the ordeal of another hectic bus ride home.

A Taiwanese man approached us and, in hesitant English, asked us if we were going to the "sleeping temple." After a few minutes of stilted conversation we ascertained that the man was speaking of overnight accommodations in a nearby building, and the rest of us were overjoyed to find that we could spend the night rather than leave that same day.

Two of us began walking up the trail towards the lodge, but the man began gesturing and smiling and pointed to my friend's camera. I called out to the two others and they came back down. My friend collected everyone's cameras, and the rest of us lined up with the man and smiled while we took pictures.

I was trying to change the film in my camera in preparation for our hike when the man approached me with his arms outstretched and a big smile on his face. I smiled back and then noticed as he came closer that his lips were puckered and his arms were closing in around me.

I was unsure what to do when confronted so suddenly. A strange part of me didn't want to risk offending him by refusing his advances since he had been so friendly. It crossed my mind that it might be his custom or a cultural aspect of which I was unaware. But as he moved closer my sense of self-preservation kicked in and I put my arm out to stop him and said, "No!" in a sharp tone, which I hoped would convey my displeasure even if he did not understand my vocabulary. I said "Thank you," and then turned in the other direction and walked away.

INSIGHT:
The student learned to think quickly, considering both the intentions of the young Chinese male or her own personal needs. The correct decision is not always obvious, but the decision to say no this time was made in a cultural context, with sensitivity to both her needs and the wants of the Chinese male.

Japan

Japanese Students. When my friend and I travelled for the day to Kyoto, we visited the Imperial Palace. The same day we decided to visit the palace, a local secondary school was also visiting on a field trip. As we paid for our tickets we immediately began to stand out, first because we are Caucasian, and second we were maybe the only four that weren't wearing navy blue uniforms. The students were all around thirteen to fifteen years old. They were *very* polite, but it soon became obvious that my friends and I were a bit more of an attraction than the palace. They looked at us and smiled, and motioned waves, and made peace signs with their hands. As we (our group) began to walk towards the exit a teacher (or older woman who we assumed was a professor) asked us in perfect English if it would be alright if some girls took a picture with us. We told the teacher we would be happy to be in photographs. After they snapped the pictures they said "thank you" in English and bowed, and smiled. We tried our best "thank you" in Japanese and bowed as well. This was a really positive experience, and I've since looked back on it and felt lucky to have interacted with the Japanese students. I hope they felt the same way.

INSIGHT:
The Japanese children tried to communicate with the American students as much as they could, although very little actual information was exchanged. However, many good feelings and emotionally positive feelings were shared by both groups from their interaction, which had profound meaning.

Critical Incident. In the West, at least where I live in Los Angeles, there seems to persist a kind of self-centered attitude revolving around looking out for one's self. You look out for yourself. Everyone else's business and problems are theirs to deal with, and left alone they do not affect you. It is sad, but true.

As it turns out, the rest of the world, especially Asian (the new Evil Empire) does not share in this attitude. Maybe we can, if we ever open our eyes, learn something from them.

I was lost. I was frustrated. I was tired. I had gotten, by myself, on the wrong train leaving Nara, Japan, in hopes of returning to Kobe. I was so angry. I wanted to lash out at something, but all I had was myself. I was standing looking dumbfounded at a Japanese railman when I felt a hand on my shoulder. There stood an elderly Japanese businessman, and he asked me in somewhat broken English if I needed any help.

It was a shocker to me. I was confused. Why would this man want to help me? Why should he care about me? I stood there looking into his eyes, confused and thinking up all sorts of creative reasons, none good, on why this random man wished to help me. Not seeing really any other option, I accepted. He not only put me on the correct train, but went out of his way to accompany me back to Kobe.

It was so alien to me, such an uncharacteristic way for the people I know, at least the ones I grew up around, to react. I sat opposite the man the entire train ride back saying little, yes, weighed down with a sense of guilt. Not guilt that I had actually done anything wrong, guilt in that if the roles had been reversed I really do not know if I would have had, for lack of better words, the strength of character to do such a selfless act.

INSIGHT:
The American student was frustrated, angry, and lost, feeling very alone when the elderly Japanese offered to help him. This spontaneous gesture provided a meaningful memory of helpfulness in Japan and taught the student about alternatives to individualistic isolation in another culture.

The Japanese Bank. Ten students walked into a bank to change money ten minutes before it was scheduled to close. The tellers turned us away explaining that they could not help all of us in the time remaining. They gave us a map of all the banks in the area and suggested we go somewhere else. Aware that every place would close in a few minutes we didn't see that as a solution to our problem. We had to get money to pay for our evening and the following morning before the banks reopened. In a few minutes we had to come up with a solution.

I noticed that the way the Japanese tellers treated the situation, they wanted to help all of us or none of us. At first we did not understand why they turned us away before helping anyone. Understanding our cultural difference helped us find a good solution. We convinced them that we would all be happy if they would exchange money for two people. I changed a lot of money for my group, and one guy from the other group changed money for them. Our only other option was to go out in search of other banks that would help us. If we did that, however, we should risk meeting closed doors. The best chance for a solution was with the bank tellers in front of us.

INSIGHT:
The students had learned new strategies and methods to accommodate individual needs in a collectivist culture like Japan. Working through a group representative was an example of reframing the task in ways that were more acceptable in Japan.

A Crowded Subway Station. It was about 5:00 p.m. in the subway station in Kyoto, Japan. Businessmen had just gotten off of work and were either going home or out to a bar to drink with their fellow office workers. The subway station was crowded due to rush hour. I was with three female friends waiting in one of the several lines that formed on the platform of the subway. There were already about ten people in front of us and about ten more in back. When the train pulled into the Kyoto station I whispered to my friends, "Alright guys, we are going to get on this one." My friends nodded and we waited in anticipation for the people getting off to get off so that we could push our way into the train. My mind was set on getting on the train, so when people started pushing all I could do was go with the flow and push my way into the doorway. The whole ten seconds in which I got smashed between the people in front and in back of me my whole mindset was not on whether my friends were on or not but rather if I could make it in. What didn't occur to me is that we *all* had to make it in. When I got shoved in I looked outside and my friends were still on the platform. At first I panicked and yelled, "Get in!" but there was no way that they could fit. I had to decide whether to stay or squeeze my way out. In that split second many thoughts popped into my mind. "I don't know where to meet them if we get separated. It's not safe to walk around by myself. How do I get out of this crowd?" But when I saw my friend's arm reach out and grab for me I wiggled my arm out and she pulled me out of the train just as the door closed. "Whew! That was a close one."

INSIGHT:
The student's decision to get on the train needed to be made immediately with little time to consider the consequences or to hesitate. Being in a hurry almost led the student to make a hasty and wrong decision.

Acceptance of a Gift. I met up with a friend who moved to Japan about a year ago. We were invited over to her boss's house for tea one afternoon. We had a wonderful time and I couldn't get over how beautiful the tea set was she was using. I, of course, complimented her on the tea set and said, "I have never seen one so beautiful and exquisite." She tried to give me the tea set after that, insisting that she wanted me to have it to remember Japan. I didn't know what to do because I couldn't accept such a gift (it was expensive), but she seemed so enthusiastic about the idea that I didn't want to offend her either.

The people involved were myself, my American friend, and her Japanese boss. My friend kept telling me that she really did want to give the tea set to me but that I could refuse it by letting her know how much I appreciated her thoughtfulness, that it would be difficult for me to get it home and that I wouldn't use it as much as she would in Japan.

INSIGHT:
The rules of being a good host in Japan were very strict and demanding. The obligation to a house guest like this student were taken very seriously. While the student was also bound by the same rules there were usually face-saving strategies that would help circumvent the rules so that extravagant gifts could be refused without anyone being embarrassed.

A Homestay in Japan. I spent my first night in Kobe, Japan, with a friend from the ship and an older Japanese woman. My friend and I had decided to sign up for a short homestay because we had heard that it was very unusual to be invited into a home in Japan. I expected to learn about the set-up of a traditional house and hopefully some helpful hints about travelling in Japan. What I ended up learning was about the gender differences in this culture.

Instead of taking us to her own home our homestay "mom" took us to her daughter-in-law's apartment. Her son was out working for the evening so we never got to meet him. We walked into the apartment and were introduced to "her son's wife." (That was how the older woman referred to her.) We sat down on a couch and the daughter-in-law brought us tea and small cakes. We thanked her and tried talking to her, but she did not speak English. Because she couldn't understand us this let the older woman discuss their marriage freely.

She explained that both worked in the city but that her son paid for all of the "important things" such as rent and car payments. She made it seem as through her son's job was much more important. Our homestay mother also expressed great disappointment because her son's wife had yet to produce any grandchildren.

During our entire conversation the younger woman was refilling our tea cups and waiting on her mother-in-law. The older woman never thanked her or acknowledged her the entire time. We got up to help clear away the dishes but were told not to. "Don't worry, she will take care of it," our homestay host told us.

INSIGHT:

Japan is a society in transition so that traditional rituals frequently come in conflict with modern values and necessities, especially in family relationships. The student recognized the family problems as an area of controversy and some sensitivity where unsolicited advice from outsiders was not welcome.

Little Ol' Lady. The day was beautiful--clear skies and a cool wind. It was our last day in Kobe, Japan. We had already been to Hiroshima, Nara and Kyoto with our fair share of language barrier difficulties. We didn't intend to run into anymore problems with languages, because we only had one hour before on-ship time and we were done. Two of us were sitting in the park across from a small strip center. It was a beautiful park area with wonderful fountains and ponds. As we were scribbling out our last postcards this little ol' lady came up to us and started speaking Japanese as though it was our first language. She was holding out a newspaper and rambling on and on. It was all in a friendly tone and it seemed to be a gift. We were dumbfounded. We didn't know what to do or say. The only thing I knew how to say was thank you in Japanese. Should I tell her we can't understand a word she is saying or just smile and play along with it all? Then suddenly I found myself partly understanding what she was saying. I heard "ship" and "American."

The whole time I was thinking, "She must be crazy. Do we look like we know word one that she is saying? How long is she going to go on? Why is she giving this to us? We can't read it! Well I guess we will just keep smiling and nodding until she's done; it seems to be working so far." This went on for sometime. She had been offering us this newspaper which must mention us at the port. It was definitely the right decision to continue smiling and let her finish. She was happy and seemed rather thrilled we accepted her gift. As she walked on she was digging through her purse, then returned and handed us two big handfuls of chocolate, smiled, and went on her way.

INSIGHT:

The more authentic the contact between a student and the Japanese host culture person, the less likely that either party would entirely understand the other because of language differences. While much of the content in such an encounter was lost, the feelings and emotions were vivid and powerful.

Visiting Hiroshima. This incident occurred in Hiroshima, Japan, right next to the A-Bomb Dome. A group of three of us, all Semester at Sea students, were all walking out of the park when a man and two women approached us. They stood there in a line, said, "Hello," smiled and bowed. We were confused as to why they had approached us. Then the man pulled a sheet of paper out of his briefcase. He kept folding and unfolding the sheet until he found the printed message in our language. It said, "The greatest happiness which one can have is to make others happy."

At this point they motioned for us to put our palms together. They then proceeded to say something in Japanese. We were then motioned to close our eyes. We did and the three people continued in their routine for about three minutes. At the end they thanked us and walked away.

I'm not sure what they were doing, but it seemed to have a religious meaning to it. I say this because I perceived them as missionaries. Obviously there was no word exchanged that I could understand.

I think I chose to stay because of the body language the people sent. They approached us in a friendly, reverent manner. I felt they were with a church organization so that added to the comfort that the people were not going to do anything bad to us. Also the surroundings helped, because of the solemn peacefulness of the park in which an awful event had occurred.

INSIGHT:
Hiroshima was a powerful symbol in relationships between Japan and the United States. Japanese and Americans meeting at such a powerful place felt the need to communicate. The student learned that there were many ways to communicate meaningfully that do not depend on sharing the same language.

I Want to Stay in Japan. On our last day in Japan my friend got back from Tokyo after having spent four days there with one of her best friends from high school. From the second I saw her I knew that something was up. I immediately asked her what happened in Tokyo. She didn't even look at me in the eye when she answered, but seemed really excited. She said she would come and tell after she got something to eat. This was during lunch that day.

When she came to sit by me the first thing she said was that she wanted to stay in Japan. Having known her for the last two or so months this really didn't surprise me. She was one of those people who got really excited about all the ports we visited. She couldn't wait to go back to those countries.

I immediately told her that if that's what she really wanted to do she should do it. I asked her what had made her decide to stay. She said that her friend had tried to convince her to stay since the first day she was there but really hadn't taken it seriously until a few days later. Her friend had tried to convince her by telling her that she could stay with her in her apartment and not pay any rent, and that it is really easy to get jobs teaching English in

Japan. What really convinced her of staying, however, was a group of people that she met one night. They were all from different countries and they spent all their time travelling from one country to another. They would live in one country for awhile and get a job or sell things they had brought from other countries. They were not rich, but they had all travelled extensively.

They talked about how they always would end up running into each other even though they never told each other where they were going. In Japan they all had jobs teaching English or Spanish and some of them also sold jewelry on the streets. They all said they wouldn't trade their lifestyles for anything. This apparently inspired her to make her decision. Since I could see her being perfectly happy living that way and travelling a lot, I supported her decision all they way. I know that a lot of people were surprised by her decision. Everybody would ask her if she was sure she wanted to stay. A lot of people thought she was crazy!

INSIGHT:

The student's experience of visiting other countries opened perspectives for seeing the world and living life more completely than many students would have thought possible before the journey. Such a voyage profoundly changed the priorities of many students by offering new opportunities and demonstrating that the student was truly free to make new choices and decisions.

When We Got Lost. When I travelled to Kyoto, Japan, with four friends from the ship we had quite an experience when we got lost. We had taken a bus from the Todoji Temple and were on our way to the Golden Pavilion. Our bus dropped us off at a corner and we were instantly confused. We had everything written down but we were unable to read any of the street signs because they were in Japanese characters. There were about four different roads that we could take, but we had no idea which one to choose.

A group of about twenty schoolchildren, about fourteen years old, were walking by and we decided to ask them for directions. I said, "Excuse me," and eight of them stopped. "Do you know how to get to the Golden Pavilion?" I asked. They just looked at me blankly, obviously not understanding what I had just asked. They noticed that I was holding a map and a sheet of phrases translated into Japanese. Two of the girls said something to me and pointed to the map. I showed them where we wanted to go and they said "Oaaah. Okay. Okay." The group then motioned for us to follow them. We didn't really know if the schoolchildren understood where we wanted to go, but we decided to follow them anyway. We were already lost and didn't have much to lose. So the five Americans followed the eight Japanese teenagers for almost a half an hour up hills and around corners. The next thing we knew we were at the front gate to the Golden Pavilion.

INSIGHT:

The students learned to ask questions and accept the feeling of dependence in a foreign culture like Japan. This was difficult for the more individualist students who were uncomfortable with dependency, but in many other cultures dependency was accepted and appropriate in relationships.

My Last Night in Japan. My last night in Japan was quite an eventful and somewhat stressful night. I was in Tokyo with a bunch of my friends and we had gone out to dinner and then decided to go to a couple of bars. One of my friends and I did not really feel like partying, and because we didn't have enough money to stay at a hotel we decided to try to get a reservation on the bullet train that night and take it back to Kobe. It was already around 10:00 p.m. and we had been warned that we probably had missed the last bullet train that ran that night. We were stubborn though and did not want to stay at a bar all night, so we made our way to the subway station and headed for the Tokyo stop, which was where we could catch the bullet to Kobe.

Once we arrived at the Tokyo stop we realized that we had missed the last bullet train and that the next one did not run until 6:20 the next morning. We really did not know what we should do at that point. Our first thought was to hang out and sleep in the Tokyo station until we had to get on the bullet train. Unfortunately, we realized that the subway station was closing in about a half an hour and would not re-open until 5:30 the next morning. We realized that if worse came to worse we could try to get a hotel room and just charge it (because we were low on cash), but neither one of us wanted to do that. We decided that our best bet was to try to find an "all-night coffee shop" where we could hang out until the next morning. Unfortunately, we had a hard time trying to communicate our intentions because no one really spoke English.

Luckily we came across this Japanese businessman at the subway station from whom we asked directions. We first asked him if he could point out the gate we needed to go to tomorrow to catch the train. He was extremely helpful and actually walked us to where we needed to catch the bullet. We then asked him if he knew of any all-night restaurants that were open. We told him that we needed to find a place that was open all night that we could hang out at until we had to catch the train. I think he was surprised and somewhat amazed at the fact that this is what we wanted to do. I think he felt sorry for us so he told us to follow him and he would take us to a place. He hailed a cab for all of us, and at this point he confesses to be "rather drunk." As we got in the cab he explained in Japanese that we were looking for an all-night restaurant and did the cabbie know where one was.

The businessman explained to us that he had a wife and a twenty-one year old daughter, and offered to put us up at his home for the night. We politely declined and said it would be easier if he could show us where an all-night restaurant was. He kept talking with the cab driver in Japanese and they kept laughing and turning around and looking at us. My friend and I began to get a little nervous because we really had acted impulsively by just jumping into a taxi with this businessman whom we really know nothing about. The fact that he was drunk made me a little nervous too, but because he had a twenty-one year old daughter I kept reassuring myself everything would be okay.

At one point the businessman turned around to us and said, "I wish I did not have a wife!" My friend and I definitely became nervous that we were not going to be taken to an all-night restaurant and instead we were going to be taken somewhere by the cabbie and businessman that would not be safe. All I could think about was how would I explain to my parents the fact that I had jumped into a taxi with a drunk Japanese man (he was not visibly drunk) who said he would show us where an all-night restaurant was. After driving for about ten minutes the cab actually did pull up to a coffeehouse. We were both extremely relieved to arrive there. The businessman insisted on coming upstairs with us to make sure the coffeehouse was okay. After saying our goodbyes to him my friend and I could not believe how nice he had been to us.

INSIGHT:
The students were more vulnerable in Japan than back in the United States without many of the back-home support systems to depend on. Japanese nationals became protective of the vulnerable students and helped them. A more arrogant and independent student might have had a more difficult time.

May I Have Your Autograph. Japan was one of my favorite ports and the learning that I did was probably more beneficial than any other port. Before Japan I had resented the Japanese immensely. Why shouldn't I have? The messages throughout the American media are mass-hysterical, "The Japanese are coming!" They have taken over our car, electronic, movie and even consumer industry. They were coming to our country searching for bargains and ruling what I considered "ours."

When I stepped off the Shinkansen train in Kyoto, I was exhausted and tired of being stared at. Groups of schoolchildren gawked at us and giggled. I just gave them a tired smile and looked for the information desk. My travelling companion pointed out that we were going the wrong way so we turned around to back track.

As we started our trek back, a number of schoolchildren, of about age twelve, came up to us. In their hands they held pink and blue bunny paper and a matching pencil. One of the uniformed girls said shyly, "Hello, would you write your name, please?" My heart melted as I took the paper from her shaking little hand and printed my name in bold letters.

Right then it all came together, these people admired us and wanted (maybe) to be like us. Also, I realized that through this whole voyage every port we'd been to, I had seen an abundance of other countries' cultures. My resentment for the Japanese was my own closed minded global selfishness.

INSIGHT:
The conflict between Japan and the United States seemed much less ominous for the students when mediated by children. The students learned that young children had the time and curiosity to be wonderful mediators for learning about Japan and finding common ground.

CONCLUSION

The fourth stage of culture shock moves from reintegration toward a more autonomous position where the students did not blame either themselves or the host culture for misunderstandings but were able to see each event in a balanced context. This stage is a synthesis of the previous three stages, incorporating elements of each previous stage. The students were now able to be proactive and had enough insight to see what had to be done, even though they might not have the skill to do it. They were becoming more competent in the host cultures and more accurate in their assessment of the cultural context.

Students who were able to achieve this balanced perspective, however briefly, describe it in very positive terms. There is little of the illusion of the first stage nor the pain of the second stage nor the anger of the third stage but rather a synthesis in a more complex but also competent role for the student in the host culture. Not all students were able to reach this fourth stage, but most of the students experienced the flash of insight this stage provides from time to time during the voyage.

The fifty-two critical incidents gathered to illustrate students in the fourth stage of culture shock demonstrate a wide range of feelings toward themselves and the host culture. The critical incidents used to illustrate the fourth stage each carried elements and traces from the previous three stages as well.

The first theme of these fourth stage incidents emphasizes a more comfortable perspective of the student herself or himself, incorporating concepts such as "spontaneous, enthusiastic, independent, appropriate, important, courageous, adventurous, communicative, humorous, generous, giving, accurate, aware, curious, prepared, sensitive, intentional, polite, effective, experienced, authentic, and competent."

The second theme in these critical incidents emphasizes a generally positive perspective of the host culture in concepts such as "friendly, memorable, receptive, hospitable, safe, fair, trusting, accommodating, leisurely, positive, and generally accepting."

A third theme describes the experiences the students had in the host cultures, using concepts such as "reassuring, meaningful, planned, potential, symbolic, invested, selective, patterned, relational, in transition, sharing, change, and providing choices."

Sometimes students who shared the same experience interpreted that experience from the perspective of different stages, depending on what was emphasized. The host/guest rules are in place for students in this fourth stage. They have some idea of what they can expect of others as well as what others expect of them.

7

The Interdependence Stage

INTRODUCTION

The last stage in most descriptions of culture shock aims at the goal of a bicultural or multicultural identity. In this almost idealized target goal, the U-curve, the individual has moved from alienation to a new identity that is equally comfortable, settled, accepted, and fluent in both the old and new cultures. There is a sense of belonging to several cultures at the same time. Even though the individual is still different from the host culture in a variety of ways, those differences do not dominate or control the individual's identity any longer. A mutual adaptation has occurred that defines the profoundly significant common ground between visitors and the host culture. The differences between the visitor and the host culture are no more or less significant than the differences between any two residents of that host culture. The new culture has been internalized to the point where the visitor accurately and appropriately acknowledges some ownership, responsibilities and privileges in that new host culture. Ideally, that fifth-stage person will be referred to as a bicultural or multicultural person.

The attitudes, emotions, and behaviors of the person in the fifth stage of culture shock will accurately build on both similarities and differences between cultures. The person will exhibit a high level of trust and authentic sensitivity to the conditions of the host culture. The person will express humor and creativity and will accurately interpret the meaning of events in the host culture. The emotions of the previous four stages will be integrated and synthesized into this new identity with each stage contributing its own essential perspective to the development. The person will build on this new identity as a "transitional experience" (Adler, 1975) in the encounter with other cultures and with an unfolding of the new self. This fifth stage then is not the end point or culmination of development but a state of dynamic tension between self and culture that opens new perspectives.

In this fifth stage, the person will have learned several insights about cultures in contact. First, each culture is a fabric of values attitudes and beliefs with its own pattern and internal consistency. Second, no single culture is inherently better or worse than any other culture but must be experienced and judged according to its own rules. Third, there is no easy measure to rate a successful/good or an unsuccessful/bad culture. Fourth, all persons are culture bound to the extent that they have truly internalized the values, attitudes, and beliefs of their home culture and are therefore products of their own culture. Fifth, each culture provides its own identity through regulating the behavior and defining the individual's personal space in the world. As the individual's cultural identity is enlarged to include more cultures, he or she draws from a larger cultural vocabulary for self-expression. This final stage incorporates aspects of all previous stages in a developmental harmony. Figure 1 (by Adler, 1975) summarizes these stages in a useful diagram.

Adler (1975) describes this transitional experience in several ways. At a perceptual level he describes the movement of personality from a symbiotic state of single reality awareness to a more complicated differential state acknowledging the interdependence of many realities. At an emotional level the transition moves from a limited dependency to a more autonomous independence or even interdependency of feeling states. With regard to self- concept, the transition moves from a monocultural to an intercultural or multicultural frame of reference. Adler (1974) suggests that increased culture contact is resulting in a new type of person whose orientation and worldview transcends that person's indigenous cultural identity, which he calls "multicultural." The multicultural person's identity is inclusive rather than exclusive in appreciating both the similarities and the differences between, among, and within cultures. This new multicultural perspective is not totally a part of nor apart from that person's home culture but rather on the "boundary," in a state of dynamic tension.

Adler's (1974) multicultural person presents a unique perspective in three aspects. First, the multicultural personality is psychoculturally adaptive, responsive to situational cultural factors, and without boundaries between the self and cultures being experienced. Truth is not judged by a self-reference criterion, nor by an absolute rigid standard nor by comparison with other cultures but by criteria which emerge uniquely from within each cultural setting. Second, the multicultural person is evolving and going through a dynamic transition, similar to Lifton's (1967) notion of protean man who is always recreating his identity. To this extent a multicultural identity is a process rather than an end point of development. Third, multicultural persons maintain an indefinite boundary to their concept of self. Consistency becomes less important than accurate and appropriate reflection of the cultural context, not captured by any single culture nor having any particular cultural home. The multicultural identity is defined by flexibility, adaptability and adjustment to the cultural context. Multiculturalism in this sense is more than having experienced many cultures. Multiculturalism requires being a part of each culture as an insider while also staying apart from each culture as an outsider.

In its extreme forms, the dangers of a multicultural identity are obvious. First, the multicultural person is vulnerable by not having boundaries for definition and protection. We depend on boundaries to define an event, experience, or a person's identity, defining who we are in relation to others. Second, the multicultural person is likely to experience a diffused identity with changing loyalties and identifications. Without a fixed cultural identity, the multicultural person is forced back on her or his own subjectivity to interpret experiences. It is easy for the multicultural person to be overwhelmed by the cultural context. Third, the multicultural person may be reduced to a sequence of unrelated roles in response to one or another cultural contexts, much like an actor or actress who can no longer remember who he or she was originally. The congruence and integrity that define identity can be lost in this multicultural adaptive process. Fourth, multicultural persons may appear to be dilettantes, changing identities without commitment to any particular culture. In this way multiculturalism can result in an escape from deeper responsibilities and involvements. Fifth, the multicultural person may take refuge in cynicism or an aloof detachment from any particular cultural context.

In a positive direction, the multicultural person provides a catalyst and facilitating function for cultural contacts, providing links between cultures. These multicultural persons provide a mediating function to society and different cultures. The construct of multiculturalism suggests a dynamic synthesis of similarities and differences among cultures.

Relatively few examples of critical incidents by student authors were found to illustrate aspects of this fifth and final stage of culture shock. The student authors of these critical incidents were able to value both similarities and differences as significant and interdependent in a new synthesis of values. They describe the full range of emotions such as trust, sense of humor, ability to love, and all other normal emotions. They describe behaviors as self-expressive and creative, allowing them to function normally without regard to either the new or the old culture. Their interpretations of this experience were to accept social, psychological, and cultural differences while freely exercising choice and responsibility for those choices. They were able to interpret meaning from both the positive and negative experiences in this new cultural setting.

Figure 1

Stage	Perception	Emotional Range	Behavior	Interpretation
Contact	differences are intriguing, perceptions are screened and selected	excitement stimulation euphoria playfulness discovery	curiosity interest assured impressionistic depression withdrawal	The individual is insulated by his or her own culture. Differences as well as similarities provide rationalization for continuing confirmation of status, role, and identity.
Disintegration	differences are impactful, contrasted cultural reality cannot be screened out	confusion disorientation loss empathy isolation loneliness inadequacy	depression withdrawal	Cultural differences begin to intrude. Growing awareness of being different leads to loss of self-esteem. Individual experiences loss of cultural support ties and misreads new cultural cues.
Reintegration	differences are rejected	anger rage nervousness anxiety frustration	rebellion suspicion rejection hostility exclusive opinionated	Rejection of second culture causes preoccupation with likes and dislikes; differences are projected. Negative behavior, however, is a form of self-assertion and growing self-esteem.

248

Autonomy	differences and similarities are legitimized	self-assured relaxed warm empathic	assured controlled independent "old hand" confident	The individual is socially linguistically capable of negotiating most new and different situation; he or she is assured of ability to survive new experiences.
Independence	differences and similarities are valued and significant	trust humor love full range of previous emotions	expressive creative actualizing	Social, psychological, and cultural differences are accepted and enjoyed. The individual is capable of exercising choice and responsibility and able to create meaning for situations.

Source: From "The Transitional experience: An alternative view of culture shock" by P. Adler, 1975, *Journal of Humanistic Psychology,* <u>15</u> (4) pp. 13–23. Used by permission.

CRITICAL INCIDENTS

Brazil

To Stay or Go. It was our first night in Salvador, and we were ready to have a good time. We had heard of a Reggae band playing at a bar, so we told the taxi driver to take us there. He knew a little bit of English and some Spanish, so we figured that between the five of us we'd be able to get where we needed to go. When we pulled up to the bar we were informed that the band had played there the previous night and that there was no entertainment tonight. We told the driver that we wanted to go to a bar where there was a band playing--Samba music we said. He proceeded to drive us for what seemed like a half an hour and finally we came to a bar, but everyone was just standing outside in the parking lot. We all got our of the car and had to decide if we wanted to stay or go. Some of our group was a little nervous, including myself, because we had no idea what this place was like.

As we were talking to the driver about maybe taking us to a different place, and finding out how much we already owed him, two girls came up to us and said they spoke English. They helped us with paying the driver and then tried to convince us that they were having a fundraiser for their graduation from medical school, that there would be great music and a lot of fun. One girl with us was a little unsure about staying, but at this point most of us wanted to because these Brazilian girls and their friends were being so nice. We assured our friend that if we were uncomfortable we could always come outside and grab a cab. I asked why everyone was outside, and they told us it was because it was still so early--when it was 11:30! It was then that we decided to stay, paid the driver, and sent him on his way.

INSIGHT:

The students had developed a sixth sense about when it was better to stay and when to leave. This decision to stay was not necessarily a rational decision but nonetheless important, if the student was to take advantage of learning opportunities in Brazil.

South Africa

A Loud Friend. When in South Africa I had the opportunity to visit some townships and squatter settlements. At one of the squatter settlements we talked with some of the residents. We asked questions, and our guide translated for us. The nine Semester at Sea students were rather hesitant. The South Africans readily answered our questions. I wondered why these local South Africans spoke so freely to us. I assumed that because we were white they linked us with the power that oppressed them, and that they would therefore resent us. After all, we were the enemy, right?

But they did not treat us like the enemy. They answered our questions. They told us everything we had the courage to ask. We asked if we could take pictures. They laughed and said yes.

As we started to walk around one man started yelling. He was very excited, and I could not understand some of his broken English. But I could make out some of it. "You, you are my friends. You, you come and you see how I live. But no one else comes," he yelled at us. After he yelled for a while, he asked us to take a picture of him. I very much wanted a picture of myself with the man. I wanted to show him that I was his friend. But I was scared. I knew he would not harm me physically, but he was yelling and it scared me. I had to decide if I wanted to share my personal space with him. I had to decide if it would be safe or if he would start yelling at me.

I handed someone my camera, and I went and put my arm around him. He continued to yell, and he put his arm around me. "No one else comes. You come, and you see. You are my friends." The picture was taken, but the man still had his hand heavily placed around my shoulder. He did not realize the picture had been taken because he had been looking around and yelling. I tried to slide away, but I could not without being rude, so I stood there. His arm was heavy, and I was a little nervous.

After what seemed like a very long time, someone told him the picture had already been taken, and he lifted his arm off my shoulder. He asked if I would send him a copy of the picture. I said yes, and he made me promise not to forget.

INSIGHT:

It was not easy to maintain the right balance of formal and informal behavior appropriate to the South African cultural context. The students became more or less formal as the situation required, reading the subtle cues in the South African's culture about which was appropriate at this time and place.

Right of Admission Strictly Reserved. We walked into a bar in Stellenbosch and I thought for a minute that I was home. The place was packed with college students from the nearby university, and I kept expecting to be greeted by a familiar face. But what I did not notice was that there were no black, colored or Indian students in the bar, and that my outwardly liberal views would not be appreciated.

I began talking to a guy named Ludwig. He was blond, blue eyed and surfed all his life. He reminded me of a typical Californian. We began with small talk and I realized he was as far from being a typical Californian as you could get. He had been in a war that South Africa fought in three years ago. He had watched his best friend die in his arms. He said that he had no future in South Africa because the education he was getting did not guarantee anything. But what surprised me the most was that he blamed his problems not on the government but on the black people. He said, "If the kafirs would only realize that they're not as good as us whites and stop causing so many problems they would be given more privileges, like the blacks in America."

It was at this point that I had to make a decision. I was very offended by the statement he had made, not only because of its falsehood but because of the outright prejudice of the statement. I was offended that he could make any correlation between apartheid and the United States, and I was shocked by his ignorance. We had been having a fairly intellectual conversation before.

Instead of losing my temper and saying something offensive to him I told him, "When you were born you had the same exact qualities, both physical and mental, as any other baby, be he black, white, or colored. It is the circumstances under which you were born that has made you different from other people, not the color of your skin." He nodded his head and I continued to have a four-hour conversation with him in which I questioned him openly about his views of blacks in America, and he voiced his fears and expectations as a young white South African. I was able to overlook his statement and put it into context with his education. I controlled my anger until we found a common ground that we could agree on and then I realized I wasn't angry at him but at the ideals he had been taught.

INSIGHT:
The student found similarities among the South Africans who appeared different and also found differences among those who appeared similar. It was essential for the student to become "cross-eyed" to see clearly by focusing one eye on the similarities and the other on the differences at the very same time.

The Taxi-Driver Teacher. Our last day in South Africa turned out to be maybe the most educational thus far. After a day of visiting townships and squatter camps I was feeling in a very festive mood. Nonetheless, all my friends wanted to meet at Bertie's Landing to enjoy a few drinks before onboard time. I was separated from the group and had to take a cab to Bertie's. When the cab pulled up I was welcomed by Arnold, a very friendly Black South African.

I told him where I was going and he was on his way. As we drove through the streets we discussed politics and the life of the Black people there in South Africa. I began to become very involved in our conversation and forgot all about the drinks and friends at Bertie's. When we pulled up to the bar I thought for a moment and realized spending time with Arnold was more important then getting a buzz with my friends. I told him to keep going, and we did. We parked at an inlet overlooking the ocean and just discussed life. I believe he was grateful to be listened to and appreciated what my views were. After about an hour he brought me to the ship. I gave him the fare and a nice tip. I felt bad for him and the way he lived, and thought the tip was a nice gesture. As I made my way to the gangway Arnold raced toward me and reached out his hand and gave me back the tip and the fare. "My friend" he said. "This one is on me. When I am able to visit America we will have another conversation and you will drive."

INSIGHT:

Once in a great while the students were lucky enough to break free from the visitor status and establish a genuine relationship with locals. This usually happened by accident rather than through planning. Lasting relationships sometimes resulted from these spontaneous contacts.

Kenya

Where to Sit. I had an interesting experience in Samburu, Kenya, that I "hope" can be classified as a critical incident. I went on a safari and enjoyed the natural surroundings, the camping, and the wildlife very much. I was on the safari with fifty other Semester at Sea students, but I pretty much went "solo." The camp was set up in this way: The Semester at Sea students all sat at long rectangular tables, underneath a canopy-type covering, with bright lights shining down on them. Just about ten steps away sat the (black African) cooks and jeep drivers, who were our tour guides. They sat on the ground facing each other in a circle. There was no canopy, no table, no shining artificial lights. They sat together talking quietly underneath the star-specked sky.

I walked out of my tent the first night and was shocked to see this blatant separation and "polarized" feeling exemplified in the camp. I got my plate of food and coffee. I was the last one to fill my plate, and a few Semester at Sea students summoned me over to join them. I glanced back and forth between the African men quietly sitting, facing each other under the stars, and the long rectangular lit-up, covered table of boisterous students. Since I had come on the safari by myself this was my chance to meet new Semester at Sea students and make some more friends, as well as possibly break through any stereotypes some of the students may have had of me.

A few students started staring at me like, "Well are you going to sit down or what?!" I couldn't help but feel torn between joining them and doing what I really wanted to do (at the risk of being imposing). I wanted to sit in the dirt with the African men and talk to them instead.

I awkwardly declined the seat offered to me by some students and walked towards the circle of men around the fire. I simply sat down with them, and a bit embarrassed, introduced myself. One thing led to another, the conversation twisted and turned, and it became an amazing night. They asked questions about me and my country, and I asked questions about them and their country. I learned so much from these seven men and enjoyed my dinner with them much more than I would have had I sat beneath glaring lights, drinking beer and playing cards with the people from the ship.

INSIGHT:
As the voyage progressed, the students were not as constrained by group pressure to stay with their own kind. They were more likely to seek out new experiences with locals and consequently were more likely to be accepted. Travelling in a group or even in pairs was easier and sometimes more comfortable, but it sometimes got in the way of making local contacts.

Come into My Home. I was involved in a critical incident in Kenya. I was with a group of twenty-eight Semester at Sea students in Masai Mara. Our tour director took us to a Masai village, which consisted of about thirty mud huts encircling a large space with a manure covered floor. I was walking around with a friend of mine from home when a Masai woman approached us and asked us to come into her hut. We were sort of far from the rest of the group and we were not sure if it was safe to enter the hut. The lady then came up and touched my arm and said, "Come in my friend." I knew that we either had to take a chance and enter her hut or walk away very quickly. At this point I decided to go into the woman's hut and look around. I grabbed my friend and said, "Come on, let's go in." Thus, I played an active role in the decision-making process.

There were many cues that led me to make this decision. First, the woman was very soft spoken and gentle when she approached us. Thus, she appeared to be a very kind woman. Also, she was carrying a baby, which led me to believe that she was a sensitive person. I also knew that we were not in any immediate danger, because she could not hurt the two of us and hold the baby at the same time. Since she and the baby were both wrapped in authentic Masai wraps, I knew that she was not a stranger and that she did belong to the village. Also, the security of knowing there were twenty-six other Semester at Sea students nearby probably helped in giving me the courage to go into the hut. In other words, I knew the woman probably would not try to steal from us or hurt us with twenty-six other students nearby. The entire atmosphere of the village was a cue in and of itself. For instance, the people were kind to us, they sang songs when we entered the village, and they did not hesitate to answer our questions. Thus, the atmosphere lead me to trust the woman and enter her hut. If I had walked away, I would have missed out on an amazing cross-cultural experience.

INSIGHT:
Different students had almost the very same experience in the Masai Village. Some students viewed that experience positively, and other students described the experience in negative terms. The voyage provided the opportunity, but experience taught the skills to take advantage of that opportunity.

India

Visiting an Orphanage. During my stay in India, shortly after I met Mother Teresa, we visited the orphanage that she started. It was early in the morning so we had to wait a little while outside. While we waited there were Indian children all around with their hands outstretched. What do you do in this situation? Especially right after visiting Mother Teresa. I had this urge to help, to give something. However, by giving them something you only teach them to beg. One of the four people that I was with was my roommate. He asked me to hold on to his camera, and he went down the street to a store. I followed him. He bought a couple loaves of bread. At this time we were being followed by seven or eight kids. The number was growing as they realized what we were doing. He and I handed out all the bread and then the kids continued to hold out their hands and say something in their language.

We were then let into the orphanage. By that time we were practically swarmed by all the kids. Most of the kids in this orphanage had something physically wrong with them. Many of them had club feet or were very sick or something, yet they were all happy. They all smiled at us and followed us around. None of the kids outside smiled. We played and laughed with the kids. They got the biggest thrill out of our cameras. As we left we all gave a little money to the orphanage. When we got into the car I think we all were in a good mood. It wasn't all because of the money we gave, but it was the time we spent with those kids and the things we felt, and saw, and heard that day.

INSIGHT:
Some students were able to identify common ground with Indian children no matter how different and strange those Indians appeared and behaved. Discovering common ground led to understanding while the inability to identify common ground created distance between students and locals.

Beggars in Madras. I went out beyond the port entrance specifically to bring food to some street children I had spent the afternoon with. I had planned on giving to seven kids, but at least twenty swarmed around me grabbing my arms and reaching for what I might pull out of my bag. I did not want to give anything if it would create hostility, but I really wanted to share my excess food with the starving children around me. After several failed attempts to get the children alone, I realized I never would. I only had a few minutes until I had to run to the ship for departure. My friends looked up at me with innocent eyes that made my heart want to give everything it could. I saw the same eyes turn to glares towards other people swarming around me. I had to decide what was more important, to give them a meal or discourage fighting. The meal seemed more important for the time, but I did not want to give the children a bad experience that would make them feel pathetic.

I had a large emotional attachment to the seven children I had spent the afternoon with. We related as friends or siblings, not provider and beggar. They took me under their wing and showed me around their home turf. They gave me fresh jasmine, peanuts, songs, a rind, and the care of true friends. I gave them M & M's, but they never asked me for anything. When I went to give them food, it was hard for me to feel our relationship change. They still related to me as friends, but I felt the distance of having something they needed. My main goal was not to give them the food, but give them whatever I could that would be best for them. It was hard to find the best answer.

I don't know any of the children's names because our communication was limited. The older boy (around 12) watched over the others; he was the first to get hostile with outsiders and the first to support other children in the small group. A girl of about the same age seemed the second down the hierarchy. She wanted food, but understood my dilemma. I had tried to give her a bracelet in exchange for a ring she gave me. When other children got upset, she gave it back to me to make peace. There was also a small girl who I was really attached to. We had been hand in hand all day. I taught her a hand clap on the beach. They were the ones I had the strongest connection with. They, with the other four children I'd been with were a closely linked group. They watched out for each other and shared adventures. I imagine they have known each other for most of their lives.

I first tried walking up the street to lose some of our followers. That only worked to collect more as we passed women and children. When the decision point came I had already tried following the advice each child offered. I looked regretfully into their eyes and said, "There is too much fighting, I cannot give anything." I felt horrible. I wanted to cry. My friends looked to me deeply with sorrowful understanding. Our eyes met for a sad goodbye before I left.

I could have taken out the food and given it to the first grabbing hands. I also could have struggled to give it only to my friends. Either situation would have created jealousy and anger that I did not want to contribute to. I could have tried to get the children in a rickshaw to drive out into the street where I could safely give them my food. That probably would have been the best solution. My time was limited, so I went sadly back to the ship.

INSIGHT:

As the student became more aware of the profound need of Indian children, she experienced more pain and inadequacy to meet that need. Naivete, inexperience, and misunderstanding protected the less-experienced students from that sort of pain.

Hong Kong and China

Questionable Generosity. In Guanzhon three other Semester at Sea students and I were out with five students from Zhonshan University. We had been walking around the night market and had stopped on a street corner to figure out what to do for the rest of the night. One of our students suggested that we go to a disco. The idea was received well by all of us American students, but with more hesitation from the Chinese students.

One of our students pulled us over and said, "One of the girls told me that they would really like to go but the cover charge is too high."

I said, "What should we do? Go somewhere cheaper?"

He suggested, "I think they really want to go to this night club but they can't afford it. I think they feel really awkward about this."

Another friend said, "Could we pay for them if it's not too much?"

I said, "Do you think it would make them feel more awkward by admitting we have more money then they do?"

We all thought about that question carefully. We did not want to insult anyone. We just wanted to have a good time with the Chinese students.

He said, "Why don't we just offer the suggestion to them and they can say what they want."

I said, "Okay, then we should also have a back-up place that we also want to go to and suggest it."

So we agreed and walked back over to the group of students. We offered to pay their way into the bar and they gladly accepted. The decision was a good one, but the situation was a bit awkward.

INSIGHT:
The students were able to give help and still avoid embarrassment. While the American students may have had more money than the Chinese students, the Chinese had the ability to provide invaluable experiences to the students in exchange.

Bikes, Paths, and People. While I was in China I did so much travelling that I was just sick of it. It really wasn't the travelling that bothered me so much, it was more travelling in a large group. For most of this trip I have been pretty spoiled. I would travel with whomever I wanted, go where I wanted and best of all, when I wanted. The trips that were scheduled into China were much too complicated for me to do alone, so I had no choice but to travel with a group.

After two days in Beijing with the group, I was so tired that when we reached Xian a friend and I decided to take the day off and travel on our own. We got up around 10:00 a.m. and decided to rent bikes and explore the city of Xian on our own.

It is really a different experience to ride a bike as a form of transportation instead of recreation, people take it much more seriously. Inevitable as it seems, we did get lost. One minute we were on a main street that was paved, had lots of traffic and lots of buildings. The next thing that I knew we were riding down this narrow dirt road. I do not think that a regular sized car could fit down it. There were fires burning in barrels. Garbage was in big piles alongside this road, or shall I say path. It smelled, and it reminded me very much of India.

There were people on this street, but they were somehow different than the other people we had seen. Now that I think of it, they weren't the ones who were different, we were. We had violated tourist laws. We were in a place, a certain part of the city, that tourists just didn't go. These people just kept staring at us. I don't think they were mean stares, maybe more like curious stares. They probably wondered, what in the world we were doing in this place. I was thinking just the same thing. I turned to my friend and said, "I think we took a wrong turn." Her response was cut short as at that moment I plowed into a cart. Thank God no one was pulling it at the time. I really felt out of place. First I came into a section of town that I was not supposed to be in, and then I crashed into one of their carts. I could just imagine what they think of Americans!

As I began to dust myself off I heard someone say, "Good afternoon." I turned around and there was a young girl, probably around twenty-one or twenty-two, looking down at me smiling. I just stared at her; I guess I didn't expect to run into someone who spoke English here. My friend took over and said, "Good afternoon," back. I commenced brushing myself off. She was saying something about a school right over there. She was pointing, but when I looked in that direction I just saw some old buildings. I began to get suspicious. She wanted us to come in and look at her school. It was supposed to be an art school. I thought to myself, why does she want us to come in there? There couldn't actually be a school in there, much less a painting school. Why was she being so nice to us, she didn't even know us? I couldn't understand why she would come up to some complete strangers on the street and want them to come into her school.

The next thing I know, I am walking into this school that didn't look like a school. Why was I trusting this person? I didn't know her. I didn't know what was on the other side of those doors. I was going against my judgment. Everything inside me said don't go. Something kept saying, "You are walking into some kind of set up." I kept walking, I don't know why.

We got to the door and walked into a very rundown, gloomy courtyard. It did not look anything like a school. I said to myself, "Okay, now you've done it. You have really got yourself into one this time." I looked up at the balcony and saw this man rushing down. Oh gees, we did it. There was no one around. The group was not supposed to be back until around 5:00 p.m. They had no idea where we were. All of our identification was back at the hotel. We were in the middle of a foreign country, and to top it all off it was a communist country!!! Just as my worst fears heightened the man said, "Hello, good afternoon." He was one of the instructors at the school.

At that moment I felt like the biggest jerk in the world. I had been so distrusting. Why did I have to act like that? What kind of person am I? Something kept me walking toward that school that day. I don't know what it was. Everything inside me said, "Don't go." We ended up having a wonderful day. We spent the afternoon talking with the instructors, having tea and looking at the students' paintings. We even ended up buying a painting to take home with us. It was a great afternoon and is probably one that I will remember for a really long time.

INSIGHT:
Getting lost became much less frightening and much more attractive to the student after making friends. Getting lost made it possible for the student to find what she was looking for in China.

Our Forbidden Conversation. One night four of us were in a Karaoke bar in Beijing when a group of Chinese people invited us to join them at their table. They had graduated from Beijing University and spoke very good English. Three out of the six of them had been out of the country, while the others had been trying to get out for a long time and were unable to do so. I focused in on a conversation with one particular man who was extremely disheartened with China's political system.

"It is irrational," he said, "that we live under such unreasonable laws." He then asked me if I was aware of the 1989 Tiananmen Square incident. I responded "Yes," and knowing that I had to be very careful not to put him in an awkward position, I simply said that it was a tragic event.

He leaned closer to me and said, "I want to tell you what I know about Tiananmen, but I must watch my back."

I knew he trusted me by this time, because we had been talking for hours about communism and democracy and social settings in America and China. It was a "critical moment" in which my decision to go further into a forbidden discussion was an easy one to make.

He told me about "this beautiful, beautiful girl" he knew who was walking through Tiananmen Square with her friends, and when stopped by the police she said that she had no weapons, and then she was immediately shot dead. He told me of the tanks that literally smashed his schoolmates. He buried his head in his hands and tears swelled up in his eyes, and then he asked me, "Are you allowed to have gatherings for demonstrative purposes or just for fun on your campus?"

My heart sank, and the lead weight of socialist China pushed down heavily on my shoulders; I quietly said, "Yes."

The look in his eyes could never be recorded on paper or even film. The grief he felt for the youth of China was immeasurable. We talked about many more things, and he told me that they are waiting for Deng Xiao Ping to die soon. That once the old men in the high seats of the government die off the young people with any knowledge of what's going on in the outside world will rise up again.

This man smacked me in the face with my precious freedom. As a "critical incident" it can be interpreted in different ways. I will never forget our "forbidden" conversation and the way I felt when we said goodbye.

INSIGHT:

As the student became more experienced abroad, he also learned a lot about back-home values and customs by comparison. Values such as freedom, which were taken for granted back home in the United States, were seen in a new light in a local Chinese culture where freedom was more constrained.

Republic of China (Taiwan)

What Americans Are Like. During my stay in Taiwan we spent the night and the next morning in a little town called Wushe, but I really wish I could have spent more time there. People were really friendly in all of Taiwan, but especially there. They would come up to us and say "hello" because that was the only word that they knew how to say.

When we were trying to order dinner a man came up to us who spoke very good English. He helped us order our food and we asked him if he would join us. It turned out that he was an English teacher at the local school. He was very excited because he didn't get to meet people who spoke English very often. He showed us around his town and then we went to his house for tea. He was a little hesitant, but he finally asked us if we would speak in his class the next day. We said we would, and he wouldn't stop thanking us.

When we woke up a little before eight o'clock the next day, it seemed like we were in a totally different town. It was alive. Everyone was busy, especially at the school. Their band was playing, and all the students were dressed in their uniforms saluting the flag. Roger, the English teacher, told me that this is how they always started their day.

When we walked into the class all of the students started yelling and cheering for us. Roger then began telling the class about our voyage. He told them that the girl I was travelling with studied psychology and that I was an anthropology and religion major. One of the students asked how old we were. I answered twenty. Then they all pointed to one of the kids in the class laughing, and said he is bigger than you. Of course almost everything they said they asked in their own language and Roger translated. They were very hesitant to speak English in front of us. The class was very informal and was a lot of fun.

One of the students asked me what I thought the difference was between American women and the women of Taiwan. I said American women were usually more outgoing, and Taiwanese women were often more reserved. Roger then translated, and it was funny because they all said, "Ohhh," at the same time. One student asked why Americans are so tall, "Is it because they play basketball?" I had to laugh at that one. They were impressed with my facial and body hair, and they commented to me how pretty American girls were. They asked if we would take pictures of all of us. We said we would and then mail some to them. They all cheered. We didn't spend that much time in the little town of Wushe, but I feel I learned a lot there and had a really great time.

INSIGHT:
This student found a "role" or purpose in the local culture which legitimized his presence better than being a temporary visitor. Helping the local teacher work with a class or volunteering to work alongside a local provided legitimacy in the local Chinese culture that otherwise would have been impossible.

Japan

Travelling Alone. Having decided to travel alone in Japan, I skipped the Semester at Sea lines in Kobe to get my rail pass validated. I bought a separate ticket to Shin-Osaka, a neighboring town, jumped on a train and took off on my own. Once I had my pass validated in Shin-Osaka, I got directions to the small town near Mt. Fuji that I wanted to go to and went to go find my train. I must have looked extremely confused while I was trying to match up the Japanese characters on my ticket with the ones on the departure board, because an elderly Japanese man decided he was going to help me, even though he didn't speak English. His manner was very abrupt and he frightened me slightly, which must have shown on my face because another Japanese man came up and began bickering at him. By this time I was confused and frightened until the second man turned to me and said, in English, "I have an American with me," so I followed him obediently.

It turned out that the American was a silver medalist in the Olympic long-jump some years ago. He was with seven Europeans, and they were all paid by Japan to race bicycles for gambling purposes. They were on the same train as me, and they paid the extra money for me to sit in the first-class car with them. Once in the train I told them were I was going, and they said there was no way I would make it there that night because I had to take two more trains and a bus to get there, and it was already dark.

They offered me a place to stay at their training camp, but I told them that I didn't think that was such a good idea. They said that they really couldn't let me go on my own at night in these small towns because so few people spoke any English, and my major warning bell went off.

I am nineteen, blond, female, and they were eight grown athletes with an interpreter. There was something definitely wrong with this picture. Yes, I was frightened of going alone in a non-English speaking community, but I was even more afraid of what would happen to me here. When the guy from

England saw the reluctance on my face, he came and sat next to me and we talked about what the heck was going on. He told me that his girlfriend had flown in two days before and that I could share a room with her. So I counted my blessings and went with these guys and their interpreter.

INSIGHT:
The student was able to accept help without embarrassment or loss of face in Japan. In a surprisingly large number of cases, the students encountered fellow countrypersons or friends of friends. Because the network of students was relatively small, international student travellers frequently encountered one another in their travels.

Whether to Trust. Three of my female friends and I were on a bus in Kyoto, Japan, on our way to the Imperial Palace. It was about 1:00 p.m. in the afternoon and the bus wasn't very crowded so we each sat in our own row, one behind the other. I was sitting in the last row and the seat behind me was empty. The two friends in the front fell asleep, and the girl directly in front of me and I started talking in English. We talked about normal items, such as our plans for the day.

Out of the corner of my eye I saw someone looking our way. I turned to see a tan, old Japanese man smiling with crooked teeth at us. I smiled back and began talking with my friend again. Soon thereafter, the old man came over and sat directly behind me and said, "Hello" in a recognizable Japanese accent. I said, "Hello," and turned back to smile at him. He was a small, friendly man with glowing white hair and obviously seemed somewhat bored with the long ride. "Where you come from?" he said. I told him, "I come from Los Angeles, California, U.S.A." "Oh," he said and smiled, "I live there long, long time ago." He didn't seem threatening with his weak appearance, but at the same time I couldn't read his motives. He laughed a lot at anything I said that wasn't even supposed to be funny.

Every time I would turn around to talk to my friend he would ask another question. "How long are you stay in Japan? Where you stay? What you do now?" Meanwhile, my friend would turn the other way and look out the window. After a few questions I felt nervous and wasn't sure if I should tell him all this information. No one is ever this friendly in Los Angeles without an ulterior motive, and I had to decide whether or not I felt comfortable trusting him.

I had to decide quickly so I would know if I would answer his questions or just ignore him. The pro's of continuing my conversation with him were that it would be a polite and interesting talk with a native and he would get a more positive impression of Americans. On the other hand, he could be a potentially dangerous figure who could hurt us if we showed signs of vulnerability. I decided that my latter ideas were overreactive situations that I experienced in Los Angles not Kyoto, Japan, so I continued my conversation with the old man. It turns out that all he wanted to do was practice his English. When it was time for him to get off at his stop he thanked me numerous times. "Thank you for listening to my bad English. Thank you," and kept bowing as he left.

INSIGHT:
The student made friends easily and found an opportunity to have a contact with a local Japanese man. The student represented a different United States perspective which was of interest to the Japanese. The importance of friendly relations with locals went beyond the convenience and pleasure of the student and became part of the student's education for a collective responsibility to others.

CONCLUSION

The fifth and final stage of culture shock is labelled the achievement of "interdependence" because at that stage the students became aware both of themselves and the cultural context around them. This is the stage where persons are supposed to achieve a bicultural or multicultural identity, although that concept has never been clearly defined. In any case, this is the last or highest stage of development in the culture shock U-curve sequence and therefore provides an end goal for persons going through culture shock.

Not everyone achieves this fifth and final stage nor are they expected to do so. In fact, the research literature emphasizes that few if any actually achieve a bicultural or multicultural identity as indicated and implied by this final stage. Nonetheless, this stage provides a hypothetical goal for the heuristic model of the U-curve and is therefore useful.

To some extent, this final stage resembles the first stage, assuming that the person was already competent and established in his or her own back-home culture before he or she ventured into the new culture. The difference is that, in this fifth stage, the person is competent in more than one culture at an equally high level of competence.

In reviewing the insights from the fourteen critical incidents used to illustrate aspects of this fifth stage it might be useful to identify the fifteen rules illustrated by those incidents that are indicative of this fifth stage. There are many more than fourteen rules or guidelines indicating the fifth stage of culture shock but, these arbitrary examples provide a sample of the complex and somewhat paradoxical style of thinking associated with this highest level.

1. The student will be able to see the relationships between problems and opportunities in each cultural context.
2. The student will be competent in both a formal and an informal perspective and will know when to follow each.
3. The student will see both similarities and differences between himself or herself and the local population.

4. The student will find the role of visitor and the role of local somewhat blurred and overlapping at times.
5. The student will distinguish the roles of host and guest according to accepted rules and will be comfortable in either role.
6. The student will be able to identify advantages and disadvantages of both the home and host cultures.
7. The student will be able to find common ground with the host culture, no matter how different it may seem.
8. The student will be able to identify priority needs and take appropriate action to meet those needs.
9. The student will be able to give help and avoid embarrassment in the process.
10. The student will be able to find what he or she wants by getting lost.
11. The student will learn about his or her own culture by studying the local cultures.
12. The student will find an appropriate place or role for himself or herself in the local culture.
13. The student will be able to request and accept help from locals without embarrassment.
14. The student will be able to make friends and to be a friend to persons in the local culture.

This list provides a sample of the process toward which the five stages of culture shock are directed. There is a dialectical or at least dialogical quality to this final stage of culture shock which is difficult to discuss in the abstract. The critical incidents from this and previous chapters help the reader identify the final stage by identifying what it is not in the previous four stages.

My graduate school advisor defined education as "something that happens by accident when you are trying to do something else." Just as it is possible for teaching to occur without learning so it is also possible for learning to occur without teaching. The formal academic courses were certainly important to the students on this voyage even though none of the "on-ship" activities were reported in the selected critical incidents. These incidents described the learning that took place informally as the students encountered host cultures. Many other examples of learning or even examples of culture shock, took place onboard the ship as it sailed around the world.

About midway through the voyage, just out of Cape Town, I asked the students to spend five minutes drawing a map of the world at the beginning of my Social Groups class. The students' maps were quite accurate in their drawing of countries and continents from the United States through South Africa, but from that point on the drawings became much more vague and distorted. The students themselves commented on how important their experiences in the countries visited thus far were to their ability to draw the countries and how this increased accuracy symbolized their increased understanding of those countries.

In another classroom simulation, after leaving Japan, I provided students with U.S. $100,000,000.00 from the United Nations Development Bank which had been "overlooked" and would revert to the U.N. General Fund in two hours unless the students could unanimously decide how to spend it. The students were organized into five groups representing geographic areas we had visited to negotiate by concensus the spending of this lump sum within the two-hour time limit. The students had prepared themselves by interviewing other faculty and resource persons on the ship as well as by extensive library readings and were both well informed and enthusiastic about the priorities of their region. They demonstrated an articulate awareness of priorities, consequences, and sociopolitical realities internationally reflecting their experiences and new insights. These were no longer abstract facts or figures but now had faces and feelings and personal identities.

Arguments for and against International Training Experiences

There are many arguments for and against the kind of international and multicultural training provided by this voyage around the world. Some of the more typical criticisms would include the following (Pedersen, 1988):

1. All multicultural training and experience is a waste of time and money when any intelligent individual should be able to adjust in a foreign culture without any preparation. The critical incidents demonstrated how persons with culturally different assumptions could disagree without either one being unintelligent.
2. Intercultural training is actually harmful because the trainee learns half-truths and develops stereotypes that have to be unlearned when arriving in the foreign culture. The critical incidents demonstrated how many stereotypes were confronted and discarded by the students based on personal experiences abroad.
3. Only training programs that teach factual information about the foreign culture are valuable in learning about what to expect. Both the formal classroom training and the informal training in host cultures complemented each other in a comprehensive learning experience for the students.
4. Failure to make an emotional adjustment to another culture is a sign of weakness and mental instability, and consequently is unlikely to be prevented by training. The critical incidents describe numerous examples of personal growth and growing maturity toward both the host and home cultures.
5. It is a waste of time to focus on one's own cultural assumptions or biases, and more time should be spent looking at the values of the foreign culture. The importance of cultural self-awareness became

clear as the students progressed through the culture shock experience.

6.   The intelligent person already knows his or her own assumptions or biases and is in control of them. culture shock demonstrated to the students the limits of their culturally biased perspective about themselves and others.

7.   There is one right answer for each situation in the foreign culture, and it does not change from time to time or place to place. As the students applied what they learned from one culture to a completely different culture, they learned the vulnerability of cultural absolutes.

8.   Any reasonable person from the foreign culture will be able to identify what would be an appropriate response to an ambiguous situation. Emotions were at least as influential as rationality in helping the students select their responses to different cultural situations.

9.   It always will be possible to identify rewarding experiences in the foreign culture because they will remind the visitor of rewarding situations back home. In some of the critical incidents, the students found new and unique rewards in the foreign culture unavailable back home.

10. If you can become less sensitive to a superficial situation abroad, you will become less caring in a more extensive exposure to foreign cultures later. The teaching/learning context of the shipboard faculty and classes helped turn even brief experiences in host countries into important learning experiences.

11. Just being in spontaneous contact with foreign nationals is presumed to enable you to learn about them and their values on your own. Support and guidance by other students, faculty, and staff helped students capture the learning insights of spontaneous contacts that would otherwise have escaped them.

12. You don't have to learn about a foreign culture once you "get the feel" of the way they do things. Some learning in the host cultures was intuitive, but the constant emphasis on analysis and interpretation of what was "felt" helped students articulate their learning.

13. Diversity creates disunity in a society. All people should be taught to believe the same absolutes to produce a homogeneous society that has strength. The strength of diversity in an international perspective was evident as students saw different solutions being proposed for similar problems of power, poverty, and politics.

14. The differences that separate us from one another somehow are a regression to some primitive earlier stage of evolutionary progress and are out of place in the ideal future where differences of ethnicity, religion, and race will be eliminated. The countries visited, where a single view of truth, was enforced demonstrated the weaknesses and injustice of any one group's imposing its will on the others.

15. When we take particular differences of race, religion, nationality, and

gender as reasons for treating people differently, we are being prejudiced if we treat people differently. The students visited many cultures where people requested or even required that they be treated differently according to gender, religion, or any of the other cultural categories.

16. The long-range drift toward secularization and rationality demands that we ignore nonrational or irrational factors inherent in religious, ethnic, and racial diversity in the name of human progress. The rules of the more industrialized countries visited were different from those in the less industrialized countries largely due to nonrational or irrational factors.

17. To emphasize cultural diversity while the world is going through crisis will aggravate the dangers of fragmentation that destroys a culture from within. The more authoritarian cultures seemed more fragile and brittle in many ways than those cultures that were more tolerant of diversity.

In addition to the negative arguments against international or multicultural training of students, there are also some positive arguments.

1. More knowledge leads to more sympathy, more sympathy will ultimately lead to more empathy, and more empathy will finally lead to improved multicultural relations. The students experienced some of this growth process in their multicultural identity development.

2. Increased multicultural knowledge will stretch people's imaginations with a net result of increased tolerance of other cultures, which will contribute toward a more secure world. Alumni from previous voyages speak of the profound impact this experience continues to make in their decisions and choices.

3. The diffusion of knowledge about other cultures will lead toward a more harmonious world, helping the different cultures become interdependent. In the best of the critical incidents, the students helped disseminate a positive impression that was welcomed and valued abroad.

4. The demonstration of how people from different cultures are interdependent on one another might contribute toward world peace as we learn to exchange what we have for what we need from others. Studying classes in psychology, ecology, sociology, or any of the other areas while going around the world demonstrated clearly the dangers of sociopolitical isolation for the future.

5. Learning about persons different from ourselves clarifies our knowledge of who we are as we learn about ourselves through others' perceptions of us. The students described the importance of their own

personal voyage toward an articulate self-identity being at least as important as the voyage to different countries.

6.   The meaning of cultures and minds can enhance progress toward a new multicultural identity. The voyage raised more questions than it answered and sent the students off toward a lifetime of seeking answers to those unanswered questions.

7.   Contact with different countries and cultures in person was less abstract and more relevant than reading about those cultures in books. The students will now associate sights, sounds, smells, and personal encounters with each country they visited in ways that books and lectures could never provide.

8.   The international experience will protect students against cultural encapsulation by their own self-reference criteria of truth. Students were challenged by persons, ideas, experiences, and choices and were forced to deal with those challenges by going outside their cultural cocoons.

Escaping Cultural Encapsulation

Persons who have not encountered other countries or cultures different from their own have a tendency to depend on one authority, one theory, one truth. These encapsulated people live in a cultural cocoon where they become insensitive to cultural variations, protect unreasoned assumptions about others, depend on a technique-oriented job description, and reject any responsibility toward others. These encapsulated people are trapped in their own way of thinking, believing that way to be universal truth. The dangers of living in such a capsule is that the structure is inflexible and resists adaptation to different people, times, and places.

A more multicultural perspective accommodates a range of culturally defined differences and assumptions. The multicultural perspective provides an opportunity to increase one's repertoire for correctly and accurately matching the right answer to the right question in the right way at the right time. The international experiences of these students will increase the accuracy of their understanding about the countries and cultures they visited. The goal is not ethnocentrism ("mine is best") nor is it relativism ("to each her/his own") but is rather a perspective defined by the fifth and final stage of culture shock where the goal is to emphasize both similarities and differences at the same time. This multicultural perspective will not occur spontaneously without guided training and experiences such as the students on this voyage discovered.

Some social scientists who specialize in the study of the future suggest that we are moving toward a future which by definition is so different from life as we know it that it is beyond our wildest imagination. It is impossible to even imagine what this future will be like. They further suggest that we, our students, and our children will not all survive this future, which will be so radically different from the present. The question, of course, is how can we prepare for a future which by definition is beyond our imagination? They finally suggest that the best preparation for the future is to put ourselves deliberately in contact with persons who are different from ourselves. Our natural tendency is to spend time with people who are like ourselves and avoid contact with persons who are different. Perhaps by increasing our contact with persons who are different from ourselves we can increase our facilitative ability to adjust, adapt, and accommodate in ways that will save us, our students, and our children when that unimagined future arrives.

The voyage continues. The critical incidents described in this book describe ways that the participating students have begun the chain reaction of events in their individual lives which will make the voyage memorable to them. The positive effects of culture shock will result in learnings and insights that could not be achieved without some of the problems and opportunities described in these critical incidents.

References

Adler, P. S. (1974). Beyond cultural identity: Reflections on cultural and multicultural man. *Topics in culture learning*, 2, 23-40.

Adler, P. S. (1975). The transitional experience: An alternative view of culture shock. *Journal of Humanistic Psychology*, 15(4), 13-23.

Albert, R. D. (1983). The intercultural sensitizer or culture assimilator: A cognitive approach. In D. Landis & R. W. Brislin, *Handbook of intercultural training: Volume II, Issues in training methodology*, (pp.186-217) New York: Pergamon Press.

Ball-Rokeach, S. J. (1973). From pervasive ambiguity to a definition of the situation. *Sociometry*, 36, 3-13.

Beker, J., Husted, S. M., Gitelson, P. M., Kamistein, P., & Adler, L. F. (1972). *Critical incidents in child care: A case book for child care workers*. New York: Behavioral Publications.

Berry, J. W. (1980). Social and cultural change. In H. C. Triandis & R. Brislin (Eds.), *Handbook of cross-cultural psychology*: Vol. 5, Social, (pp. 211-79). Boston: Allyn & Bacon.

Berry, J. W. & Kim, U.(1988). Acculturation and mental health. In P. R. Dasen, J. W. Berry, & N. Sartorius, *Health and cross-cultural psychology*, 207-236. Newbury Park, CA: Sage.

Berry, J. W., Poortinga, Y. H., Segall, M. H., & Dasen, P. J. (1992). *Cross-cultural psychology: Research and applications*. Cambridge, England: Cambridge University Press.

Brislin, R. W. & Pedersen, P. B. (1976). *Cross cultural orientation programs*. New York: Gardner Press.

Brislin, R. (1981). *Cross cultural encounters*. New York: Pergamon Press.

Brislin, R. W., Cushner, K., Cherrie, C., & Yong, M. (1986). *Intercultural interactions: A practical guide*. Beverly Hills, CA: Sage.

Brown, F. (1989). *Reentry*. Los Angeles: Korean Federation of Los Angeles.

Burger, J. M. (1990). *Personality*. Belmont, CA: Wadsworth Publishing Company.

Byrnes, F. C. (1966). Role shock: An occupational hazard of American technical assistants abroad. *Annuals of the American academy of political and social science*, 368, 95-108.

Calia, V. F. & Corsini, R. J. (1973). *Critical incidents in school counseling*. Englewood Cliffs, NJ: Prentice Hall.

Church, A. T. (1982). Sojourner adjustment. *Psychological Bulletin*, 91, 540-72.

Coffman, T. L. (1978). Application for a postdoctoral research training fellowship submitted to the Duke University Center for the Study of Aging and Adult Development.

Coffman, T. L. & Harris, M. C. (1978). *Transition shock and the deinstitutionalization of the mentally retarded citizen*. Paper presented at the 102nd annual meeting of the American Association on Mental Deficiency, Denver, CO.

Coffman, T. L. & Harris, M. C. (1984). The U-curve of adjustment to adult life transitions. Paper presented at the meeting of the American Psychological Association, Toronto, Ontario, August 25, 1984.

D'Ardenne, P. & Mahtani, A. (1989). *Transcultural counseling in action*. London: Sage.

Dunbar, E. (1992). Adjustment and satisfaction of expatriate U.S. personnel. *International Journal of Intercultural Relations*, 16, 1-16.

Fiedler, F. E., Mitchell, T. R., & Triandis, H. C. (1971). The culture assimilator: An approach to cross-cultural training. *Journal of Applied Psychology*, 55, 95-102.

Fivars, G. (1980). *The critical incident technique: A bibliography*. Palo Alto: CA: American Institutes for Research.

Flanagan, J. C. (1954). The critical incident technique. *Psychological Bulletin*, 51, 327-58.

Flanagan J. C. & Burns, R. K. (1955). The employee performance record: A new appraisal and development tool. *Harvard Business Review*, 33 (5), 95-102.

Furnham, A. & Bochner, S. (1986). *Culture shock: Psychological reactions to unfamiliar environments*. London: Methuen.

Furnham, A. (1988). The adjustment of sojourners. In Y. Y. Kim and W. B. Gudykunst, *Cross cultural adaptation, Current approaches, International and Intercultural Communication annual, Vol. XI*, 42-61. Newbury Park, CA: Sage.

Gudykunst, W. B. & Hammer, M. R. (1988). Strangers and hosts: An uncertainty reduction based theory of intercultural adaptation. In Y. Y. Kim and W. B. Gudykunst, (Eds.) *Cross-cultural adaptation: Current approaches*, 106-39, Newbury Park, CA: Sage.

Gullahorn, J. T. & Gullahorn, J. E. (1963). An extension of the U-curve hypothesis. *Journal of Social Issues*, 19 (3), 33-47.

Guthrie, G. M. (1975). A behavioral analysis of culture learning. In R. W. Brislin, S. Bochner, & W. J. Lonner (Eds.), *Cross-cultural perspectives on learning*. New York: Wiley.

Hammer, M. (1992). Research, mission statements, and international student advising offices. *International Journal of Intercultural Relations*, 16, 217-36.

Juffer, K. A. (1987). The first step in cross-cultural orientation: Defining the problem. In M. Paige, *Cross cultural orientation: New conceptualizations and applications*, 175-192. Lanham, MD: University Press of America.

Kealey, D. J.(1988). *Explaining and predicting cross- cultural adjustment and effectiveness: A study of Canadian technical advisors overseas*. A thesis submitted to the Department of Psychology in conformity with the requirements for the degree of doctor of philosophy. Queens University, Kingston, Ontario, Canada, September 1988.

Kealey, D. J. (1989). A study of cross-cultural effectiveness: Theoretical issues, practical applications. *International Journal of Intercultural Relations*, 13, 387-428.

Kim, Y. Y. (1988). *Communication and cross-cultural adaptation*. Clevedon, England: Multilingual Matters Ltd.

Lesser, S. O. & Peter H. W. S. (1957). Training foreign nationals in the United States. In R. Likert and S. P. Hayes (Eds.), *Some applications of Behavioral Research*. Paris: UNESCO.

Levine E. S. & Padilla, A. M. (1980). *Crossing cultures in therapy: Pluralistic counseling for the Hispanic*. Monterey, CA: Brooks/Cole.

Liebhart, P. (1985). *Discovery*. Pittsburgh, PA: Institute for shipboard Education.

Lifton, R. (1967). *Boundaries*. New York: Vintage.

Lysgaard, S. (1955). Adjustment in a foreign society: Norwegian Fulbright grantees visiting the United States. *International Social Science Bulletin*, 7, 45-51.

Oberg, K. (1958). *Culture shock and the problem of adjustment to new cultural environments*. Washington, DC: Department of State, Foreign Service Institute.

Oberg, K. (1960). Cultural shock: Adjustment to new cultural environments. *Practical Anthropology*, 7, 177-82.

Pedersen, P. B. (1988). *A handbook for developing multicultural awareness*. Alexandria, VA: American Counseling Association.

Ruben, B. D. & Kealey, D. J. (1979). Behavioral assessment of communication competency and the prediction of cross-cultural adaptation. *International Journal of Intercultural Relations*, 3, 15-47.

Sauser, W. I. (1987). Critical incident technique. In R. Corsini (Ed.) *Concise encyclopedia of psychology*, 272. New York: John Wiley & Sons.

Smalley, W. (1963). Culture shock, language shock, and the shock of self-discovery. *Practical Anthropology*, 10, 49-56.

Sodowsky, & Plake, B. S. (1992). A study of acculturation differences among international people and suggestions for sensitivity to within-group differences. *Journal of Counseling and Development*, <u>71</u> (2), 53-59.

Stephan, W. G. & Brigham J. C. (1985). Intergroup contact: Introduction. *Journal of Social Issues*, <u>41</u> (3), 1-8.

Stephen, C. W. & Stephen, W. G. (1992). Reducing intercultural anxiety through intercultural contact. *International Journal of Intercultural Relations*, <u>16</u>, 89-106.

Sue, D. W. & Sue D. (1990). *Counseling the culturally different: Theory and practice*. 2nd Ed., New York: John Wiley & Sons.

Torbiorn I. (1982). *Living abroad: Personal adjustment and personnel policy in the overseas setting*. Chichester England: John Wiley & Sons.

Triandis, H. C. (1971). The perception of interpersonal disagreement between supervisors and subordinates. Paper presented at NATO Symposium on Leadership and Management Appraisals, Brussels, Belgium, August 1971.

Index

Accidents, fear of: pedestrians, 159; scooters, 66-67; traffic, 66-67,159

AIDS, 40-41, 51

Alcohol, drinking of: 64, 98, 138, 144, 158; under the influence of, 29, 31, 33, 43, 45, 92, 131, 175-176, 182, 205

Amazon, trips to the, 40-42, 85, 88, 143, 209

Anger: by students towards host cultures, 77, 86-87, 103, 123, 134-135, 145, 146, 159, 168-169, 174, 181, 189, 193, 252; by host cultures towards students, 53, 71, 84, 102-103, 123

Animals: bats, 41, 42, 88; bears, 121, 214; bugs, 75, 82, 85, 96, 108, 157, 163, 218; cats, 81, 82; elephants, 53, 102, 219; fish, 42, 96, 116, 141; hippopotamus, 144; insects, 107; ostriches, 44, 45; snakes, 74; spiders, 88, 143; tarantulas, 41, 88

Apartheid, 46, 91,94, 96, 149, 151, 153, 213, 252

Bargains, 105, 180; bargaining, 85, 100, 104, 160, 175; bartering, 54, 105

Bathroom customs: holes in the ground, 106; long skirt versus short skirt, 122; no privacy, 123-124, 143

Begging, by host cultures, 38-39, 44, 58, 109-112, 117-118, 169, 172, 255-256

Behavior: by host cultures, 47-49, 53, 71, 77, 82, 84, 89, 96, 100-103, 145, 146, 151, 159, 162-163, 168-169, 176, 181, 200, 255; by mobs, 110; by students 29, 34, 77, 123; safe and unsafe, 63-64

Bible, 62-63

Bigotry, 153-154

Birthday, 119, 120

Body language, 34, 42, 58, 125, 174, 183, 239

Brazil, travelling to, 34, 35, 37-43, 81, 83, 86, 88-90, 135, 139-141, 144-146, 208, 209, 211, 212, 250

Breaking the law, 43, 187, 189, 190

Calcutta, travelling to, 108, 117, 169, 220, 221, 224

Canadian International Development Agency (CIDA), 8

Candomble ceremony, 35

Cape Town, travelling to, 45-47, 49, 90-93, 95-98, 148, 149, 151, 153, 215, 264

Caracas, travelling to, 26, 30,

81, 135, 137, 138, 204, 206, 207

Carnivals, 43, 82, 141, 209

Chapman College, 23, 24

Cheated, feelings of being, 39, 106, 123, 158

Children: begging by, 88, 90, 107-108, 117-118, 169, 172; feeling sorry for, 63, 91, 94, 97, 108-111, 117-118, 255-256; positive experiences with, 61, 224-225, 234, 242, 255-256; sexual exploitation of, 67; stealing from students, 82, 84

Communication, 43, 57, 68; positive experiences of, 51; nonverbal, 33-34, 43, 50, 60, 69, 167, 133, 209, 239. *See also* Language barriers

Coup, 32

Critical Incidents: cross-cultural counseling, 17; culture assimilator, 18, 19, 22; general culture assimilator, 19; eighteen general themes, 19; methodology, 15, 16, 17; reporting format applied by students, 17; stage-one, 26

Cross-cultural awareness, 107, 146

Crossroads, 48, 50, 90, 91, 213

Culture shock: accepted assumptions, 11; acculturative stress, 7, 8; approaches, 9; definition of, 1-15; educational model, 2; eight deficit explanations, 5; feared negative consequences, 6; five explanations, 6; five-stage educational and developmental process, 3; four-stage description, 3; growth experience, 7; initial contact, 3;

J-curve, 26, 199; medical model, 2; negative consequences, 6; seven stages of adjustment, 2; six classes of predictor variables, 8; six indicators, 22; three-stage process, 3; U-curve, 3, 4, 11, 12, 14, 26, 134, 199, 245, 263; W-curve, 2, 4

Customs, differences in, 9, 33, 40, 42, 47, 48, 54-57, 87, 100, 113, 120, 122, 124-125, 128, 131, 176, 181, 185, 206, 211, 214, 226

Dancing: by children, 67; by host cultures, 37-38, 90, 140; by students, 32-33, 144, 151, 204, 231

Dead bodies, 85, 118

Desmond Tutu, 91, 215

Disabilities, 44, 49, 50, 97, 107, 111

Discrimination: ethnic, 30, 59, 198-199; sexual, 174

Drugs, 28, 101, 102, 172, 173

Embarrassment, feelings of, 30, 52, 59, 63, 80, 92, 96, 123, 132, 148, 158, 178, 179, 182, 189, 194, 198, 212, 232, 237, 253

Etiquette, 121, 206, 229

Families, 68, 164, 178, 207, 210, 220

Fear: of animals and bugs, 41, 53; of being lost, 89, 113-114, 129, 235, 258-259; of bodily harm, 34, 36-37, 48-49; of diseases, 36, 63; of rape, 31, 63-64, 219; of strange surroundings, 203; of swimming in the Amazon, 42

Fishing, 42
Flying, 47, 53, 66, 87, 97, 106, 142, 211
Food, encountering new, 121, 188, 218, 228-229
Forbidden City, 124, 186
Friendship: development of, 23, 29, 76, 99, 104, 163, 214, 220, 229, 252-253; friendliness shown by host cultures, 40, 51, 59-60, 75-76, 104, 107-108, 119, 129

Gender issues, 56-57
Gift giving, 54, 75-76, 206, 213, 220, 237, 238
Government issues, 46, 154, 206, 207, 216, 219, 228, 252, 259
Guilt, feelings of, 44, 67, 84, 94, 97, 102, 130, 133, 159, 235

Hang gliding, 210, 211
Harassment, 81, 82, 170
Helplessness, feelings of, 36-37, 50-51, 79, 82, 83, 89, 95, 99, 103, 110, 112, 116-117, 128, 129, 133, 147, 150, 170, 188, 232
Hiroshima, 76, 129, 130, 238, 239
Homestay, 57, 59, 60, 112, 115, 225, 226, 237, 238
Hostile behavior: by host cultures, 33, 39, 47, 59, 116, 199; by students, 34, 198
Hosts, 1, 18, 35, 54, 121, 199, 203, 223, 226, 228, 229, 272
Humor, 75, 105, 232, 245, 247, 249

IESA, 30, 34, 137
Immigration, 70, 176, 215
Imperial Palace, 234, 262
India, travelling to, 55-61, 107, 109-118, 164, 166, 168-174, 220-229, 255, 258
Innocence, 159, 181
International University Cruise, Inc., 23
Invasion of privacy, 46

Kissing, by host cultures, 63, 64, 131, 144, 233
Kobe, travelling to, 26, 76, 126, 127, 132, 191, 192, 194, 198, 235, 237, 238, 241, 261

Language barriers, 33-34, 39, 43, 59, 113, 127-128, 131, 141, 160, 186, 189, 206-207, 210-211, 232, 238. *See also* Communication
Local traders, 53-54
Lost, geographically, 207, 240, 257-259; possessions, 87, 192
Lying, 46, 66, 85, 108, 118, 128, 145, 159

Machismo, 137
Madras, travelling to, 57-59, 109-111, 114, 117, 118, 164, 166, 167, 169, 170, 172, 173, 220, 222, 223, 227, 255
Malaysia, travelling to, 61-66, 119-122, 174-177, 230
Mombasa, travelling to, 50, 51, 54, 55, 99, 100, 103, 104, 159, 161, 162, 216
Money: changing of, 34-35, 169; cruzeiros, 38, 39, 84, 140, 145; discussions of, 80; exchanging of, 38-40, 126; feeling cheated, 38-40; giving of, 49-50, 63; rupees, 58, 115-117, 165, 166, 168, 171, 225
Monuments, 60, 129, 130
Mother Teresa, 117, 221, 222,

224, 255
Museums, visits to, 129, 130,
   189

Nudity, 47, 64-65

Peer pressure, 74, 75, 212
Peking University, travelling to,
   70, 124, 184, 186
Penang, travelling to, 66, 74-176,
   230
Picture taking, 38, 46, 48-49,
   53-56, 58, 65, 66, 69, 71, 91,
   96, 100-102, 110, 116, 120,
   135, 140, 179, 180, 192, 194-
   195, 213, 222, 233, 234, 251,
   255, 261; camcorders, 99,
   100
Physical contact, 100, 169
Police, interactions with, 72, 81,
   124-125, 135, 149, 151, 152;
   184, 191-192, 259
Poverty, 44, 46, 58, 82, 91, 94,
   96, 97, 103, 105, 107-112,
   117-118, 137-138, 183, 190,
   207, 209, 213, 224-225, 228

Racism, 50, 59, 77, 96-97, 133,
   147, 148-154, 193, 197-199,
   252
Rejection, feelings of, 2, 6, 7,
   57, 134-135, 197-199
Religious beliefs, 35, 56, 59,
   171, 207, 260, 266, 267
Republic of China (Taiwan), 71,
   125, 188, 232, 260
Restaurant: host culture behavior
   in, 37, 39, 43-44, 91, 126-
   127, 148, 152, 176, 196-197,
   198-199; student behavior in,
   32, 175, 189,
Rio de Janeiro, 145, 210

Safari, 52-54, 101, 103, 105,

106, 156-159, 163, 217-219,
   253
Safety, feelings of, 37, 45, 49,
   61, 101, 108-110, 139-140,
   211-212
Samburu Village, travelling to,
   163, 217
Sexual issues, 47, 60-61, 67,
   131-132, 158, 178; prostitutes
   and AIDS, 41
Shop owners, interactions with,
   161, 179, 227, 228
Snake Alley, travelling to, 74
South Africa, travelling to, 44,
   45, 47-49, 90-93, 95-99,
   147-153, 161, 212, 214, 215,
   218, 250-252, 264
Spanish language, 33, 34, 43, 81,
   135, 136, 138, 139, 202, 203,
   208, 240, 250
Squatter camps, 46, 48, 95, 213,
   214
Stereotypes, 6, 18, 61, 77, 162,
   164, 253, 265
Stolen objects, 66, 135, 192; by
   host cultures, 82, 136; by
   students, 182
Subways, 129, 206, 236, 241

Taipei, travelling to, 74, 75, 126,
   188, 190
Taxi Driver, interactions with,
   43, 74, 80, 85, 90, 98, 135,
   160, 161, 174, 198, 215, 221,
   227, 241-242, 250
Temples, 55, 56, 61, 109, 110,
   112, 119, 164-166, 171, 173,
   174, 224, 230, 233, 240
Thailand, travelling to, 67, 177,
   231
Tiananmen Square, 124, 184, 259
Tokyo, travelling to, 76, 77, 127,
   129, 191, 198, 239, 241
Toroko Gorge, travelling to,

71-73, 125, 189, 233

Tourist, 3, 27, 32, 54, 65, 69, 77, 82, 87, 95, 103, 105, 108, 119, 135, 190, 191, 194, 207, 258; tourism, 67, 70, 77, 211

Transportation, 71, 72, 129, 176, 230, 257; airplane, 48, 56, 87, 114, 128, 142, 143, 209; bikes, 257; buses, 28, 31, 41, 46, 51, 56, 57, 59, 66, 75, 86, 89, 90, 96, 107, 118, 135, 136-138, 141, 143, 162, 176, 177, 180, 184, 186, 188, 190, 202-204, 208, 212, 213, 228-230, 233, 240, 261, 262; boats, 66, 84, 90, 96, 98, 111, 143, 152, 154, 160, 181, 192, 227, 228; hitchhiking, 73; motorcycles, 71, 72; railways, 95, 192; rickshaws, 164, 166, 169, 172, 173, 256; scooters, 66, 189; taxis, 27, 28, 43, 45, 48, 50, 74, 80, 85, 86, 90, 92, 93, 97, 98, 100, 101, 102, 104, 105, 108, 111, 117-119, 135, 139-141, 149, 150, 152, 153, 159-161, 166-170, 174-178, 198, 202, 207, 215, 221, 225, 227, 241, 242, 250, 252; trains, 57, 62, 63, 70, 71, 76, 95, 107, 110, 111, 113-115, 125-128, 189, 191, 192, 194, 216, 217, 227, 228, 232, 233, 235, 236, 241, 242, 261; trolleys, 205; vans, 35-37, 53, 54, 97, 141, 151, 213, 215

Trust, feelings of, 16, 28, 42, 51, 52, 60-62, 99, 128, 165, 175, 182, 211, 218, 225, 227, 245, 247, 249, 254, 262

U-curve, 2-4, 11, 12, 14, 26, 134, 199, 245, 263, 271, 272

Ugly American, 29, 46, 80, 81, 86, 140, 194

Unfairness, feelings of, 123, 147, 148, 161, 162, 200

Vendors, interactions with, 37-39, 61, 102-103, 104, 122, 123, 126

Venezuela, travelling to, 29, 30, 32, 33, 80, 135, 136, 138, 139, 202-208

Violence, 61, 85, 151, 219

Vulnerability, feelings of, 54, 74, 120, 262, 266

Water, safety of; 46, 64, 65, 87, 99, 108, 116, 222, 223, 225, 229

About the Author

PAUL PEDERSEN is professor of education in the department of counseling and human services at Syracuse University, Syracuse, New York. He has authored and edited a number of books, including *Handbook of Cross-Cultural Counseling and Therapy* (Greenwood, 1985), and with Allen Ivey, *Culture-Centered Counseling and Interviewing Skills* (Praeger, 1993).

ISBN 0-313-28782-1

EAN

9 780313 287824

90000>

HARDCOVER BAR CODE